Checkmate in Berlin

Checkmate in Berlin

*The Cold War Showdown That Shaped
the Modern World*

GILES MILTON

JOHN MURRAY

First published in Great Britain in 2021 by John Murray (Publishers)
An Hachette UK company

1

Copyright © Giles Milton 2021

Maps drawn by Rodney Paull

A CIP catalogue record for this title is available from the British Library

Hardback ISBN 978-1-529-39315-6
Trade Paperback ISBN 978-1-529-39316-3
eBook ISBN 978-1-529-39318-7

Typeset in Bembo MT 11.5/14 pt by Palimpsest Book Production Limited,
Falkirk, Stirlingshire

Printed and bound in Great Britain by Clays Ltd, Elcograf S.p.A.

Hardback endpapers: The Brandenburg Gate, Berlin, 1945.
Photo Trinity Mirror/Alamy Stock Photo.

John Murray Press policy is to use papers that are natural, renewable and
recyclable products and made from wood grown in sustainable forests.
The logging and manufacturing processes are expected to conform
to the environmental regulations of the country of origin.

John Murray (Publishers)
Carmelite House
50 Victoria Embankment
London EC4Y 0DZ

www.johnmurraypress.co.uk

For George

Contents

CONTENTS

PART IV: The Siege

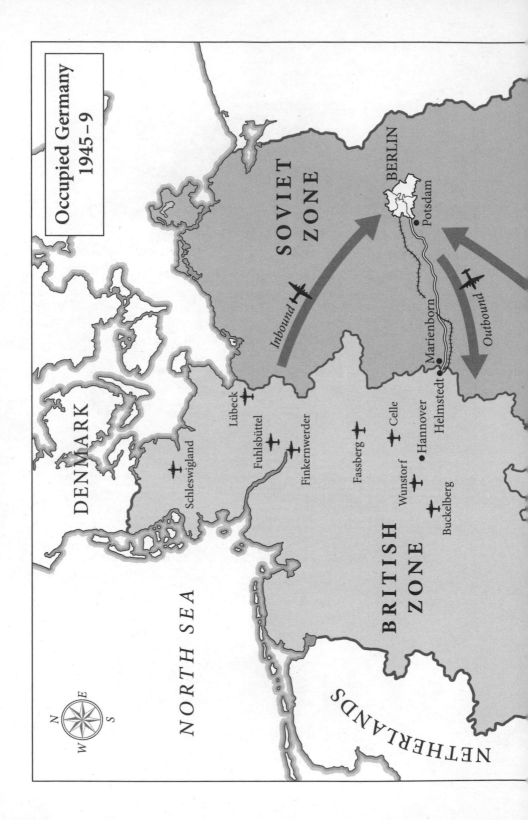

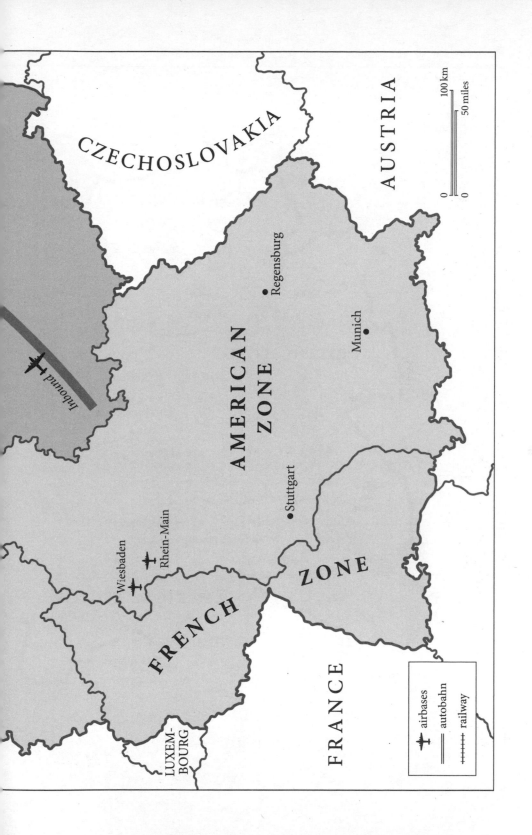

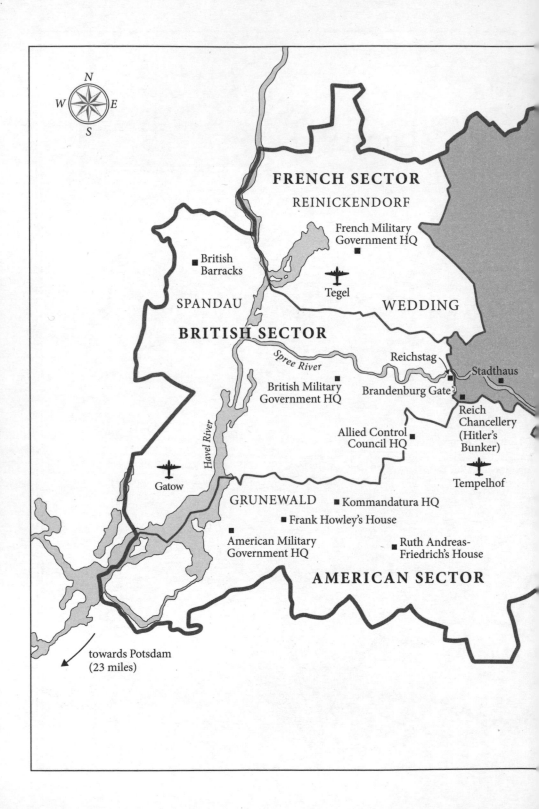

Four-Sector Berlin
1945–9

0   8 km
0   5 miles

SOVIET
SECTOR

Soviet Military
Administration HQ

KARLSHORST

Klingenberg
Power Station

Spree River

If we lose Berlin, we may as well kiss Germany and Western Europe goodbye.

Colonel Frank Howley, commandant,
American sector, Berlin

I don't like the expression Cold War. This war is hot as hell.

General William Donovan,
director of America's Office of Strategic Services

One foot wrong now and it's World War Three.

General Sir Brian Robertson, deputy military governor,
British occupation zone, Germany

Principal Characters

American

Franklin D. Roosevelt
Thirty-second president of the United States (1933–April 1945) and one of the 'Big Three' wartime leaders, along with Winston Churchill and Joseph Stalin.

Harry S. Truman
Thirty-third president of the United States (April 1945–53). Overseer of a major shift in American foreign policy that led to the post-war Truman Doctrine and the Marshall Plan.

General Lucius D. Clay
Military governor of the American zone of Germany (1947–9), serving on the Allied Control Council. Previously served as deputy military governor.

Colonel Frank 'Howlin' Mad' Howley
Commandant of the American sector of Berlin (1947–9); previously served as deputy commandant. Leading American representative on Berlin's Kommandatura.

George Kennan
Distinguished American diplomat who urged a policy of containment against Soviet expansion. Author of the famous 1946 'Long Telegram'.

General William H. 'Tonnage' Tunner
Commander of the Berlin Airlift (1948–9).

British

Winston Churchill

British prime minister (May 1940–July 1945); Britain's principal representative at both the Yalta and Potsdam conferences. Delivered his 'Iron Curtain' speech in March 1946.

Ernest Bevin

British foreign secretary (July 1945–March 1951), serving in Clement Attlee's post-war Labour government. An architect of both NATO and the Federal Republic of Germany.

General Sir Brian Robertson

Military governor of the British zone of Germany (1948–50), serving on the Allied Control Council. Previously deputy military governor.

Brigadier Robert 'Looney' Hinde

Deputy director of British Military Government, Berlin (1945–8). Leading British representative on Berlin Kommandatura.

Lieutenant Colonel Harold 'Tim' Hays

An early recruit to Military Government Greater Berlin Area, serving 1945–51. Author of the unpublished memoir, 'Nach Berlin' (To Berlin).

Soviet

Joseph Stalin

Marshal of the Soviet Union and one of the 'Big Three' wartime leaders, he pursued a post-war policy of aggressive Soviet expansion in Eastern and Central Europe.

Vyacheslav Molotov

Stalin's minister of foreign affairs (1939–49); the key Soviet negotiator at both the Yalta and Potsdam conferences.

Marshal Georgy Zhukov
Leading Red Army commander in the 1945 Battle of Berlin and first military governor of Soviet-occupied Germany.

General Nikolai Berzarin
First Soviet military governor of Berlin, 1945.

Colonel Sergei Tiulpanov
Head of the Soviet Military Administration's propaganda bureau (1945–8).

General Alexander Kotikov
Commandant of the Soviet sector of Berlin (1946–50). Leading Soviet representative on Berlin Kommandatura.

Pro-Soviet Germans

Walter Ulbricht
German Communist leader who returned to Berlin from Moscow in 1945. Helped found the Socialist Unity Party and later became leader of the German Democratic Republic (East Germany).

Wilhelm Pieck
Leader of the German Communist Party who spent his wartime in exile in Moscow. Later served as president of the German Democratic Republic (East Germany) (1949–60).

Otto Grotewohl
Leading member of the Social Democratic Party; promoted the party's merger with the Communist Party, thereby creating the Socialist Unity Party. Later served as the de facto head of the German Democratic Republic (East Germany).

Berliners

Ruth Andreas-Friedrich
Berlin-based journalist and member (together with her companion, Leo Borchard) of the Uncle Emil anti-Nazi resistance movement. Diarist and author of *Berlin Underground 1938–45* and *Battleground Berlin 1945–8*.

Ernst Reuter
Vigorously pro-western mayor of Berlin (1947–53) and symbol of 'free' Berlin. Celebrated for his rousing 1948 speech pleading with the world not to abandon Berlin.

Wilhelm Furtwängler
Principal conductor of the Berlin Philharmonic Orchestra (1922–45 and 1952–4). His return to Berlin in 1946 would expose wide differences in the Soviet and western approaches to denazification.

French

General Marie-Pierre Koenig
Commander of French forces in the French occupation zone. Served on the Allied Control Council.

General Charles Lançon
Commandant of French sector of Berlin (March–October 1946). French representative on Berlin Kommandatura.

General Jean Ganeval
Commandant of French sector of Berlin (1946–50). French representative on Berlin Kommandatura.

Prologue

Crimea, February 1945

TWILIGHT ARRIVED EARLY in the Crimean mountains, with dusk falling at four-thirty and darkness shortly after. A lone road crossed this gloomy terrain, one whose high altitude hairpins made for a forbidding drive in the glacial depths of winter. In such a season, and at such an hour, the 'Route Romanov' was normally deserted.

But this was no normal day. On the afternoon of Saturday, 3 February 1945, the alpine twilight was pierced by the shrill glare of carbide headlamps. Two Packard limousines were grinding their way around the precipitous flank of the Roman-Kosh massif, the vanguard of a snaking column of jeeps and trucks that stretched for more than a dozen miles into the rear. Inside those two lead vehicles sat Franklin D. Roosevelt and Winston Churchill – American president and British prime minister – en route to the Crimean resort city of Yalta. Here, they were to meet with their wartime ally, Joseph Stalin.

The Big Three leaders held the world's fate in their hands in that final winter of war, masters of a rapidly advancing front line that stretched from the coast of Brittany to the shores of the Black Sea. Now, at Yalta, they were hoping to thrash out a new global order. Under a bruised February sky they were to be the architects of a whole new world, reshaping it in their collective image. Nazi Germany was to be dismembered, along with its shattered imperial capital, and the frontiers of Europe redrawn. Never before in history had the spoils of war been subject to such scrutiny, nor laced with such brooding drama.

The fighting was far from over in those early months of 1945 and the Wehrmacht was putting up stiff resistance on both the eastern and western fronts. Yet the Allies were advancing inexorably towards the Fatherland, a giant pincer movement of their million-strong armies closing in on the German capital. With their eventual victory all but assured, it was time to plan the peace.

Stalin had selected Yalta for this latest conference, having rejected all the other proposed venues because of his fear of flying. In happier times, the Crimean resort might have provided the ideal setting for a week of virtuoso diplomacy. Its backdrop of snow-sculpted mountains looked majestic when lit by the rays of a winter sun and the climate was so temperate that palm trees flourished along the Black Sea littoral. But Yalta had been devastated by war and was now a blighted ruin, gutted by the retreating Wehrmacht and despoiled of its fin-de-siècle charm. When the rain swept in from the Black Sea, it was depressingly, unremittingly bleak.

Roosevelt and Churchill had flown into the Crimea escorted by a phalanx of Spitfires and P38 fighter escorts. Churchill was first on the ground. Dressed in his military greatcoat and officer's cap, Britain's wartime leader was chomping on an eight-inch cigar and grinning mischievously at the white-gloved guard of honour.

It was some time before the president emerged from his plane. Paralysed by polio in his late thirties, he was confined to a wheelchair that had to be lowered from the fuselage in a specially constructed caged elevator.

Among the many onlookers at the airfield that freezing afternoon was Captain Hugh Lunghi, a young interpreter from the British Military Mission in Moscow. He was shocked by the physical condition of the president, who seemed a 'gaunt, very thin figure with his black cape over his shoulder'. His face was 'a sort of yellow, waxen and very drawn, very thin, and a lot of the time he was sort of sitting, sitting there with his mouth open'.[1] There was a reason why the president looked so ill: he had recently been diagnosed with acute congestive heart failure, a condition for which there was no cure. Yalta was to be his epitaph, as he knew.

Grand-scale diplomacy requires a grand-scale entourage and Yalta was to outshine all of the previous wartime summits in both scale and extravagance. Touching down at Saki within minutes of the two leaders was an aerial armada of twenty-five transport planes – codename Mission No. 17 – bringing 750 accredited participants. Among them were Churchill's most trusted confidants, including his Foreign Secretary, Anthony Eden, and his chief of staff, General Sir Hastings 'Pug' Ismay. Roosevelt's delegation was of equal calibre, led by his Secretary of State, Edward Stettinius, and his special adviser, Harry Hopkins. Hundreds of others were following in their wake: field marshals, generals, ministers, soldiers, aides, advisers, translators, stenographers, secretaries, signallers, cooks and stewards. Roosevelt brought eighteen bodyguards, as well as his presidential outriders, nicknamed 'the Crazy Gang' by the British secretarial staff. Churchill's closest entourage was more modest, consisting of his physician, Lord Charles Moran, his valet, Frank Sawyers, and his adoring daughter, Sarah.

British military victuallers were so alarmed by reports of the primitive conditions in Yalta that they decided to transport everything necessary for the eight-day conference: dinner plates, tablecloths, paper napkins, wine glasses, tumblers, pepper-pots and thirteen sugar bowls. Aware that the wheels of diplomacy require frequent lubrication, they also shipped an ocean of alcohol, including a thousand bottles of whisky and gin. Churchill recommended whisky as a salve for everything: 'Good for typhus,' he said, 'and deadly on lice.'[2]

Everything had to be transported overland from Saki airfield to Yalta, a six-hour drive over mountainous terrain. At the head of this cortège were the two leaders travelling in their separate limousines; they were followed by the convoy of trucks and jeeps. Security was paramount. Stalin had ordered the route to be lined with the troops of two Soviet divisions, all armed with American Lend-Lease Springfield rifles. Each soldier stood in sight of the next one, along the entire eighty-mile route.

It was an extraordinary sight, or so it seemed to Roosevelt's interpreter, Charles Bohlen. 'As the presidential car passed,' he noted, 'the soldiers, many of them girls, snapped to the Russian salute – an abrupt move of the arm to put the rifle at a 30-degree angle from the body. Repeated thousands of times, the salute was most impressive.'[3] Churchill was rather less enamoured with the drive, for the route was unpaved and there were potholes so deep that they juddered the spine. 'Christ,' he said to his daughter after an hour on the road, 'five more of this.'[4]

The British delegation was to be housed in Villa Vorontsov, former residence of Prince Mikhail Vorontsov, some five miles outside Yalta. It was an architectural oddity, part Scottish baronial castle, part Moorish fantasy palace, which met with Churchill's approval. Indeed he was so taken with the sculpted imperial lions standing guard over the entrance portico that he tried (unsuccessfully) to purchase them. Sir Alexander Cadogan, Permanent Undersecretary of State, was less impressed. 'A big house of indescribable ugliness,' he said, with furnishings that had 'an almost terrifying hideosity'.[5]

The villa had been a ruin until just a few days earlier, stripped of its furniture, light-fittings and door handles by the departing Wehrmacht. More than a thousand Soviet workmen had been requisitioned to repair the place, and 1,500 wagons of furniture had been transported from Moscow's grandest hotels, the Metropol, Splendide and National. While Churchill and his closest advisers were housed in comfort, conditions remained primitive for everyone else, with mattresses so infested with bed bugs that they had to be fumigated with DDT. Sanitation was minimal. 'If you were a spectator along the bedroom corridors here at about 7.30 in the morning,' wrote Sarah Churchill in a letter to her mother, 'you would see three field marshals queuing for a bucket.'[6]

The American delegation was housed closer to the centre of Yalta in the Livadia Palace, an Italianate mansion constructed by Tsar Nicholas II at ruinous expense just six years before his abdication. In happier times, the tsar's eldest daughter, Grand Duchess Olga, had danced quadrilles in the White Ballroom on the occasion of her sixteenth birthday, her necklace sparkling with thirty-two diamonds and pearls.

Now, the palace was playing host to a very different gathering. President Roosevelt was assigned the tsar's private suite, a yellow satin-panelled bedroom with a huge wooden bed inlaid with mythical beasts; the adjacent billiard room was his private dining room and the imperial audience chamber his study. He was delighted, declaring that he had 'all the comforts of home'.[7]

As Roosevelt and Churchill were settling in to their lodgings, Stalin was busy preparing for the first day of the conference at his headquarters in the Koreiz Villa. This had once been the summer home of Prince Felix Yusupov, orchestrator of Rasputin's murder, and came equipped with a newly built bomb shelter whose roof was reinforced with three metres of concrete and sand. Stalin was terrified of assassination and had to be reassured that not even an eighty-pound bomb could pierce the shelter.

The conference schedule had been structured so as to make the best use of the available time. There was a great deal to be decided. 'The immense task', said Churchill, 'of the organisation of the world.'[8] The Big Three themselves would thrash out the broad sweep of their collective vision in daily plenary sessions; these were to be held each afternoon in the Livadia Palace. The foreign ministers and their aides would then search for solutions to the many areas of dispute.

Each of the three leaders brought his own demands. Stalin's most pressing goal was to retain his vast territorial gains in Poland and install a pro-Soviet government in the country. This was to cause much wrangling over the days that followed and dominated the agenda for seven of the eight plenary sessions. The Soviet leader held the upper hand, for his troops had already overrun Eastern and Central Europe, and much of Poland, Czechoslovakia, Romania, Bulgaria and Hungary was under Red Army control.

President Roosevelt had two principal aims: to persuade the Soviet Union to join the war against Japan, which was proving so costly in American lives, and to cajole Stalin into accepting his proposals for a new organisation, the United Nations. He believed that such a body was the only means of avoiding future global conflict.

Churchill's overriding goal was to preserve the integrity and status of both Great Britain and her empire, which still ruled over a quarter of the world's population. He also had strong views on Poland, on whose behalf Britain had first declared war on Nazi Germany. Above all else, he was determined to prevent post-war Europe from being dominated by the Soviet Union.

Stalin played the host to perfection, allowing his guests to settle into their lodgings before paying them a courtesy call the following afternoon, Sunday, 4 February. It was exactly 3 p.m. when his armour-plated Packard swept to a halt outside the Villa Vorontsov, the vehicle's three-inch-thick glass windows distorting the seated figure inside. Stalin was dressed in a high-collared khaki tunic with a marshal's gold star embroidered on the shoulder straps.

This was the fourth time that Stalin and Churchill had met and they greeted each other with what appeared to be genuine warmth. 'Both seemed glad to meet again,' thought Arthur Birse, Churchill's interpreter, 'and they talked like old friends.'[9] Yet behind the scenes, the chicanery had already begun. Prior to the arrival of both the president and prime minister, listening devices and directional microphones had been concealed in the principal rooms of both the Villa Vorontsov and the Livadia Palace. Members of the British Military Mission in Moscow – all too familiar with eavesdropping – recommended discussing sensitive issues in the bathrooms, with the taps gushing water to drown out their conversations.

Stalin appeared in fine humour, yet behind the smiling facade was an ingrained distrust of both Churchill and Roosevelt. Just a few months earlier, he had described the prime minister as 'the kind of man who will pick your pocket of a kopeck if you don't watch him!' As for the American president, he said that Roosevelt 'dips his hand only for bigger coins'.[10] It was an apt metaphor coming from one who had robbed a bank in his twenties. When Stalin stole, he did so on a grand scale.

The Soviet leader went from the Villa Vorontsov to the Livadia Palace in order to greet the American president, who had dressed for the occasion in a pale suit and flowered tie. 'Smiling broadly, the President grasped Stalin by the hand and shook it warmly.' So wrote Charles Bohlen, who was watching the body language of the Soviet leader closely: 'His face cracked in one of his rare, if slight, smiles . . . [He] expressed pleasure at seeing the President again.'[11]

Roosevelt led Stalin into his red-velvet-lined study and made a jugful of dry martini, a ritual he often performed at the White House. As he passed a cocktail to Stalin, 'he said apologetically that a good martini should really have a twist of lemon'.[12] Stalin said nothing, but the next day a huge lemon tree was flown in from Georgia, its branches laden with two hundred ripe lemons.

Roosevelt made conversational small talk about their last meeting at Tehran, recalling Stalin's jest about how he wanted to execute fifty thousand German officers at the end of the war. It was a remark that had disgusted Churchill. Now, the president sided with the marshal, expressing his hope that Stalin would make the same grim toast at this conference. According to Bohlen, it was by no means an innocent remark. It was Roosevelt's subtle way of 'showing Stalin that the United States was not joining Britain in any united nego-tiating position'. For good measure, Roosevelt criticised the British for being 'a peculiar people [who] wished to have their cake and eat it too'.[13]

The first plenary session of the Yalta Conference took place later that afternoon, with the delegates gathering at 5 p.m. in the imperial ballroom of the Livadia Palace. The Big Three sat at their assigned places around a large round table covered in a cream damask cloth, with their foreign secretaries seated to their right and their inter-preters and closest advisers clustered around them. A fire crackled in the huge conical hearth and the bright winter sun tipped through the six arched windows. Stalin invited Roosevelt, as the only head of state, to act as chairman.*

America's ambassador to the Soviet Union, Averell Harriman, sensed a peculiar dynamic between the two men. 'I think Stalin was afraid of Roosevelt,' he said. 'Whenever Roosevelt spoke, he sort of watched him with a certain awe. He was afraid of Roosevelt's influ-ence in the world.'[14] Harriman noted that Stalin never displayed the same sense of awe when talking to Churchill.

President Roosevelt graciously accepted Stalin's offer to chair the conference, telling the assembled group that they would 'cover the map of the world' over the days that followed. But they were to begin with a briefing on the current military situation, inviting the most senior military figures to give a presentation on the ongoing advance into Germany.

The Soviet army's advance was remarkable. Since launching its assault towards Germany's eastern frontier on 12 January, it had pushed forward some three hundred miles and taken a hundred thousand prisoners. It also had a new jewel in its crown, a bridge-head over the River Oder near Küstrin, on the Polish-German

---

* The respective heads of state of the Soviet Union and Great Britain were Mikhail Kalinin and King George VI.

frontier. It was a moment of great strategic significance. Berlin, the glittering prize, lay just sixty miles to the west.

General George Marshall spoke for the western Allies, briefing on the destruction caused by American and British bombers and giving an upbeat assessment of the ongoing offensive. But the fact remained that the Americans and British were still west of the Rhine and more than 350 miles from Berlin.

Once the general had finished, Churchill raised the question of the following day's agenda, proposing that it should be devoted to 'the future of Germany, if she had any'.[15] Both Roosevelt and Stalin agreed to this.

Much of the post-war planning for Germany had already been done. The three leaders had discussed various possibilities at their previous meeting in Tehran, in November 1943. They had agreed that Germany should be divided into three zones of occupation, one for each of the victorious Allies, with the capital likewise divided into three sectors. The detail was to be fine-tuned by a secret London-based body known as the European Advisory Commission and led by a trio of diplomats, one American, one British, one Russian.

These diplomats had swiftly agreed on generalities, with the Soviet Union getting the east of the country, and Britain and America getting the west. They had also agreed that Berlin should be split on an east–west axis, with the Soviets controlling the capital's eastern districts and their British and American partners getting those in the west. But there remained many small-scale battles to be fought and won. To aid them in plotting the exact dividing lines, the Geographical Section of the General Staff equipped them with a gigantic street map of Berlin.[16] It was on such a grand scale – 1:25,000 – that it came in four sheets, each measuring six feet by three.

The Soviet representative pushed his territorial claims as far as Mitte, the central district of the city, forcing a generous bulge into the boundary of the Soviet sector. This gave the Russians the historical core of Berlin, along with the city hall, parliament and other machinery of government. The Americans and British voiced no objection to this, for their western share also came with potential assets. The Americans gained the huge Tempelhof airfield, along with the residential suburbs of Zehlendorf, while the British secured the north-west quarter of the city, including Spandau and Charlottenburg. They also got the Grunewald, with its woodland, pretty boating lakes and fine Wilhelmine villas.

But there was one glaring problem with their agreed dividing lines. The frontier of Soviet-occupied Germany lay 110 miles *west* of the capital, meaning that Berlin's western sectors would be surrounded by territory controlled by the Red Army. This would not be a problem so long as the British and Americans remained on good terms with their Soviet partners. But if relations were to falter or break down completely, the western sectors of Berlin would be completely cut off.

The diplomats had also planned how Berlin was to be run. It was to have a three-power governing body, the Kommandatura, headed by three soon-to-be-appointed commandants, one American, one British, one Russian. With this decision they had created posts for three old-style regents with the power of Roman pro-consuls and the authority of oriental satraps. These commandants would hold the lives of three million inhabitants in their hands. They would also shoulder the responsibility for preserving friendly relations between the three occupying powers.

On the second day of the Yalta Conference, Monday, 5 February, the leaders turned their attentions to the fate of Germany and its capital. Stalin wanted the country rendered 'impotent ever again to plunge the world into war'[17] and demanded the country's dismemberment, but Churchill stalled for time. 'The actual method of tracing lines is much too complicated a matter to settle here in five or six days,' he said. 'We are dealing with the fate of eighty million people and that requires more than eighty minutes to consider.'[18]

President Roosevelt reminded his two comrades of the work of the European Advisory Commission, pointing out that the London-based diplomats had already agreed upon the zones and sectors of occupation, but that these had yet to be approved by the three respective governments. Churchill raised the issue of whether or not France should be granted an occupation zone, given that 'their participation was essential to keeping the peace after the war was won'.[19] Stalin dismissed this suggestion. 'We cannot forget that in this war, France opened the gates to the enemy.'[20] Yet he eventually accepted that the French government should be included in the division of the spoils, so long as its slice was carved from the British and American sectors.

At this point, the conversation took an unexpected turn. Stalin asked Roosevelt how long American troops would remain in Europe after the end of the war. The president was swift in his response: 'Two years would be the limit.'[21] This came as an unwelcome shock to Churchill. He had been counting on America's military presence for the security of post-war Europe. If US forces were indeed demobbed, as Roosevelt had just said they would be, it would leave the Red Army the only great military force on the continent.

Each of the three leaders brought his own negotiating style to Yalta and these were the subject of much comment by the multifarious note-takers attending each day's deliberations. Britain's Permanent Undersecretary of State, Sir Alexander Cadogan, had no doubts as to who was the conference winner. 'Uncle Joe is much the most impressive of the three men,' he said. 'He is very quiet and restrained.' He was also a good listener. 'The President flapped about and the P.M. boomed, but Joe just sat taking it all in and being rather amused. When he did chip in, he never used a superfluous word and spoke very much to the point.'[22]

Cadogan's opinion of Stalin was shared by Anthony Eden, who said that Stalin was 'the toughest proposition of all', playing the conference room with impressive skill. 'Of course the man was ruthless and of course he knew his purpose. He never wasted a word. He never stormed, he was seldom even irritated. Hooded, calm, never raising his voice, he avoided the repeated negatives of Molotov . . . By more subtle methods he got what he wanted without having seemed so obdurate.'[23]

Churchill, by contrast, made a poor impression and was constantly criticised by his own team for having failed to read his briefs. 'The PM got rather off the rails,' noted Cadogan after listening to his intervention in a discussion about the United Nations. 'Silly old man – without a word of warning to Anthony [Eden] or me, he plunged into a long harangue about [the] World Organisation, knowing nothing whatever of what he was talking about and making complete nonsense of the whole thing.'[24]

Roosevelt also tired of Churchill's constant monologues – 'too many speeches',[25] he said to James Byrnes – yet Roosevelt himself was not immune from making long-winded discourses. Bohlen, his interpreter, grew increasingly exasperated. 'The President rambled on about the Germany he had known in 1886, when small, semi-autonomous states such as Darmstadt and Rothenburg thrived.'[26]

Matters were not helped by the fact that Roosevelt was growing sicker by the day. By the sixth day of the conference, he had weakened to such an extent that Stalin and his closest aides held discussions with him as he lay on his sickbed. 'He was clearly tired and drained,' wrote one of those aides. 'We sat with him for maybe twenty minutes, while he and Stalin exchanged polite remarks about health, the weather and the beauties of the Crimea. We left him when it seemed that Roosevelt had become detached, strangely remote, as if he could see us, yet he was gazing somewhere into the distance.'[27]

It had been decided that each of the statesmen would host a banquet during the course of the conference. Roosevelt had given the first dinner at the Livadia Palace on the opening night of the conference. Stalin gave his banquet on the fifth day. It was held in the fifty-foot-long dining room of the Yusupov Palace and the tables were furnished with china and crystal from Moscow's finest hotels. The Soviet leader was in his element, hailing the 'good, very good' agreement that he had struck with Roosevelt over the Soviet Union's entry into the war against Japan. He had got exactly what he wanted: territorial gains at Japan's expense and a Soviet foothold in north-east China. Buoyed with success, he described the American president as 'the chief forger of the instruments which had led to the mobilisation of the world against Hitler'. He also proposed a toast to Churchill, hailing him as 'the bravest governmental figure in the world'.[28] And then came a toast to the comradeship that had enabled the three leaders to work together as unlikely partners.

'I want to drink to our alliance,' he said, 'that it should not lose its character of intimacy, of its free expression of views. In the history of diplomacy I know of no such close alliance of three Great Powers as this, when allies had the opportunity of so frankly expressing their views.' But he warned that such unity of purpose would be more difficult in peacetime. Their duty was to ensure that post-war relations would be 'as strong as they had been in wartime'.[29]

Churchill responded in gushing language. 'It is no exaggeration or compliment of a florid kind', he said, 'when I say that we regard Marshal Stalin's life as most precious to the hopes and hearts of us all. There have been many conquerors in history, but few of them have been statesmen, and most of them threw away the fruits of victory in the troubles which followed their wars.'[30]

Sir Alexander Cadogan felt that Churchill's exuberant tone was due to the prodigious quantity of alcohol he had consumed – 'buckets of Caucasian champagne', he said, 'which would undermine the health of any ordinary man'.[31]

By the seventh day of the conference, the three leaders had raced through the agenda and resolved many of the issues. The future of Poland, the UN, and the war with Japan had all been decided upon, and they had also agreed to sign the protocol on the splitting of Germany and Berlin.

That night was the occasion of Churchill's banquet, which he intended to be a night to remember. Six days of lavish feasting had taken its toll on everyone, but there was to be no respite. The first course of dinner included caviar, sturgeon, salmon and suckling pig with horseradish sauce. This was followed by vols-au-vent stuffed with game, two soups, fish in champagne sauce, mutton shashlik, pilau rice and wild goat. The third course included roast turkey, partridge and quail, and was followed by a dessert of ice cream, fresh fruit and petits fours. There was alcohol in abundance. A special shipment (codename Yalta Voyage 208) had been delivered. It included a consignment of 1928 Veuve Clicquot champagne, along with several hundred bottles of Rhineland wine, and the British ambassador in Moscow had also sent a case of exquisite 1928 Chateau Margaux.

When Churchill delivered his toast to the Soviet leader, he was as gracious as ever. 'There was a time when the Marshal [Stalin] was not so kindly towards us,' he said, 'and I remember that I said a few rude things about him, but our common dangers and common loyalties have wiped that out. The fire of war has burnt up the misunderstandings of the past. We feel we have a friend whom we can trust, and I hope he will continue to feel the same about us.'[32]

As it grew late the guests began to leave. 'They broke it up at about 12.30,' said Jo Sturdee, one of Churchill's secretaries, 'and as the Marshal was leaving, the dear old PM led us in three cheers.'[33] It was a rousing end to a highly successful evening.

There remained one final session at which the three leaders discussed their conference communiqué to the press and the wider world. It set out much of what had been agreed upon, with Germany's future spelled out in brutal terms: unconditional surrender, trial of war criminals, disarmament, reparations and the establishment of zones of occupation. The three leaders agreed that the communiqué should be broadcast simultaneously in their three capitals on the following day, 12 February.

As the conference wound to a close, there was a valedictory luncheon at which everyone was in high spirits. Roosevelt seemed particularly upbeat; his parting words to Stalin were, 'We will meet again soon, in Berlin!'[34]

Churchill was similarly jubilant, convinced that the three of them had avoided the potential catastrophe of a fall-out between east and west. 'Sombre indeed would be the fortunes of mankind if some awful schism arose between the Western democracies and the Russian Soviet Union.'[35]

Those in the American delegation were even more optimistic, with Roosevelt's special adviser, Harry Hopkins, feeling as if they had saved the world. 'We really believed in our hearts that this was the dawn of the new day we had all been praying for and talking about for so many years. We were absolutely certain that we had won the first great victory of the peace – and, by "we", I mean *all* of us, the whole civilized human race.'[36]

PART I

Uneasy Allies

I

The Road to Berlin

COLONEL FRANK 'HOWLIN' Mad' Howley was a living legend to the men serving under him, a blunt-spoken Yankee with a dangerous smile and a disarmingly sharp brain. He commanded an outfit named A1A1, splendid shorthand for a group led by such a high-spirited adventurer. The task of this unit was to sweep into newly liberated territories and impose order on chaos, repairing shattered infrastructure and feeding starving civilians.

Colonel Howley had won his spurs in the chaotic aftermath of the D-Day landings in June 1944. Appointed to run the wrecked port of Cherbourg, he swung into town like a benevolent dictator, abolishing the kangaroo courts that were dealing out rough justice to collaborators, and ruling over his new fiefdom with a rod of iron. His second big job had been to organise the feeding of five million hungry Parisians after the city's liberation in August 1944. He knew how to get things done: no bureaucracy, no red tape, no rules – unless they were his own. His success earned him plaudits from far and wide, as well as the Legion of Merit, the Croix de Guerre and the Légion d'Honneur. Howley may have played the cowboy, but he cared deeply about people's welfare.

His team was still running food supplies into the French capital in the autumn of 1944 when he was paid a visit by the American commander, Brigadier General Julius Holmes, at his offices at 7 place Vendôme. Their conversation was perfunctory but purposeful.

'Frank,' asked Holmes, 'how would you like to go to Berlin?'

'Fine,' shrugged Howley. 'The job is done here and I'd like to stay on the main line east. Berlin sounds good to me.'[1] This brief exchange was all it took for him to land one of the biggest jobs in the post-war world.

He certainly had the required levels of dynamism. He was a curious mixture of firebrand and intellectual, a man always on the alert like 'a very large, trim eagle, ready to swoop if necessary'.[2] In the years before the war, he had excelled as an all-American footballer (he was known as Golden Toe). His sporting prowess had come to an untimely end when he crashed his motorbike at reckless speed and broke his back and pelvis. He was fortunate to make a full recovery.

Sportsmen do not always make intellectuals, but Howley was invariably the exception to the rule. He taught himself five languages, studied Fine Art at the Sorbonne and went on to establish a successful advertising company in the midst of the Great Depression. 'He has the knack of being able to do anything he tries, a bit better than anyone else,' said one of his classmates at New York University.[3]

Now, he was to lead the American contingent of the joint British-American Military Government for Berlin, whose task was to run the western sectors of the divided German capital. He would also serve on the three-power Kommandatura, which was to deal with issues that concerned the city as a whole. As such, he would frequently be dealing with his Soviet partners.

Howley swiftly recruited his team: his chief aide, Lieutenant Colonel John Maginnis, had been the first of his A1A1 recruits to land in Normandy, while his principal marksman (hired as a precaution) was Captain Charles Leonetti, a former FBI sharpshooter with a formidable track record. Within weeks, Howley had employed scores of experts and specialists with the necessary skills to run a city that was in ruins.

His Berlin team was not a combat unit, nor was it intended to fight its way into the city: it would be supported by the British and American armies. But Howley was expecting trouble en route and instructed everyone to use their own system of shoot-to-kill. He also insisted that the men should be at peak physical fitness. To this end, he established a gruelling muscle-training programme.

'I had three or four judo experts, and every officer and enlisted man learned all the dirty tricks of close-in fighting.' The older members were spared 'the rough tumbling acts',[4] but even they had to learn how to protect themselves in hand-to-hand combat.

To his great delight, Howley 'picked up' a young French linguist, Helen-Antoinette Woods (she had married an Englishman), who was both sharp and talented. 'I had some misgivings about bringing a girl along,' he confessed, 'but decided if she was willing to take the chance, I couldn't be so ungallant as to refuse a lady.' Besides, it made him feel good. 'My prestige was upped by having this chic, capable French girl in my office.'[5]

Woods herself was desperate to go to Berlin. 'There were all kinds of complications, of course, because Allied women were not allowed to go into Germany.'[6] Howley brushed these complications aside. He gave her a steel helmet, a pistol and a bodyguard and told her she would be the first Allied woman to enter Berlin.

Howley knew that carving up one of the great European capitals into three separate sectors would prove a logistical nightmare, for the city's gas, water, sewage and electricity networks did not respect the sector boundaries. If supplies were to be restored, it would require the British and Americans to work closely with their Soviet allies. Food was an even greater problem. Berlin was dependent for fresh meat and vegetables on the rich farmland in Brandenburg and Pomerania, provinces that lay to the east of the city. These were already in the hands of the Red Army, meaning that the western Allies would be dependent on Stalin's continual goodwill if they were to feed the population.

Howley's greatest concern was the fact that Berlin lay 110 miles inside the Soviet-occupied zone of Germany, turning it into an island surrounded by a sea of red. The only land route into the city was by road or rail, passing through territory controlled by the Red Army. Frank Howley thought it so vital for his team to reach the city in advance of the Soviets that he proposed a mass parachute drop into Berlin, just as the Americans and British had done in Normandy, with his A1A1 adventurers landing alongside the First Airborne Division. But it was such a bold proposition, and so fraught with risk, that Allied commanders dismissed it as unworkable.

The British contingent of Berlin's Military Government was led by Brigadier Robert 'Looney' Hinde, a precision-dressed cavalry officer whose outlook and deportment had been shaped by his years in British India. Hinde had learned Urdu and Pashtu in Kashmir, fought border skirmishes on the North West Frontier and played polo with his fellow cavalry officers in Rawalpindi, whacking the ball with such chutzpah that he was selected to represent Great Britain in the 1936 Berlin Olympics.

His sporting rivalry against the Germans had taken a more serious turn with the outbreak of war. Posted to North Africa with the 15th/19th King's Hussars, he found himself playing a deadly game of cat and mouse with Rommel's Afrika Korps. Always in the vanguard, he led his scout car on crazed dashes through enemy lines, churning clouds of hot sand into the desert skies. 'Don't shoot,' he would signal back to his men. 'It's me!'[7]

Hinde was offered the Berlin appointment in the aftermath of the battle for Normandy in the belief that he had all the necessary qualities: 'Dash, decisiveness, wisdom, supreme courage and deep responsibility.'[8] He also had a deliciously whimsical streak that had earned him his nickname, Looney, along with an insatiable passion for butterflies. 'Anyone got a matchbox?' he asked during a battlefield briefing in Normandy, having just spied a rare species of caterpillar. His stressed junior officer snapped that it was no time to be studying nature. 'Don't be such a bloody fool, Mike,' said Looney. 'You can fight a battle everyday of your life, but you might not see a caterpillar like that in fifteen years.'[9]

Brigadier Hinde was initially based in Wimbledon, from where he began hiring recruits for his contingent of Military Government. Some were civilians – intelligence operatives, linguists, lawyers and engineers, with years of expertise in their field. Others were soldiers hardened by five years of war. The recruitment process itself was undertaken by young women from the Auxiliary Territorial Service.

Brigadier Hinde's overriding priority was to forge a close working relationship with his Soviet allies. This was government policy and it was his duty to ensure it was followed to the letter. He put out feelers to his Soviet partners in the first weeks of 1945, eager to make contact in advance of their meeting in Berlin, but received no answer. He was disappointed – a reply would have been courteous – but brushed it off as an unfortunate oversight on their part.

He was determined not to prejudge the Soviets and was disquieted to hear some of his recruits talking about them in derogatory fashion. He urged them to be more open-minded. 'I have noticed a tendency to regard Communists with suspicion almost automatically,' he said, before informing them that the Soviets had 'many sincere and able men among them, who have a valuable contribution to make'.

His team were to be flag-bearers for Britain's role in the post-war world, something that concerned Hinde as much as it did Churchill: 'The example we set is a matter of the greatest importance. The prestige of the British Empire has never been higher than it is today, and it is up to us to see that in no case are we instrumental in lowering it.'[10] As he eyed up his full-blooded young recruits, he could only hope they would be able to resist the temptations that would surely be on offer in Berlin.

One of Brigadier Hinde's first appointees was a snappy young lieutenant colonel named Harold 'Tim' Hays, a whirlwind of a man with gaunt features, a smart peaked cap and a devotion to work that was 'far beyond the normal line of duty'.[11] Amidst his many duties, Hays set himself the unofficial task of recording the adventures of the newly formed Berlin team, noting the highs and lows of everything that was to come. His typescript account, still unpublished after almost eighty years, is a unique chronicle of the extraordinary events that were to follow.

Hinde's team expanded rapidly in its first few weeks and it was not long before there was a real urgency to their work, 'prompted by the imminent collapse of the enemy'.[12] This urgency increased when they received orders to move to France in the opening weeks of 1945: it was here, some forty-five miles to the south-east of Paris, that the fastidious brigadier was to meet his American deputy, 'Howlin' Mad' Howley.

As soon as Colonel Howley was informed that Brigadier Hinde's team was en route, he made it his business to find accommodation for both his own men and those of the brigadier. Howley alighted on the village of Barbizon, an hour's drive from Paris. It was a place he knew well, for he had spent his weekends there in the late 1920s while studying at the Sorbonne. A bucolic idyll in the heart of the

Fontainebleau forest, it had a scattering of guesthouses and a lot of wild boar.

Never one to vacillate, Howley drove his fleet of jeeps down from the French capital, requisitioned all the largest private houses and hotels (along with their cooks, cleaners and other domestic staff) and then 'posted armed guards on all buildings' in order to deter any other branch of the army from trying to oust him. 'In wartime,' he told his men, 'possession is not nine-tenths of the law, it's ten-tenths.'[13]

Within hours his American team was in full command of the place, swaggering down the main street like outlaws in a Western. The Stars and Stripes fluttered from Howley's headquarters in Grand rue and American jeeps and half-tracks were parked up in the street. By the time Brigadier Hinde's unit arrived from Wimbledon, Howley ruled the roost. Harold Hays couldn't help feeling they had been completely outsmarted by the Americans, especially when it came to finding accommodation. 'It was simply a question of retaining the best for themselves and handing the remainder over to the British element.'[14]

The first meeting between Hinde and Howley had all the makings of a disaster. The American colonel was aggrieved at having to answer to an old-school brigadier with the cut-glass accent of a home-counties squire. 'Serving under anyone has always been irksome to me,' Howley wrote in his diary. 'Having been given a choice, I would never have served under a British officer.' He was also infuriated at not having been promoted to a rank similar to Hinde. 'I was only a colonel, representing the most powerful nation in the world.'[15] It was a humiliation that rankled.

Brigadier Hinde was no more convinced about having an American deputy. Americans had no subtlety; no sense of finesse. They ate jam for breakfast and left their buttons unpolished. Worse still, they had no staying-power. Little wonder that it was the British, not the Americans, who had acquired an empire.

The omens were bad, but the meeting itself proved a revelation. When the two men came face to face there was an instant attraction that was to develop into a deep friendship. Hinde had a profound admiration for Howley's bravado, while Howley was won over by the brigadier's intense energy. The two commanders were diametrically different yet curiously alike: two impatient warriors who jointly held the fate of Berlin in their hands.

Teamwork was everything – that was Howley's mantra. The biggest problem facing the Berlin team, as he saw it, was the snooty arrogance of Hinde's 110 recruited officers. 'Without exception they are members of the landed gentry and conservatives,' he said. 'Emotionally they find it difficult to kowtow to rich Americans lacking the gentlemanly qualities they consider important.' Indeed they seemed to view all Americans 'as barbarians, and had a top-heavy idea of class distinction'. Howley thought their behaviour was due to their spending too much time in India, 'dealing with colonial inferiors'.[16]

Yet the eighty Americans serving under Howley came with their own prejudices. 'I don' like the Britishers,' said one G.I. to Harold Hays. 'You fellers can't eat, can't drink, can't talk and can't walk properly. Yer just crude. Doggon it, we spend hours back home breakin' the kids from eatin' like you.'[17]

Howley felt that such animosity was a serious problem: it was imperative that the team present a united front when dealing with its Soviet allies. If ever the situation in Berlin turned sour, it was vital that his men and those of Brigadier Hinde could work together as close comrades. He wanted people who 'knew and liked each other, so that when we ran into difficulties on the job in Berlin, we had only the troubles to iron out [because] the personality angle was solved'. To this end, he organised bonding experiences that included wild-pig hunts, climbing expeditions and nocturnal outings to Paris. 'A minimum of chicken-shit', as he put it, and a maximum of fun. He even adopted two baby boars – the Smith Brothers – as mascots of the Berlin team and vowed to carry them all the way to the German capital.

His approach worked to perfection. '*They* learned to respect us,' he said in reference to the British, 'and *we* learned to respect them.' British sangfroid, it transpired, was only skin-deep. Brigadier Hinde's men played hard and worked hard, and this made them 'the best fellows in the world after business hours and we soon began to have spontaneous dinner and cocktail parties'.[18]

★

The Berlin team faced one serious handicap that could not easily be rectified: very few recruits had ever visited the city they were going to save. Brigadier Hinde had spent a few days there during the Olympic Games eight years earlier, but he had been based in Charlottenburg to the west of the city where Hitler had built the new Olympic stadium.

A version of Berlin had been served up in British and American cinemas over the last six years. Daily Pathé newsreels had made familiar the city's monuments: the domed Reichstag, the fortified Reich Chancellery and the majestic sweep of the Unter den Linden festooned with Nazi swastikas. For many in the Allied team, the German capital stood as a symbol of darkness at the heart of Hitler's 'thousand-year Reich'.

One recruit, Wilfred Byford-Jones, had visited Berlin shortly before the outbreak of war and recalled watching Hitler's storm-troopers marching down the Unter den Linden with clockwork precision, accompanied by 'fiercely pompous Prussian music'.[19] Another member of the team, George Clare, had also visited pre-war Berlin, albeit in very different circumstances. His family were Jewish refugees from Vienna and were among the very few to have been granted refuge in the Irish Free State: they had come to the German capital to collect their immigration visas.

Clare told his comrades how he had been beguiled by Berlin's irreverent charms. Few Berliners were ardent Nazis and he felt that the capital 'wore its brown shirt sloppily, unbuttoned and with collar open'.[20] This was a historical truth: in the city elections of 1933, held two months after Hitler became chancellor, the Nazis had won little more than a third of the vote.

Clare's knowledge of Berlin was very much the exception. For most of those en route to the German capital, whether British or American, they might have been heading to the moon.

Colonel Howley took charge of logistics for the Berlin assignment, considering himself the most qualified person. He certainly proved a master of his brief during those long weeks in Barbizon. 'We sent to London for air-bomb-damage pictures, learned from maps and charts exactly how the sewers were laid out, how much coal was needed to pump them, where the water lay in the 1,300 deep wells throughout the city.' His men studied the schools, hospitals and the language. 'We even tried to locate, also from air pictures, a building where we could set up a joint headquarters with the Russians.'

The more he came to understand the city, the more he realised that the task ahead would be infinitely more challenging than Cherbourg or Paris. 'I knew that Berlin would be a tough job,' he said. 'I knew what hunger was and what thousands of orphans on your hands could mean. I was familiar with the scabby look of scabies.' He also knew 'that Berlin was getting the real treatment and was going to be a mess'.[21]

The team was getting firmly into its stride when an unexpected visitor pitched up in Barbizon. Dr Walter Dorn was a military expert from the American Psychological Warfare Division and he had just returned from the front line of the advancing American army. He brought news that caused serious alarm. The countryside to the east of Barbizon was overrun with millions of displaced people, many of whom were violent and most were without possessions or food. Rape was commonplace, murders widespread. Dr Dorn also warned that the Germans were 'unable to appreciate that we came as conquerors and not as liberators', adding that there would be severe problems in finding anyone suitable to take over the offices previously held by Nazis.

'He blew a gaping hole into all our previous training,' said Harold Hays. 'It was the most illuminating talk that we had on the subject, shedding much light in dark places.'[22] Only now did the men realise that they had a potentially life-threatening mission on their hands. They would be working in an apocalyptic war-zone in which their presence would not always be welcome. Colonel Howley's judo and pistol training might prove useful after all.

As spring arrived in Fontainebleau forest, Hinde and Howley were brought the latest news of the Allied advance into Germany. General Patton's Third Army was making a great thrust south-east towards Czechoslovakia, while the British and Canadians were heading for the northern cities of Bremen and Hamburg. The American First Army, under the command of General Courtney Hodges, was also making rapid progress as it advanced through the central zone of Germany towards the Renaissance town of Torgau, on the River Elbe. One of Hodges's divisions, the 69th Infantry, had pushed so far east that it was tantalisingly close to the Russian front line. Less than five miles of no man's land lay between them and the Red Army.

Among the soldiers in this dangerous slice of territory was a young sergeant named Alfred Aronson, whose comrades had recently fought their way into Leipzig. Aronson had been surprised by the welcome they received from the local civilians, but it soon became apparent that this was not because they were pleased to see the Americans but because they were terrified by the rapid advance of the Red Army.

'Are the Russians coming? Are the Russians coming?' The same question was repeated over and over. Aronson sensed that they were fearful of 'retaliation for what the German soldiers had inflicted on the Russians – a vengeance to even up the score.'

After a few days in Leipzig, Aronson and his men advanced to the town of Trebsen on the River Mulde, some 125 miles from Berlin. Here, they awaited the order to push further east. But Aronson's patrol commander, Lieutenant Albert Kotzebue, was keen to lead a reconnaissance mission into no man's land. 'We're going to go and see if we can find some Russians,' he joked. He was also intrigued. For three and a half years he had followed the progress of the Red Army without getting any sense of what the Russians were like. Now, he was going to find out.

That very afternoon, on Tuesday, 24 April, Lieutenant Kotzebue led his patrol into uncharted territories. They spent their first night bivouacking in the town of Zehren, then drove their jeeps down to the River Elbe. As they reached the water, Kotzebue spotted what appeared to be Russians on the other side. He fired green flares into the sky, a signal (agreed upon between the western Allies and the Russians) to identify his men as American. Before long, Russian troops began congregating on the riverbank. There was great excitement on both sides. Ten months after the landings in Normandy – and some twelve weeks since the Red Army crossed the eastern border into Germany – they were making history. 'Through waving and whistling and hollering, we got to meet one another.'

The Russians soon got the pontoon ferry into action, hauling the American jeeps and men across the sluggish river. It was an agonising few minutes before they stepped ashore on the eastern bank. Communication was a problem. Very few of the Russians spoke English and the only Russian speaker in Lieutenant Kotzebue's patrol was a young medic named Corporal Stephen Kowalski. The rest tried to communicate by 'using pig Latin and waving our hands and saying *Nostrovia*, which was a word that everyone seemed to like'.[23]

Aronson was immediately struck by the shambolic appearance of the Russian soldiers. Their uniforms were in tatters and they were using horse-drawn cavalry pieces. The more he studied them, the more he was astonished. 'We couldn't have imagined how they could have advanced so well against the might of the Germans with such primitive weaponry.'

One of the Russian soldiers fetched some vodka and began pouring generous glassfuls. They drank a toast to each of the three wartime leaders 'and then we drank a toast to each other and then we drank a toast to everyone else'. The vodka performed wonders. 'Those Russian toasts,' said a swampy-headed Aronson, 'it isn't just a sip. It's bottom's up.' Within a few minutes, their historic meeting had turned into a raucous party with the festivities enhanced by the appearance of female Russian soldiers.

The onset of evening was the cue for yet more vodka, along with music and dancing. 'There were harmonicas and concertinas – the first night was a riot.' Aronson and company exchanged buttons and patches from their uniforms before drinking yet more shots of vodka. 'Everyone was clapping everybody on the back and very happy to see one another,' said Aronson's comrade, Jim Kane. 'We were all buddies.'

When the Americans staggered into town to find somewhere to sleep they made an unwelcome discovery. They were accustomed to requisition the most luxurious houses and pass the night in the comfort of a German bed, but the Russians had trashed everything. 'Beds, chinaware, they just threw everything out of the buildings. It looked like a disaster zone.'[24] Aronson and his men had no option but to sleep on the floors of these ransacked homes. It was their first note of disquiet and made them wonder if these Red Army soldiers were nothing more than a band of gangsters.

Bleary-eyed and sore of head, Aronson and company awoke the next morning and prepared to head back to base. They later discovered that a second American patrol (led by 2nd Lieutenant William D. Robertson) had met up with the Russians some hours before they had, thereby winning the accolade of being the first officially to link the western and eastern fronts. It was two days before this news was released. The delay was to allow for a simultaneous announcement by the three Allied leaders. 'We meet in true and victorious comradeship,' was their message to the world.[25]

Brigadier Hinde's contingent of Military Government left Barbizon in early April and set off eastwards on the trail of the advancing army. His men were stunned by the scale of destruction. Bridges, railway junctions and canals had all been reduced to rubble by Allied airpower. In the words of Harold Hays, there were 'sunken barges in the river, power standards leaning drunkenly, shattered rolling stock, empty shells of buildings and hundreds of tons of scrap metal lying around'.

They were instructed to halt at Namur, where they requisitioned an undamaged chateau. Everyone felt restless and frustrated. 'So near to our German destination, yet so far,' said Hays. 'We began to think we should never get to Germany at all.'

But they soon received orders to continue their advance and it was a more cheerful Hays who led the team into Aachen, one-time imperial capital of Charlemagne. This was their first German city and thus a milestone of sorts. 'We were elated and whistled jokingly the Horst Wessel,' the Nazi party anthem. Hays's comrade, Major Jeffrey, was so beside himself with excitement that he babbled away 'in a mixture of French, German and Hindustani'.

Their high spirits lasted until they reached the wrecked centre of Aachen. 'We caught our breath in chilled astonishment,' said Hays. He had lived through the London blitz and seen entire terraces of houses destroyed by the Luftwaffe. 'But all conceptions of the power of aerial bombardment were scattered to the winds as we threaded our way tortuously through the heaps of rubble that once represented the city of Aachen.' Not even the shells of buildings remained standing. On one of the few walls still upright, there was graffiti daubed in white paint: '*Hitler ist Kaputt.*'

Their sense of shock intensified as they pushed deeper into Germany, passing streams of destitute refugees, 'walking, cycling, pushing barrows and riding heavy-laden in farm carts'. A freezing rain was driving in from the east 'and as these parties moved along the roads in their hopeless quest for shelter, one felt a surge of pity'. The Berlin team was witnessing a biblical-scale exodus, a trudging mass of humanity with nowhere to go and nothing to eat. 'Poor sods,' murmured one of Hinde's recruits, before adding sardonically, 'but they deserve everything coming to them.'

The sights witnessed by Harold Hays became little vignettes of horror in his chronicle: a demented woman dragging herself through the ruins, 'her swollen feet bound in blood-soaked rags'; three youths 'with the unmistakable and awful imprint of starvation and scurvy stamped on their pinched features'; an elderly German couple 'quietly weeping while they faced the rubble of a totally demolished dwelling in Paderborn, their entire worldly possessions resting pathetically behind them in a dilapidated perambulator'. Hays had been taught to hate the Germans; now, he felt nothing but pity for them.

Hinde's team pushed on into the Ruhr, Germany's industrial heartland. It had only recently been seized from the Wehrmacht and the scars of warfare were everywhere visible. The old town of Essen had been particularly hard hit and Hinde's convoy of trucks could get through only by blasting a passage with explosives. The mighty Krupps factory was damaged beyond repair, with 'concrete floors hanging like carpets in the sun'. It looked as if a malevolent giant had gone on a rampage. 'Girders everywhere and shattered boilers, gas containers, pipes and pumps, furnaces, locomotives, strewn about like discarded toys.'[26]

It was bitterly cold by the time Hinde's men swept into Düsseldorf, still 350 miles west of Berlin and only recently liberated by the 94th US Army Division. Their arrival coincided with that of Goronwy Rees, a young intelligence officer undertaking an inspection of liberated Germany territory. His experiences in Düsseldorf offered a first glimpse of the nightmare that would face the Berlin team once it reached the German capital.

The atrocious weather was grimly appropriate. 'It was pouring from a leaden sky the colour of dead ashes,' wrote Rees, 'and in this downpour the ruined empty streets had the mournfulness and melancholy of some tragic funeral dirge, as if we had come to attend a burial ceremony.' The place was completely deserted. 'In this dead city there was nothing any longer to support life, neither food, nor water, nor shelter, nor heating.'

Düsseldorf had been temporarily placed under the command of a British officer who had requisitioned the only undamaged building in town. Untrained and unqualified, this anonymous lieutenant colonel possessed limitless power. 'By one of those magical trans-formations which occur in war, he found himself the administrator and absolute ruler of an area containing over one million human beings who had suddenly been deprived of the means of existence.' But he was a ruler without the means to rule. Rees said that he 'might just as well have been dropped from the skies in the middle of tropical Africa and told to get on with the job of governing some primitive tribe living on the edge of starvation'. [27]

While Rees chatted with the lieutenant colonel, Harold Hays went in search of accommodation. There were few buildings intact and his men spent that night in the cellar of a blitzed building, with sleet tipping through the glassless windows.

As Brigadier Hinde's men pushed their way towards Düsseldorf, Colonel Howley's Americans had been heading for the Ninth Army headquarters at Gütersloh, an industrial city some 250 miles west of Berlin. For Howley, the division of Military Government into two separate entities was a moment of personal triumph. He had never wanted to be a deputy and now, less than four months after first meeting Hinde, he was the de facto commander of his own eighty-strong team. He attributed his success to 'a lack of diplomacy, bluntness and directness of what I said and thought'. [28]

He was particularly pleased to have acquired a magnificent Horch Roadster that befitted his new status. It was a veritable beast of a machine with huge headlamps, shimmering chrome-work and a bonnet the length of a bed. 'The biggest and best car in Germany,' he said.[29] When driven at speed, it purred like a lion. One of his aides had found it hidden under a haystack and requisitioned it in a bold act of daylight robbery. 'He hitched his jeep to the bumper,' said Howley, 'and brought the roadster back to me.'

As Howley and his men headed eastward, they grew increasingly excited by the prospect of meeting soldiers of the Red Army. 'We had nothing but good wishes for our friends, the Russians.'[30] He had met his first Russian a few weeks earlier in an encounter that had been less than propitious. He was steering his staff car towards army headquarters when a complete stranger leaped onto the vehicle's running board. 'More in surprise than anger, I swung a left hook to his jaw and knocked him back into the road.' Howley assumed the man was an enemy German and was extremely surprised to hear him shouting, 'Russky! Russky!' It transpired that he was a newly liberated prisoner of war in want of a lift. Howley's passenger, an English lieutenant colonel, looked on in astonishment. 'My God, colonel,' he said, 'you've just bashed the first Russian we've met.'[31]

Howley was welcomed at Gütersloh headquarters by Colonel Craigy, a staff officer with the Ninth Army. 'Thank God you're here,' he said. 'I've been trying for weeks to get SHAEF* to release you and your unit to me.' He gave Howley some welcome news. 'We've had three bridgeheads across the Elbe. There's nothing between us and Berlin but an SS regiment in Potsdam.' He assured Howley that the first Allied troops into Berlin would be American. 'If we get our orders tomorrow we can be in Berlin before Saturday.' He added with a smile, 'Can you join us?'[32]

'We can join you and we will,' promised Howley. He meant it. He had been among the first American troops into both Cherbourg and Paris. Now, he intended to lead the vanguard into Berlin.

But his triumphant entry into Berlin was unexpectedly thwarted. Six months earlier, General Eisenhower had insisted that Berlin was 'the main prize' and therefore the Allied armies' ultimate objective. 'We should concentrate all our energies and resources on rapid thrusts to Berlin.' Now, in a dramatic change of policy, he dismissed

---

* SHAEF: Supreme Headquarters Allied Expeditionary Force.

Berlin as 'nothing but a geographical location'.[33] The primary task of the western Allies, he said, was the complete destruction of Hitler's remaining forces.

Howley was furious. 'The last great decision in history to be made on such a limited basis,' he said, 'ignoring political consequences.' Impatient for action, he reiterated that he was 'available and more than ready to go'.[34] If and when he got the green light, he would make a headlong dash for Berlin.

2

Flag on the Reichstag

THE HOTEL LUX on Moscow's Gorky Street was the ultimate house of secrets, a labyrinth of deceit in which conspiracies were planned, revolutions hatched and murders plotted with chilling detachment. From the outside, the building's wedding cake facade conveyed an air of faded imperial grandeur. It had been built at a time of tsarist splendour and no amount of drab Stalinism could diminish its bourgeois opulence. Once inside, guests were invited to enjoy the perfumed luxuries that had long since vanished from Moscow's other hotels: fine dining, tailors' repair shops, a private laundry and a well-equipped infirmary.

Each guest was obliged to carry a *propusk* or identity card complete with photo. There was good reason for the security. The Hotel Lux was a mecca for spies and revolutionary activists from across the globe. In its curtained salons, Polish brigands rubbed shoulders with Spanish Communists and Soviet propagandists.

The hotel had been a hotbed of plots since 1921, when it had hosted a congress of the Communist International. The Hungarian activist, Gyula Háy, found staying there an enthralling experience. 'Within its walls, the cauldrons of the world revolution bubbled and seethed non-stop.'[1] If you wanted to plan an insurrection or topple an elected leader, the Lux was the place to come.

In the spring of 1945, the hotel became the headquarters of Moscow's Berlin Group, a secretive band of German-born revolutionaries supported by Stalin. They were charged with infiltrating themselves into the German capital within hours of the Red Army capturing it. Once there, they had two important roles to play, one official and one very much unofficial. The official role was benign: to root out the remnants of Nazism and lay the groundwork for

33

a new and democratic system of government. The unofficial role was more nefarious. In the words of their group leader, Walter Ulbricht, 'it's got to *look* democratic, but we must have everything in our control.' He intended to outwit the western Allies by seizing control of the city's institutions, including the Berlin police. 'The best thing will be for us to divide ourselves up and each take over a particular district in Berlin,' he told his group at a planning session. 'We can then meet in the evenings and each report on his district.'[2] Ulbricht's team was to be helped in its work by some of the brightest stars in the Soviet military, generals whose medal-bedecked chests were evidence enough that they were accustomed to winning.

Walter Ulbricht was the éminence grise of this little band. A Communist to his fingertips, he had impeccable revolutionary credentials. He had fled to the Soviet capital eight years earlier, when life in Hitler's Germany grew too dangerous for comfort, and was soon smuggling anti-Nazi agents back into Berlin. In Moscow, Ulbricht became known as Comrade Cell on account of his gift for organising networks of underground agents.

Some questioned if he was the right man for a mission that would require charm and charisma. Attired in the shapeless suit of a party apparatchik, Ulbricht was chillingly deficient in both. 'I seldom saw him laugh,' said one in his circle, 'and I do not remember ever having detected any signs of personal feelings.'[3] Another concluded that he was 'not a nice man . . . a tireless weaver of intrigues'.[4] This intriguing had left him a loner: 'from his schooldays onwards, he never had a single personal friend.'[5] He had managed to acquire a wife, known as Comrade Lotte, but she was loathed by everyone at the Lux.

Ulbricht had the dogmatic asceticism of a desert monastic. He didn't drink, didn't socialise, didn't eat meat or fish. His mealtime preference was for raw vegetables, a dietary regime that even his most diehard comrades found hard to stomach. According to one, 'he never gave cocktail parties, never had affairs and even gave up smoking as [being] a drain on his revolutionary activities.'[6] When he spoke, he did so in a curiously high-pitched voice, dispensing revolutionary wisdom in his sing-song Saxon dialect. His judgement was final and irrevocable. 'He has the last word always, interrupting everybody [and] heckling speakers he dislikes.'[7] He was the prototype for so many future leaders of Eastern Europe: grim, ashen-faced and entirely devoid of humour.

Those in Ulbricht's inner circle were similarly lacking in human warmth. His policing expert was 'entirely without humour' while his cultural affairs commissar, Otto Winzer, was a 'cold, acid type of Stalinist official who would remorselessly carry through every directive'.[8]

In this sea of menacing greyness there shone but one bright light. Wolfgang Leonhard was an impressionable twenty-three-year-old who had been on a voyage of discovery ever since his mother pitched up in Moscow as an exile from the Nazis in 1935. Indoctrinated in the Karl Liebknecht School for anti-fascists, Leonhard was next sent to an elite college for would-be revolutionaries in Russian Bashkortostan where he studied alongside Žarko Tito, son of Yugoslavia's future president.

His spell there might have extinguished every last spark of revolutionary idealism. Instead, Leonhard emerged as a cheerily naive optimist who believed that the end of the war would bring a radical change to Stalinism: 'more leisurely, pleasant, tolerant, democratic and flexible'.[9] He was singing from a very different hymn sheet from Walter Ulbricht.

On Friday, 27 April 1945, the Berlin group was summoned to a meeting in Ulbricht's second-floor bedroom in the Hotel Lux. He told them they were to fly to the German capital within the next few days. 'Everything ready?' he asked each one in turn. 'Everything completed?' He next turned to the practicalities of their mission, providing details about transport and money. 'He opened his briefcase and took out a bundle of bank notes which he distributed among us. "Here's a thousand roubles each as pocket money",' Leonhard remembered him saying. This was a large sum, the equivalent of a month's wages. 'And now here are two thousand German Reichsmarks for each of you for your first expenses in Germany.'

Two days after this meeting, the group was invited for farewell drinks in the suite of rooms occupied by Wilhelm Pieck, chairman of the German Communist Party in exile. He filled each of their glasses with vodka before giving the toast. 'Comrades!' he roared, 'To our future work in Germany!'

And that was it. Their years in Moscow were almost at an end. On the following day at 6 a.m. sharp they were to meet at the side entrance of the hotel, where a bus would pick them up and take them to the airport. 'I was still dizzy with excitement when I got back to my room,' wrote Leonhard. 'For a long time I could not sleep.'[10]

He had good reason to be excited, for that very day the first Red Army tanks had pushed their way into the centre of Berlin, reaching Potsdamerplatz. They were now less than a thousand yards from the Brandenburg Gate.

Soviet forces had advanced with lightning speed since launching their offensive in the third week of April. Two huge army groups were converging on the city from the south and east, while a third was wheeling in from the north. On Friday, 20 April, Hitler's fifty-sixth birthday, Marshal Georgy Zhukov's one-and-a-half-million-strong army had begun shelling the city centre from their positions in the northern suburbs, while Marshal Ivan Konev's forces were approaching the city's southern outskirts. The Red Army had soon encircled the German forces that remained in the city, trapping the beleaguered defenders.

On 29 April, Hitler married Eva Braun inside his fortified bunker, with Goebbels and Bormann acting as witnesses. The Führer's hand was shaking so badly when he signed the register that his signature was illegible. Elsewhere in the bunker the febrile atmosphere was fuelled by alcohol, sex and blind panic. Hitler's secretary, Traudl Junge, was deeply shocked when she ventured upstairs. 'An erotic fever seemed to have taken possession of everybody,' she said. 'The women had discarded all modesty and were freely exposing their private parts.' She knew – as did Hitler – that the curtain was about to fall.

A menacing drumroll heralded the Red Army's arrival in the southern outskirts of Berlin. In prosperous Potsdam, a forty-minute drive from the city centre, Paul Hoecke and his wife Valerie were desperately anxious about their three children: seven-year-old Hermann, Olga, four, and Irina who was just two. Whenever young Hermann looked out of his bedroom window he could see a blaze of artillery barrages lighting up the night sky. 'The flashes became so frequent that they merged into a continuous glare across the horizon, like a lightning storm that went on and on.'

The Hoecke family had particular reason to fear the arrival of the Soviet army. Valerie was herself Russian, one of millions who had fled their homeland in the aftermath of the Bolshevik revolution. Her German husband, Paul, had converted to Russian Orthodoxy and was now a priest serving Berlin's community of exiles. In Nazi Germany, these exiles had been given refuge because of their vehemently anti-Communist credentials. Now, those credentials placed them at grave risk.

Just a few months before, the Hoeckes had moved out of Berlin and into a new home in the Russische Kolonie, a Russian-style suburb of Potsdam. It was safer than Berlin, but they felt increasingly exposed as the war rolled ever closer. By that third week of April the night sky to the north-east 'had a dull pulsating glow to it, proof that the battle was already raging over there'. Alarmingly, the southern sky was also aflame. This could mean only one thing: 'We were already surrounded.'

On Wednesday, 25 April 1945, as General Konev's forces approached Potsdam, the Hoecke parents sought a safer place of refuge. Close to their home was the Schloss Cecilienhof, home to Germany's former ruling family, the Hohenzollerns. Paul Hoecke knew the secretary of Princess Kira Kirillovna (the Russian wife of Prince Louis von Hohenzollern) who offered them shelter in the vaulted wine cellar.

Young Hermann noticed anxiety on the faces of those already assembled underground. 'When we got there, we found people had already set up camp all over the floor, among the wine racks, piles of coal and stacks of dusty old furniture.' Menacing shadows stalked the dimly lit vaults, with the only lighting coming from Hindenburg tallow lamps. The muffled din of explosions boomed through the brickwork, along with the moan of incoming shells. And then, imperceptibly at first, the noise of war came to a halt.

'The faint sounds of gunfire we had been hearing for what seemed like hours faded away and were replaced by total silence above our heads and around us.' Everyone knew it heralded the imminent arrival of the Soviet forces. 'As we held our breath, many of the people around us instinctively put out their lights, leaving the cellars pitch dark.' Silence. Complete silence. Hermann Hoecke was scared. In the darkness, he could hear someone whispering, '*Die Russen! Die Russen sind hier!*'

He was crouched at the bottom of a long flight of stairs that led up to the courtyard. The stairway was sealed at the top by a heavy door that offered a protection of sorts against shellfire and shrapnel. Suddenly, and quite without warning, the door was flung open and light flooded down the stairwell.

'Momentarily blinded, I could only discern a couple of dark silhouettes crouched in that bright rectangle, but their voices were quite clear. They were yelling, "*Davay! Davay! Alle heraus!*" And their accent was distinctly Russian.' It was clear to all what it meant. 'Come on! Come on! Everyone out!'[11] The Red Army had captured Potsdam. And the residents' lives now hung in the balance.

The Hoecke family was ordered out of the cellar, along with everyone else. Two Red Army soldiers led them into the courtyard of the palace, where fires were burning in huge metal drums. The afternoon had passed in a flash and it was already growing dark. Young Hermann Hoecke watched nervously as a drunk Soviet infantryman began strumming a balalaika. 'He stared at me with glassy eyes, a fixed grin on his face, as he bellowed out unintelligible snippets of some song.'[12] One of his hands was wrapped in a thick, blood-soaked bandage.

No one knew what would happen next and all feared the worst. But after being held for a few tense hours, everyone was told to return to their homes. The Hoeckes were to pass a terrifying night listening to the cries of women begging for help.

The panic in Potsdam was nothing to the terror in Berlin itself. For months the family of seven-year-old Helga Schneider had been hiding in a cellar beneath their housing block in Lothar-Bucher-Strasse, close to Berlin's botanical gardens. Young Helga's horizons were limited to a foetid underground room shared with a dozen or more neighbours. Among the crowd was her stepmother, Ursula, her younger brother Peter and 'Opa' her step-grandfather, as well as Frau Kochler, the concierge, and Kochler's twelve-year-old son, Rudolf. Opa was emaciated from lack of food. 'His fingers were long and white, like those of a corpse, and his clothes appeared to be holding him up.' Ursula had once been a knock-out blonde: now, her hair 'had assumed the indefinable colour of dust'.[13] Others were in even worse shape. Fourteen-year-old Erika, a refugee from the countryside, was suffering from acute tuberculosis and kept coughing up blood. To Helga's eyes, 'her skin was so transparent that the outlines of her bones showed through it.'[14]

This little community had lived underground for weeks, with only the occasional foray into the streets to fill their water-cans at the standpipes. The outside world had become a hostile battleground where shells, shrapnel and mortar fire endangered anyone who dared to leave their cellar. When the young German journalist, Marta Hillers, poked her head outside in a nearby district she saw defeat all around her. 'I stood in the doorway and watched some soldiers pass by our building, listlessly dragging their feet.' They were in a pitiful state, she saw. 'Some were limping. Mute, each man to himself they trudged along, out of step . . . Stubby chins and sunken cheeks, their backs weighed down with gear.'[15]

Berliners snatched at the whispers of desperate refugees pouring in from the east. They were whispers to chill the blood. 'We tried wearing headscarves,' sobbed one young girl from Landsberg, 'but at fourteen it's hard to turn yourself into an old woman.'[16] Rape. The word was unspoken, but it was on everyone's minds.

By the last week of April, Berlin had ceased to function; there was no government, no electricity, no transport and precious little gas. Essential supplies had run out long before. In the Schneider cellar they had no more toilet paper – a serious sanitary problem given that everyone had dysentery. They resorted to using pages ripped from Nietzsche and Shakespeare. 'When a culture ends up in the shit,' remarked one of those living there, 'a people is finished.'[17]

On the rare occasions when the wireless could be cranked into life, the news was grim. The Soviets were in the suburbs. The Soviets had taken the Teltow Canal. The Soviets had occupied Tempelhof. 'Opa and Herr Mannheim were constantly glued to the radio trying to pick their way through the flood of information. Deutscher Rundfunk was suddenly interrupted one day, right in the middle of a news item.' The silence that followed could mean only one thing: the enemy had captured the nearby radio station.

When the Russians finally arrived on the 28th, they did so brusquely. The door to the cellar in which Helga Schneider and her family were hiding was kicked open by a booted foot and 'we found ourselves face to face with six Russian soldiers, all aiming submachine guns at us. Two of them had shaven heads, three wore fur caps, and one had black curly hair and a beard that came down over his chest.' The soldier with the beard asked peremptorily: 'Here *soldaty germanskie?*'

No one responded; they were too terrified.

'*Soldaty germanskie?*' the solder repeated, this time with real menace in his voice.

Young Helga's step-grandfather managed to stammer a reply. 'No soldiers here.'

The Soviet infantryman looked furious. He spat out his response. 'You lie!' he snapped. 'If *soldaty germanskie* here, you *kaputt!*'[18]

The six soldiers pointed their submachine guns at the assembled group. '*War kaputt!*' screamed one of them. '*Hitler kaputt!*' He demanded the watches of everyone in the room. 'You give *urri* or you *kaputt!*'

They all hurried to hand over their watches, with the exception of one old man in the cellar who snivelled into his jacket and said it was the only remaining memento of his wife.

'You cry for *urri?*' shouted the soldier. 'You idiot! Better weep for your city.' He tore the watch from the old man's wrist.

After stealing the watches, one of the soldiers reached into his pocket and handed a loaf of black bread to young Helga. And then the six of them went back upstairs shouting '*Hitler kaputt!*'

'There was stunned silence. Then relief. Bewildered agitation . . . [and] finally everyone was talking at once and there was a mood of jubilation.' Frau Kochler the concierge seemed to speak for everyone when she said, 'If those are the barbarians Goebbels was talking about, they've got my vote.' Another of the women shed tears of joy. 'And they didn't touch any of the women!'[19]

She soon regretted those words. Shortly afterwards two very different Soviet soldiers burst into the cellar. Drunk and heavily armed, they snarled at the terrified occupants before turning to the two teenage girls, sixteen-year-old Gudrun and fourteen-year-old Erika. 'You *Fräulein*! You *gut*! You come with me!'

Gudrun's mother protested and was kicked in the stomach. Erika's mother begged to take her daughter's place and was beaten unconscious. Young Helga Schneider buried her face in a jacket and opened her eyes only when it was all over and the soldiers had left. Gudrun was carried to a camp bed. 'She was trembling, her teeth were chattering and her eyes were wide and staring.' Erika, feeble from acute tuberculosis, was in an even worse state. She had begun to haemorrhage and no one was able to staunch the flow of blood. 'She gripped her mother's hand and kissed it. But the kiss stiffened and she died biting her mother's fingers.'[20]

Closer to the city centre, at the Elisabeth Hospital on Lützowstrasse, nurse Kaethe Eckstein glanced out of the window and saw the muzzle flares of approaching Russian artillery. 'There were fearful screams from the rear wing of the hospital. I heard shots and hand grenades going off. I rushed out into the corridor.' The sight was one she would never forget. 'Wounded men with their bandages falling from them were dragging themselves along the corridors and crawling on all fours up the stairs, shouting, "The Russians are here."' Eckstein and her fellow nurses, all nuns, had nowhere to hide. 'Most were on their knees praying. Others were running about in terror.' There was to be no escape from the sexual violence now unleashed upon them. 'Everywhere there were Russians dragging away nurses or female patients, pulling off their clothes, pouring whisky over them, shooting at the wall.' Nurse Eckstein managed to escape and hide in the cellar of an adjacent building. When she eventually emerged, the hospital was a smouldering ruin with iron-framed beds poking through the rubble. 'And lying upon them, horribly charred, were the burned bodies of human beings.' Shells had scored a direct hit on the building, setting fire to everything inside. 'By the buckles, pistols and the charred remains of boots, we could tell that the Russians in their madness had been burned to death with the women they had raped.'[21]

Thirty minutes to the south, on Kaiserallee, thirty-three-year-old Friedrich Luft had anticipated the rapes and contrived a solution of sorts, albeit a macabre one. When his two female neighbours were killed by Russian shellfire, he wrapped their bodies in rugs and left them outside in the courtyard. He hoped this would provide protection for the women hiding in the attic.

A group of Soviet soldiers soon came banging on the door. 'Where are your women? We want your women! *Frau! Frau!*'

Luft displayed remarkable composure, leading the soldiers to the two corpses. He unrolled one of the rugs and said sadly, 'This is my *Frau*. I can't supply you with any women. These are the only women.'

An abrupt change came over the soldiers, one that astonished Luft. 'They made the sign of the cross and said little prayers and then kissed me because they thought I was a widower and gave me cigarettes and bread.' He then watched as they headed off like a pack of wild dogs, 'and probably got what they wanted at the next house or the next street'.[22]

Herr Luft was unaware that Soviet soldiers were being actively encouraged to take their revenge on the Germans. The final directive issued by the Political Administration of the Red Army was chillingly clear: 'On German soil there is only one master – the Soviet soldier, he is both the judge and the punisher for the torments of his fathers and mothers.'[23]

Shortly after lunch on Monday, 30 April, Adolf Hitler and Eva Braun shook hands with their closest staff before retiring to their private suite. At 3.30 p.m., a single shot was heard. When bunker staff entered the room, they found Hitler slumped on a sofa and drenched in blood. He had shot himself through the mouth. His new wife had also killed herself, by swallowing a capsule of cyanide.

Much of Berlin was in Soviet hands by that last day in April, but the Reichstag itself was still held by enemy troops. This was the greatest prize for every Soviet soldier because it was seen as an emblem of Nazism, even though it had scarcely been used during the twelve years of the Third Reich. Soviet generals wanted the red banner of victory raised over the building, aware that such an image would send a powerful message to the world. The timing of the Reichstag's capture was also on their minds. The following morning would be May Day, the Soviet national holiday. To seize the building on such a day would be irresistibly symbolic.

Earlier that morning, Soviet troops had fought their way into the basement of the nearby 'Himmler's House', the Ministry of the Interior building on Moltkestrasse. After several hours of heavy fighting, the last pockets of German resistance were flushed from the upper floors. This gave Soviet soldiers a commanding view of the Reichstag, just 400 metres away. But they were 400 metres of extreme danger, for the adjacent Königsplatz was a blighted no man's land littered with burning tanks and half-tracks.

Rumour begat rumour that afternoon. At 2.25 p.m., General Vasily Shatilov was told that Soviet troops were already inside the building. He phoned the news through to General Vasily Kuznetsov, who in turn phoned Marshal Zhukov. 'Our Red Banner is on the Reichstag! Hurrah Comrade Marshal!'[24] It was untrue. Soviet soldiers had not yet made it to the doors of the building, let alone the cavernous interior.

Among those in the vanguard was a platoon of war-toughened warriors led by Captain Vladimir Makov. His four men were Alexei Bobrov, Alexander Lysimenko, Gazetin Zagitov and Mikhail Minin. They had fought together for two years and they had also vowed to die together. Twenty-three-year-old Minin was particularly turbo-charged, a thick-jawed heavyweight who had fought his way from Leningrad to Berlin.

As night fell, Minin noticed an increasing reticence among soldiers to go on the attack. 'Nobody really wanted to die that night because the war was already won.'[25] Even the promise of medals brought forth few volunteers. Captain Makov's platoon was the exception.

At 9.30 p.m., Soviet artillery unleashed a barrage of fire at the Reichstag. Five minutes before it was scheduled to end, Makov and his four men vaulted from a window of the interior ministry and sprinted across the Königsplatz. Dodging intense gunfire they dived for cover, caught their breath, then made a second dash towards the Reichstag entrance, leaping up the wide granite steps that led to the main doors. Sergeant Zagitov dragged a wooden beam to the entrance and rammed the bolted doors. These gave way after a few heavy blows and the five of them dashed inside. They were soon joined by other platoons that followed in their wake.

Makov's platoon secured the atrium and began a fighting advance to the upper floors, with Sergeant Minin in the vanguard. 'We threw hand grenades into all the corridors opening onto the stairs and raked everything with machine gun fire.' When they reached the top of the building they found an attic with a trapdoor. Zagitov shone his torch upwards and saw a cargo winch with two massive chains hanging down from the roof. 'The links of the giant chain were so big that they could be used as footholds. One by one we started climbing up.'[26]

Sergeant Zagitov led the way, with Minin closely behind. The latter was clutching the large red flag he had been given by his senior commander. A few more steps and they reached the dormer window that opened onto the roof. In the light of an exploding shell, Lysimenko saw the Goddess of Victory sculpture they had used as a landmark earlier that day.

Minin said they should hang their Soviet red flag from this sculpture. But first, he wanted to ensure they would be recognised for their deed. 'There, on the roof and in the dark, I scribbled our names on the banner with a pen: my name and those of Zagitov, Bobrov and Lysimenko.' He then tied the flag to a long metal rod and attached it to the sculpture. It was 10.40 p.m. on Monday, 30 April. 'Comrade General,' shouted Makov down the wire to Major General Perevertkin, 'my lads are the first to hoist the Victory Banner on the Reichstag roof.' With characteristic insolence, he added that they stuck it 'into the crown of some bare-assed whore!'[27]

There was but one problem. No one had brought a camera.

Photographic images are an essential component of modern warfare and a well-staged propaganda picture will remain in the public consciousness for long after the fighting is finished. Such were the thoughts of the Soviet photographer Yevgeny Khaldei, who had much admired the iconic photo of American marines raising the Stars and Stripes at Iwo Jima, taken two months earlier by Joe Rosenthal.

Rosenthal's image had not been staged: he had been in the right place at the right time. Khaldei was unwilling to trust his luck. His employment with the Soviet news agency, Tass, required him to produce a succession of striking images. Just a few hours earlier, as Red Army troops were fighting their way towards the Reichstag, he began planning an iconic image of the Soviet flag flying over the building.

Unable to find a large enough flag for his photo, he hitched a ride back to Moscow on one of the many military planes flying back and forth. He bought a large red tablecloth and asked his uncle, a tailor, to sew a hammer, sickle and yellow stars onto the cloth. The next morning, 2 May, saw him back on a plane to Berlin, arriving in the capital shortly after the Reichstag had been cleared of its last German defenders.

He led three soldiers up to the roof, clambering up stairs still sticky with blood, and persuaded one of the men, eighteen-year-old Aleksei Kovalev, to lean out from the parapet of the building while holding the huge homemade flag. Perched above him, and clutching his Russian-made Leica Rangefinder, Khaldei squeezed off thirty-six frames. 'I was euphoric,' he would later say. 'This is what I was waiting for, for 1,400 days.'[28]

Within hours he was back in Moscow and developing the pictures, intensifying the smoke and darkening the sky to make them yet more dramatic. His editor asked him to scratch out one of the two watches on the wrist of the soldier helping Kovalev to mount the parapet, given that they had clearly been looted.

The photograph was first published in the Russian magazine *Ogonek* and then rapidly diffused around the world. The image was as perfect as the timing, coming just two days after Hitler's suicide. Khaldei's photograph delivered a clear message to the world: the Soviets, and they alone, had won the battle for Berlin.

For Khaldei's part, the photograph marked the closure of a grim chapter in his life. Just a few years before his father and sisters had been brutally murdered by the Nazis. This was his sweet revenge.

★

The sky was a smouldering yellow, with sulphurous smoke drifting through the shells of houses. The spring sunshine burned hot. In the Landwehr canal, rotting corpses exuded a sickly stench that hung in the air like a toxic cloud. Death was everywhere in that first week of May: 'Sweet, heavy, oppressive,' wrote Ruth Andreas-Friedrich, a resistance activist who dared to venture outside in the company of a friend.[29] 'We clamber over bomb craters. We squeeze through tangled barbed wire and hastily constructed barricades.' In the nook of a wall she noticed an old man, pipe in one hand, lighter in the other. 'Why is he sitting so still? Why doesn't he move at all?' The two of them took a closer look. 'A fly is crawling across his face. Green, fat, shiny. Now it crawls into his eyes . . . something slimy is dripping onto his cheeks . . . it wasn't only yesterday he died.'

In Hauptstrasse, Hafenplatz and elsewhere the stench of corpses was overlaid with the tang of stale urine. 'These victors feel free to piss on any wall any time they choose,' wrote Marta Hillers. 'Puddles of urine on the stairwell, on the landings, in the entrance hall.'[30] When Ruth Andreas-Friedrich managed to sneak back to her wrecked apartment at 6 Hünensteig Strasse, she found it smeared with excrement. 'An unbearable stench assaults us. Torn-open drawers, knocked-over closets, broken chairs, soiled tables. We wade through clothes and kitchen utensils. Phonograph records are breaking under our feet, empty pill containers and broken bottles.'[31] As she crossed the room, she slipped on human faeces.

The Soviet war correspondent, Konstantin Simonov, kept a chronicle of the horrors he witnessed in the days that followed the city's capture. When he entered an underground bunker next to the Berlin Zoo he flashed his torchlight into the gloom. Its corridors were choked with the stiff corpses of men and women who had committed suicide after an alcohol-fuelled orgy. One dead SS general lay on a bed with a half-finished bottle of sparkling wine wedged stiffly between his thighs. His glassy eyes stared blankly back at Simonov when caught in the beam of his torch.

Simonov clambered over a wall and found himself inside the zoo. The dazed zookeeper led him to the hippopotamus basin, where one of the hippos lay dead and bloated in the water, the stabiliser of a grenade protruding from its swollen belly. The other hippo wallowed sadly in the stagnant water. 'It doesn't want to go near the corpse, as if it knew the danger,' wrote Simonov in his diary.

In happier times, the nearby ape house had echoed with the whoops and cries of children. A sign proudly declared that it was home to the largest gorilla and chimpanzee in Europe. Simonov poked his head inside. Both had been shot dead and lay on the concrete floor in a pool of thickly congealed blood. The zookeeper was distraught, 'standing there and shaking his head without saying anything'.[32]

When Ruth Andreas-Friedrich and three friends ventured outside for a second time, they saw a lone white ox lumbering through the rubble. They were so desperate for food that they dragged the animal into a nearby courtyard and killed it. Within seconds, emaciated Berliners began scrabbling out of the surrounding ruins and fighting over the spoils.

'They came running with buckets. With tubs and vats. Screaming and gesticulating they tear pieces of meat from each other's hands.' Someone wrenched out the liver, others snatched at the dripping tongue. '"The tongue is mine . . . the tongue . . . the tongue!"' Five blood-covered fists angrily pull the tongue out of the ox's throat.' At the rear of the beast, a shrill-voiced woman hacked off the tail and fled the scene in greedy triumph. Frau Andreas-Friedrich felt profoundly depressed. 'Is this the moment we have awaited for twelve years? That we might fight over an ox's liver.'[33]

It was dangerous to remain outside for long, for Mongol conscripts prowled the wreckage, their glazed eyes filled with menace. They lurched drunkenly into the shells of private homes, raping in gangs. Marta Hillers was repeatedly raped in the first weeks of May. She was unsparing in detailing her ordeal, wanting the world to know what she was forced to endure: 'The one shoving me is an older man with grey stubble, reeking of alcohol and horses . . . He carefully closes the door behind him . . . No sound. Only an involuntary grinding of teeth when my underclothes are ripped apart . . . Suddenly his finger is on my mouth, stinking of horse and tobacco. I open my eyes. A stranger's hands expertly pulling apart my jaw. Eye to eye. Then, with great deliberation, he drops a gob of gathered spit into my mouth.'[34]

When Fräulein Hillers managed to visit her nineteen-year-old friend, Gerti, she learned that the teenager had also been subjected to multiple rapes. Once finished, her three attackers rummaged through the kitchen cupboards and found a jar of jam and some ersatz coffee. 'Laughing, they spooned the jam onto Gerti's hair and once her head was covered they sprinkled it generously with coffee substitute.'[35]

Some ninety thousand women would seek medical assistance as a consequence of rape, but the actual number of assaults was certainly far higher. Many were too ashamed to report the abuse; many took their own lives. A few dared to resist. When a Soviet soldier shouted over to Hildegard Herrberger, she gave him a piece of her mind. 'Piss off!' she shouted. 'Lick my arse!' She soon realised her mistake. 'Arse, arse, good, good,' was the Russian's response.[36]

As the violence against women intensified, a few Russian soldiers tried to intervene. Colonel Grigori Tokaev arrested two conscripts raping a German girl and dragged them to the army control point. The captain on duty ordered Tokaev to release them immediately. '*Pobeditelei ne sudiat*,' he said. 'Victors are not to be judged.'[37]

One Soviet general who entered the city with Marshal Zhukov said he had no problem with his soldiers 'making it hot for those Herrenvolk women'.[38] As far as he was concerned, the women deserved to be raped. His only concern was that his troops might contract venereal disease.

As the Russians completed their takeover of the city, a bizarre rumour began to spread through the underground shelters of Berlin. Marta Hillers first heard it from the wife of the liquor distiller, who had heard it from 'a reliable, very secret source'. The rumour, if true, was sensational. 'The Yanks and Tommies have quarrelled with Ivan and are thinking of joining with us' – the Germans – 'to chase Ivan out of the country.'

Could such news be true? Could the western Allies really be contemplating an attack on the Soviet army? 'Scornful laughter and heated discussion,' said Fräulein Hillers. 'No one knew what to believe.'[39]

The rumour was not confined to Berlin. Ronald Mallabar, a private in the Durham Light Infantry, was en route to the German capital and looking forward to drinking vodka with his victorious Soviet counterparts. He was aghast to hear the same astonishing story doing the rounds of Hamburg. Several well-connected Germans let slip that 'we were about to re-arm *them*' – the Germans – 'and go into Russia and attack the Russians.'[40]

It would later transpire that these rumours were true – that is, they contained a grain of truth. As the Red Army tightened its control over Berlin in the first week of May, Winston Churchill ordered his Joint Planning Staff at the War Office to plan a massive ground, air and naval offensive against Soviet forces. The prime minister had long held that Stalin represented the greatest threat to the security of post-war Europe, despite having toasted him as 'a friend whom we can trust' at Yalta less than three months before.[41] The fact that the Soviet marshal was reneging on so many of the agreements struck at the conference, most notably the promise to hold free and fair elections in Poland, was vindicating Churchill's contention. If the western Allies could inflict a rapid and crushing defeat on the Red Army, then Stalin would have to rethink his planned domination of Eastern Europe.

Operation Unthinkable was conceived as a military thrust deep into the heart of Soviet-occupied Europe, with the aim of imposing upon Russia 'the will of the United States and British Empire'.[42] The strategic architect of this land offensive was Brigadier Geoffrey Thompson, an ex-commander of the Royal Artillery with professional expertise in the terrain of Eastern Europe. His battle-plan envisaged a massive drive eastwards towards Berlin and beyond, with forty-seven British and American divisions driving the Red Army back to the Oder and Neisse rivers, some fifty-five miles to the east of Berlin. This was to be followed by a climactic battle in the countryside around Schneidemühl (now Pila, in north-west Poland).

It would be an armoured clash on a massive scale, far larger than the battle of Kursk where six thousand tanks had fought on the Kursk salient. Operation Unthinkable was to involve more than eight thousand tanks and would utilise American, British, Canadian and Polish forces. In the words of the brigadier, 'we should be staking everything upon one great battle in which we should be facing very heavy odds.'[43]

Those odds were indeed heavy. The Soviets had 170 divisions available that spring, whereas the western Allies had just forty-seven divisions. Thompson reckoned that the defeat of the Red Army would require the use of additional forces and he knew exactly where to find them. He proposed rearming the Wehrmacht and SS and using them to fight alongside the Allies. This would add another ten divisions to the western army, with all of them hardened by six years of warfare.

This is where his plan came unstuck. Churchill's chief military adviser, General Hastings Ismay, was horrified by the idea and said that such a policy would be 'absolutely impossible for the leaders of democratic countries even to contemplate'. He reminded Brigadier Thompson that the government had spent the last five years telling the British public that the Russians 'had done the lion's share of the fighting and endured untold suffering'.[44] To attack these erstwhile allies so soon after the end of the war would be 'catastrophic' for public morale.

Field Marshal Sir Alan Brooke was equally appalled and considered the brigadier's offensive to be an act of supreme folly. 'The chance of success [is] quite impossible.'[45]

Their hostility would eventually kill off Operation Unthinkable, with the chiefs of staff officially rejecting the plan on 8 June. Churchill regretted their decision, telling Anthony Eden that if Stalin's territorial ambitions were not dealt a definitive blow 'before the US armies withdraw from Europe and the Western world folds up its war machines, there is very little prospect of preventing a Third World War'.[46] He also warned his chiefs of staff that the Red Army would soon be an invincible force. 'At any time that it took their fancy, they could march across the rest of Europe and drive us back into our island.'[47]

The chiefs of staff remained unmoved. They wanted nothing more to do with Operation Unthinkable and enclosed the strategic plan in a grey government-issue folder marked 'Russia: Threat to Western Civilisation', along with its accompanying charts, tables and statistics. It remains in that folder to this day, with each page stamped in red ink with the words 'Top Secret'.

It would later transpire that Winston Churchill was not alone in his belief that the wartime struggle had yet to run its course. 'America is now the primary enemy,' said one of Marshal Zhukov's generals at the time of the capture of Berlin. 'We have destroyed the base of Fascism. Now we must destroy the base of Capitalism – America.'[48]

3

Red Berlin

AT EXACTLY 6 a.m. on the last day of April, a bus pulled up outside the side doors of the Hotel Lux. It had come to collect Walter Ulbricht's group of revolutionaries and take them to Moscow airport, from where a military plane would carry them to Berlin.

The wind-blasted Moscow streets were deserted at such an early hour, but the city was already decorated in preparation for the upcoming festivities. The following day was May Day and shops were bedecked with flags, bunting and political slogans.

As leader of the Berlin group, Walter Ulbricht knew exactly what was to be done on their arrival in the German capital. 'We had worked out all the details,' he said, 'from the setting up of the administration to the organisation of culture.'

Wolfgang Leonhard, the youngest member of the group, felt a surge of excitement as he and his comrades were whisked through Moscow airport and onto an American Douglas transport aircraft acquired through the lend-lease programme. Within minutes, the engines were fired and they were off, heading towards a city that none had visited for more than a decade.

After a ninety-minute flight they landed at a military landing strip in Karlau, far to the east of Berlin, where they were met by a small fleet of vehicles. Leonhard was impressed. 'The cars carried little red flags and Soviet army signs; the chauffeurs were in Soviet uniform.' After a long drive through desolate countryside, their little convoy reached the town of Bruchmühle, twenty miles east of Berlin: this was the headquarters of the political staff of Marshal Zhukov's army.

Leonhard and his comrades were billeted in a requisitioned house and given ration tickets normally reserved for senior officers in the

Red Army. At one point, much to Leonhard's surprise, a Soviet soldier introduced them to a colleague as the new German government. 'I almost gasped! What was it he had said? *The new German government?*' He was unsure as to whether or not it was a joke.

Leonhard was delighted to be back on German soil and impressed by the professionalism of the Red Army. It was somewhat disquieting, therefore, to find himself in a gloomy conversation with his new German housemaid. 'You must understand', she whispered, 'that in the last few weeks we've been through a terrible time.'

Leonhard and his comrades assumed that she had been roughly handled by retreating Nazis, but the truth was harder to swallow. 'I didn't mean the Nazis,' she stuttered. 'You must realize that when the Russians arrived here . . .' And thus began a terrible litany of rape, violence and plunder.

None of them believed her. Several mocked her stories and one said she was spilling Nazi propaganda. Leonhard alone felt she was speaking from experience. 'In my heart of hearts, I had reconciled myself to the fact that she was really telling the truth.' If so, and if such stories extended to Berlin, then their work to win the hearts and minds of Berliners had just become a lot more complicated.

On 2 May, the group's small column of cars set out from Bruchmühle towards Berlin, taking them through the outlying suburbs. Leonhard was stunned by the devastation. 'The scene was like a picture of hell – flaming ruins and starving people shambling about in tattered clothing; dazed German soldiers who seemed to have lost all idea of what was going on; Red Army soldiers singing exultantly and often drunk.'

The headquarters of the Berlin group was to be 80 Prinzenallee in Lichtenberg, an unscathed building equipped with stenographers, secretaries and a fleet of cars and attendant drivers. Within hours of arriving, Ulbricht gave the group a detailed briefing about the work ahead. Their aim was to establish an administration in each of the city's twenty districts, one that reflected the district's political outlook. 'In the bourgeois quarters,' he told them, 'we must appoint a bourgeois [mayor].'[1] But such mayors were to be nothing more than figureheads. Real power was to lie in the hands of the deputy mayor, a Communist, who would control all future appointments.

In this way, Ulbricht's team would be able to extend its influence over the whole of Berlin.

'You will also have to find one completely reliable comrade in every district whom we shall need to build up the police,' said Ulbricht. Leonhard was in no doubt that they were involved in an unprecedented power grab. The goal was 'to build up the [Communist] Party, making it the most organised party, the most militant party, the most active party . . . and gradually take over the whole situation'.[2] This needed to be done before the British and Americans entered the city.

Leonhard was excited about the mission ahead, especially when Ulbricht took him to a meeting of Communist activists who had run the anti-Nazi resistance. The only discordant note came when Ulbricht refused to countenance abortion for women who had been raped, since it would be tantamount to admitting that the Red Army had done the raping. The local Communists were shocked by his lack of compassion, but Ulbricht refused to back down. 'There can be no question of it! I regard the question as closed.'

Leonhard was unsettled to hear Ulbricht laying down the law 'in a tone which permitted no contradiction', but he nevertheless threw himself into his work. 'Within a few days, we had established in every district of Berlin a sort of active nucleus,' he said.[3] He also helped establish a fledgling executive, or Magistrat, composed of sixteen members. It was to be led by a municipal architect named Arthur Werner, hand-picked for the role by Ulbricht himself.

Werner was taken aback to be offered such an important post. Indecisive and apolitical, he could only think he had been given the job because he was relatively well known in Berlin. He accepted immediately, unaware that he had been chosen precisely because he was so ineffectual. 'Coughing and slurping,' said one, '[he] is hardly capable of delivering his Goethe-quotation-filled speech during the five-minute council meeting.'[4] As with all of Ulbricht's appointments, real power was to lie with the deputy. In this case it was Karl Maron, a manipulative workaholic who had been trained for the role in the Hotel Lux.

Ulbricht's years in Stalin's Russia had taught him the tricks of totalitarian rule. Of overriding importance was the appointment of a dependable chief of police. He had already selected his candidate. Paul Markgraf had won his spurs as a dashing Prussian captain in the Wehrmacht's 24th Panzer Division, fighting his way across Soviet Russia with such distinction that Hitler himself had pinned the Knight's Cross to his chest. After his capture at Stalingrad, Markgraf displayed a ruthless pragmatism by abandoning Nazism and declaring himself a Communist, joining the newly formed League of German Officers. The League comprised captured soldiers who had decided to throw in their lot with the Soviet regime.

Markgraf may have changed his political colours, but he retained the looks and physiognomy of a Nazi loyalist: 'A young man, well over six feet tall, with slick pale hair and hard, unblinking blue eyes.' So wrote the American journalist Emmet Hughes, who would later interview him in Berlin. Renowned for his consumption of schnapps, Markgraf had cultivated 'a veneer of culture' and could chat with ease about Goethe, Schiller and Shakespeare. He knew that advancement in life required two important qualities: 'servility towards superiors, severity towards inferiors'. Hughes thought him 'the perfect reincarnation of the medieval German mercenary'.[5] Markgraf immediately accepted the post of *Polizeipräsident*, aware that it would elevate him to one of the most important positions in the German capital. He had just weeks to create a police force in his own image: hard-line, ruthless, effective. He set about the task with relish.

Berliners knew nothing about the arrival of Walter Ulbricht and received no news from the outside world. Like creatures emerging from hibernation, they tentatively crawled out of their cellars and blinked into the spring sunshine. Seven-year-old Helga Schneider had spent more than four months underground, living in squalid semi-darkness with her grandfather, stepmother and brother. Now the fighting was at an end, they poked their heads outside and found themselves gazing on a hellish spectacle: 'An expanse of burning ruins whose glow turned night to day.'

Young Helga took a final glance at the room that had witnessed such harrowing abuse. She would never forget those wretched and terrifying months, but others were to bear far deeper scars. Sixteen-year-old Gudrun, raped in that very cellar, remained in a state of profound shock. 'The poor thing had still not recovered the power of speech.' The mother of the dead teenager Erika was consumed by grief. Her only possession was 'the cardboard suitcase in which she still kept her poor daughter's clothes'.

Fräulein Schneider accompanied her grandfather into the streets, keeping a sharp lookout for drunken Soviet troops. '[We] scoured abandoned courtyards and mounds of rubble in search of nettles, edible roots or dandelion leaves, which we ate in salads.'[6] In exchange for a Chinese porcelain tea service, they managed to acquire a little vegetable oil.

The lack of food was of equal concern in the Potsdam household of Paul and Valerie Hoecke, who were surviving on watery broth. They were fortunate that their co-tenant, Frau Wach, managed to supplement this meagre diet by judicious flirting with Soviet officers.

Russian Orthodox Easter fell on 6 May in 1945, a rare moment of celebration for the Hoecke family. Eight-year-old Hermann watched his father head to church, 'wearing his black *talar*, the priest's cassock, that I had rarely, if ever, seen him wear before'.

Easter passed without incident, but life took a sinister turn the following weekend. Two uniformed Russians knocked on the front door and demanded to see Herr Hoecke. 'They appeared to be military' – at least they did to young Hermann's eyes – 'but wore those infamous leather greatcoats, the hallmark of the NKVD.' Polite but firm, they insisted that Paul Hoecke accompany them for questioning. As the three of them left the house, Hermann also went outside, shading his eyes against the afternoon sun as he watched them walking downhill towards Nauener Chaussee. 'Just before they disappeared from sight behind the church, I waved to Father, but he never looked back.'[7]

The Red Army's takeover of Berlin followed a tradition that dated back to the tsarist regime. The first general to enter a besieged city was customarily handed the keys to the place and so it was with the German capital. Colonel-General Nikolai Berzarin had been in the vanguard during the battle, leading his 5th Shock Army into the heart of the city. Now he was appointed commandant of Berlin, the master and overlord of a capital in ruins.

'Fat, brown-eyed, arch and with white hair, although he is young.' So wrote the celebrated writer and journalist Vasily Grossman. 'He is clever, very calm and resourceful.'[8] Berzarin was also cocksure and flamboyant, notorious for driving through conquered territories at breakneck speed on his gleaming American Harley motorbike. When he reached Berlin, he acquired a trophy bike, a Zündapp KS-750, to which he attached a large green sidecar. He called it his Green Elephant and took great delight in racing through the treacherous streets of Berlin.

Berzarin spoke fast and sweepingly, with punchy phrases and magniloquent boasts. He certainly hit the ground running, taking charge of his new fiefdom with the same energy he had displayed in capturing the place. Grossman spent a day shadowing him and said his work was akin to 'the creation of the world'.[9] In the first days of his rule, his team developed an effective way of dealing with captured Nazis. 'SS men who had been denounced were summarily executed and their bodies dumped in the streets with an X stitched across their backs by machine-gun bullets.'[10] But Berzarin soon performed a volte-face, declaring that he cared little about a person's past as long as they had useful skills. '*Bürgermeisters*, directors of Berlin's electricity supply, Berlin water, sewerage, underground, trams, gas, factory owners . . .'[11] Grossman watched in astonishment as a queue of former Nazis was given immediate employment by the Soviet Military Administration.

General Berzarin's most pressing task was to clear the main thoroughfares of rubble. With no mechanised vehicles at his disposal, he relied on conscripted labour, largely women, who were forced to work in fifteen-hour shifts. The reward for this back-breaking toil was a bowl of cabbage soup. Among the workers was young Gerda Schmidt, whose green eyes and striking good looks had made her an early victim of Soviet brutality: she was raped with a knife to her throat. Now, she was forced to dig decomposing corpses out of a mud-choked subway as punishment for having been a member of the League of German Girls. She and her fellow workers 'were ordered around with whips like slaves' and if she stopped momentarily to rest on her shovel 'she was screamed at and threatened with a beating'.[12]

Marta Hillers was another conscript, arriving at the Rathaus assembly point with a bucket and dustpan. 'The rain kept coming – now a light drizzle, now a substantial downpour.' Her knitted dress was soon completely waterlogged. 'Nonetheless we kept on scooping and shovelling, filling bucket after bucket with dirt so there wouldn't be a break in the chain of hands . . . Once a cart was loaded, four of us shoved it up to the trench.'[13]

No sooner had the first thoroughfares been cleared than food supplies were brought into the city. Fräulein Hillers received her first rations on 19 May: groats (crushed grain), dried pork and a little sugar. 'The groats were full of husks, the sugar is lumpy since it got wet and the meat is stiff with salt. But it's food nevertheless.'[14]

Ruth Andreas-Friedrich had to wait a further four weeks before receiving any protein. '"It's because of the transport difficulties," explained the butcher as he ladled some semi-liquid meat onto a scale. "Sausage," the shop assistant informs me. "Liver sausage! I'd urgently advise you to eat it soon."'[15]

Berzarin's energetic rule soon bore fruit. The first buses began running within five days of the German surrender; just a day later, a line of the U-Bahn subway was partially reopened. Electricity flickered into life on 6 June, a source of great joy to Frau Andreas-Friedrich. 'An hour ago the lights went on . . .' she wrote in her diary that evening. 'One who has never been deprived of them cannot possibly understand what it means.'[16]

Tap water also began running, brown at first but soon gushing bright and clear. By that first week of June, post-war Berlin even had its first newspaper, *Die Tägliche Rundschau* (The Daily Review). Berliners immediately dubbed it *Die Klagliche Rundschau* (The Pitiable Review) because it was filled with Soviet propaganda. In the inaugural issue, there was a personal message from Stalin to the inhabitants of Berlin thanking them 'for their generous gifts' to his soldiers.[17] It was a bitterly ironic message for all who had been robbed and raped.

Propaganda was one of Berzarin's priorities, as Friedrich Luft was to experience first hand. Having informed the authorities that he was a journalist, he found himself invited to the newly opened Society for Soviet-German Friendship, established less than two weeks after the German surrender.

'All of a sudden, these big doors were opened and I saw the biggest and most lavish buffet I have ever seen, with caviar, cakes, butter and meat, and all sorts of foods.' Until a few days previously, Luft had survived in his cellar by sucking water out of the radiators.

For some invitees the temptations proved too much. 'I saw a famous theatre critic, an elderly gentleman, eating as much as he could get into himself, and after a few minutes he just fell back, green in his face, and collapsed.' He was trampled underfoot as everyone scrambled towards the food. Among the crowd was a Protestant bishop. 'He had a big plate in one hand and with the other hand he dug into the cake, the caviar and the herring – whatever he could reach.'[18] When his plate was full, he started cramming the food into his pockets. By the time he had finished, his giant silver cross was clogged with caviar and cream.

Luft was grateful for the food that day, but it wasn't long before he felt the first tinge of disquiet about Berzarin's new regime. He was told that each apartment block in the city was to have a warden whose task was to observe everyone who lived there. After twelve years of Gestapo intrusion, Luft found such institutional prying deeply alarming.

And it didn't stop there. Every scrap of intelligence was to be processed in General Berzarin's headquarters in the Karlshorst district of the city, which had been transformed into a fortified military compound. Among those who worked here was Gregory Klimov, a major in the Red Army. 'For security reasons, Karlshorst lived in a state of semi-siege. The whole district was ringed with guard posts. All street traffic was forbidden after 9 p.m.'[19]

This rapidly developed into Berlin's Kremlin, the headquarters of the Soviet Military Administration for the city itself, as well as for the rest of Soviet-occupied Germany. According to one employee, Grigori Tokaev, it was the hub from which every command was issued. 'Through my hands flowed top secret telegrams, orders, instructions and directives from the General Staff and from the Kremlin . . . we were the brain and nerve centre.'[20] Karlshorst held the fate of the city in its hands.

★

An urgent priority for Nikolai Berzarin was to discover the fate of Adolf Hitler, for there was no certain news as to whether he was dead or alive. Berzarin delegated this task to Colonel Vassily Gorbushin, who was to investigate Hitler's final hours.

Gorbushin spoke no German and was therefore reliant on the only female in his team, a twenty-five-year-old army interpreter named Elena Rzhevskaya, whose melancholic eyes had witnessed a world of suffering since she entered Berlin with the first wave of troops.

There were countless stories about Hitler's supposed flight from Berlin, all unproven, and it was some days before Rzhevskaya tracked down a key witness. Harry Mengershausen was one of Hitler's SS bodyguards and he was adamant that the Führer had killed himself. More importantly, he had seen the corpses of both Hitler and Eva Braun being burned in the garden of the Imperial Chancellery.

Soviet troops had only recently disinterred two burned corpses from a shallow grave in the Chancellery; Mengershausen's account suggested these were the bodies of Hitler and Braun. 'This was the missing link in our story,' wrote Rzhevskaya. 'A participant in, or witness of, the burning.'[21]

The post-mortem of these gruesome cadavers was undertaken by the appropriately named Dr Faust Shkaravsky, a military surgeon working at Mobile Field Surgical Hospital No. 496. 'The remains of a male corpse disfigured by fire was delivered in a wooden crate,' reads his autopsy report.[22] The doctor found fragments of glass in the cadaver's mouth that seemed to have come from a thin ampoule. There was no obvious bullet wound in the badly mangled skull and he concluded that death was caused 'by poisoning with cyanide compounds'.[23] In a notable aside, he recorded that the corpse had only one testicle.

Shortly after the autopsy, Elena Rzhevskaya was summoned to Colonel Gorbushin's office and handed a crimson box with a soft satin lining, 'the kind that is used for perfume bottles or cheap pieces of jewellery'. Curious, she asked what was inside. Gorbushin told her it contained Hitler's jaws 'and I should answer for their safe-keeping with my life'.

She slipped the box into her inside pocket, aware that she had been entrusted with a grim but priceless relic. The contents contained potentially indisputable proof of Hitler's death, for she knew that no set of teeth is ever identical. All she now had to do was find Hitler's dentist.

This was easier said than done. The dentist in question, Professor Hugo Blaschke, had fled to Berchtesgaden, but his thirty-five-year-old assistant, Käthe Heusermann, was known to be still in town. It was she who had held the miniature mirror inside Hitler's mouth while Professor Blaschke undertook fillings and bridges.

Fräulein Heusermann was soon tracked down by Gorbushin's team, but she promptly burst into tears when told she was to be interrogated, perhaps because she had already been twice raped by Soviet soldiers. Once calmed by Rzhevskaya, she revealed that the X-rays of Hitler's jaws were almost certainly to be found in Professor Blaschke's surgery inside the Reich Chancellery. It was to the Chancellery that they now made their way.

'We had only one torch between the three of us,' said Rzhevskaya. 'It was dark, deserted and rather frightening.' The massive oak doors had been splintered by shell blasts, and chandeliers had crashed to the floor, scattering crystal droplets across the red marble. But Käthe Heusermann knew her way around this 'tomb of the Pharaohs', as she called it, and she led them down to the cubicle in which Professor Blaschke had performed his surgery.

'The beam of the torch picked out a dentist's chair, a sofa with an adjustable headrest and a tiny desk.' More importantly, it picked out a cabinet that housed the dental records, including the all-important X-rays of Hitler's teeth. 'We were lucky,' said Elena Rzhevskaya, 'desperately lucky, that the tempest which had swept through the bunker only a few days ago had left this little cubby-hole untouched.' She was no dental expert, but even she could see that the X-rays were a perfect match with the jaws in her box. Käthe Heusermann was able to confirm this. 'They are the teeth of Adolf Hitler.'[24]

Fräulein Heusermann would never have uttered these words had she known the terrible fate that was to befall her. She was arrested, transferred to Moscow and held in solitary confinement without trial. Six years would pass before she was finally tried, found guilty and condemned to a decade in a Siberian gulag.[25] She wouldn't be repatriated to Germany until 1955. There was a grim logic to her incarceration. Stalin was intending to conceal the truth about Hitler's suicide, stoking rumours that he might have escaped from Berlin. In this way, the Führer could be used as a propaganda weapon against the western Allies.

Less than a fortnight after the conclusive Soviet enquiry into Hitler's death, the American president's diplomatic adviser, Harry Hopkins, arrived in Moscow. At one point during his conversation with Stalin, Hopkins said he was looking forward to visiting Berlin and jokingly added that 'he might even be able to find Hitler's body'. Stalin said this was unlikely, since 'Bormann, Goebbels, Hitler and probably Krebs had escaped and were in hiding'.[26] Later in that same conversation, he was to repeat this falsehood, reiterating to Hopkins his conviction that the suicide stories were untrue and 'that Hitler was still alive'.[27]

Ever since General Alfred Jodl had signed the German surrender on Monday, 7 May 1945, the armies of the western Allies had been halted on a line that stretched from the Baltic in the north to Bavaria in the south. Lieutenant General William H. Simpson's Ninth Army had come closest to Berlin, with his troops stationed on the River Elbe, some fifty miles west of the capital. Colonel Frank Howley's contingent of Military Government remained much further west in the provincial town of Gütersloh, some 250 miles from his goal.

Howley was impatient to get on the move. 'My unit was all keyed up and ready to go,' he said. 'We had requisitioned a fleet of German cars which we had repainted and housed in special garages.' Yet the order to advance was not forthcoming and he was warned that 'many questions remained unsettled'.[28] It was deeply frustrating. He had long been relishing the idea of meeting his Soviet allies, having formed a clear idea of what they would be like: 'Big, jolly, balalaika-playing fellows who drank prodigious quantities of vodka and liked to wrestle in the drawing room.' He was looking forward to sharing that vodka before getting down to business. 'I optimistically raised my glass and expressed complete confidence that we were going to be firm and fast friends,' he said. 'It never occurred to me that it could be otherwise.'[29]

Brigadier Hinde was equally frustrated at not being invited to enter the German capital. He had now been in his job for the better part of six months, yet he and his team were even further from Berlin – some 350 miles west of the capital – than Howley and his men. Harold Hays felt 'a sense of suppressed excitement, in anticipation of the next move'. Before long the excitement had become so suppressed that everyone was searching for thrills to keep boredom at bay. Hays himself borrowed a jeep and drove up to the Harz Mountains, travelling through land destined to become the frontier zone between the British and Soviet sectors of occupied Germany. News from Berlin had already reached the villages here, and there was a real sense of fear. 'It was as if everyone and everything was waiting for something cataclysmic to happen, and nature itself was holding its breath.'[30]

Hinde used his time wisely, studying anything that might help him in the daunting task ahead. He had never been to the Soviet Union, and he spoke no Russian, but he was a keen admirer of Russian literature and had read many of the nineteenth-century classics of Dostoevsky, Tolstoy and Chekov. 'The Russians are not Englishmen who speak a different language,' he told his team. 'They are [a] wholly different people, with a wholly different outlook, traditions, history and standards, and at a wholly different level of civilisation.' It was crucial for his men to form friendly relations with their Soviet allies, in order to break down the 'barrier of suspicion'.[31] In common with Frank Howley, the brigadier was keenly looking forward to working with his Soviet allies.

4

Loot

IN THE GREAT sieges of the Middle Ages, cities that submitted without a fight were spared destruction while those that resisted attack faced an orgy of bloodshed and plunder. It had been thus when the Crusaders captured Jerusalem in 1099 and when Sultan Mehmed II seized Constantinople in 1453. Berlin now faced a similar fate, except that the traditional three days of pillage were to be stretched into two long months. Soviet soldiers had a large window of opportunity to snatch their spoils before the British and Americans rode into town.

The commands issued from Soviet headquarters in Karlshorst were unambiguous. 'Take everything from the Western sector of Berlin,' ordered one senior official. 'Do you understand? Everything! If you can't take it, destroy it. But don't leave anything to the Allies. No machinery, not a bed to sleep on, not even a pot to pee in!'[1] General Berzarin also issued a public decree to Berliners dictating that all personal valuables were to be surrendered to the new administration, including radios and telephones.

Not everyone on the Soviet side agreed with the ransacking of Berlin. Colonel Grigori Tokaev watched with mounting alarm as small-scale pilfering escalated into something on a far grander scale. Writing about it years later, he recalled that 'watches, rings and other personal valuables were shamelessly filched from Germans in the public streets in the name of "Soviet liberation" and radio sets were stolen from houses like apples from an orchard.'[2]

Once these smaller items had been looted, soldiers moved onto bigger catches. Sofas and beds were requisitioned and packed up, awaiting transportation to Russia, along with sewing machines, bathroom taps and bicycles. 'What men could not take, they destroyed,' said Tokaev. 'Mirrors, refrigerators, washing-machines, radio sets, bookcases – anything not easily transported was riddled with bullets.'[3]

Ruth Andreas-Friedrich first heard Berzarin's decree ordering the mass confiscation of private property in the second week of May. Notices were posted on public buildings ordering the surrender of items such as telephones and typewriters. 'Those who won't give them up will be shot.' When she went to the local collection point, she was confronted by a sorry sight: 'Rain is dripping onto the mahogany veneer of all the Blaupunkt and Telefunker, the Philips and Siemens super radios. They are piled, one on top of another, and stacked in corners . . . barely a quarter of it will still be usable after confiscation.'

When she entered Pariser Platz, she saw a swarm of soldiers looting the famous Hotel Adlon, helping themselves to gold-plated mirrors, plush armchairs and mattresses. Just a few days later, she was in the city's outskirts and saw a vast procession of heavily laden trucks heading towards Russia. 'For four years their stuff had been rolling from East to West,' said her friend, Walter Seitz. 'Now, ours is rolling back.'[4]

Much of it would never reach its destination, for many railway tracks leading east had been torn up as war booty and few trains were getting through to Russia. 'Huge crates piled up at the railroad stations, each bearing an address in Cyrillic letters – addresses in Moscow, Odessa and Kharkov,' wrote one observer. 'But even while more and more crates were being delivered to the stations, the Berliners knew that the pianos, telephones and radio sets inside them would never reach their destinations.'[5]

For a fortunate few, the indiscriminate looting brought unexpected windfalls. In Potsdam, Valerie Hoecke was informed by a neighbour that someone, probably a Soviet looter, 'had dumped what looked like an entire library on the side of the gravel road leading to the Alexandrowka Colony'. The neighbour suggested that the books 'could be used as fuel for the stove'.[6] When Frau Hoecke went to investigate, she found them to be valuable, with bookplates that indicated that they had once belonged to the illustrious Von Jagow family. She sent her children out to collect them and they spent much of that afternoon carting them home. The haul included complete sets of Voltaire and Rousseau, the collected works of Dostoevsky and volumes on ancient Greece and Rome.

Berlin's Soviet commander, Nikolai Berzarin, was quick to summon experts from Moscow to help in the systematic pillaging of Berlin's greatest artistic and cultural treasures. The German capital's museums were concentrated on Museum Island in the heart of the city. Here was the Kaiser Friedrich Museum, the Pergamon Museum and the Altes (Old) and Neues (New) Museums. The city was also home to the Museum of Decorative Arts, the Ethnological Museum and the Schlossmuseum, along with many other galleries and imperial palaces.

The Nazi regime had moved the most priceless treasures into the city's anti-aircraft towers or *Flaktürme* – vast concrete fortresses constructed on multiple levels. Two of the largest were at the Berlin zoo and in the Friedrichshain district. The Friedrichshain *Flakturm* had become a storehouse for the magnificent collection of Renaissance masterpieces from the Kaiser Friedrich Museum, including canvasses by Caravaggio, Tintoretto, Cranach and Rubens – 411 gigantic works that constituted the highlights of the collection. Also moved there were 160 smaller Italian paintings, 400 sculptures (by Donatello and other Florentine masters) and 10,000 antiquities and glass objets d'art.

The zoo *Flakturm* also held some of the greatest wonders of western civilisation: the massive Pergamon Altar from Asia Minor, three crates of Trojan gold from the fabled Schliemann Collection and the famous head of Queen Nefertiti from the Egyptian Museum. There was also Chinese porcelain, Japanese sculpture, terracotta figurines and thousands of rolled-up drawings, including Botticelli's illustrations for the *Divine Comedy* and Grünewald's studies for the Isenheim Altarpiece.

Nikolai Berzarin had been told about these depositories by Walter Ulbricht and he went to visit the zoo *Flakturm* within hours of the city's capture. Here he met Dr Wilhelm Unverzagt, director of the Museum of Pre- and Early History, who had appointed himself unofficial guardian of the place. When he confessed to Berzarin his fears about looters, the Soviet commander promised that 'very soon the Special Committee will remove everything to storage.'[7]

Berzarin realised that if he were to take advantage of this unique opportunity for plundering, speed was essential. According to the post-war plans for Berlin, the zoo *Flakturm* was to fall within the British sector of the city. It seemed obvious to the Soviet commander that the British would lay claim to all the museum treasures not removed prior to their arrival.

Marshal Zhukov agreed with Berzarin that the work should begin immediately and summoned the head of SMERSH, the all-powerful military counter-intelligence agency. 'You have twenty-four hours to evacuate everything from the Zoo Flakturm,' he said. When told that this was impossible due to the quantity of booty, Zhukov modified his order. 'If not in twenty-four hours, [then] in forty-eight hours everything must be removed.'[8]

Army sappers were moved to the site in order to cut down trees adjacent to the *Flakturm* and blast a large hole into the concrete side-wall. They then manoeuvred a mobile crane next to the building to enable them to remove the massive stone blocks that formed the Pergamon Altar. 'Forty soldier-workmen joyfully attacked the sculptures with pickaxe and crowbar. The friezes were ripped anew from their walls, loaded upon flat cars, and were never seen again.' So noted one observer, who watched the sculptures being packed into wooden crates. 'About a hundred other first class Greek sculptures and architectural pieces, from Olympia, from Samos, from Priene and Miletus, from Didyma and Baalbek, brought by the devoted labour of archaeologists to Berlin, went with them.' The removal men were directed in their work by the art historian Viktor Lazarev, who had been flown in from Moscow. The quantity of treasures removed from the building left everyone stunned. 'Seven thousand Greek vases, eighteen hundred statues, nine thousand antique gems, sixty-five hundred terracottas, the Tanagra figurines and thousands of lesser objects were removed from the Department of Greek Antiquities alone.'[9]

This marked the beginning of the greatest looting spree in history. Byzantine altars, Coptic textiles, Italian sculptures and French armoury – all were loaded into crates and moved to an abattoir in the Soviet sector of the city. The works of Mantegna, Goya and

Ghirlandaio were removed from Museum Island, along with Raphael's *Sistine Madonna* and canvasses by Van Dyck and Caravaggio. These were followed by thousands of medieval manuscripts and seven million rare printed volumes. One eyewitness saw iron strongboxes spilling over with priceless coins from antiquity.

'All things must be transported to Moscow immediately,' urged Viktor Lazarev. 'Immediately send to Moscow everything that was removed from the Zoo Flak Tower and the museum objects situated in our depositories.'[10] Lazarev was aware that Berlin was also home to private collections, many of which had been seized by leading Nazis. He now ordered that these be tracked down and confiscated. His team did exactly that, seizing works from the famous Koehler and Gerstenberg collections, including El Greco's *John the Baptist* and Goya's *Portrait of Lola Jimenez*.

In this frantic bout of pillaging there were inevitable tragedies and the most terrible of these occurred on 5 May when a fire broke out in the Friedrichshain *Flakturm*. The Soviets claimed it was an act of arson undertaken by fanatical SS officers, while others said it was started by thieves carrying flaming torches into the gloomy interior. Whatever the truth, the resulting inferno consumed many of the greatest treasures of western civilisation: canvasses by Fra Angelico, Rubens and Reynolds, as well as tens of thousands of antiquities.

At the end of May the first trophy train left Berlin for the long overland journey to Moscow. A few weeks later, a military cargo plane transported the Trojan gold, along with treasures from the Ethnological Museum. Over the weeks that followed, hundreds of booty trains left from Lichtenberg station, all overflowing with priceless treasures. The Soviet trophy brigades also took the opportunity to stash aboard their own private loot: radios, violins, furs and bicycles, as well as carpets, tapestries and pianos.

Soviet curators were stunned when they received the Berlin museum treasures. The Pushkin Museum received 3,000 gigantic crates filled with looted art. The State Historical Museum in Moscow received a further 12,500. No one had realised that Berlin would yield so much booty.

★

Not everyone on the Soviet side approved of the stripping of Berlin's museums and nor did they agree with the private looting being undertaken by Red Army soldiers. One senior colonel discussed the matter with Marshal Zhukov, arguing that the looting was a stain on the Soviet army's already tarnished reputation. Zhukov agreed that 'these indecencies sullied our victories', but he did nothing to bring them to a halt.[11] There was a good reason for this. In a city of looters, he was the looter-in-chief, stripping the richest Berlin palaces of their heirlooms and hereditary silver for his own personal use.

The private plunder he sent back to Russia was on such an eye-watering scale that it did not go unnoticed. The first hint of trouble came when a train heading from Berlin to Odessa was stopped, searched and found to contain eighty-five crates of furniture, all of it being sent to Zhukov's home address. This news was forwarded to Stalin, who ordered an undercover search of Zhukov's Moscow apartment and his dacha in nearby Rublevo. The search was conducted by Viktor Abakumov, head of state security, who was shocked when he forced an entry into Zhukov's dacha. In the dimly lit interior, the bolts of rich cloths and damasks looked like the ill-gotten booty from the hold of a Spanish argosy. Silks, brocades and sables were piled to the ceiling. There were priceless tapestries and carpets from the Potsdam palaces (forty-four in total) along with classical paintings, porcelain tableware, Holland & Holland hunting rifles, and silverware. 'Not a single thing of Soviet origin,' noted Abakumov's official report.[12]

But the loot stored in the dacha was, in the words of that report, just 'a drop in the ocean'.[13] Hundreds more treasures were found in Zhukov's Moscow apartment: fob-watches, cigarette cases and pendants, all of gold, along with diamonds and precious chains.

Central to the ensuing investigation was a suitcase that Zhukov was alleged to have handed to General Vladimir Kryukov, husband of the famous folk singer Lidia Ruslanova. This suitcase was eventually found in her possession: it contained more than two hundred cut diamonds and scores of emeralds, sapphires and pearls. The general had also helped himself to nearly 240 pounds of gold and silver.

Zhukov, Kryukov and Ruslanova would eventually get their come-uppance, with demotion, humiliation and imprisonment in a gulag. But their nemesis lay far in the future: throughout the spring of 1945, Zhukov was preoccupied with the logistics of looting one of Europe's greatest capitals.

Berlin was still smouldering when one of Berzarin's senior officers pitched up unannounced at the scientific laboratory of Manfred von Ardenne, arguably the most brilliant physicist of his generation. Von Ardenne seemed to have it all: an aristocratic pedigree, a supercharged brain and an ability to conjure inventions that both stunned and delighted his contemporaries. In 1928, when still just twenty-one, he inherited a slice of the dynastic fortune and used the money to set up his own Berlin establishment, the Research Laboratory for Electron Physics, which soon attracted some of Germany's greatest physicists. His self-built equipment included a revolutionary electron microscope, a machine for separating isotopes and a sixty-ton cyclotron – a type of particle accelerator used for atomic research. In short, he had the brain, laboratory and staff that made him an extremely valuable asset to anyone who could find him in the ruins of Berlin.

Shortly before the arrival of the Red Army, von Ardenne had been encouraged by his colleagues to flee the city and re-establish his laboratory in one of Germany's western regions. Large numbers of scientists from Berlin's prestigious Kaiser Wilhelm Society had already headed west, reasoning that it would be better to be captured by the Americans or British than by the Russians. Among these fugitive scientists were two Nobel Prize winners, Otto Hahn and Werner Heisenberg, both experts in atomic physics.

Manfred von Ardenne declined to join his colleagues, in part because of his political convictions. An ardent anti-Nazi, he saw little to fear in the Soviets. 'I knew what the territorial divide was going to be between the Soviet Union and Western powers,' he would later say, 'and I decided to stay on the Soviet side.'[14]

Von Ardenne's principal concern during the battle for Berlin had been the safeguarding of his laboratory and staff. All the scientific equipment was moved into an underground bunker in the Lichterfelde

70

district of the city and the bunker's entrance was then concealed beneath charred and broken furniture.

The whereabouts of the underground bunker were soon brought to the attentions of the Soviet Academy of Science and Manfred von Ardenne found himself courted by an important guest. General Avramii Zaveniagin was the Soviet Ministry of the Interior's representative for atomic research, a charmingly persuasive man who arrived at his laboratory with an enticing offer – the directorship of a Moscow-based research institute, where he would be provided with unlimited funds and state-of-the-art equipment. Von Ardenne knew a gift horse when he saw one. 'It only took me a few seconds to accept this surprising proposal.' He agreed to fly to Moscow to discuss his terms of employment.

Forty-eight hours later, he and his wife Bettina were driven to an airfield outside Berlin, where a converted Douglas transport plane (equipped with luxury sofas and pile carpets) awaited them. 'We said goodbye to our children with relatively light hearts, because we were only going for two weeks in order to discuss this contract.'

The first alarm bell sounded when they were met by their interpreter at Vnukovo military airport. In her opening words she expressed surprise that they hadn't brought their children. 'It made us quite pensive,' confessed von Ardenne.

Any doubts were swept away by the excitement of arriving in the Soviet capital, where the snow-covered palaces looked like the stage-set for an enchanted fairy tale. A chauffeur drove them through a thickly forested area known as Silverwood before bringing the car to a halt outside a large dacha. 'And then,' said von Ardenne, 'it was surprise after surprise.'

Just a few hours earlier, they had been struggling to survive inside their underground laboratory. But here in Silverwood there was a panoply of luxuries. 'A whole staff was there, ready to look after us: a chef in a white hat, two maids and someone in charge of the heating.'

The von Ardennes were invited to eat as soon as their luggage had been brought in from the car. 'The door to the dining room opened dramatically and we were bathed in light; our gaze was caught by the festive table with its white tablecloth.' Von Ardenne felt as if nothing was quite real. 'During the war, as far as food was concerned, we were used to the most humble portions.' But here, the table was set for a feast. 'A strong soup with cream, roasted chickens, white bread, butter, lots of hams, several kinds of cheese, dessert, wines, vodka, beer and coffee.' Von Ardenne had a momentary pang of guilt as he thought of his family back in Berlin, but it didn't last for long. 'We decided to enjoy it,' he said.

As the days passed, the von Ardennes grew increasingly concerned as to when they might rejoin their children in Berlin. No meetings had been set up and their interpreter had no news of the promised contract. And then, three weeks after their arrival, Frau von Ardenne saw a car pull up outside the dacha. When the door was opened she got the surprise of her life. 'It's the children!' she yelped. They had been brought to Moscow with her husband's sister, Renate, and another relative. They were not the only arrivals. Renate told them that all the inventors, physicists and lab technicians, as well as everything from the laboratory (packed into 750 huge wooden crates), were on their way to Moscow from Berlin – the first delivery of many millions of pounds of reparations that were to be transported from Berlin to the Soviet Union.

A few days later, Manfred von Ardenne was reunited with his staff and equipment, including the cyclotron. He was pleasantly surprised at the careful fashion in which everything had been packed. 'Even the most fragile optical instruments arrived without damage.' There was only one disquieting note. 'After all this news, we realized that our return to Berlin was no longer a topic for discussion.' For the foreseeable future, von Ardenne and his team were to be based in the Soviet Union.

This was to be their gilded cage. In return for working on isotope separation – a field in which the Soviets lagged behind the West – they were to receive first-class food and lodgings. Berlin belonged to the past, and Manfred von Ardenne was unsure if he would ever see the city again.

Back in Berlin the looting continued apace. Once the city's railway tracks had been stripped and loaded into crates, the Soviet dismantling teams moved on to the trains and carriages, removing everything from metal ashtrays to the brown-grey plush of the second-class seats. Window latches, luggage racks and light-bulb sockets were also packed into crates.

In the first week of June, the Soviet Military Administration issued a decree dictating that every house had to fly the flags of the four victorious nations. This led to a flurry of anxiety as people searched for the necessary coloured cloth and tried to remember how many stars there were on the American banner.

Decaying corpses were being dug from the ruins in ever increasing numbers, but there were no coffins available so each cadaver was placed in a cardboard box covered with black-out paper and adorned with a rudimentary tinfoil cross. After the briefest of ceremonies, the dead were buried in communal graves.

A rare piece of good news came on 8 June, when it was announced that a section of the S-Bahn transit railway was reopening. It was a welcome development in a city too large to be easily crossed on foot.

In the third week of June, Ruth Andreas-Friedrich stepped into the street and was confronted by a disturbing sight. 'Red flags greet us. They wave from all the buildings. Some are at half-mast, others carry black crepe.'[15] She asked passers-by what had happened. Some told her that Zhukov was dead, others said it was Stalin.

The truth was rather different. It was General Berzarin who was dead, killed in a high-speed, alcohol-fuelled motorcycle accident. He had been riding his Zündap 'Green Elephant' motorbike at more than seventy miles per hour down Schlossstrasse when he slammed into an army truck. His skull was smashed and his chest crushed, causing instantaneous death.

'How unfortunate for the man,' said Ruth to her friend, Walter Seitz. 'He certainly wasn't the worst.'

'How unfortunate for *Berlin*,' corrected Seitz, who knew little of the museum looting that Berzarin had overseen. 'He was certainly one of the best.'[16]

General Eisenhower was increasingly eager to get Allied forces into Berlin in order to stake their claim to the western sectors of the city. Shortly before General Berzarin's fatal crash, on Tuesday, 5 June, Eisenhower had flown into the German capital in the company of his British and French counterparts, Field Marshal Bernard Montgomery and General Jean de Lattre de Tassigny. Also present was Eisenhower's deputy, Lucius Clay, who kept a note of everything that happened that day. He was beginning to realise that the Russians were masters of geopolitical chess.

Eisenhower and company landed at Tempelhof in the late morning, flying in several different planes as a security precaution. A ceremonial guard of honour snapped a smart salute as they were inspected by Eisenhower and Clay. 'The first Soviet military unit I had seen,' wrote Clay. 'In splendid physical condition and well disciplined.' The only person missing was Marshal Zhukov. Clay was surprised by his absence but not unduly alarmed. He assumed the Soviet commander would be awaiting them at his Karlshorst headquarters.

The convoy of vehicles that chauffeured them across the city was positively presidential. Equipped with armed guards and motorcycle outriders, it drove at speed along narrow alleys that had been bull-dozed through the rubble. Clay was genuinely shocked by the state of Berlin. 'A city of the dead,' he wrote. 'I had seen nothing quite comparable in western Germany.'

Zhukov was still absent when they arrived at Karlshorst. Lunch was served by Red Army matrons, and a couple of minor officials greeted the western commanders. Eisenhower was by now growing testy, 'impatient with the delay and with the unexplained lack of courtesy'.[17] Several more hours were to pass before Marshal Zhukov finally appeared, at 5 p.m., greeting his fellow commanders as the first among equals. Clay noted that his physiognomy and bearing 'indicated that he had become accustomed to wield power and authority'.[18] But the marshal had another attribute that went un-noticed by Clay. He was a master of getting his way. 'Always the man from the East,' noted a British intelligence officer. 'Ice-cold, remote, his mind in Moscow.'[19] That same officer added that he was 'something resembling a viceroy'.[20]

He certainly proved a master choreographer on that particular day, inviting his guests to sign various protocols in front of the world's media, 'in the glare of flashlights and with photographers everywhere'.[21] Zhukov ensured he was always seen in the most favourable light.

Under the terms of the protocol signed at Yalta, the British and Americans had the right to occupy their zones of Berlin with immediate effect. But Zhukov refused to allow any Allied troops into the city until the American army had withdrawn from the provinces of Saxony and Thuringia, which were to fall within the Soviet zone of occupied Germany. 'The quicker they move,' he said, 'the quicker the entry into Berlin.'[22]

Zhukov also declined to meet any French representatives, with the exception of General Jean de Lattre de Tassigny, until the boundaries of the French sector had been agreed upon. The marshal was treating his guests as bit-part players whose presence in Berlin was merely to be tolerated. When Montgomery spoke to Zhukov, comparing his El Alamein triumph to the Red Army's victory at Stalingrad, the marshal begged to correct him. 'I did not want to belittle the merits of the British troops,' he wrote in his memoirs, but he nevertheless took the opportunity to tell Monty that El Alamein was a mere small-scale victory whereas Stalingrad 'had a vast strategic significance'.[23]

Every victorious general requires a celebratory banquet and Zhukov was no exception. With an affability that felt patronising to his guests, he ushered them all into his Karlshorst banqueting hall where a long table was furnished with delicacies: caviar, smoked salmon, pickled fish and enough vodka to toast a hundred victories. These toasts were to prove interminable to the British and American generals. 'If the ability to enjoy vodka comes from experience,' said Clay, 'I never passed the first stage.'[24]

Eisenhower listened to the Red Army choir, followed by Zhukov's oration, before making his own short speech. He was brief and warm, yet clearly unhappy at Zhukov's stage management of the day's events. He told Clay he was furious about 'the hours of delay which he did not believe conformed to the dignity of his position as a representative of the United States'.[25]

In his final words to Zhukov, Eisenhower expressed regret 'that the long delay had prevented an earlier start as he now had to thank his hosts and say goodbye'. He was due back in Frankfurt that night. Yet he did wring one concession from the Soviet marshal. In twelve days' time, Frank Howley was to be allowed to enter Berlin with his advance team of A1A1 adventurers.

PART II

Troubled Waters

5

Arrival of the Allies

FRANK 'HOWLIN' MAD' Howley was stationed in Halle, some hundred miles to the south-west of Berlin, when he was given the green light to head to the German capital. His mission was for reconnaissance purposes: reconnoitre the districts of the city assigned to the Americans and prepare for the arrival of the First Airborne and Second Armoured Division troops. It was 17 June and Howley was firing on all cylinders. Seven weeks after the Russians took control of the city, the Americans were finally moving into their sector.

Howley knew that he would be writing himself into the history books. He also knew that this had been the dream of every soldier since the D-Day landings. To mark the occasion, he vowed to arrive in such style that his Russian allies would remember it for the rest of their lives. 'It was my intention', he said, 'to make this advance party a spectacular thing.'[1]

His team had expanded greatly since their time in Barbizon. It now comprised some five hundred people, including intelligence officers, logistics experts and secretarial support. He had also acquired 120 vehicles, mostly jeeps, half-tracks and ten-ton trucks.

Howley decided to abandon all the vehicles requisitioned from the Germans, since most were covered in dents. 'I didn't want the Russians to see a miscellaneous collection of vehicles representing the American army.'[2] His was to be an all-American convoy, and he ordered each jeep and truck to be scrubbed, polished and touched up with paint. He also arranged to have several hundred American flags printed and placed in the windscreen of each vehicle, along with canvas flags on the right front mudguard of each lead car. The convoy was equipped with a supply lorry laden with ten thousand bottles of wine and whisky to help them celebrate their historic arrival.

Every convoy needs to be led from the front and Howley's was no exception. Riding in the vanguard of this proud unit was the colonel himself, driving his magnificent Horch Roadster. He was most impressed when the other vehicles swung into line behind him. 'Quite a parade,' he mused, 'with a company of the Second ('Hell on Wheels') Armored Division bringing up the rear and formal-looking machine guns bristling from the half-tracks.'[3]

The great armoured column fired its engines on the morning of 17 June and began roaring eastwards towards the autobahn. 'We moved along in gala spirit,' wrote Howley.[4] As the vehicles advanced, the half-tracks flung a swirl of dust into the late spring air, visible for miles around.

The excitement mounted as they neared Dessau, where a small pontoon spanned the River Mulde. This marked the frontier between the American and Soviet zones of occupied Germany. Once they crossed the bridge, they would be entering territory controlled by the Red Army.

As Howley steered his convertible Horch onto the rickety bridge, he noticed a giant arch on the far bank, 'with huge pictures of Lenin and Stalin gazing down upon us'. These were flanked by a banner with a Cyrillic inscription that read, 'Welcome to the Fatherland.' He felt as if they were entering a land 'that had been annexed by the USSR'.

A Russian officer was awaiting them on the far side of the bridge. He guided them towards a much larger bridge that traversed the River Elbe. There, a phalanx of Russian guards snapped their salutes.

Howley's crew had been expecting a trouble-free trip to Berlin, but they now came across an unexpected snag. 'Suddenly we were confronted by a road block, a red and white pole leaning across the road.' Howley's instinct was to push it aside with one of the half-tracks, but he chose discretion over valour. 'We didn't want to break the pole or force the guard.' This was just as well, for he was directed to the Russian border control where a Soviet officer named Colonel Gorelik was awaiting him.

'Won't you sit down and have a drink with us?'

Howley was keen to press onwards to Berlin but thought it polite to accept the colonel's offer. 'German champagne was served and toasts drunk. We thanked our host and prepared to depart.' But his departure was blocked by the Soviet colonel.

'You cannot go just yet. There is a formality.' He then stood up and strode over to the window. 'How many vehicles, officers and men do you have?'

Howley provided him with the figures, whereupon Gorelik shook his head.

'The agreement says 37 officers, 50 vehicles and 175 men.'

'What agreement?'

'The Berlin agreement.'

Howley had heard of no such thing. 'Perhaps you are confusing some off-hand estimate made by one of our officers?'

'There is [an] actual agreement,' said Colonel Gorelik.

This detonated Howley's short fuse. 'Look . . . we have orders to go to Berlin. These orders cover every unit and they don't say, "If the Russians are willing." Let's be frank. You are keeping us from going to Berlin and I want to know who is responsible.'

Colonel Gorelik snapped his response: 'My superior ordered this.'[5]

Howley was tempted to ignore the colonel and press on to the capital, using force if necessary. 'I don't think the Russians would have fought,' he said, 'but if they had, I would have had enough troops to protect ourselves.'[6] After several fraught phone conversations with the First Airborne's general, Floyd Parks, he was told to proceed to Berlin with a much-reduced column of thirty-seven officers, fifty vehicles and 175 men.

It was late afternoon by the time he climbed back into his Horch Roadster and began the final leg of the journey under Russian escort. As his party neared Berlin they encountered thousands of troops, along with horse-drawn wagons laden with the spoils of war. 'The dirtiest I have ever seen,' noted Howley. 'More of a mob than an army.'[7] Unshaven and unkempt, these Mongolian conscripts looked askance at the American column. 'They didn't salute. They didn't answer our salutes. They didn't respond to our questions.'[8] Howley felt the atmosphere change dramatically. 'We were certainly not treated as Allies, but felt that we were in enemy territory.'⁹

It was twilight by the time they approached the outskirts of Berlin. Howley had assumed the Russian escort would lead them into the centre of the city, but it suddenly swerved off the main road and headed for the suburb of Babelsberg. Instead of seeing the Brandenburg Gate and the Reichstag, Howley's men found themselves in an enclosed compound surrounded by Soviet troops. 'Prisoners,' he said, 'instead of welcomed Allies.'

When he asked what was happening, he was given a blunt warning. 'We were not allowed to leave.' He was also warned that the entire area 'was under the control of Russian police [who] reported directly to Stalin'.¹⁰

Howley walked over to one of the barriers with his interpreter, Pat Artzeruni. 'Is this the boundary of the American section?' he asked.

'I don't know,' said the Red Army guard.

'Is this the limit of the compound?'

'I don't know.'

'Can we get past?'

'*Nyet!*'¹¹

It was just as Howley suspected: he was caught in a trap from which there was only one way out. On the following day, he climbed back into his Horch motorcar and set off on a return journey to Halle. When he finally arrived, he assembled his officers and men and gave them a debriefing on everything that had happened.

'Gentlemen,' he said, 'we are never going to Berlin.'¹²

It would fall to General Lucius Clay, Eisenhower's deputy, to have a second meeting with Marshal Zhukov on 29 June, in order to thrash out a solution to the mounting tensions between the Russians and the Allies. The Soviet marshal agreed that each occupying power should be allowed to station twenty-five thousand troops in the city, but he proved obdurate when Clay raised the issue of access to Berlin. He refused Clay's request for the use of multiple railway lines into the capital and insisted on restricting access to one highway and two air corridors, which were to be monitored by Soviet forces.

Lucius Clay accepted Zhukov's restrictions, aware that Washington's priority was continued cooperation with its Soviet allies. Besides, he thought it inconceivable that the Red Army would flex its muscles over the fate of Berlin. 'We were sitting over there with the greatest army that had ever been seen,' said Clay. 'Nobody was concerned about anybody blocking us on roads and railways.'[13] He was nonetheless troubled by Zhukov's response when he asked for the assurances to be put in writing. 'Nonsense!' said Zhukov. 'A formal agreement of that kind isn't necessary between friends and allies.'[14]

News of the Soviet restrictions caused a stir when it reached Brigadier Hinde's team. Harold Hays considered it 'a nightmarish problem' that had not been properly thought through. He took another look at his map of Germany, with the occupied zones clearly marked, and saw 'the whole problem shown up in bold relief'. Without free access across Soviet-occupied Germany, Berlin 'was an island surrounded by a Red Sea'.[15]

Frank Howley got his second green light for Berlin on 30 June and set off the following morning, clambering once again into his Horch Roadster. This time he was confident of success, for it was as if the entire American army was on the move. The autobahn that linked Halle with the German capital was 'the highway to Bedlam . . . jam-packed with tanks, trucks and other vehicles, Military Government people and troops, all hurrying toward the previously forbidden city'.[16]

When a lone Red Army officer tried to halt Howley's vanguard advance, he was given a swift lesson in American authority. One of Howley's men jumped from his car 'and personally deposited the struggling Russian in the ditch to allow our column to pass'.[17] This time there were no hitches. Howley's detachment finally pulled into Berlin in the late afternoon, by which time a summer storm was pelting huge raindrops from the thunderous sky.

There was mayhem as thousands of troops poured into the ruined city. Howley's aide, Lieutenant Colonel John Maginnis, was not impressed. 'Undoubtedly history's most unimpressive entry into the capital of a defeated nation by the conquering power,' he said.[18]

Colonel Howley's A1A1 unit was better prepared than most, carrying field equipment and tents. The colonel directed his men to the forested Grunewald district and ordered them to pitch camp. 'Under the dripping trees, I pulled up my vehicles in a protective circle, as in the old covered-wagon days on the prairie, and posted guards. Not a Russian, not a German, could have interfered with us.'[19]

He was still accompanied by his chic Parisian interpreter, Helen-Antoinette Woods, who had changed out of her trousers and into a skirt because she was fed up with being sexually harassed. 'Even the most polite British and American soldiers would whistle at me when I wore slacks.' She was becoming less chic by the day and matters were scarcely helped by bivouacking in a forest. 'It's very difficult to hang up one's skirt and to keep one's dresses looking well pressed when one is sleeping in the Grunewald and it is raining every day.'[20]

One of Howley's intelligence officers, William Heimlich, was sent on a recce of the rain-washed city and was depressed by what he found. 'Apartment buildings were gutted by fire and explosives . . .' he said. '[It] looked like a cemetery of giants.' The few people out on the streets were pale and malnourished. 'Shocked into utter silence. They moved about the city like zombies. They were starving, that was clear.'[21]

Those who had known Berlin before the war were left reeling by the scale of the destruction. The American correspondent Curt Riess had spent his youth in Berlin; now, he found his old stamping grounds had been wiped from the map. 'The great Opera House was a heap of rubble, so were the Hedwigskirche and the Herrenhaus, the Prussian House of Lords.' Nothing was left standing: 'Gone too was the school I had attended, the house where my parents had lived, the house where my grandmother had spent her last years. It seemed to me that a great part of my life was completely and utterly gone.'[22]

On the morning of 2 July, the day after his arrival, Colonel Howley was invited to what he would later describe as a 'high noon' meeting with the new commandant of the Soviet sector of Berlin, General Alexander Gorbatov.[23] Brigadier Hinde had also been invited, along with his deputy; it was their first post-war visit to the city. Howley was amused to see the two of them 'decked out in shiny whistles [and] glistening Sam Browne belts'.[24] He assumed it was the British way of creating an impression. He preferred full combat fatigues.

The Soviet general lacked the showmanship of his deceased predecessor, General Berzarin, but was nonetheless a punchy operator. 'A red-faced fiery soldier who pounded the table, in anger flushed the colour of beet borsch and forced his will upon others.' Howley thought him quite stupid, for 'he seldom seemed to grasp the real importance of an issue under discussion'.[25] After bragging about Soviet progress in repairing the city's infrastructure, he produced a large map of Berlin and pointed to the twelve districts to be handed over to the British and Americans, as agreed at Yalta. He then asked Howley when he would be ready to move his team into these areas.

'Right now,' snapped Howley.

General Floyd Parks was also at the meeting and urged caution, proposing 4 July, Independence Day and the American national holiday.

'Agreed,'[26] said Gorbatov.

When he asked the same question of the British, Brigadier Hinde had to demur. 'He could set no date for occupying their sector,' he said, because he was unsure of British troop movements.[27] He hoped it would be within the next week. The assembled group also discussed the French, who had yet to receive a sector of Berlin. It was agreed that their advance party, currently en route to the city, should stay in the British sector pending a decision on the exact boundaries of their districts.

Howley was intrigued as to how the relationship between the western Allies and the Soviets would develop. 'We differ from them in almost everything,' he wrote in his diary. 'Here in Berlin we have married the girl before we have courted her. It's like one of those old-fashioned marriages when the bride and groom practically met each other in bed.'[28] As he and the others left the meeting, General Parks turned to Howley with a smile. 'Well, we've got the ball now, Howley,' he said. 'Can you handle it?'[29]

★

Frank Howley set to work that very afternoon, recruiting 1,200 German labourers to fix up billets. No longer would his men have to camp out in the Grunewald; Berliners were turfed out of their homes with a moment's notice. When still in Barbizon, Howley had told his men that possession was ten-tenths of the law. Following this maxim to the letter, he helped himself to a rambling Wilhelmine villa in leafy Dahlem. It was a house fit for a regent, a solid cake of a building with a grand portico and four gigantic urns decorating the stone-lined pediment.

Howley sent his senior officers on a fact-finding tour of the six American districts they were to command. When they reported back to him later that afternoon they spilled a sorry tale of looting and theft, with the Soviets engaged in grand-scale industrial pillage. 'They had dismantled the refrigeration plant at the abattoir, torn stoves and pipes out of restaurant kitchens, stripped machinery from mills and factories, and were completing the theft of the American Singer Sewing Machine plant when we arrived.'

The dismantling teams had done their work without any specialist tools. 'Crowbars were often used to tear out machinery, which could have been removed simply by unbolting it. Valuable lathes and precision tools were stacked in open railroad cars to rust in the rain.'[30] Nor were the Russians showing themselves to be friendly allies. John Maginnis spoke to a group of them and was far from impressed: 'A baffling combination of childishness, hard realism, irresponsibility, churlishness, amiability, slovenliness and callousness.'[31]

The afternoon of 4 July had been set aside for the official hand-over ceremony, when General Gorbatov was to welcome the Americans into their sector of the city. This was to take place at the former Adolf Hitler SS barracks, swiftly renamed McNair Barracks, with two Red Army companies to welcome the guest of honour, General Omar Bradley. To Howley's disappointment, Gorbatov declined to attend in person and sent his deputy instead.

General Bradley's opening speech was warm and generous: he praised the Red Army's fighting prowess and 'expressed the hope for lasting peace and friendship'.[32] Everyone expected Gorbatov's deputy to offer similar sentiments, but he replied 'by practically claiming for Russia credit for winning the war singlehanded'.[33] He informed the American troops that 'the Russians broke the back of the German army at Stalingrad', and added that the Red Army 'would have gone on to victory, with or without American aid'.[34] The message was clear: '*They* had won the war.'[35]

Howley was astonished by the speech. '[It] stunk with self-praise and belittlement of us,'[36] he said, adding that the men of the First Airborne were left with their mouths wide open, 'wondering if we had heard his incredible insults correctly'.[37]

It was to be the first in a series of snubs. Later that day, Marshal Zhukov sent a curt message to General Parks informing him of a dramatic change of plan. The American sectors of the city would not be handed over until the Allied Kommandatura – the governing body – had been constituted.

Howley advised Parks to ignore Zhukov's message. 'It's just another excuse for the Russians to gain time and finish looting our sector before we move in.'[38] He proposed sending American troops into the districts they had been promised, as previously agreed. 'Okay Howley,' said General Parks. 'Go ahead, but don't get into too much trouble.'[39]

Howley always relished confrontation and this promised to be a showdown on a grand scale. He summoned 'the toughest and most competent of my detachment commanders', including John Maginnis, Lieutenant Colonel Hart and Major Ring. These were the men charged with running individual districts in the American sector. Aware that the Russians rarely got up before noon, Howley decided to spring them an early morning surprise. 'We move in at daybreak and set up Military Government,' he told his commanders. 'Don't get into a fight, but protect yourselves if you have to.'[40] It was a high-risk strategy, for it was possible the Russians would resist the American action. 'We didn't know whether they would start a gun fight or whether they would arrest the detachment commanders.'[41]

His commanders swept into their appointed districts at dawn on the following morning, securing key buildings, seizing mayoral offices and raising the Stars and Stripes. They also posted two ordinances: the first declared the establishment of American Military Government, the second announced penalties for crimes committed against Americans. Within hours, Howley received news of their success.

'By the time the Russians woke up . . . the whole thing was an accomplished fact.'[42]

The Soviets fumed and issued threats, but each of the American district commanders gave a stock answer: 'We are soldiers, as you. Therefore we obey our orders.'[43] In Tempelhof district, a detachment of Red Army soldiers began ripping down the American ordinances. 'Don't budge an inch,' yelled Howley down the phone, before jumping into his Horch and paying an unscheduled visit to the Soviet deputy commandant, General Nikolai Baranov, who received a full blast of his fury. The Soviet general sniffed the wind and decided to back down. 'He was faced with a *fait accompli* . . .' said Howley. 'There was nothing he could do but acquiesce.'[44] Nine weeks after the Red Army had captured Berlin, a third of the city was finally in American hands. It was time for the British to play catch-up.

Brigadier Hinde's team was stationed in Wolfenbüttel, some 150 miles west of Berlin, when it received orders to proceed to the German capital. Billeted near them in the surrounding countryside were twenty-five thousand British troops also destined for the city. All began heading eastwards on the morning of Wednesday, 4 July.

Hinde's team set off in advance of the soldiers, leaving Wolfenbüttel at 7.45 a.m. and travelling on a prescribed route through thick drizzle that turned the roads to liquid glue. Also travelling in the vanguard was Harold Hays, noting everything that happened.

They soon got ensnared with the Seventh Armoured Division and found themselves travelling at a snail's pace. It took five hours to cover the twenty miles to the Helmstedt–Marienborn border that marked the crossing point into Soviet-occupied Germany. The Allied side of the frontier was marked by red and white oil-drums and a Union Jack flying from a makeshift pole. It was just like the frontier outposts that Brigadier Hinde had visited in the Hindu Kush. On the Soviet side there flew an enormous red flag, the assembly point for a large number of Soviet troops. Richard Brett-Smith, a twenty-two-year-old captain with the 11th Hussars, studied them with as much curiosity as they studied him. '[They] examine our passes upside down, and smilingly, expectantly, cadge cigarettes, return our looks of appraisal and astonishment, and politely salute as we drive on.'[45]

To the *Daily Mail* correspondent Edwin Tetlow, the advance on Berlin was one of romantic adventure. 'Cossack horsemen, cavorting in the early morning drizzle and shouting their traditional war-cries, gave us a rousing welcome. They were exercising their horses, sending great clods into the air as they performed their unrivalled tricks of horsemanship.'[46]

The four-lane Helmstedt to Berlin autobahn was rather less romantic, 'a never-ending ribbon of concrete, fringed occasionally by trees'. The British column of vehicles found itself sharing the highway with Soviet plunderers. 'Out of one lorry project the legs of a grand piano, another is entirely filled with sheep, a third appears to be a mobile field kitchen in full blast.' So wrote Captain Brett-Smith, who had never seen anything like it: 'Armchairs, kitchen chairs, sausages, hams, pots and pans, shoes, dresses and furs, and sacks bulging with some unidentifiable but prized commodity, are all crammed together in glorious hugger-mugger, and the beaming faces of the human occupants hint that they are returning from a profitable treasure hunt.'[47]

As Brigadier Hinde's column rolled into Potsdam, locals began congregating at the side of the road. 'They waved and smiled [and] some of them threw flowers.'[48] They clearly viewed the British as liberators rather than occupiers. At the entrance to Spandau, in the west of the city, the road was adorned with placards bearing such slogans as 'Salute the Glorious Red Army Which by Its Bravery and Skill has Freed Europe from the Fascist Terror'.[49] To the soldiers of the Seventh Armoured Division, the 'Desert Rats', such placards seemed calculated to offend.

The tanks and half-tracks pushed onwards into the heart of Berlin, where the soldiers were to receive an official welcome from General Lewis Lyne, commander of British forces in Berlin. The Desert Rats made such a fine impression that Edwin Tetlow felt a burst of patriotic pride, especially when he noticed their jeeps and Bren gun carriers showing 'the dents of battle and distance through the glowing coats of fresh paint'.[50] As they neared the Brandenburg Gate, the sun burst out from behind a wall of cloud, a sign of providence for many of the men.

Captain Brett-Smith felt it was a moment to be savoured. 'Berlin has been for so long the hub around which so many hopes and fears and jokes and allusions revolved, that only by reaching the city can we really seem to have won the war.' He had fought through both France and Belgium, yet the German capital had always been at the forefront of his mind. 'Twelve months ago the armoured cars began to carry the chalked inscription *à Berlin* which pretty French and Belgian girls scrawled on their plating . . . Today, unreal as it seems, this has come true.'[51]

Every Berliner would remember glimpsing his first Allied soldier, whether American, British or French. Nine-year-old Manfred Knopf had been awaiting this moment ever since looking on in terror as his mother was raped by Red Army soldiers. To his eyes, the Americans and British troops might have dropped from another world. 'They looked more like movie stars compared to Russian soldiers; the way they were dressed, in the way they behaved themselves, [they were] like gentlemen.'[52]

As the armoured column passed through the city centre, the troops all turned towards a raised dais and snapped the victory salute to General Lewis Lyne. 'The cars sweep by, the cameras whirr, the General stands stiffly to attention and salutes.'[53] The pageantry was something to be savoured, for the men were to get a reality check when they arrived at the Von Seeckt barracks in Spandau. The barracks had been used by the Soviets prior to their arrival and had been left in an indescribable state. 'There were quantities of rancid fat and decaying meat in one kitchen, so that the bluebottles and flies, which were bad enough in the others, were legion here: so were the maggots.' The other kitchens were inches thick in potato peelings, rotting vegetables and empty tins, while the waste pipes were blocked with food and bones. The smell was so bad that the *Daily Telegraph*'s war correspondent, no stranger to grim experiences, was violently sick.

The damage was more serious in the living quarters. The Russians had removed every stick of furniture, including beds, chairs, cupboards, light bulbs, plugs, door handles and taps. Resigned to sleeping on the bare ground, Captain Brett-Smith and his comrades tried to get some rest. This was not easy, for the stillness of dusk was broken by 'zooming mosquitoes and an antiquated Russian biplane that chugs and coughs about over Gatow. Later, what sounds like bursts of machine-gun fire can be heard away in the city to our east, and nearer at hand, odd shots and muffled shouts.'[54]

Brigadier Hinde's team was also trying to get some rest. They had peeled off from the main convoy shortly before the welcome from General Lyne and headed to the residential suburb of Wilmersdorf. Here, they requisitioned a huge villa that had formerly belonged to the industrialist, Hugo Stinnes. 'It was as bare of furniture as could be, with the minimum of sleeping accommodation, but we ate, and we chatted, until at last we settled down to sleep in any old corner not already occupied.' So wrote Harold Hays that evening. 'Our main feeling was one of high adventure. We had arrived and there was work to be done.'[55] Seven months after leaving Wimbledon, and 700 miles from home, Brigadier Hinde's Berlin team had at long last reached its goal.

Brigadier Hinde's tenure as deputy director of British Military Government began that very evening. Officially he was subordinate to General Lewis Lyne, commandant of British forces in the city, but Hinde was to be responsible for much of the day-to-day business of running the British sector, as well as dealing directly with his Soviet counterpart. It was just as well that these duties fell to him, not Lyne, for Hinde was to remain in the city for the next three years whereas the general would be out within weeks.

It was a post that came with a personal price-tag for Hinde: indefinite separation from his beloved wife Evelyn. They had already been apart for seven long months and he had no idea when he would see her again. Nor had he seen his four children, Bill, Elisabeth, Cathryn and Victoria, who were growing up with a father who was always absent. War had divided many families and peace was to divide some of them even more.

Hinde's fiefdom was one of enviable size and wealth – at least, it was on paper. He ruled over six of the finest districts in the city, from Spandau in the west to Tiergarten in the centre, and was custodian of some of the city's most notable monuments, including the Victory Column and the Charlottenburg Palace. His sector also included the Grunewald forest with its undamaged villas and the boating lakes of the Havel and Tegel.

More enticingly, the British sector contained the city's economic jewels, with the most famous being the Siemensstadt, or Siemens City, one of the largest industrial complexes in the world. There was also AEG's vast generator plant and the Bergmann-Borsig machine-tool factory. Hinde had no idea if any of these plants were still intact. Nor did he know the condition of the city's 570,000 inhabitants for whom he was now responsible.

He awoke early the following morning, Thursday, 5 July. His first action was to send Harold Hays on a reconnaissance tour of the British sector, aware that very little could be done until he had on-the-ground intelligence about the condition of the six districts under his control.

Hays had witnessed destruction on a grand scale while en route to the German capital, but he was nevertheless stunned by the scale of the wreckage. 'What the air forces had done to the city beggars belief,' he wrote that day. 'Row after row of bomb-blasted buildings, with burned out tanks and vehicles everywhere . . . The devastation was frightful and the further we pushed on, the more appalling it appeared.' Most buildings were burned-out shells, while many had completely collapsed. 'All the government buildings surrounding the Wilhelmstrasse were just so much useless rubble, blasted in most instances beyond recognition.'[56]

When Hays arrived at the Rheinmetall-Borsig industrial plant, which covered twenty-five blocks, he found that the Russians had been there before him. It had been stripped of all its heavy machinery, and broken floor bolts lay where there once had been state-of-the-art equipment. 'There is no question of our producing anything,' said the factory's forlorn German manager. 'Our productive capacity is absolutely nil.'[57]

It was a similar story with the sector's textile mills and sugar refineries. They had been looted, ransacked and trashed, along with all the company offices. 'Every safe in the city had been cracked by the oxy-acetylene flame,' said Hays, 'and every desk had been care-lessly ripped open.' It was as if the Russians had spent the previous two months systematically looting everything of value. 'With a thoroughness which left one staggered, the Russians had combed official Berlin from end to end and there was little that newcomers could do but scratch their heads and marvel or curse as they viewed the results.'

Further reconnaissance brought further bad news. When Hays ventured into the Grunewald, he stumbled across a charred scrapheap of trashed vehicles, their skeletal frames twisted beyond repair. This was the municipal bus fleet, sabotaged by fanatical Nazis carrying out Hitler's 'Nero Decree' – dictating that everything of use must be destroyed.

But it was the parlous state of Berlin's health service that caused Hays the greatest concern. Forty-three of the forty-four hospitals in the British sector were severely damaged and none had any anaesthetics, antibiotics or anti-bacterials. An outbreak of virulent typhoid was threatening to become an epidemic, as was diphtheria, and six out of every ten new-born babies were dying from dysentery. Hays was warned that 'insufficient chlorine was available for the water supply' – such as it was – 'and that unless the most energetic steps were taken to remedy this, the possibility of epidemics was very great.' Pitiful sanitation was compounding the problem. More than five hundred mains pipes had been shattered, along with drains and sewers, and the flooded streets frothed and bubbled with human effluent. 'Flies, flies and more flies,' wrote one local resident, 'black, blue and fat.'[58] The Russians had restored the principal supply pipes in their area of the city, but had left the British and Americans to repair those in their own sectors.

Brigadier Hinde's team expanded greatly over the days that followed, with scores of additional experts assigned to serve with the British Military Government. The brigadier could also call upon the services of the twenty-five thousand soldiers, sappers and army engineers who had taken the salute from General Lyne. And there was an advance guard of the women's Auxiliary Territorial Service, whose first two members had just arrived in the city. Hilda Witchell and Peggy Quinney were excited about having reached their destination, but profoundly shocked by the nightmarish scenes that greeted them. 'Three miles with no building standing,' said Witchell of their drive through the outskirts. 'People were lying in the gutter.'[59] She noticed something else that unsettled her. Berlin was a city that no longer had any cats, dogs or birds, for all had been eaten by starving Berliners.

Hinde ordered the British troops to start clearing up that very first morning, bulldozing rubble, repairing power lines and burst pipes. They were hindered by the atrocious summer weather, which brought heat, humidity and torrential rain. 'The day invariably ended with a thunderstorm,' wrote James Chambers, an officer with the Royal Engineers, who was sickened by the stench of putrid corpses that followed each downpour. 'The smell was terrible. It was everywhere. You could almost taste it in your food.'[60]

Food supplies were brought in by truck from depots in the western-occupied zones of Germany, and coal was brought from the mines of the Ruhr. Armed troops were sent to guard the coal stocks, for looting was rife, and food was distributed through a hastily installed rationing system. The basic ration provided a daily subsistence of just 1,504 calories and was dubbed the 'death card' by Berliners.

Brigadier Hinde sent Harold Hays back into the Grunewald with orders to requisition the finest undamaged villas for himself and his officers. For Hays and his team, it was the most rewarding search for lodgings they had ever undertaken. It required no agents and no fees. Armed with a stash of requisition forms, they simply seized the choicest accommodation in town. 'Germans in Grunewald were turfed out of their houses at an hour's notice to make way for us, while the mess building' – the villa formerly belonging to the industrialist Hugo Stinnes – 'quickly accumulated the necessary carpets, tables and chairs, crockery, etc.'

Within hours the Berlin team was housed in style, with Brigadier Hinde installed in a regal Weimar-period villa with lofty ceilings and a huge principal salon. Also requisitioned were a cook, cleaner and washerwoman, as well as a chauffeur named Schneimann who laid his hands on a fine black Mercedes with red leather trim. Where it came from was anyone's guess: in post-war Berlin, it was better not to ask.

The requisitioning did not make Hinde's men popular with the local population. 'It meant much wailing and tears on the part of the Germans,' noted Hays, but he felt little sympathy. 'Where people went to, and how they fared, was obviously no concern of ours.' He pointed out that the Germans had treated their conquered populations in similar fashion. 'The chickens had merely come home to roost.'

One of Brigadier Hinde's key priorities was to fix up Deutschland House, a five-storey, yellow-painted property on Adolf Hitler Platz (hastily renamed Reichskanzlerplatz), selected as the headquarters of the British Military Government. It was still functioning as the head office of the Leuna Oil Company when Hays first pitched up on the morning of 5 July. When informed that their offices were being confiscated, the Leuna directors protested – in vain: they were turfed out into the street, along with employees who were at that very moment arriving for work.

Hinde's men wasted no time in getting rid of every trace of the former occupants, as Hays recorded with indecent relish. 'Leuna Oil Company documents and files were disposed of by the very simple procedure of throwing them out of the windows into the courtyard below, where they were collected by the company's staff.'

Everything else in the building was too useful to be junked. 'All the office material, furniture and furnishings were immediately seized for Military Government use and were lost to the Leuna concern forever.' Hays conducted a swift recce of the building and found it in better condition than most in Berlin, although shell damage had blown out the windows. On being told of a nearby builders' merchant with a large stock of glass, he promptly requisitioned the lot, causing the owner 'to splutter a bit and, in spluttering, he denounced another dealer as a hoarder'. Hays drove over to this second dealer and commandeered all his glass as well. In this way, he said, 'we were able to requisition enough glass to cover all our immediate requirements.'

Later that day there was a brief but unseemly breakdown in British discipline as everyone in the Berlin team sought the best offices: 'The scramble for good desks was really something to remember.'[61] But in a surprisingly short space of time, British Military Government was up and running.

★

Brigadier Hinde was undaunted by the scale of the crisis he was facing, contending that even the most insurmountable problems could be overcome by the rigid application of British common sense. From his analytic brain there now emerged a blueprint for Berlin that was to be issued to everyone in his team. 'In this way,' he said, 'we may hope to avoid mistaking the wood for the trees.'

This blueprint, entitled *Military Government: British Troops Berlin*, provided a framework for how his men were to work. It covered all the most pressing issues facing the city's traumatised population, including law and order (there was none), Nazis in hiding (there were many) and the challenges of governing a city in which the entire infrastructure had collapsed. Hinde felt that the biggest problem facing his team would be power-sharing with the other three nations, particularly the Russians. With the exception of post-war Vienna, Berlin was to be the only place in the world 'where members of the four nations work together, eat together and give orders to the Germans as an integrated whole'. It was a unique political experiment that had never before been attempted.

It had already been decided that Berlin's different sectors were to be jointly run by the Kommandatura, in which Hinde and Howley would be working closely with their Soviet counterpart. There was no room for failure. 'The Allied Kommandatura is an experiment in co-operation which *must* succeed,' said Hinde. If the western Allies fell out with their Soviet counterparts, then disaster would surely ensue.

Hinde reminded his team that they would need to be consummate diplomats, showing 'the maximum tact and understanding towards the other Allies, especially the Russians'. To this end, he urged them to mix with their Soviet comrades in the makeshift bars and clubs of Berlin. 'Get to know them socially by having meals together,' he said. 'Only by so doing will we be able to find out what they are thinking about.'[62]

Marshal Zhukov summoned his American and British allies to another meeting at Soviet military headquarters on Saturday, 7 July. It was an occasion that none of the participants would forget, for the marshal was poised to give the western leaders a masterclass in gunboat diplomacy, with the emphasis on the gunboat. There were few niceties, apart from his addressing his guests as gentlemen, and not much charm. 'The most perfectly cool, persistent negotiator, with a clear policy that had a broad answer for most problems.'[63] Such was the opinion of one British intelligence officer studying Zhukov at close quarters.

The Americans were represented by General Lucius Clay, Frank Howley and a few others, while the British fielded General Roland Weeks and Brigadier Hinde, along with several advisers. The French had not been invited.

Zhukov wrested control of the meeting at the outset by appointing himself chairman. 'Well gentlemen,' he began, 'shall we start business?' The word 'business' wrong-footed his guests, who had assumed they were attending an informal weekend discussion. 'The two delegations seemed a little stunned,' noted Howley. 'If they thought it was going to be a social call, that fantasy went out of the window immediately.' Zhukov was armed with briefing notes, whereas Clay and Weeks had arrived empty-handed. 'It was obvious that both were unprepared.'

Howley was expecting the worst, but even he was shocked when Zhukov announced that all contentious issues in Berlin were to be settled unanimously by the four commanders, with each having a veto over the others. Howley interjected, telling Zhukov that such a plan was unworkable. 'The British, French and Americans may agree on a million things,' he said. 'But there will be many on which the Russians won't agree.'[64] He insisted that each commandant have autonomy over his own sector, the only workable solution to four-way-power rule, and was stunned when Lucius Clay gave him a public dressing-down.

'You are entirely wrong,' said Clay. 'I have just come from Washington and it certainly *is* the intention of our government to administer Berlin on a unanimous basis.' Howley felt like 'a brash uninformed junior in that Olympian company of omniscient generals'.[65] Clearly, he was wildly out of step with American foreign policy towards Berlin.

Zhukov now produced a printed agreement setting forth everything he had just proposed. Howley read it before sliding it back to Clay.

'As a legal document it stinks,' he said. Clay ignored him and signed his name at the bottom, 'thereby indicating that he had no intention of quibbling about commas, periods or anything else'. He justified his actions by reminding Howley of Washington's insistence that 'mutual understanding' among the four ruling powers was the over-riding objective.[66]

The Soviet marshal saved his most spectacular bombshell for the end. 'Now gentlemen, we will discuss the question of food and coal you will supply for the maintenance of Berlin'. Howley described Zhukov's words as 'an icy blast from the steppes.' Berlin had always been fed from the rich farmland to the east of the city – from Brandenburg and Pomerania – which were both under Soviet control. It was inconceivable that the Americans and British could feed the 1,650,000 inhabitants in their sectors of the city with only the use of a single road and rail link.

Even Lucius Clay balked at Zhukov's demand, informing him that there was currently no large bridge over the River Elbe. The marshal's deputy responded with a cynical smile. 'What have you been doing since the Yalta Conference?' he asked. 'Why don't you clean up the bridges and use them? That's what we do.'

And that was it. 'Well gentlemen,' said Zhukov, 'the meeting is now ended.' He invited everyone to a celebratory banquet at which Lucius Clay presented him with an engraved pistol. Zhukov glanced at the gift, offered a frigid smile and handed it to an aide.

Howley felt the marshal had 'wrung everything from us but our gold teeth'. His verdict on the meeting was blunt: 'After the vodka fumes were dissipated and the caviar savor vanished, our leaders discovered their pockets had been picked . . . It was round one for the Russians.'[67] He knew that if the western Allies were to stand up to the Soviets, they would have to start fighting dirty.

6

Life on the Edge

ERLINERS FACED A tense few days as they waited to discover
into which sector their neighbourhood would fall. At her ruined
lodgings in the Steglitz district of the city, Ruth Andreas-Friedrich
was discussing the likely division with her daughter, Karin, and
friends Dagmar Meyerowitz and Dr Walter Seitz.

'Steglitz remains Russian,' asserted Frau Meyerowitz, although she
offered no evidence to support this. Dr Seitz disagreed. 'Steglitz will
be American. They are taking the entire south. The west becomes
English. Russia keeps the east and the French will get the north.'
He reached for a blue pencil and scored the likely boundaries onto
a map of the city, much as the trio of diplomats had done in London
almost two years earlier.

'Let's hope that they stay in agreement with each other,' said
young Karin. 'If these four start fighting . . .' Her voice trailed off
before she could finish. 'Then we've had it,' concluded Dr Seitz.

So many questions remained unanswered. 'Will they erect barriers?
Will one have to pay duty?' They also wondered if they would be
permitted to cross from sector to sector. 'We have a hundred questions and, once again, are sure of only one thing – that we don't
know anything.'[1] But they got answers soon enough, for signs began
to spring up all over the city delineating the boundaries of each
sector. Ruth Andreas-Friedrich's lodgings were in the south-west of
Berlin and therefore fell inside the American sector. It was a rare
piece of good news.

On the same side of the city, Hildegard Herrberger was growing
anxious. 'We literally prayed, "Please let us be taken over by the
Amis or by the English! Please let it happen, but not – for goodness

sake – by the Russians!"'[2] She got her wish: the Neukölln district of the city also fell within the American sector.

The boundary signs erected by the Americans were written in giant capital letters: YOU ARE LEAVING THE AMERICAN SECTOR, and were much photographed. The wording was also given in Russian and French, with a German translation in smaller lettering. But there were hundreds of other panels marking individual crossing points, along with instructions for those entering a new sector. One gigantic Soviet placard carried a political slogan: 'Long Live the Anglo-Soviet-American Alliance Against the German Fascist Aggressors.' It was a text that still had some currency in the early weeks of July. 'In those days,' said Captain Brett-Smith, 'East and West were cautiously feeling their political way and had not yet finally decided to jettison their short-lived alliance.'[3]

Other signs, handwritten, tattered and wind-blown, were forlorn pleas for help. 'Mothers seeking their sons, wives seeking their husbands, children seeking their parents.' So wrote journalist Curt Riess, who added that all were 'seeking people who might be tramping over the highways of Europe or lying in unknown graves'.[4]

Dorothea von Schwanenflügel had been delighted to discover that her family's house fell within the American sector. 'We are able to freely move around the streets again,' announced her father with a rare smile. But the family's joy was short-lived, for they soon saw newly erected signs carrying a proclamation from General Eisenhower. It reminded Berliners that the Allies came as occupiers, and that there was to be no fraternisation. 'We could not believe what we read,' said von Schwanenflügel.[5] She had assumed they were being liberated. Instead, they were to be further ostracised. The fact that Eisenhower himself was of German stock made it yet more painful.

The division of the city did nothing to hinder freedom of movement, for there were few physical checkpoints at the boundaries of each sector. Curious British and American soldiers began visiting the Soviet districts of the city, while Red Army troops started to frequent the bars springing up in the western sectors. It was as if everyone was eyeing everyone else up, intrigued, yet wary and filled with trepidation.

It was one thing to cross the city by day, quite another to do so by night. The streets were dangerous in the hours that followed the 11 p.m. civilian curfew and Captain Brett-Smith said that 'only foolhardy spirits ventured unarmed into the Russian sector at night, where the fall of darkness and the rattle of machine-gun fire usually coincided.' He would lie awake in his Spandau barracks and listen to the bursts of staccato gunfire. 'One often heard shooting across the Havel, and several times anonymous bodies were washed up on the British side.' The Russians had found that the most effective way of clearing the streets for the nocturnal curfew was to let rip with their machine guns. 'The fact that some of their allies might be on the pavements did not worry them.'[6]

It was inevitable that accidents would happen and one of the more tragic blunders involved Ruth Andreas-Friedrich's partner, Leo Borchard, a professional musician who had been born in St Petersburg and emigrated to Berlin after the 1917 revolution. His impeccable anti-Nazi credentials had endeared him to the city's first governor, General Berzarin, who had appointed him senior conductor of the newly reconstituted Berlin Philharmonic. In a city renowned for its classical music, this post elevated Borchard to instant stardom.

As the summer heat arrived in earnest, he and Frau Andreas-Friedrich were invited for drinks in the Grunewald with a music-loving British colonel. It was an enjoyable evening: they ate white bread sandwiches (a luxury in such lean times) and consumed too much whisky. As the clock ticked towards 11 p.m., Ruth Andreas-Friedrich began to get jumpy. 'Curfew in fifteen minutes,' she said.

The colonel offered to drive them back to their apartment, unaware that his chosen route would take him along a thoroughfare on which American and Russian soldiers had exchanged gunfire the previous evening. Tensions had been running high at the sector boundaries, where volatile troops were equipped with loaded weapons. Many of these soldiers were jumpy and nervous, suffering the after-effects of the stresses of combat. Many were also drunk.

Frank Howley was so concerned about security that he had ordered all vehicles travelling across sector boundaries to be stopped and searched, an order unknown to the British colonel driving his guests home. As the car hurtled towards the S–Bahn bridge near Bundesplatz, at the sector boundary, Andreas-Friedrich glimpsed flashlights in the darkness. Next she heard a sound of stones being hurled against the car: 'Tack-tack-tack . . . tack-tack-tack.' This was followed by a loud bang, the screech of brakes and carnage. 'Something is being spattered around my face, hits my arms and shoulders with biting force.'

The car careered to a halt beyond the underpass and Andreas-Friedrich flung open the door and ran to the passenger side. Borchard had been hit through the head by an American bullet and blood was pulsating from his brain. 'I hear it dripping like a gutter, I see it flow. It is sticky. It sticks to my hands and my feet. Everywhere . . . everywhere.'[7] Within seconds, her beloved partner was dead.

The posthumous concert of Tchaikovsky's Fifth, for which Borchard and his orchestra had been rehearsing, was deeply moving. The British colonel was as grief-stricken as everyone else. 'He will get a coffin,' he said to Andreas-Friedrich. 'And a hearse will take him to his own grave in the cemetery.'[8]

In those first weeks in the German capital, the behaviour of British and American soldiers did little to endear them to their Soviet counterparts. One of the first notable incidents occurred when an American combat engineer named Major Kasparazycki was invited to a restaurant by two Red Army commanders. As they gulped down 'some noxious liquid which smelled like gasoline' one of the Soviet officers asked the American major why he had brought along only two of his friends. Fuelled by liquor, Major Kasparazycki bragged that 'three Americans are equal to twelve Russians'.

This proved too much for the most senior Soviet colonel, who immediately challenged him to a fight. Kasparazycki rose to the occasion and punched the man unconscious, at which point another Russian stepped forward to take his place. He, too, was knocked to the ground. And so it continued until the American major had beaten six of the twelve.

News of the affray soon reached Frank Howley, who listened with undisguised relish. '[It was] the kind of boisterous, rough-and-tumble party the Russians loved in the early days,' he said. 'They acquired considerable respect for American stamina.'[9]

Brigadier Hinde's men were equally combative, with the most high-spirited being the garrison soldiers, bored senseless after the adrenaline rush of conflict. When a Red Army looter pulled his gun on one British sergeant, he was taught a swift lesson. The sergeant 'knocked it out of his hand with the butt of his rifle, then knocked out the looter's front teeth with the same weapon'. As a coup de grâce, he grabbed the soldier 'by the seat of his pants and the scruff of his neck . . . and kicked him over into Soviet territory'.[10]

Captain Richard Brett-Smith experienced a more alarming situation on the boundary between the British and Soviet sectors. He was walking his dog along the banks of the Havel when he found himself facing a platoon of Red Army frontier guards. '*Zu Hause!*' screamed the officer in heavily accented German. '*Schnell! Schnell!*'

Brett-Smith subscribed to the traditional British fashion of dealing with foreigners. 'I am an English officer,' he bawled, 'this is the British sector, what the hell you bloody Russians are doing here with your pissarse exercises without our permission I don't know, but I suggest you push off to your own sector!'[11] The Soviet soldiers immediately backed down, yet Brett-Smith was left with the impression that these so-called allies were not as friendly as they had been made out to be.

As the weeks passed, the clashes between rival soldiers became increasingly serious. When Sergeant James Chambers emerged from a cinema late one night, he found himself walking into a ferocious gun battle between British and Soviet troops. 'Bullets were flying everywhere.' It transpired that a band of Russian marauders had entered the British sector intent on looting whatever they could find: 'Alcohol, food, anything,' said Chambers. 'It was like the Vikings. Pillage and rape.'[12]

Rape remained a serious concern, especially when gangs of drunken Red Army conscripts strayed into the British or American sectors to commit their crimes. As the frequency of such incidents increased, Frank Howley took dramatic measures to protect his fiefdom. 'We started shooting,' he said. 'The men of the Second Armoured Division were fine soldiers. You couldn't expect them to stand by and watch women being raped and kids frightened out of a year's growth.'[13]

Matters came to a head with a murderous incident at Potsdamer station, which stood just inside the Soviet sector but whose approach track ran through the American sector. Howley was brought news that a wayward platoon of Soviet soldiers had held up an overloaded train as it was pulling into the station. 'The train was coming from either Silesia or Czechoslovakia, with refugees who swarmed in the coaches like bees, packing the inside and clinging to the roofs.' As they jumped down from the train they were stopped by the Russian platoon, who stole their watches, jewellery and cash. It was fortunate for the refugees that one of Howley's finest men, the ex-FBI sharp-shooter Captain Charles Leonetti, happened to be at the station. He was so disgusted by what he was seeing that he decided to intervene, shouting abuse at the Russian soldiers and thereby prompting a volley of poorly aimed bullets. It was a volley they would regret. Leonetti blasted a single bullet into the air as a warning signal and then 'let them have it'.[14] His first four shots killed two of the Russians and wounded another; his subsequent shots caused the rest to flee from the scene.

News of the incident incensed General Gorbatov, who immediately telephoned Howley and launched a blistering verbal attack, 'charging us with murdering – they love the word "murdering" – Soviet citizens and Soviet soldiers'. Howley sent General Parks to see the Soviet commander rather than going himself, a wise decision given Howley's impetuous nature. Parks delivered a brief lecture on the lawless days of the Wild West. It was worth assuming, said Parks, 'that a man who draws his weapon intends to shoot you'.[15] He also urged the Russian general to put his house in order, criticising him for having such a rabble under his command. 'You must control and discipline your troops,' he said. 'You can't expect us to let them run wild in our sector, looting and shooting.'[16]

Brigadier Hinde faced a daunting challenge during his first weeks in Berlin, with his team struggling to repair the infrastructure of the British sector with inadequate tools and supplies. Yet there were tangible signs of progress. A round-the-clock convoy of food trucks was soon pulling into Spandau barracks, while hastily repaired locomotives brought increasing quantities of coal from the Ruhr. Water pipes and sewers were repaired, and power was restored. When Captain Brett-Smith made a reconnaissance tour of the capital he found it improving at a remarkable rate. 'There were still dead Panthers and Tigers [tanks] making landmarks in certain streets, and T34s and Shermans as well,' he said. 'But the roads had been mended [and] their obstructions mostly removed.'[17] Most impressive was the fact that the electric light and gas services had been partially restored.

Hospitals had also begun receiving medicines. When Hinde first arrived in the city, one of his intelligence officers had warned that Berlin 'was on the brink of the worst scourge of disease and pestilence since the Middle Ages'. This was no hyperbole: thousands of makeshift coffins had been constructed 'in readiness for the fatal casualties'.[18] But swift action by Hinde averted an immediate catastrophe. Forty tons of DDT was imported to kill lice, along with vast quantities of disinfectant. Hinde also brought in urgently needed medicines: five million units of insulin, thirteen million aspirin tablets, four and a half million anti-bacterial tablets and a huge tank of diphtheria anti-toxin.

He escalated the process of rubble-clearing during those foetid summer months using teams of soldiers and local inhabitants. 'The difference was staggering,' noted Harold Hays on returning to Berlin after a visit to England. All the Soviet placards had been removed and replaced with signs 'directing the troops to what seemed an endless number of clubs'.[19] These had sprung up within days of the western Allies entering the city: Roxy's, Bobby's, Chez Ronnie, Rio Rita and the Embassy, as well as the Royal, the Blue-White and Femina. 'In all of them,' noted Captain Brett-Smith, 'the drinks were expensive and the girls cheap.'[20] And herein lay Brigadier Hinde's biggest headache.

The extent of the problem was revealed by Wilfred Byford-Jones, a young British intelligence officer only recently arrived in Berlin. He took himself off to Chez Ronnie's and was astonished by what he found. 'One blinked upon entering, after seeing the heaps of rubble, the jagged ruins against the sky and the hundreds of homeless people.'[21] The bar had a jazz band, dance floor and an army of snappily dressed waiters. It was also equipped with starched white tablecloths and newly upholstered chairs. But the real draw of the place was the abundance of young German women.

Byford-Jones knew that fraternisation was forbidden. Allied soldiers were prohibited from talking to Berliners and most certainly banned from flirting with them. This latter offence carried the hefty fine of $65, a sum that led to the propositioning of Berlin girls becoming known as the '65-dollar question'.[22]

'Do you know German women have been trained to seduce you?' read an army pamphlet issued to Allied troops. 'Is it worth the knife in the back?'[23] The soldiers in Chez Ronnie's ignored such warnings, just as they ignored the ban on fraternisation. 'Copulation without conversation is not fraternisation,' they quipped.[24]

Byford-Jones learned several new expressions that night, all coined by the Americans. A 'frat' was a German girlfriend, while 'to go fratting' was to pursue available women. A 'frat sandwich' was an army-issue corned-beef sandwich, appetising enough to lure many a half-starved fräulein into bed. One British lieutenant contended that 'corned beef was more precious than diamonds to Germans', as were chocolate, cigarettes and nylons, all available to Allied soldiers in almost limitless quantities.[25] It made them lords of all they surveyed. A night with a German girl cost five cigarettes; twenty-five packets purchased a state-of-the-art Leica camera.[26]

The ensuing breakdown in morality threatened to undermine everything that Brigadier Hinde had sought to achieve. He was prepared to turn a blind eye to overindulgence in the officers' mess and accepted that high-jinks were part and parcel of army life. But he expected his hand-picked team to deploy a stiff resolve when exposed to the temptations of the flesh. 'It is imperative that the conscience of all British personnel must be clear,' he told them.[27] He was to be sorely disappointed when he learned of the scenes taking place in Chez Ronnie's, where British and Americans alike were behaving with a complete disregard for the rules.

One G.I. gave Byford-Jones an exuberant account of his exploits, beginning with a blast against the army authorities. 'Somehow or other we'd been led to believe that a German girl was fat and ugly, with fanged teeth, who beat her fist on *Mein Kampf* and shouted "Heil Hitler, I am a Nazi."' The truth was so very different. 'When we came up against our first 19-year-old Rheinland blonde with blue eyes, pink cheeks, plaits, and very desirable, we were just clean bowled over. No one could help it, biology being what it was.'

Another American said the troops deserved unlimited sex after fighting their way from Normandy to Berlin. 'The girls were pretty and they didn't wear much, just light-coloured summer frocks, and we'd been living through hell, living hard, in the open. Yes, it wasn't long before Army Div. was worn out.'

British soldiers recounted similar stories. 'Here you've got girls competing for you,' bragged one young lad. 'Strewth, you could have a dozen if you wanted, and I don't mean prostitutes.' He described Berlin as a sexual paradise, but Byford-Jones detected a more disturbing story beneath the banter. 'These girls will take any treatment and they treat you like a king,' whispered one soldier. 'Doesn't matter if you keep them waiting half an hour . . . They are thankful for little things, a bar of chocolate or a few fags . . . it's like giving these girls the moon.'[28]

Lieutenant Byford-Jones felt sorry for the women of Berlin, yet not all were selling their bodies out of necessity. Some were happy to find themselves in the arms of a soldier who brought frivolity and optimism to a city devoid of both. Berlin was also devoid of eligible German men. In the Lichterfelde district – population fifteen thousand – there were only eighty-one German males between the ages of sixteen and twenty-one. In Tempelhof, there was just one man for every ten young women and most were in a state of decrepitude, having returned to Berlin from the battlefront on foot. 'They shamble around like walking ruins,' wrote Ruth Andreas-Friedrich in her diary. 'Limbless, invalid, ill, deserted and lost.' Many had been left disabled by the war. 'Sometimes all that's left is the trunk. Amputated up to their hips, they sit in an old box supported by wheels.'[29]

Among Brigadier Hinde's most qualified recruits was George Clare, the Jewish refugee who had first passed through Berlin in

1937 while en route to the Irish Free State. He had been intending to serve British Military Government with upstanding professionalism, but he changed his mind when he saw what was taking place in his Tiergarten mess. No sooner was it dark than all his comrades scuttled off to their rooms with a local girl in tow. 'They were cementing Anglo-German relations at the grass-roots with their girlfriends,' he wrote. 'International friendships were being celebrated in high style all over the place. One never went into any bedroom, including one's own, without knocking first.'[30]

Clare found himself pursued by a voracious partygoer named Anita who made it abundantly clear that she was 'an experienced woman' looking for the sort of fun that she'd enjoyed before the war. Clare stepped up to the mark with relish, enjoying the kudos of being actively pursued by a woman.[31]

The downside to the womanising soon became apparent. 'Syphilis and clap all over the place,' whispered one anxious serviceman to Byford-Jones. 'That's why a guy's got to be careful.'[32] Another added that the Red Army rapes had bequeathed a nasty surprise on young women already traumatised by abuse: 'a particularly virulent type of Asiatic syphilis which was rather unpleasant because you tended to swell up. It was like elephantiasis, all your joints and limbs and face and everything swelled up.'[33]

Venereal disease, or VD, was joshingly referred to as Veronica Dankeshön by the young Allied soldiers, but they knew it was no joke. The worst afflicted ended up looking like the Michelin man and required lengthy and uncomfortable treatment. That same officer told Byford-Jones that Russian syphilis was a serious condition, and 'very different from the normal American blob-on-your-knob kind of stuff'.[34]

Brigadier Hinde's men were also using Berlin's burgeoning black market to make serious amounts of cash, buying and selling illicit goods with the German civilians and the Soviet soldiers. This became a problem too big to ignore and the brigadier addressed his team in the tone of an admonishing headmaster. 'We have been apt in the past to talk about the Black Market rather light-heartedly and to tend to regard it as something of a joke,' he said, but it was

The Big Three wartime leaders at the Yalta Conference, February 1945. Stalin played his hand with skill against an ebullient Winston Churchill. President Roosevelt was ill and close to death.

In Yalta's aftermath, Colonel Frank 'Howlin' Mad' Howley was tasked with planning the occupation of Berlin's American sector. Promoted to commandant, he was to fight a four-year battle against the Soviets.

Brigadier Robert 'Looney' Hinde was deputy director of British Military Government. Unlike Frank Howley, he sought a close working relationship with the Soviets.

Soviet tanks sweep into Berlin, April 1945.
Terrified Berliners hid in their cellars as the battle raged around them.

The battle for Berlin was brutal and intense.
Here, Soviet troops fight their way towards the Reichstag.

Soviet troops celebrate victory in front of the Brandenburg Gate.
Berliners were fearful of drunk and violent Red Army soldiers.

This iconic image of the Soviet flag over the Reichstag was staged by
photographer Yevgeny Khaldei. He later edited the image, removing one
of the two looted watches on the wrists of the lower soldier.

Tens of thousands of refugees poured into Berlin in May 1945. Fleeing from Soviet-occupied territory to the east, they were homeless, hungry and desperate.

Berliners were close to starvation in the aftermath of war. Here, two women search a rubbish dump for scraps of discarded food.

The Soviets introduced ration cards and mobile soup kitchens to feed Berlin's starving civilians. The basic ration – 1,504 calories a day – was dubbed the 'death card'.

American tanks enter Berlin at the end of June 1945. It marked the beginning of a fraught relationship with their erstwhile Soviet allies.

British forces take the salute from General Lewis Lyne as they enter Berlin on 4 July 1945. Some twenty-five thousand British troops would be stationed in the city.

Potsdam Conference, July 1945. A confident President Harry Truman sits between Joseph Stalin and Prime Minister Clement Attlee. Britain's scowling foreign secretary, Ernest Bevin (*back row, second left*), meets his Soviet nemesis, Vyacheslav Molotov (*back row, right*).

The four-power Kommandatura, established to run post-war Berlin, became the setting for a bitter power struggle between the western allies and the Soviets.

General Alexander Kotikov, commandant of Soviet Berlin from 1946 to 1950. Ruthless, brilliant and often genial, he went to war with his American opposite, Colonel Frank Howley.

Kommandatura meetings were always tense. Here, Brigadier Hinde and General Herbert sit opposite Colonel Frank Howley (*back to camera*). Howley despised Herbert for his refusal to support the airlift.

Brigadier 'Looney' Hinde (*right*) is served food at a lavish Kommandatura tea-break. While Berliners starved, Allied officers feasted on lobster, caviar and champagne.

The Kommandatura decided on broad sweeps of policy, delegating the detailed work to four-power committees like this one, dealing with public health.

The first Soviet military governor of Berlin, General Nikolai Berzarin leaves his Berlin-Karlshorst head-quarters. Berzarin died in a high-speed motorbike crash just weeks after his appointment.

The Allied victory parade, Berlin, 7 September 1945, was a propaganda coup for the Soviets, who reneged on an agreement about the number of parading troops and tanks.

A bemedalled Marshal Georgy Zhukov stands with General George Patton at the Allied victory parade. Zhukov insisted on addressing the crowd and infuriated Patton by extolling the fighting prowess of the Red Army.

no longer a laughing matter. 'Nothing could be more derogatory to our prestige and nothing could more effectively sabotage the objectives of Military Government in Germany than indulgence in black market activity.'[35]

His words once again fell on deaf ears, for the black market proved an irresistible temptation. Among those making extensive profits was Len Carpenter, a red-blooded British civilian who had escaped from a German prisoner-of-war camp and sneaked into Berlin – uniquely, perhaps – when the Soviets were still in sole control of the city. With the arrival of the western Allies he ought to have reported his presence to British Military Government; instead, he continued his freebooting existence, lodging in an abandoned flat in Charlottenburg and cadging meals from a nearby army cookhouse. 'No one ever asked me who I was or what I was doing there.' Everyone assumed he was part of Brigadier Hinde's outfit.

Carpenter was a rakish wheeler-dealer who thrived in the chaos of four-sector Berlin. 'I was living a lovely life,' he later admitted. 'I'd sleep till about half past eleven in the morning, then Boscherling [a German banker friend] and I would go down to the Kurfürstendamm where we'd have lunch. We would invariably pick a couple of girls up and take them back to the flat for the afternoon.' Those after-noons were the prelude to a punishing schedule of overindulgence. 'We'd push them out of bed at about teatime, four or five o'clock, and at about seven o'clock at night we'd go out for dinner.' After once again eating for free at the army mess, Carpenter would start the process over again. 'I would invite more German girls in for a cup of tea or a drink, but some nights really I was so knackered I would just slap their thighs and say "cheerio" and that was the end of it – I just hadn't the energy.' One of the reasons why he was 'so knackered' was because he also had a regular girlfriend.

Carpenter was among the first to pioneer Berlin's black market, making huge amounts of cash from the illicit trade in food, alcohol and cigarettes. 'I started by buying NAAFI* goods from English soldiers and selling them to Germans, and getting cameras and suchlike from Germans and selling them to English soldiers.' He

* NAAFI: Navy, Army and Air Force Institutes

soon had a viable racketeering business, which included procuring young women for those in need. 'Very soon the British soldiers were bringing the German girls I had introduced into my flat in Kastanienallee in Charlottenburg,' he said. 'Of course they were doing it all over my furniture and my lovely silk-brocaded chaise-longue – still with their boots on!'[36]

Len Carpenter soon found himself in competition with British, American and Soviet soldiers. It was so easy to make money from cigarettes, the city's most sought-after currency, because they were far more valuable than the debased German mark. British troops were issued with fifty cigarettes a week and could buy a further two hundred at duty-free prices. They could also buy cheap chocolate and soap. These commodities were then used to purchase sex, Leica cameras, antiques, paintings and tapestries, Meissen china and German marks. The marks were then exchanged for sterling or dollars at the favourable army exchange rate, delivering an instant profit. 'People were going home on leave and cashing huge amounts of cash into English money,'[37] said the young sergeant, James Chambers.[38]

It was the same for American troops, many of whom sold their watches to Soviet soldiers for vastly inflated prices. Within four months of arriving in Berlin, they had sent home around eleven million dollars, more than they had received in pay.

'Finding the black market was no problem,' said George Clare. 'It came to you.' He was astonished at the ubiquity of an underworld that never stopped giving. 'Everywhere and anywhere, in the streets, in cafes, on the underground, on the tram, indeed right outside the entrance to the Winston Club, Germans stopped you asking if you had cigarettes to sell.' His friend, Jock, grinned as he stuffed another two hundred army-issue cigarettes into his knapsack. 'Why ever did we two idiots not want to come to Berlin!' he said. 'It's paradise!'[39]

The largest black-market areas were in the Tiergarten and the Alexanderplatz, where one could find all the principal players, including the Grosschieber (or big-time operators), the go-betweens, illicit bankers and money-launderers. 'The racketeers were to be seen as bold as brass at any time of day or night,' wrote Captain Brett-Smith. At the lowest end of the hierarchy were the 'rat-like sharp-faced little men of the sidewalks', dealing in cheap cast-offs, while at the other end of the scale were the big-time operators: 'large pale men with fishy eyes drinking *Schwindelkognak* in the Royal or Ronnie's, hardly distinguishable on the surface from Ruhr steel magnates'.[40]

Wilfred Byford-Jones investigated the dealers engaged in trading antiques and uncovered a disturbing tale of exploitation and profit. 'The Americans are our best customers,' said one such dealer, 'far better than the Russians. The Russian prefers modern things like bicycles, telescopes, radio sets. The Americans buy on an average, according to what we have computed, over one million marks' worth of antiques every week in Berlin alone.'[41] They paid in food, cigarettes or alcohol, with cigarettes being the currency of choice. It was no accident that one of Berlin's most popular cabaret acts was called 'Alles für 10 Zigaretten'.

'Who among the Germans actually smokes the cigarettes?' asked Byford-Jones on first arriving in the city. The answer was simple: they were too valuable to be smoked and it was only in the cabaret clubs such as Henry Benders that young servicemen could be seen lighting up Camels and Players. 'Each cigarette they smoked represented one day's pay for the German waiter who served the smoker.'[42]

Before long an entirely new industry had developed: the collection of butt ends in order to manufacture new cigarettes. Those who engaged in this practice, 'called Kippensammler, all had their beats like prostitutes', said Byford-Jones. Many were child orphans who hung around the entrances to officers' clubs and messes. Waiters also kept a close eye on their cigarette-smoking clientele. Most kept a bag beneath the bar, 'into which they put the ends they assiduously collected from the ashtrays, just as in the old days they had put away their tips'.[43] This 'cigarette currency' was so ubiquitous that Brigadier Hinde's quest to stop its usage was doomed. His men were making vast amounts of money, while Berliners were dependent on the black market to keep themselves alive.

The leader of the Lux Hotel revolutionaries, Walter Ulbricht, had displayed a steely sense of purpose since his arrival in Berlin, focusing his energy on gaining mastery of the city's key institutions. He had done so with the active support of the Soviet Military Administration, but his work was now complicated by the arrival of the western Allies.

Frank Howley's agents were keeping a close eye on the Soviet-trained revolutionaries, reporting back each new piece of intelligence. The first alarm bell sounded when it was discovered that Ulbricht's police chief, Paul Markgraf, was a Nazi-turned-Communist. 'In this way,' said Howley, 'the Berlin police force was added to the Communist ranks, giving them a powerful weapon.' Next it was discovered that Ulbricht had placed the judiciary in the hands of a Communist activist named Mittag. Herr Mittag had no legal training – he was a locksmith by profession – but he had years of experience in coercion. Howley's assessment of the chief judge was scathing. 'In the United States, I doubt if Mittag, controller of all courts, would have got through grammar school.'

Ulbricht had also created a Free German Trade Union Federation, a body that was anything but free given that all union members were required to join. 'It bore no resemblance to the unions of the United States,' observed Howley, who was told it was 'an organisation with dictatorial powers'.

As each new snippet of intelligence reached Howley's desk, a clear pattern began to emerge. Something deeply sinister was taking place under his nose. All the institutions established in the first weeks of the Soviet occupation had the veneer of being democratic, but whenever Howley's agents looked at them more closely, they were found to be nothing of the sort. The city was in the hands of 'a puppet Communist body headed by Moscow-trained Germans'.

No less disquieting was the discovery that the mayor, Arthur Werner, had no authority whatsoever. 'Real power was in the hands of Soviet tools such as Deputy Mayor Maron', one of the Hotel Lux revolutionaries.[44] Frank Howley's liaison officer witnessed a graphic display of Karl Maron's ruthlessness while visiting the mayoral headquarters. Throwing a batch of papers onto Werner's desk, Maron ordered them to be signed.

'But I haven't read them yet,' protested Werner. 'You cannot expect me to sign them without reading them.'

'Sign!' commanded Maron and Werner did as he was told.

More surprising, but no less sinister, was Ulbricht's treatment of the many left-wing groups that had sprung up in the city since its capture. Instead of welcoming them as fellow travellers, Ulbricht viewed them as rivals. 'We must break them up at all costs,' he told his Hotel Lux comrades. 'You must ensure their immediate dissolution.' When one of them questioned the wisdom of such an action, Ulbricht revealed his autocratic streak. 'They are to be dissolved,' he snapped, 'and at once.'[45]

The youngest of the Lux group, Wolfgang Leonhard, had no doubt as to what was taking place. Ulbricht was creating a Stalinist system that would brook no criticism. Comrades who declined to toe the party line were to be eliminated rather than tolerated. Those who knew something of Ulbricht's background were not surprised. His job during the Spanish Civil War had been to liquidate anti-Stalinist fighters in Spain's Republican army.

The Hotel Lux group was now joined in Berlin by Wilhelm Pieck, head of the exiled German Communist Party, who had served valedictory vodkas in his Moscow bedroom just a few weeks before. An unknown figure to most Berliners, news of the arrival of this carpenter-turned-activist soon appeared on Wilfred Byford-Jones's radar screen. The British intelligence officer sought out Pieck at a Soviet sector rally and found him 'a squat, blotchy-faced white-haired man about seventy', with a resolute expression and wily eyes.

Pieck was as dogmatically stubborn as Walter Ulbricht and similarly lacking in joie de vivre. 'His physique had not been broken by concentration camps,' noted Byford-Jones, 'and his convictions had been strengthened by indoctrinations administered during his long stay in Russia.'[46] Pieck was close to Stalin, both ideologically and personally, and had been encouraged to return to Berlin and 'reinstate Communism in the capital'.[47] Pieck's goal was to turn the Communist Party into a mass movement that could sweep to power through the ballot box, albeit with the aid of coercion, bribery and relentless propaganda.

Byford-Jones trailed the German revolutionaries with the assiduousness of a private detective, aware that he was witnessing the opening moves in a secretive power grab. 'The real political battle in Berlin was at first underground,' he wrote. 'One could live there as a foreigner and not be aware that a classical struggle between an international Communism and the forces which will ever oppose it was in progress.' He was dismayed by the policy emanating from London, whose politicians seemed entirely ignorant of the situation on the ground. '[They] watched developments a little puzzled as to where the Russian bear was heading,' he said, 'ever hoping for the best.'[48]

Harold Hays had also been keeping a close eye on Walter Ulbricht and was increasingly convinced that Berlin would be the stage for a violent struggle between east and west. He had seen enough to conclude that Ulbricht's revolutionaries represented an existential threat to the western sectors of Berlin. 'Communism to them is not just a political dogma,' he said, 'but a holy crusade.' He felt they would be prepared to use force to achieve their goal, although he added an important caveat. 'They are led by cunning leaders who prefer to attain their victory by other means . . . propaganda, false-hood, calumny and every evil which can be stirred up by the written or spoken word.'[49]

Frank Howley agreed with Hays, having already concluded that American policy towards Berlin was as misguided as that of the British. Stalin's apparatchiks were simply not playing by the same rules. Howley was equally aware that when it came to dealing with the Soviets, the traditional American way of doing things was wholly inadequate. 'They will promise anything, sign anything, provided it benefits them, and will scrap the pledge the moment it doesn't.' It was a world away from life in Philadelphia, where Howley had his advertising business. 'American business life is carried on by checks, which imply trust. The Russians are ideologically incapable of such a system, because they would dishonour their signatures the next day, if it happened to be expedient.'[50]

Howley's first weeks in the German capital had opened his eyes in a way he had never thought possible. 'I had come to Berlin with the idea that the Germans were the enemies,' he wrote. '[But] it was becoming more evident by the day that it was the Russians who really were our enemies.'[51] This realisation placed him in a dilemma. Should he continue to follow Washington's misguided policy, or should he develop his own, more combative approach, one that risked rousing the fury of Joseph Stalin? It didn't take him long to find the answer. But before he could make his first move, he had to await the outcome of the much-vaunted Potsdam Conference.

7

Dividing the Spoils

THE POTSDAM CONFERENCE was to begin in the third week of July 1945, five months after Stalin, Churchill and Roosevelt had last met for their discussions at Yalta. That previous conference had taken its toll on Roosevelt's declining health and observers were shocked to see how frail the president looked on his return to America. He continued to pay close attention to the unfolding events in Europe and was outraged to learn that Stalin was already breaking his Yalta commitments; so outraged, indeed, that he sent the Soviet leader an indignant rebuke. The marshal replied by accusing the president of plotting a separate peace with Hitler. Roosevelt was incensed. 'Frankly,' he said, 'I cannot avoid a feeling of bitter resentment towards your informers, whoever they are, for such vile misrepresentation of my actions or those of my trusted subordinates.'[1]

It was the president's last communication with Stalin. On 12 April, he complained of a terrible headache. Shortly afterwards he collapsed unconscious and died within hours of a massive brain haemorrhage. He was sixty-three years of age.

The new president was Harry S. Truman, Roosevelt's vice president of just eighty-two days, whose views on foreign policy were completely unknown both to the American people and to America's wartime allies. Truman had no experience of foreign affairs and had only ever travelled abroad once, on a troopship in 1918. Churchill was so alarmed by the dramatic political developments in America that he sent Eden to sound out the new president's views.

Eden was impressed by Truman's grasp of European affairs and by his conviction that post-war Europe should not be dominated by any power hostile to democracy. 'We shall have in him a loyal collaborator,' said Eden after that first meeting, 'and I am much heartened by this first conversation.' But the new president was to be tested to the limits by the sixteen-day gathering in Potsdam.

The principal task facing the three victorious leaders was to establish a post-war consensus in Europe, with a focus on the occupation of Germany and Berlin, and the fate of Soviet-occupied Poland.

The setting for these discussions was both regal and homely: Cecilienhof was in Potsdam, a half-hour drive from Berlin. The last imperial palace of the Hohenzollern dynasty, whose end had come with the abdication of Kaiser Wilhelm II in 1918, it was a mock-Elizabethan fantasy, replete with stone portals, diamond-paned leaded windows (all ersatz Tudor) and a battalion of red-brick chimneys. In preparation for the conference, the Russians had furnished it with items scavenged from across Berlin, including solid Prussian armchairs, Wilhelmine side-tables and Murano glass flutes for the anticipated champagne toasts.

The conference room itself was sombre, with dark panelling, red drapes and a large round table (made to order at the Luxe furniture factory in Moscow) with room for fifteen chairs. 'An oasis of material comfort in a desert of devastation,' thought Joan Bright, the same doughty administrative officer who had led the British hospitality corps at Yalta.[2] She was preparing for the arrival of the delegation from London and was pleasantly surprised to note that each of the fifty newly requisitioned houses had been provided with a Steinweg or Bechstein grand piano.

The arriving delegates were led by Stalin, Churchill and Truman, with the stakes far higher than on previous occasions when leaders from the three countries had met as wartime allies. Potsdam was to pitch them into an intense contest in which the winner stood to gain control of large areas of Europe, either directly or as spheres of influence. The French were once again not invited, and would not be formally offered a sector of Berlin until 30 July, by which time the conference was almost at an end.

All diplomacy is coloured by personality and never was this truer than at Potsdam. Stalin arrived in a blaze of triumph, the undisputed master of Berlin. He had only recently awarded himself the title of 'generalissimo' and came dressed in the fashion of a tin-pot dictator:

'Like the Emperor of Austria in a bad musical comedy,' wrote a member of the British delegation, 'cream jacket with gold braided collar, blue trousers with a red stripe.'[3]

Truman was nattier in his choice of attire: white shirt, a polka-dot bow tie and a double-breasted dark suit, all neatly set off with two-tone summer shoes. 'He seemed like a chairman of the board,' said one, a pertinent observation. Truman played the conference as if he were running a multinational company.[4]

And then there was Churchill, who stomped into town clutching a silver-topped cane and dressed in his favourite military costume, with brass buttons and a stiff peak cap. He was followed by a pin-striped regiment of Foreign Office mandarins equipped with briefcases, umbrellas and homburgs. They were instantly recognisable as British: indeed they looked as if they had just stepped off the early morning commuter train from Sevenoaks.

The arrival of each of the leaders was carefully choreographed for maximum effect. President Truman swept into Potsdam in unmistakably presidential fashion, 'an immense cortège, outriders on motor-cycles forming a vanguard, then armoured jeeps, the President's car with G-men crouched on the running-boards and finally a wagon-load of armed men prepared to give all-round covering fire, the whole proceeding at speed with sirens and whistles blowing importunately'.[5]

Stalin's arrival was no less theatrical. His fear of flying had led him to travel by train across western Russia, Lithuania and East Prussia. His cortège was a sight to behold, for Stalin had ordered four opulent carriages from the imperial train to be removed from their museum and hitched to a Soviet locomotive. He arrived with the pomp and circumstance of a hereditary autocrat. Once in Potsdam, he travelled in a bullet-proof car along roads lined with saluting armed guards. In this game of one-upmanship, observers found it hard to decide who created the greatest impression.

Churchill's means of transport was altogether more modest, as it had been at Yalta. When he arrived at the Cecilienhof Palace on the first day of proceedings, he did so accompanied by a single plain-clothes detective. As a piece of theatre, it cleverly undercut both the president and the generalissimo. The message was clear: he did not require the vanities and outward trappings of power.

Each of the three leaders came with an ace card, or so it seemed to those watching from the side-lines. Stalin's ace was his army, which was already in possession of huge swathes of Eastern Europe – far more than it had controlled at the time of the previous conference. It was as if he had got what he wanted before even starting to play the game.

Truman's ace was top secret and had the potential to trump everything, but he was as yet unsure if or when he would be able to deploy it. Everything depended upon a coded telegram he was expecting from America.

Churchill's ace was the vast German naval fleet, which had been captured in its entirety by the British. But the prime minister felt he had a second winning card, one more personal and idiosyncratic. It was his vast experience, his breadth of knowledge and his ability to speak extempore on any subject thrown at him. Others on his team feared that this was in fact his greatest weakness. When Churchill was swept along by emotion, as he had been at Yalta, he could be erratic and irrational.

Churchill's other weakness, which he acknowledged, was that he was awaiting the results of the British general election. It had been called on 5 July, but the outcome would not be known until 26 July, the ninth day of the conference, because of the time taken to count the votes of overseas service personnel. Churchill hovered between confidence and despair. With the outcome in the balance, he had invited the leader of the opposition, Clement Attlee, to accompany him to Potsdam.

It was not just the personalities of the three key players that made Potsdam's high-level diplomacy so unique. It was also the fact that the corridors and antechambers of the Cecilienhof Palace were filled with diplomatic voyeurs watching the proceedings with observant eyes – men and, to a lesser extent, women – who kept a metaphorical score-sheet of each day's winners and losers. Their letters and diaries allow for an intimate peek into the last great summit of the Second World War.

The conference was scheduled to open on Tuesday, 17 July, but the groundwork began to be laid on the preceding morning when

Churchill paid a visit to President Truman at his lakeside villa in Babelsberg – his 'Little White House' as he styled it. Churchill was perpetually exhausted, or so it seemed to his physician, Lord Moran, who had accompanied the prime minister to his lodgings upon their first arriving in the city, as he had done at Yalta. 'Without removing his hat, Winston flopped into a garden chair, flanked by two great tubs of hydrangeas, blue, pink and white. He appeared too weary to move.' After catching his breath, he barked, 'Where is Sawyers? Get me a whisky.'[6]

He was in better spirits when he called on Truman, whom he had met once before, fleetingly, in Washington. Truman set the meeting for 11 a.m., which led Churchill's daughter, Mary, to announce gaily to the presidential party that her father 'hadn't been up so early for years'. Truman later wrote a terse aside in his private diary: '*I'd* been up for four and one-half hours.'[7]

Churchill knew that a warm personal relationship with the American president was crucial to success and he bubbled with charm, offering compliments and soothing words. Truman smiled warmly, but his diary reveals scepticism behind the smile. 'He gave me a lot of hooey about how great my country is and how he loved Roosevelt and how he intended to love me etc., etc.' Truman viewed Churchill as both clever and charming, but too gushingly sycophantic. 'I am sure we can get along if he doesn't try to give me too much soft soap.'[8]

When Lord Moran later asked Churchill what he made of Truman, the prime minister approvingly declared him to be a man who took no notice of delicate ground. 'And to illustrate this, the PM jumped a little off the wooden floor and brought his bare feet down with a smack.'[9]

Both president and prime minister toured Berlin that afternoon, a visit that left Truman aghast. 'We saw old men, old women, young women, children from tots to teens carrying packs, pushing carts, pulling carts, evidently ejected by the conquerors and carrying what they could of their belongings to nowhere in particular.' He was profoundly depressed by the spectacle and placed the blame squarely on Hitler's shoulders. 'This is what happens when a man overreaches himself.'[10]

Churchill's tour took him to the Reich Chancellery, where the group passed through a seemingly endless maze of wreckage that left Lord Moran feeling nauseous. 'It was like the first time I saw a surgeon open a belly and the intestines gushed out,' he said, a sensation heightened by the stench of rotting cadavers. The prime minister was recognised by many and his presence elicited a mixed response from Berlin's populace. 'Some of the crowd looked away, others glanced at him with expressionless faces, one old man shook his fist, a few smiled.'[11]

Churchill and his party were led deep inside Hitler's bunker, where the air was foetid and the floors still littered with detritus. Wilfred Byford-Jones had only recently visited and left a vivid description of the wreckage. 'Red upholstered furniture, broken and burned, lay about the floor of inlaid gold mosaic. A massive Swastika, at which two heavy gilded eagles clawed savagely, lay amid broken glass, brass fittings, shattered marble and the remnants of a moulded ceiling.' This underground labyrinth was permeated with the malodorous stench of death and much of it was inches deep in stagnant water. It was also infested with rats, 'some as fat as groundhogs, which scooted and slithered up and down the one long room'.[12]

Accompanying Churchill into the bunker was Lord Moran, who helped himself to two Iron Crosses, and Sir Alexander Cadogan, the permanent under-secretary for foreign affairs, who pocketed a chunk of marble to use as a paperweight. Churchill wanted nothing: he seemed mentally and physically exhausted by the visit. He slumped into a dust-covered gilt chair near the bunker's entrance and mopped the sweat from his brow. 'Hitler must have come out here to get some air and heard the guns getting nearer and nearer,' he mused to no one in particular.[13]

When Truman returned to his lodgings later that afternoon he was handed the telegram he had been waiting for: TOP SECRET. URGENT. FOR COLONEL KYLES [sic] EYES ONLY. The message was as cryptic and bizarre as the heading. OPERATED ON THIS MORNING. DIAGNOSIS NOT YET COMPLETE BUT RESULTS SEEM SATISFACTORY AND ALREADY EXCEED EXPECTATIONS. Truman knew exactly what it meant. The 'operation' was the testing of the atomic bomb at Alamogordo in New Mexico and the 'diagnosis' suggested that it had worked to perfection. America was a nuclear power and Truman had just secured his ace.

The president met Stalin the following day, when the generalissimo paid a visit to Truman's lodgings, bringing Foreign Minister Vyacheslav Molotov and Pavlov, the same interpreter he had used at Yalta. One of Truman's advisers left a vivid portrait of Stalin at this time, describing his low-slung frame, rough-skinned face and the square-cut tunic that hung from his shoulders like an oversized sack. 'The teeth were discoloured, the moustache scrawny, coarse, and streaked. This, together with the pocked face and yellow eyes gave him the aspect of an old battle-scarred tiger.'[14] After the usual courtesies the two leaders discussed the conference agenda, but Truman was still thinking about his tour of Berlin and he asked the Soviet leader how he thought Hitler had died.

Stalin's response reveals that he was prepared to play dirty: he told Truman that 'he thought Hitler was still alive and living in Spain or Argentina.'[15] This was a lie, of course: the Soviet leader had certain proof that Hitler had died in Berlin. When pressed on his assertion, he reiterated his belief 'that the Führer had escaped and was in hiding somewhere'. He added that 'careful search by Soviet investigators had not found any trace of Hitler's remains or any other positive evidence of his death.'[16] *Izvestia*'s report of Stalin's comments went even further, asserting that the Soviet leader believed both Hitler and Eva Braun to be living in a castle in Westphalia, in the British-occupied zone of Germany. This was an invidious accusation, as the American *Newsweek* correspondent, James O'Donnell, pointed out. Stalin was once again 'blackguarding an ally that had been fighting Hitler from the very first day of the war'. Worse still, the Soviet leader 'was virtually accusing them of harbouring a living Hitler'.[17]

Truman was surprised by Stalin's claim, for he had been assured that Hitler was dead, but his general impression of their first meeting was positive. 'I can deal with Stalin,' he wrote. 'He is honest – but smart as hell.'[18] That 'smartness' was all too apparent just four hours later, when the three leaders met together for the first time in the Cecilienhof Palace. The opening scene had been meticulously choreographed by the Soviet organisers, who had gone so far as to decorate the main courtyard with hundreds of red geraniums in the shape of a gigantic star. One of Truman's advisers, George Elsey, had arrived in advance of the president and couldn't help noticing that as one set of troops was planting the flowers, another set was ransacking the outbuildings. 'Lorries were drawn up just looting, taking absolutely everything out of the palace except the rooms where the conference was being held – light fixtures, plumbing fixtures, books, furniture . . .'[19]

Churchill's inner team included his foreign secretary, Anthony Eden, and Sir Alexander Cadogan – both of whom had accompanied him to Yalta. Clement Attlee also attended. Truman came with his secretary of state, James F. Byrnes, and his military adviser, Admiral William Leahy, while Stalin brought Molotov and his deputy, Andrey Vyshinsky.

Stalin seized control of the conference from the outset, nominating Truman as chairman and then setting forth an agenda. One of the British delegation, Walter Monckton, thought it a masterful performance. Stalin was 'often humorous, never offensive; direct and uncompromising'.[20] He was determined not to be deflected by his Allied rivals.

The subject of the keenest discussion was once again the fate of Germany and Poland, with the Polish border proving as contentious as it had been at Yalta. Stalin had the upper hand, for his army already controlled much of the territory he coveted. He had helped himself to 70,000 square miles of eastern Poland; in exchange, he had given the acquiescent Polish government the former German territories of East Prussia, Silesia, Pomerania and East Brandenburg. Their German populations were being swiftly expelled to the western zones, causing a massive logistical headache for the British and Americans.

When Stalin also demanded his share of the German naval fleet, still in British hands, Churchill told him that 'weapons of war are terrible things and that the captured vessels should be sunk'. Stalin's eyes flickered with mischief as he delivered his riposte. 'Let us divide it . . .' he said with a smile. 'If Mr Churchill wishes, he can sink his share.'[21]

Churchill's advisers were shocked by the prime minister's lacklustre

performance. Eden was particularly incredulous to hear him surren-
dering the German fleet, his only tangible advantage. '[I] urged him
not to give up our few cards without return,' he wrote. 'But he is
again under Stalin's spell. He kept repeating, "I like that man."' It
was a curious sentiment to come from the mouth of someone who,
just a few months earlier, had been planning Operation Unthinkable.

Later that evening, Anthony Eden delivered a stern lecture to
Churchill, telling him that he was being artfully manipulated. 'In
particular, [I] urged him to try to resist giving in to Stalin, who
knows *exactly* how to manage him.'[22]

Sir Alexander Cadogan was equally appalled by Churchill's performance, writing a despairing letter to his wife. 'The PM, since
he left London, has refused to do any work or read anything . . .
if he knows nothing about the subject under discussion, he should
keep quiet or ask that his Foreign Secretary be heard.' But Churchill
rarely asked Eden to speak in his place. 'Instead of that, he butts in
on every occasion and talks the most irrelevant rubbish and is giving
away our case at every point.'

Cadogan thought that Truman, by comparison, was 'quick and
businesslike' and able to deal with subjects concisely.[23] Truman had
his own private reasons for rattling through the conference agenda.
'I'm not staying around this terrible place all summer just to listen
to speeches,' he wrote in his diary.[24]

Those speeches invariably came from Churchill. No sooner had
Truman finished his deliberations than Churchill would launch into
yet another monologue. 'Every mention of a topic started Winston
off on a wild rampage from which the combined efforts of Truman
and Anthony [Eden] with difficulty restrained him.'[25]

Churchill's behaviour grew so erratic that it became a talking
point of the conference. He interrupted, rambled and failed to grasp
what Stalin was saying, perhaps because he was drinking so heavily.
'Tired and below his form,' thought Sir William Hayter, a member
of the British delegation. 'He also suffered from the belief that he
knew everything and need not read briefs.' When Truman declared
one of the sessions to be finished, Cadogan noted that Churchill
'wanted to go on talking at random and was most disappointed –
just like a child with a toy taken away from it'.[26]

The point scoring spilled over into the socialising that took place each evening. At a soirée hosted by Truman at his lakeside villa, classical music was provided by a pianist and violinist specially flown in from Paris. Stalin gave his own party the following night and made a point of having two pianists and two violinists flown in from Moscow; they played Chopin, Liszt and Tchaikovsky. Truman congratulated them on their playing, although he couldn't help noticing that they 'had dirty faces . . . and the gals were rather fat'.[27] He estimated their weight to be about two hundred pounds apiece.

The food that evening was pure indulgence in a city that was starving. 'Stalin gave his state dinner . . .' wrote Truman in a letter home. 'It was a wow. Started with caviar and vodka and wound up with watermelon and champagne, with smoked fish, fresh fish, venison, chicken, duck and all sorts of vegetables in between. There was a toast every five minutes until at least twenty-five had been drunk.'[28]

Churchill was bored by Stalin's musical soirée and sidled over to Truman. 'When are you going home?' he whispered in his ear. But the president was finally enjoying himself and had no intention of leaving. Churchill drank, smoked cigars and plotted his revenge, promising to Admiral Leahy that he would 'get even' the following evening.[29] He proved true to his word. At the banquet he hosted, he ordered the RAF band to blast their brass throughout the entire dinner, deafening the assembled diners with an Irish reel, 'The Skye Boat Song' and countless others. Even Stalin's patience cracked and he begged Churchill for something lighter.

Back in the conference chamber President Truman had yet to play his ace, for he was choosing his moment with care. The moment finally came at the end of the day's session on 24 July. Having warned Churchill, he decided to tell Stalin that America had successfully detonated a weapon of immense power, one that would prove a game-changer in international geopolitics.

'I was perhaps five yards away', wrote Churchill, 'and I watched with the closest attention the momentous talk. I knew what the President was going to do. What was vital was to watch its effect on Stalin.'[30]

Truman spoke to the Soviet leader in a low voice. 'I casually mentioned to Stalin that we had a new weapon of unusually destructive force.' Stalin's reaction was strange. '[He] showed no special interest. All he said was that he was glad to hear it and hoped we would make good use of it against the Japanese.'[31] Truman could not be sure if Stalin realised he was talking about an atomic bomb. Churchill thought he did not. 'I was sure that [Stalin] had no idea of the significance of what he was being told.'[32]

But Churchill was wrong, if Marshal Zhukov's account of the incident is to be believed. He recalled Stalin returning to his villa that same evening and recounting exactly what the American president had said. Molotov listened attentively and responded in a flash. 'We'll have to talk it over with Kurchatov.' Zhukov understood the meaning as soon as he heard the name of Russia's leading atomic scientist. 'I realized they were talking about research on the atomic bomb.'[33]

Churchill and Attlee left for London on 25 July in order to learn the results of the general election. Churchill's mood was morose and morbid. 'I dreamed that life was over,' he wrote on that last night in Potsdam. 'I saw – it was very vivid – my dead body under a white sheet on a table in an empty room . . . Perhaps this is the end.'[34]

In one sense it was. The Labour Party won the election with a landslide and Churchill would not be returning to Potsdam. 'It will be strange tomorrow,' he said to his wife, Clementine, 'not to be consulted upon the great affairs of state.'[35] The new prime minister, Clement Attlee, immediately flew back to Berlin, along with his newly appointed foreign secretary, Ernest Bevin. The immaculately groomed, ever-courteous Anthony Eden was to be succeeded by the pugnacious and overweight offspring of a servant girl and an unknown father. Bevin was a former lorry driver who had helped found the Transport and General Workers' Union. 'Short and stout, with broad nose and thick lips, [he] looked more suited for the roles he had played earlier in life than for diplomacy.'[36] So thought Dean Acheson, at that point Truman's assistant secretary of state. Bevin's first words to the official Potsdam greeting party, spoken in his clotted West Country brogue, were suitably blunt. 'I'm not going to have Britain barged around.'[37]

He and Attlee took their places at the Potsdam table and would remain in discussions for another six days. 'But the magic had gone,' thought Joan Bright, 'and the term "Big Three" had lost its meaning.'[38] If Bevin had been there from the outset, his presence might have made a difference to the outcome of the conference. He was a combative negotiator – 'far tougher than Eden', thought the conference interpreter Hugh Lunghi – and Stalin was visibly wary of him.[39]

But by the time of Bevin's arrival it was too late to gain more than a few minor concessions. Stalin had already trampled over his western rivals and would leave the conference with almost everything he wanted, including a huge expanse of territory carved from eastern Poland, a Soviet-backed Polish government, massive reparations from both the Soviet occupation zone of Germany and the western-controlled zones, the expulsion of German populations living beyond the new eastern borders of Germany and sovereignty over the former Prussian city of Königsberg. He even got his third of the German naval fleet.

The Red Army was also in de facto control of much of Central and Eastern Europe, making Stalin the undisputed master of a vast swathe of territory. Just five months before, at Yalta, Churchill had given a congratulatory toast to the Soviet leader. 'There have been many conquerors in history . . . and most of them threw away the fruits of victory in the troubles which followed their wars.'[40] Stalin had certainly not squandered the fruits of victory on this occasion, as Churchill well knew.

No less worrying to Churchill – now leader of the opposition party – was the catastrophic state of the newly liberated countries of Western Europe. All had highly volatile populations who glimpsed salvation in the resurgent Communist parties. These parties had offered steely resistance to Nazi rule ever since the outbreak of war and now sought to exploit their unrivalled moral authority.

In France, the Communists were undergoing a surge in popularity and gearing up to become the country's largest political party: their leader, Maurice Thorez, had spent the war in Moscow and was an intimate of Stalin. In Italy, the party had amassed two and a quarter million members. In Norway, Finland, Denmark and Belgium,

Communist membership was also increasing rapidly. For Churchill, this resurgence of the extreme political left represented his worst fears. One false step could see the whole of Western Europe falling under the Communist yoke, leaving Stalin as the undisputed master of the entire continent.

On 2 August, Stalin, Truman and Attlee signed the Potsdam Agreement, providing a blueprint for the governance of both Germany and its occupied capital. It also outlined the policy principles by which the country was to be treated, with the emphasis on demilitarisation, denazification, decentralisation and disarmament, along with reparations, the dismantling of industry, and the reorganisation of the police and judiciary.

From his desk at nearby Soviet military headquarters in Berlin's Karlshorst district, Major Gregory Klimov viewed the outcome of the conference as a triumph of Soviet diplomacy. His country's negotiators had 'won concessions from the Western Allies to an extent that the diplomats themselves had not expected'. This was partly because the British and Americans had dealt with the Soviet delegation as if they were still friendly allies, but also because Truman, Churchill and Attlee 'had not yet got to the bottom of the methods of Soviet diplomacy' – uncompromising and resolute. It now fell to Klimov and his fellow Soviet functionaries in Berlin 'to extract full value from the advantages won by Soviet diplomacy'.[41]

It takes courage to speak truth to power and it is often the meekest individuals who dare to raise their heads above the parapet. In the aftermath of the Potsdam Conference, that role fell to a deeply private individual named George Kennan, the forty-one-year-old chargé d'affaires at the American embassy in Moscow.

Kennan had the dolorous air of a wandering scholar, with sad blue eyes, a huge forehead and a scalp 'as bald and smooth as a marble bust'.[42] Beneath that scalp lay a sharp intellect and highly perceptive brain. During his years in the Soviet Union, Kennan had witnessed horrors he would never forget, with Stalin's Great Purge set firmly in the foreground of this tableau of bloodshed. He had met the Soviet leader on a number of occasions and found him 'simple, quiet, unassuming' and lacking any trace of charisma.

But outward appearances could be deceptive, as he well knew. 'An uninformed visitor would never have guessed what depths of calculation, ambition, love of power, jealousy, cruelty and sly vindictiveness lurked behind this unpretentious facade.'

That facade hid something else that the observant Kennan had been quick to notice: Stalin had an 'immense diabolical skill as a tactician'. His unassuming air had been carefully contrived so as to be 'as innocently disarming as the first move of the grand master at chess'. Kennan said it was all part of his 'brilliant, terrifying tactical mastery'.[43]

As reports from the Potsdam Conference flooded into Kennan's in-tray at the embassy in Mokhovaya Street, he was shocked by what he read. Truman, Churchill and Attlee had been comprehensively outsmarted on every issue. Kennan viewed the reports 'with unmitigated scepticism and despair', not least because of the naivety of the western leaders. 'I cannot recall any political document the reading of which filled me with a greater sense of depression than the communiqué to which President Truman set his name at the conclusion of these confused and unreal discussions.'[44]

For the present, Kennan expressed his thoughts to no one other than his long-suffering wife, Annelise, who (said Kennan to his father) had 'the rare capacity for keeping silent gracefully'.[45] He also fumed into his private notebook, whose pages were soon replete with litanies of anger. 'We should entertain no false illusions,' he wrote in one entry. 'We are basically in competition with the Russians in Germany.'[46] It was a competition that would surely lead to war.

As he reflected on the wider consequences of Potsdam he once again set pen to paper. This time he was writing for a wider audience, pouring his intellectual brilliance into a draft report that he intended to be political dynamite. Like Frank Howley, George Kennan hoped to bring about a U-turn in American policy towards the Soviet Union: in his view, it was the only way to save Berlin from Stalin.

There was to be a final humiliation for the western Allies that summer, one in which Colonel Frank Howley and Brigadier Hinde were to find themselves unwilling participants. The occasion was a huge international parade along the Unter den Linden to celebrate victory over Japan, which had finally capitulated after the bombing of Hiroshima and Nagasaki. Truman's 'new weapon of unusually destructive force' had brought the Second World War to a close on 15 August, just thirteen days after the end of the Potsdam Conference.

The idea of an Allied victory parade was first suggested to Colonel Howley by General Floyd Parks, commander of the First Airborne. When Parks also mentioned it to Zhukov, 'he fairly leaped at the idea'.[47] Such was his enthusiasm that he proposed that Eisenhower, Montgomery and the French commander, General Marie-Pierre Koenig, should also take part – the first official recognition that the French were to play a role in Berlin.

The aim of the parade was to celebrate the participation of the four nations in defeating Nazi Germany, with the individual countries having an equal share in the pageantry. To this end, it was agreed that each nation should contribute a thousand soldiers and a hundred vehicles, although the type of vehicle was not specified.

The date was set for 7 September, some five weeks after the end of the Potsdam Conference, and it was eagerly anticipated by everyone involved. But the ensuing event didn't play out as the western powers were expecting, leading Frank Howley to describe it as 'one of the strangest parades I ever saw on the European continent'.

The first setback came when Eisenhower, Montgomery and Koenig were unable to attend, enabling Zhukov to steal the show. The Soviet marshal declared that it was important for someone to address the assembled crowds, insisting that it should be a senior military commander. 'It was pretty obvious who was going to do the orating,' said Howley. 'Zhukov announced that he would make the speech himself.'[48]

He certainly dressed for the part on the day of the parade, wearing pale-blue trousers with yellow stripes, a dark-green blouse and a bright red sash. But it was his medals that really drew the eye. 'Across his chest,' wrote Howley, 'and almost down below his hips, hung so many decorations that a special brass plate had to be worn to house this immense collection, giving the appearance of being riveted to the Russian's chest.'[49]

Howley had grown used to seeing Soviet generals bedecked with medals, but he felt that on this occasion Zhukov was taking self-aggrandisement to new extremes. They included 'the highest decorations the Soviet Union has, as well as the highest decorations from the Allies . . . down near his hip hung something of gold as big as a saucer.'[50] One G.I. turned to Howley and said with a smile: 'That's the God-damnedest Roxy doorman I've ever seen!'[51]

General Patton was there to represent Eisenhower and was attired in more sober fashion, dressed in a simple combat jacket with a minimum of ribbons. Captain Brett-Smith was observing Patton closely and noticed that he had two pearl-handled revolvers stashed in his belt, adding a touch of the bandit to the overall look.

As the ceremonies began, the two commanders became engaged in a subtle game of one-upmanship. 'Zhukov planted himself in the centre of the platform, jealously guarding his position, and each time Patton shifted his feet the Russian eyed him nervously, then moved nearer the front of the platform.'[52] By the end of this shuffling act, Zhukov's paunch was hanging indelicately over the rail.

His speech extolled the fighting prowess of the Red Army, thereby infuriating General Patton. When the Soviet marshal spoke of Germany and Japan, saying that 'two black centres of aggression have been defeated', Patton snarled in a loud voice, 'There's still a third!'[53]

The military parade began in earnest once Zhukov had finished speaking, with a march-past of the thousand troops from each nation. Howley was particularly proud of his fellow Americans. 'The 82nd Airborne, with white gloves stuck through their shoulder straps, white parachute silk scarves and polished guns slung on their backs looked very dressy.' The French came next, perfectly choreographed, and were followed by British soldiers led by a major with an immaculately upturned moustache. Howley thought he looked like a 'handsome rogue out of Kipling's books' and was particularly impressed when, at the command of 'eyes right', the men in his troops all turned and scowled at Zhukov. 'It's easy to see in men like that why there's been a British Empire for hundreds of years.'[54]

So far, the parade had gone more or less to plan, although Zhukov had infuriated the western Allies by stealing the limelight. But when it came to the procession of vehicles, the Soviet marshal had contrived a plan to showcase the military superiority of the Red Army. The Americans, British and French had agreed to limit themselves to light armoured cars, but not so the Russians. 'With a dreadful clanking of steel treads against concrete, 100 giant new Stalin tanks rumbled into view and rolled down the historic street past the reviewing stand.' The Unter den Linden reverberated with the menace of engines and the stench of diesel. 'As they passed in review, the shiny muzzles of their big guns pointed up to the sky.'[55] It was a display of raw military might, one that completely upstaged the Americans, British and French.

Zhukov felt he had scored a significant propaganda victory. 'A particularly memorable sight,' he later wrote in his memoirs, and one that reminded everyone 'of the victory of Soviet arms in the place from where the blood-thirsty Fascist aggression had spread to the whole of Europe'.[56]

General Patton watched the Soviet tanks with narrowed eyes, furious at Zhukov's menacing stunt. 'They might look good enough tanks,' he said to the British commander, General Eric Nares, 'but don't worry. If they start shooting, I'm on your side.'[57]

8

Let Battle Commence

FOUR THOUSAND MILES from the Berlin victory parade, the curtain was lifting on an event so unforeseen and dramatic that it was to send shockwaves across the world. The prelude to the drama had taken place two days earlier when Igor Gouzenko, a cipher clerk at the Soviet embassy in Ottawa, took the momentous decision to defect to the West. His move was unprecedented – the first defection of the post-war period – and was rendered all the more sensational by the fact that he had spent his final hours at the embassy stuffing 109 highly incriminating documents inside his shirt. With these documents, he hoped to cause a sensation.

His defection was an uncharacteristic move for a man who had the background and bearing of a loyal Communist Party functionary. Gouzenko had joined the Komsomol or Young Communist League at sixteen and graduated into coding and deciphering before being initiated into 'a strange, single-purposed world of secrecy and discipline'. He would eventually wind up working for the Moscow headquarters of military intelligence, the nerve centre of Soviet spying. This headquarters, he said, 'both directs the activities and reaps the harvest of espionage information from agents planted all over the world'.[1]

Gouzenko bore all the trademarks of a party apparatchik. Stern and steely-eyed, he had clamped features that hinted at an inner ruthlessness. But Gouzenko was more enigmatic than his contemporaries and had a childlike curiosity that had passed unnoticed when he was vetted for service. It was a failure that was to cost the Soviets dearly.

Gouzenko was posted to the Soviet embassy in Ottawa in the summer of 1943. Operating under the codename Corby, he was given a frank résumé of his work objectives: 'The undermining of democratic countries from within [and] the designing of a plan for delivering major crippling blows when the time becomes ripe.'[2]

Gouzenko travelled to Canada with his wife, Svetlana, and their baby son Andrei. After the deprivations of wartime Moscow, the prosperity of Ottawa proved a giddy revelation. The couple were mesmerised by 'the abundance of clothing, candies and luxuries of all kinds'. When Gouzenko and Svetlana headed into downtown Ottawa, the gleaming automobiles 'left us gaping in astonishment'.[3] People also spoke their minds in a way that was inconceivable in Moscow, a novelty that was initially unsettling. As the weeks passed, the Gouzenkos began to wonder how they might remain in this seeming paradise.

They lived in an apartment at 511 Somerset Street. Each morning, Gouzenko set off on foot to the embassy at 285 Charlotte Street, an imposing red-brick villa with an elegant white portico. From the outside it looked no different to a thousand other suburban villas, but behind the facade there lay a sinister secret.

Gouzenko was assigned to work in the most secret place of all, Room 12, on the embassy's second floor. One of a suite of rooms dedicated to nefarious pursuits, it was sealed from the rest of the embassy by a double steel door concealed behind a velvet curtain. 'Having passed through this first door,' recalled Gouzenko, 'I must wait until a second door, bigger and boasting more steel than the first one, was opened by the guard.'

This provided access to the embassy's inner sanctum: 'Once inside this second door, I was in a carpeted corridor from which several more steel doors opened into small rooms. The windows of each room had been painted white, to make them opaque and they were protected by steel bars and shutters that were closed and locked at night.'[4]

Gouzenko's boss was the military attaché Colonel Nikolai Zabotin, codename Giant, whose polished speech and well-groomed appearance hinted at his privileged background. His vodka shots were drunk to his favourite Berlin-inspired toast: 'To America . . . Yesterday our allies, today our neighbours, tomorrow our enemies!'[5]

Gouzenko also worked alongside Vitali Pavlov, whose official role was second secretary. In reality he was no such thing. He was the

NKVD chief for Canada, a devious operator known by his code-name, Klim. A further nineteen diplomats were also members of the NKVD or GRU.

In this forbidden wing of the embassy a radio blared music throughout the day in order to 'drown conversations which might be overheard by others of the trusted unit'.[6] There was also a huge incinerator; big enough, said Gouzenko, 'for the hurried destruction of large quantities of documents, codes, ciphers, telegrams and dossiers on agents'. When he expressed surprise at its size, he was told that 'it is big enough and powerful enough to consume the body of a man.'[7] The warning was clear: if he betrayed the embassy's secrets he would end up inside.

'In this setting,' wrote Gouzenko, 'I played my role for over a year in the world-wide drama of Russian espionage . . . through my hands began to pass documents of the most secret nature.' A number of these contained detailed intelligence on America's atomic research programme and had come from an impeccable source, a scientist working on the programme.

Gouzenko worked diligently for more than a year, cultivating contacts and gathering secrets. But he was increasingly troubled by the thought that his espionage was part of 'a big and threatening pattern designed to bring this Canada, this United States, this democracy under Soviet domination'.[8] As his passion for espionage waned, his attachment to Canada increased. He also continued to be seduced by the material wealth of Canada. He wanted to stay.

He had been in the country for two years when he was informed by Colonel Zabotin that he was being recalled to Moscow. He was shocked. 'Something happened inside me,' he said. 'A strange voice spoke through my mouth – the dam I had built across the mind finally broke!' When he returned to his wife that September evening he was fizzing with excitement. 'We won't go back!'[9]

But this was easier said than done. His first idea was simply to disappear somewhere in the wilderness of Canada. But this was tantamount to suicide, for he knew he would be hunted down by NKVD agents. The only possibility of preserving his life, and that of his wife and young son, was to defect. To do so successfully would require him to expose the Soviet spy ring in Canada.

He knew there could be no turning back once he had set the ball in motion: he and his family would have to live the rest of their lives under assumed identities. But if he failed to convince the Canadian authorities and was caught by the NKVD, he risked ending up inside the embassy's incinerator.

Igor Gouzenko's route to treachery began on the evening of Wednesday, 5 September 1945 when he left his apartment and headed to the Soviet embassy. There was nothing unusual about his working late, for telegrams to Moscow often had to be sent in the evening.

Over the previous weeks, he had marked 109 documents that blew the lid on Soviet espionage: 'telegrams, notes and memoranda that contained names and described spy planning or activities. These I marked by folding over the upper right corners.' Gouzenko's intention was to smuggle these documents out of the embassy and take them to the editor of the *Ottawa Journal*, whom he trusted more than the local police. After revealing their explosive content, he would ask for the editor's help in defecting.

He arrived at the embassy a little after dusk, dressed in a blue serge suit and white shirt. He was sweating profusely and his nerves were on the qui vive. His anxieties increased yet further when he discovered that Vitali Pavlov was also working late that night. 'My blood seemed to freeze.'[10] But he remained composed as he headed to the secret cipher room. No one else was about and he was able to take the incriminating documents from their folders. 'I opened my shirt and carefully distributed the documents inside.' The buttons bulged somewhat when he walked, but 'the evening was so warm I felt a sloppy looking shirt wouldn't arouse undue interest'.[11]

Leaving the building with these documents was to test his nerves further. 'One wrong move could mean the complete ruination of all our plans.'[12] But he aroused no suspicions as he bid goodnight to the security guards and took a tram to the offices of the *Ottawa Journal*.

'Outside the building I stopped to mop my brow and make sure no one was following me.' So far, so good. He entered the atrium and took the lift to the sixth floor. And this was the point at which Gouzenko's plan hit a snag. The newspaper staff had left for the evening and the only person on duty was an elderly night-editor. 'I took out the stolen documents and spread them out on the desk. As I did so, I explained who I was and that these were proof that Soviet agents in Canada were seeking data on the atomic bomb.'[13] The night-editor stared at the documents through his eye-glass, saw they were in Russian and shook his head. 'This is out of our field,' he said. 'Sorry.'[14] He told his unwanted visitor to take them to the police.

Aware of the need to plead his case to a senior official, a troubled Gouzenko headed to the Ministry of Justice building in the hope of contacting someone – anyone – of importance. But the staff had left for the night and the on-duty policeman said nothing could be done until morning. Gouzenko had no option but to return home, aware that embassy staff would probably discover the missing documents in the morning. He had just a few hours to work out a new plan.

He returned to the Ministry of Justice as soon as it opened but although his story was listened to with some interest, the minister expressed no enthusiasm in seeing him in person. In growing desperation, Gouzenko returned to the *Ottawa Journal* (this time with his wife and son) and secured a few minutes with a junior reporter. She looked through his documents and then showed them to the editor, but the outcome was the same. 'I'm terribly sorry,' she told him. 'Your story doesn't seem to register here. Nobody wants to say anything but nice things about Stalin these days.'

Gouzenko was fast losing hope: it was now early afternoon, time enough for the embassy staff to have noticed the missing documents. He and his wife returned to their apartment and were relieved to find it untouched. But when Gouzenko looked down into the street he got a shock. 'Two men were seated on the bench in the park directly opposite and both were looking up at my window.' A few minutes later, there was a bang on the door and a voice shouted his name. It was Lieutenant Lavrentiev, Nikolai Zabotin's right-hand man.

The Gouzenkos kept perfectly silent, biding their time. When they heard Lavrentiev retreat downstairs, Gouzenko dashed along the internal corridor and thumped on the door of his neighbour,

Sergeant Harold Main. The sergeant listened sympathetically to his appeal for help. 'Get your wife and boy, Gouzenko, and bring them over here. I'm going to get the police.'[15] As an officer in the Royal Canadian Air Force, Sergeant Main knew the authorities would take him seriously.

They did. Two constables appeared within minutes and interviewed this would-be Soviet defector. Having accepted his story and credentials, they told him not to leave Sergeant Main's flat: Gouzenko and his family were to be placed under immediate police protection. But he was still not out of danger. Later that night, four Soviet embassy staff could be heard smashing down the Gouzenkos' front door. The constables appeared within minutes and demanded to know what they were doing. One of them, the NKVD chief, Vitali Pavlov, told them the apartment belonged to a member of the Soviet embassy. 'He left some documents here and we have permission to look for them.' After a furious row in which the constables accused Pavlov of breaking and entering, the Soviets angrily departed.

At the break of dawn Gouzenko was escorted to the Ministry of Justice building where he was interrogated by officers of the Royal Canadian Mounted Police. After lifting the lid on Soviet espionage, he told them how he had seen two NKVD officers monitoring his apartment from a park bench. One of the Canadian officers smiled and explained that the two were actually Canadian policemen sent to shadow him. 'You weren't quite as neglected as you thought.'[16] The Canadian prime minister, William Lyon Mackenzie King, had personally ordered Gouzenko to be watched and followed, having been informed by one of the people he had approached that the Russian was touting an explosive story of high-level espionage.

The Canadian prime minister's involvement in the Gouzenko affair had started with inglorious indifference. 'The man might be only a crank trying to preserve his own life,' Mackenzie King had said to his under-secretary for external affairs, Norman Robertson, when first told of Gouzenko's attempt to defect.[17] He didn't grasp the urgency of the Gouzenko affair until the following day, when Robertson gave him a detailed breakdown of the top-secret intelligence contained in the documents handed over by the Russian. A codename that cropped up frequently was 'Alek' – clearly a central player. 'Alek handed over to us a platinum with 162 micrograms of Uranium 233 in the form of acid, covered in a thin lamina.'[18] It did not take long to discover that Alek, who also used the moniker of Primrose, was none other than Dr Alan Nunn May, a top-level British physicist working on nuclear fission in Montreal. Robertson warned the prime minister that the documents revealed 'an espionage system on a huge scale . . . to a degree we could not have believed possible'.

Mackenzie King was deeply disturbed by the implications of such a vast spy ring and foresaw 'a complete break-up of the relations that we have been counting upon to make the peace'. He was especially concerned to learn that staff at the Soviet embassy were paying great attention to the demobilisation of Allied troops in Western Europe. 'There was no saying to what terrible lengths this whole thing might go.'[19]

Three weeks after Gouzenko's defection, Mackenzie King flew to Washington in order to inform President Truman of the covert Soviet activities. In the privacy of the Oval Office, he told the president of the momentous events that had taken place. 'We owed it to the United States,' he would later write, 'as well as to the United Kingdom, to let those highest in authority in these two countries know all that we possessed in the way of information regarding R.E. [Russian espionage].'[20]

President Truman's response was characteristically businesslike. Working on the assumption that 'there must be similar penetration' in the United States, he proposed an urgent investigation. 'Every care must be taken to get full information before anything at all was disclosed.' He stressed the importance of the three affected countries (the United States, Canada and Britain) working together and told Mackenzie King that 'whatever action should be taken, it should be at the highest level, between Attlee, himself and myself.'[21] Nothing was to be made public until they had identified every suspected Soviet agent in North America.

Back in Berlin, Colonel Frank Howley was unaware of Gouzenko's defection, but he knew he would have to fight hard to save the

German capital from Soviet domination. He was increasingly strident in his criticism of official American policy, which he described as 'appeasement of the Russians at any price in an attempt to win them over'. He was also irritated by reminders from Washington that his role was to 'allay their suspicions and to gain their friendship and cooperation'.[22] He had privately vowed to take a more combative approach, even if it meant crossing swords with the White House and State Department. 'There is only one way to deal with gangsters, Russian-uniformed or otherwise,' he said with a scowl, 'and that is to treat them like gangsters.'[23] He would later describe lying awake at night, 'trying to think up ways to keep the Russians from stealing the city from under us'.[24]

The opening shots of the ensuing power struggle were fired in the Allied Kommandatura, the four-power body established to run Berlin. It had been officially convened in the first week of July 1945, but it had proven near impossible to find a building in which it could meet. The Americans eventually suggested the half-ruined headquarters of the Nazi Labour Front in their sector of the city. It stood on Kaiserswerther Strasse in suburban Dahlem, and was a large brick building whose modernist interior and Art Deco ornaments proved agreeable to everyone. Within days it was reglazed, replastered and repainted by 250 American workmen. As a finishing touch, Howley got them to erect four white flagpoles at the front of the building – one for each nation, including soon-to-arrive France.

The building's main entrance opened into an atrium of polished granite, with a sweep of stairs that led to the principal chamber on the first floor. The meeting room itself was sober and functional, furnished with a long banqueting table, twenty armchairs, upholstered in blue, and several rows of smaller seats for the advisers, stenographers and interpreters. This wood-panelled chamber was to be the stage for events that were, in the words of Frank Howley, 'as portentous in world implications as [those held in] the Hall of Mirrors at Versailles'.[25]

When the weather was fine, the sunshine tipped liquid gold through the plate-glass windows. But when thunderous skies plunged the room into gloom, the only light came from the three chandeliers whose bulbs flickered and dimmed in tandem with the intermittent electricity supply. Hanging over the room – morning, noon and night – needed was a swirling wreath of blue-grey cigarette smoke.

The key players in the Kommandatura were not the sector commandants, as might have been expected, but their deputies, including Colonel Howley and Brigadier Hinde. While the commandants oversaw the garrison troops based in the city, the deputies became 'the wheel-horses' of the Kommandatura.[26] It was they who undertook most of the day-to-day work in Berlin and who were to fight tooth and nail with the Soviets over the city's destiny.

Rarely have combatants found themselves seated in such close proximity. Colonel Howley sat next to his Soviet counterpart, with Hinde opposite him and his French comrade in the adjacent chair, all of them surrounded by advisers. Howley regarded himself as the first among equals of this four-square phalanx, a do-or-die warrior who attended meetings in full combat-dress. If his clothing and boots sent an unambiguous message that he was on the warpath, his blunt tongue would do even more to turn the Kommandatura into a bear-pit.

His American compatriots had a sneaking admiration for the bellicose fashion in which he represented his country's interests. Among the admirers was William Heimlich, a senior figure in US intelligence, who listened, his jaw dropping in amazement, as Howley fired off one of his explosive tirades. 'Well of course I don't expect you to tell me the truth,' was a typical opening salvo to his Soviet counterpart. 'You lie. You always lie, and no matter what you're going to tell me it's not going to be the truth.'[27] Heimlich averred that Howley's approach won the grudging respect of the Soviets, but it also earned their deep-seated enmity. It was not long before they viewed him as a formidable enemy, with Berlin's Soviet-backed newspapers variously describing him as a 'terrorist' and 'provocateur of civil war'.[28]

Howley's lack of decorum was viewed with disquiet by the British team, who felt he was inflaming an already tense situation. Harold Hays had enjoyed Howley's ebullient spirit during their time in Barbizon but he now found him 'thrustful, intolerant and impetuous, with a great love of showmanship and publicity'. Above all, he thought him 'extremely self-centred and individualistic'.[29]

The colonel had developed the habit of staging impromptu press conferences at which he delighted the assembled journalists with titbits of explosive gossip. These briefings infuriated the British and French, especially when Howley presented himself as the only soldier with enough swagger to save the city from Stalin. Equally infuriating was his conviction that Uncle Sam was always right. 'To him,' wrote Hays, 'the American Way of Life was the ne plus ultra in democracy and he could be just as aggressive on this point as the Russians were on Communism.'[30]

Seated opposite Howley at the Kommandatura table was the scrupulously fair-minded Brigadier Hinde. He came equipped with enough old-school charm to disarm even the frostiest of Soviet interlocutors. Less combative than Colonel Howley and more attuned to the conventions of diplomacy, he attended meetings in immaculate service dress, all 'white flannels and shiny leather belts'.[31] It was his way of showing that there was a 'right way' of conducting the weighty affairs of state.

Brigadier Hinde's negotiating style was that of an even-handed cricket umpire, with Colonel Howley noting that the British team 'was inclined to show great annoyance at anything smacking of twisted truth'. He had grown fond of Hinde over the previous seven months, but remained exasperated by the brigadier's stiff-buttoned colleagues. 'They talk our language but mean different things by the same words,' he wrote in his diary. 'When they seem the most "huffy-duffy", they are the most clever.' He viewed them as exotic relics of Britain's imperial heritage. 'They seem so similar to us that we forget how completely sold on the Empire they are, how devoted to the King and Queen, and how little they really think of democracy.'[32]

In criticising their negotiating style, Howley was missing an important point. Brigadier Hinde's goal that summer was to remain on good terms with the Soviets. This was the policy of the British government and it was his duty to carry it out, as he constantly reminded his team. He knew it would be a formidable challenge, for relations were already starting to fray. 'Peace is showing, as war did not, how easily the Four Power Alliance can fall apart. It is our job to work through the difficulties and hold it together.'[33]

The French were the last to take their seat on the Kommandatura, just as they had been the last to arrive in Berlin. After weeks of negotiations at the time of the Potsdam Conference, they were offered two Berlin districts carved from the British sector, Reinickendorf and Wedding. There was an element of 'last come, last served' to the offer. Reinickendorf stood on the periphery of the city and was isolated from the urban centre, while Wedding was a fiercely proletarian shamble of ruins. 'One of Berlin's unpleasant areas,' wrote one, 'a jumble of tenements, factories and bars.'[34]

The French had nonetheless arrived in style, marching into the city in July 1945 under the leadership of the splendidly named General Geoffroi-Marie-Otton du Bois de Beauchesne who pitched up with his horse, his tricolour and ten senior advisers. It was unfortunate that he was not yet ready to occupy his sector, and neither did he have a garrison to command. Nor, for that matter, did he have anywhere to lodge until Frank Howley took pity on him and lent him a spare bedroom in his own Dahlem villa.

Brigadier Hinde treated the arrival of General de Beauchesne as one more nuisance to be endured. He disliked the French to such an extent that he refused to have their wines served at his dinner table. He also found them deficient in all the traits of character that had swept Britain to greatness. 'The French are naturally the victims of a sense of inferiority,' he told his team, 'and anxious at the same time both to assert themselves and to follow a lead.' He advised his men to humour their French colleagues and treat them as equal partners in an obviously unequal relationship. 'Devote all your tact to them. Do not be worried by the occasional outbursts of bitterness.'[35]

Among the many French officials to arrive in Berlin that summer was a former resistance activist named Renée Bédarida. When she first toured the ruined districts handed over by Brigadier Hinde, she felt the French had drawn the short straw. '*Apocalyptique!*' she wrote in a letter home. 'Not a street nor a building remains intact; homes ripped open, facades standing isolated.' She also felt that General de Beauchesne and his advisers were very much the junior partners in the running of Berlin. 'Among the western allies, the French held a secondary position,' she said. 'The occupiers who really counted were the two big players, the Americans and British.'[36]

The French sector was indeed a meagre fiefdom but it came with a golden ticket, as Howley was quick to point out. The French 'were no longer sitting at meetings simply as spectators', he said. 'They were now the fourth power of the Kommandatura, without whose approval nothing in Berlin could be ordered.'[37]

General de Beauchesne was shortly to retire and he was replaced by General Charles Lançon, a boorish warhorse slated by Howley as being 'completely lacking in imagination and entirely unprepared by background for the political and economic struggle in Berlin'. Howley found him unsuitable on every level. 'Socially he was not well chosen for the Berlin social whirligig . . . [and] he failed to have the loyalty of his staff.'[38] Lançon spent much of his time learning Russian, German and English, and his role on the Kommandatura was 'almost of no significance' except for the fact that he often sided with the Russians.[39]

Howley's criticism was unduly harsh. French interests in those early days were not the same as those of the Americans and British, with the result that the French often backed the Russian position. The French foreign minister, Georges Bidault, was hoping to seize large areas of German territory along France's eastern border – including the Saarland – and he intended these land-grabs to be 'no milder than those of the East'.[40] From the French point of view, Moscow's seizure of territory had set a useful precedent.

The Soviet team on the Kommandatura was led by an incoming lieutenant-general named Dmitri Smirnov, who made a good impression on everyone at the first meeting. Howley described him as 'a very charming man with a skin of detachment', but he soon discovered that this detachment was used to devastating effect.[41] Smirnov was in the habit of smiling placatingly before launching verbal assaults in which, said Howley, he would 'wade in and cut us to pieces'.[42]

Smirnov arrived in Berlin with a team of commissars whose grasp of facts and figures astonished the representatives of the other powers. He was also aided by a team of shadowy political officers, probably

NKVD, whose roles and identities were never fully explained. 'The most senior of these', said Howley, 'was a sallow, chain-smoking commissar aged about thirty-six, introduced as Mr Maximov, whose true identity was so shrouded in mystery that Western minute-takers were not even allowed to know his first name.'[43] *Daily Telegraph* journalist, Anthony Mann, was fascinated by this quixotic character. 'Despite his somewhat sinister appearance, Maximov appeared at one meeting of the Kommandatura carrying a sprig of white lilac, which he raised delicately to his nostrils from time to time as the recriminations proceeded.'[44]

Colonel Howley took relish in writing about his Kommandatura colleagues. Three years of studying Fine Art in Paris had honed his powers of observation and he produced scores of witty pen portraits tainted by personal prejudice. His description of the Soviet deputy, Andrei Yelizarov, was particularly colourful. The colonel was described as 'a big, powerful bruiser who had married a sister-in-law of Lenin and had forthwith become the father of an astonishing sixteen-pound baby . . . Yelizarov was more Russian than caviar. He seldom smiled and when he did smile it was like ice breaking up on the Yukon in spring.'[45]

Howley's descriptions chime with the transcripts of the Kommandatura meetings, whose typographed pages record every word spoken by the four deputies.

Brigadier Hinde was the most well-mannered of the four, or so it seemed to Howley, and always impeccably polite. But he could fire a blistering salvo when facing unfair play. 'Absolutely insufferable and unthinkable!' he fumed after learning of a Soviet smear against King George VI. 'It has been an offence, not only to the Royal Family, but to every member of the British community in Berlin, as well as in England.'[46]

And then there were the grandstanding monologues of Colonel Howley, along with frequent pleas for food breaks. 'Hell's blazes!' he exclaimed during one meeting that spilled into a mealtime. 'I'm getting to the point where I will accept anything.'[47]

A telling comment: this was exactly what the Russians intended.

★

The first wrangle between the four representatives came at their inaugural meeting in July 1945, when they tried to reach a consensus on a working timetable. Colonel Howley proposed a brisk 9 a.m. start, saying that 'Americans got up early, ate lunch at noon and avoided night-work as much as possible.'[48] Brigadier Hinde wanted it delayed until after his morning conference, at around 10 a.m., but this was still too early for the Russians whose working day never began before noon.

The outcome of this tussle, so trifling yet so telling, was to shape the pattern of things to come. The Soviets won the day by refusing to budge. The meetings were to start late morning and run through everyone else's lunchtime, with implications that Howley had already noted: 'The Americans and British were so darned hungry that they would agree to anything.'[49]

Those early sessions were dominated by the problem of feeding Berlin's inhabitants. All agreed that the neediest should get the most calories, but there was no consensus over who was most in need. The Soviets said it was the professional classes, including political leaders, while Howley insisted it was the elderly and infirm. Turning to his Soviet counterpart, he said: 'You can't kick a lady when she's down.' The Russian flashed him an indulgent smile. 'Why my dear Colonel Howley,' he replied, 'that is exactly the best time to kick them.'[50]

Another bone of contention was the continued dismantling of factories and power plants. Howley and Hinde were dismayed to see Soviet trains arrive daily at Tempelhof freight yard and load up with dismantled equipment, far more than had been sanctioned by the Potsdam agreement. 'So savage was their cannibalizing of power plants and so wholesale their theft of generator equipment that only the strongest representations saved Berlin's remaining power supply.'[51] In what Howley described as 'a hot session', he expressed his outrage at their organised looting. The Soviet team answered with shrugs, telling him 'their orders were orders from a higher authority.'[52]

Harold Hays's account of Soviet tactics in the Kommandatura matches that of Frank Howley. 'Words in common use are given a sinister twist,' he wrote after one heated meeting, 'and an interpretation which only a warped mind could conjure up. Simple phrases are distorted or torn from their context.'[53] The Soviet team was equally mistrustful of the westerners, accusing them of eavesdropping, espionage and dirty tricks. 'Cunning' was the terse assessment of one Soviet official.[54]

Over the course of that autumn and winter, the four deputies wrangled over all the most pressing issues: food, looting, shootings, the arrest of Nazis and the intractability of the Berlin Magistrat, established by the Soviets in the first days of their occupation. This executive body was supposed to be directed by the Kommandatura but this was to prove impossible, for the leader of the Lux Hotel revolutionaries, Walter Ulbricht, had it firmly in his grasp. He had no intention of taking orders from the western Allies.

The Soviet delegation won most of the battles in those early months. Then, once they had got what they wanted, they would invite the other three delegations into the adjoining dining room where the tables were charged with smoked meats, caviar and vodka. Howard Hays felt that the Russians' conviviality masked a plot to force their will on the western Allies. 'No matter how friendly they may have appeared or how friendly they wished to be,' he said, 'Communism was the goal.'[55]

9

Enter the Overlords

SWEEPING THROUGH THE streets of Berlin that autumn in a flash of chrome and steel was a magnificent royal-blue Fleetwood Cadillac. It flew the scarlet rectangular flag of a four-star general on its right fender and had a grille like the jaws of a monster. Inside this leviathan of the roads sat the American military commander, General Lucius Clay, who was destined to play a decisive role in the future of Berlin, Germany and the West.

General Clay had been serving as General Eisenhower's deputy when he had first intervened in the city's affairs at the infamous July meeting with Marshal Zhukov. This was the occasion at which Clay had bowed to Zhukov's demand that each power should have a veto over the actions of the other three. It had also seen him publicly rebuke Frank Howley, a humiliation that the rambunctious colonel would never forget. Now, as the autumnal skies brought drizzle to the German capital, Clay found himself struggling to cope with one of the most challenging jobs of the post-war world.

He was America's principal representative on the Allied Control Council, the body charged with running the four zones of occupied Germany.* Just as the four sectors of Berlin were jointly governed by the Kommandatura, so the four zones of Germany (American, British, French and Soviet) were jointly governed by the four-power Allied Control Council. These two bodies were to work closely together, with the latter having the final say over any unresolved issues concerning the capital. It made Lucius Clay and his fellow commandants the most powerful voices in Berlin.

---

* His official role was that of deputy to General Eisenhower, but, as with the Kommandatura, it was the deputies who undertook much of the day-to-day work.

It also put Clay on a collision course with his fellow American, Frank Howley.

Clay's appointment had initially unnerved him, as he would later admit in his memoirs. 'As I sat in the plane flying across the Atlantic, I had time to wonder whether the task ahead could be accomplished, and what experience, talents or training that were mine could give me any hope of confidence.'[1]

That hoped-for confidence was undermined by his awareness that he was an anomaly in the American army, a senior general who had never done any fighting. One colleague snorted that Clay had 'never commanded anything with more firepower than a desk'.[2] This was true but unfair: his expertise lay in logistics and supply. He was an organiser par excellence who had been in charge of American military procurement since 1942. Although the job lacked the guts of combat, it was of vital importance to the war effort. For three long years of war, Clay had kept millions of soldiers supplied with everything they needed. The experience would stand him in good stead for Berlin.

'The most able fellow around this town'[3] – such was the opinion of the Washington-based Henry Morgenthau when he was secretary of the treasury. Clay also had a streak of ruthlessness that led American newspapers to view his German assignment with glee. '[It] served the Germans right for losing the war,' gloated the *Baltimore Sun*.[4]

Clay had no knowledge of Germany and spoke no German. Nor did he have any experience in dealing with the Soviets. When he first arrived in Berlin, he did so clutching a slim document, JCS 1067, which set out the broad sweep of America's occupation policy. Its terms were identical to those imposed on the German capital. Germany was an enemy state that must be permanently prevented from waging war. The economy was to produce only enough to provide a basic livelihood for the population and any significant economic recovery was viewed as undesirable. Fraternisation was strictly forbidden and all former Nazis were to be excluded from public life. In short, both city and country were to be permanently crushed by the Allied occupiers.

Clay had been granted near limitless powers with which to rule his empire. In the words of one contemporary, his position was 'the nearest thing to a Roman proconsul the modern world afforded'.[5] Others went even further. 'He looks like a Roman Emperor and he acts like one,' noted a columnist in the *Observer*.[6] Seventeen million lives would depend on Clay's ability to conjure food from thin air and he was also the ultimate arbiter of whether convicted Nazis were to be hanged or spared. 'I approved the death sentences of more than two hundred war criminals,' he said after facing criticism for commuting the death penalty for Ilse Koch, the so-called Bitch of Buchenwald.[7] Those to be hanged were sent to the gallows on a nod and a wink from Clay.

Everyone had an opinion about Lucius Clay – for, against, but never neutral. 'A formidable man, Napoleonic,' thought the veteran British diplomat, Harold Nicolson, who found him delightful company.[8] Few shared this opinion. 'Lucius is an autocrat by nature,' said one acquaintance. 'If we lived in an earlier age, he would be a baron or duke. He would be a benevolent one, but he'd be an autocrat nevertheless.'[9] Others were more damning. 'Lucius is the most arrogant, stubborn, opinionated man I ever met . . . [he] had a definite opinion about everyone. Good or bad. Yes or no.'[10] A feverish workaholic, Clay chain-smoked and toiled twelve hours a day, seven days a week. According to one American radioman in Berlin, he used to work himself into a state of utter exhaustion. 'He skipped lunch because he considered it a waste of time. Instead, he had twenty cups of coffee and two packs of cigarettes.'[11] He never went to cocktail parties because he considered them frivolous. 'Social chit-chat was just of no interest to him.'[12]

He surrounded himself with experts but rarely required their services because he already had the answer to every question. Whenever he didn't get his way he would tender his resignation, constantly and repeatedly. 'He used to resign two or three times every week in the years I worked for him,' said his aide, Edloe Donnan.[13] Over the course of five years, he clocked up scores of resignation letters. They were never accepted by Washington.

Behind his stubborn facade was a quick-thinking realist who soon saw the impracticability of directive JCS 1067. Clay dismissed the idea of dismantling German industry as 'a lot of damn foolishness', given that the country's survival would be dependent on the reopening of factories. No less important was the fact that Germany was a vital market for American goods. 'The cost to the United States was going to be terrific unless we could get the thing moving again,' he said in an interview some years later.[14]

Clay was under the strictest orders to work as a partner of the Soviets and was repeatedly reminded of this imperative by President Truman and his secretary of state, James F. Byrnes. Clay passed on this message to all who served beneath him. 'You occupy the testing ground of international cooperation,' he told his senior officers in a speech that summer. 'The experiment in Germany cannot be permitted to fail.'[15] Berlin's American intelligence expert, William Heimlich, said that Clay clung to the notion that the Soviet Union was a friendly power and was 'determined that we would get along with them'.[16] His aide went even further, saying that he would never utter a word 'that would jeopardise the relationship between the USA and the Russians'.[17]

It was a policy that put him in fierce opposition to Frank Howley, the self-styled master of Berlin. Where Clay wanted compromise, Howley wanted confrontation. Where Clay urged restraint, Howley fought for resistance. 'It is all very well poking our heads in the clouds and saying the Russians are misunderstood,' said Howley, '[but] such rationalizations fail to alter the fact that by our standards, or by any standards of common decency, they are liars, swindlers and cut-throats.'[18]

These two combatants found themselves wrangling from the very outset, fighting from their respective corners with intense competitiveness. Their opinions were so polarised – and their egos so polished – that it was unclear how they could possibly work together, especially if relations with the Soviets turned sour. Yet work together they would surely have to do.

The British representative on the Allied Control Council was General Sir Brian Hubert Robertson, deputy to Field Marshal Bernard Montgomery. In a city where cars were visible symbols of status, General Robertson's vehicle was even more eye-catching than that of Lucius Clay. It was a magnificent light-green and silver Rolls-Royce

Phantom III – so plush, so indulgent, that it was as if he was being driven around Berlin in the drawing room of his St James's club.

General Robertson was the very caricature of a British officer, complete with starched uniform, polished buttons and a bristling moustache. He had been to the right sort of school (Charterhouse), undergone the right training (Royal Military Academy) and had the right pedigree (a father who was a distinguished field marshal). At the age of twenty he had been packed off to British India where, in common with Brigadier 'Looney' Hinde, he had spent his leisure hours playing polo and going pig-sticking.

Robertson had not only the background of the archetypal soldier, but also the bearing of the archetypal gentleman. 'He did all the right things, whether it was playing polo or tennis, reading the lesson in church [or] doing the *Times* crossword.' He was also meticulous about deportment, 'and immaculately turned out for every occasion and time of day'.[19]

His wartime service had been hectic but lacking in glamour. Like Lucius Clay, he was a master of logistics and had kept supply lines open in the searing deserts of North Africa. With the armistice came new employment: a leading role on the Allied Control Council. As such, he was to find himself in a frontline battle with the Soviets.

There were those who questioned Robertson's suitability for the job. Some suggested he was too decent to realise when he was being hoodwinked; others said he was too honest to smell a rat. Was this really the man to do battle with Stalin's most devious players? Gaunt, austere and grimly formidable, Robertson was described as 'a rather Olympian figure'[20] whose 'imperturbability was as solid as the cliffs of Dover'.[21]

His devoted wife Edith never called him 'Brian' or (heaven forbid) 'Darling'. Rather, she referred to him as 'Himself', a form of address that suggested a weary acceptance of her husband's overbearing manner. Robertson told his Berlin secretary, Anne Jackson, that there were only two rules in life: 'BHR [Brian Hubert Robertson] comes first in everything' and 'NOTHING MUST EVER GO WRONG.'[22] The fact that Jackson wrote it in capital letters suggests that Robertson said it with imperious force.

Like so many of the British in Berlin, Robertson possessed a mindset imbued with a patrician grandeur forged in imperial India: it was no accident that the *Manchester Guardian* referred to him as 'the Viceroy'.[23] In Spandau as in Simla, natives were to be taught to marvel at the superiority of the British Empire. In one of the general's more eyebrow-raising speeches, he expressed forthright views on German men and women, whom he personified as 'Fritz' and 'Greta'.

'He is a very curious fellow, this Fritz – sentimental, emotional, easily led, selfish, without any sort of humour as we understand it.' In a candid piece of advice to those serving under him, Robertson said that 'in our official relations with the Germans we should be fair and just and extremely firm . . . know Fritz for what he is and treat him accordingly.'[24] He would have been horrified to learn that his men were rather more interested in getting to know Greta and treating her accordingly.

The general never recorded his opinion of Brigadier Hinde, nor Hinde of Robertson, yet they certainly had shared outlooks and goals for they had been chipped from the same imperial block. The most important of these goals in the autumn of 1945 was to remain on friendly terms with the Soviets. In common with Lucius Clay, General Robertson reminded his officers that the Russians were vital allies and that 'we should put up with almost anything to get on good terms with them.'[25]

Robertson's country residence during his tenure in Germany was Schloss Benkhausen, a magnificent moated castle that had been the ancestral seat of the baronial Bussche-Ippenburg dynasty until it was requisitioned by the general's staff. His Berlin residence, formerly owned by the well-known German industrialist Oscar Henschel, was a lofty mansion in Hohmann Strasse at the edge of the Grunewald. It was smaller than Schloss Benkhausen but no less splendid. This was where he spent much of his time in the company of his wife, Edith, and their young daughter, Fiona, both of whom had accompanied him to Germany. 'Why', asked that perceptive six-year-old, 'do only the British live in whole houses?'[26] It was a good question and one that could not easily be answered.

The general had also requisitioned his own train, which allowed him to flit back and forth from his country residence. It was, said one, 'a well equipped diesel railcar, with a sitting room, dining room and three bedrooms, with a bathroom etc. – formerly the property of Dr Josef Goebbels'.[27] The ever-stringent Lucius Clay was taken aback by the extravagance of Robertson and his circle. 'They have set up shop in their zone as if they are somewhere in darkest Africa.'[28]

India might have been a better analogy. Just as life had been comfortable during Robertson's time in the Raj, so it was to be luxurious in Berlin – a dizzying circuit of cocktail parties and champagne receptions (Marlene Dietrich pitched up at one soirée). At his Berlin villa, Robertson was attended by his personal butler, aptly named Fritz, who served pink gin and punch at the general's frequent parties.

Luxuries, victuals and rare spirits were flown in from Denmark in the general's private Dakota aircraft. And there were other, less conventional means of obtaining meat for the pot. 'There was very little fresh food in Berlin,' wrote Robertson's aide-de-camp, 'so General Robertson allowed occasional night time forays by his personal staff to bring home some rabbits, shot rather unsportingly from a Cadillac' – a car the general had acquired from the Americans.[29]

Serving as Robertson's deputy chief of staff was Major General Alec Bishop, another veteran of British India. Bishop said that Berlin's officer class soon slipped into a comfortable routine with sailing excursions on the Havel and regular hunting outings with the illustrious Count von Spee, starting 'with a breakfast of stewed pheasant and claret'.[30] Bishop was most impressed to see that the count was decked in magnificent furs and the head forester and his attendants attired in immaculate green livery. There were a few Germans, it seemed, who had been left untouched by the war.

The headquarters of the Allied Control Council was in Berlin's Kammergericht, a splendorous five-hundred-room palace that had once housed the highest court in Prussia. It was close to the city centre, some four miles from the Kommandatura building. In Nazi times it had been the People's Court of Judge Roland Friesler who, fifteen months before, had screamed abuse at those accused of trying to assassinate Hitler in the July Plot.

The building had been in ruins when America's Second Armoured Division took it over in July 1945. The roof had caved in, the two upper floors were rubble and there was no heating, lighting or water. This was swiftly rectified and the palace was ready for business by the end of the summer. It was here that Clay and Robertson were to meet with their French and Soviet counterparts, and where the countless committees and working groups met for business.

'In all the world there is no other home quite like it,' wrote the American journalist, Thomas Falco, upon first entering the refurbished building. He wandered through the corridors with the feeling of having landed in a world of surreal abundance. The principal restaurant, which served six hundred meals daily, was a place of particular luxury. 'Fresh cut flowers brighten the tables [and] a six-piece string ensemble, directed by the former first concert master of the Staedtische Oper [Berlin City Opera] will play almost anything on request, from swing to symphony.'[31]

The multilingual headwaiter had more than three decades' experience working in New York's Hotel Astor and Berlin's Kaiserhof, and certainly knew how to put on a spread. The bar was 'done in creamy white and salmon', with each nation contributing to supplies: cognac and champagne from the French, gin and Scotch from the British, whiskey from the Americans and vodka from the Russians. It was to this comfortable bar that Lucius Clay and Sir Brian Robertson often retired, along with the French and Soviet commandants. It was the latter of these, Marshal Sokolovsky, who was to prove the most enigmatic.

Marshal Vasily Sokolovsky was a veteran soldier who had been in the vanguard of the first Soviet troops to enter Berlin. The dazzling display of medals bolted to his chest was a reminder of his martial prowess, while the chest itself was as broad and solid as a slab of masonry. But this was where the Soviet stereotype came to an end: Sokolovsky's smile radiated good humour and his eyes flashed with vitality. He was very different from the typical Soviet apparatchik and a world apart from the devious Lieutenant-General Smirnov and his colleagues on the Berlin Kommandatura. Even his choice of car was surprising. Instead of driving a Soviet-made Moskvich

400 or ZIS limousine, as might have been expected, he motored around Berlin in a luxury, American-made LaSalle sedan.

Worldly and urbane, Sokolovsky sparkled with jokes, witty aphorisms and folksy Russian proverbs. Even more impressive was the way in which he peppered his speech with quotes from the novels of Jane Austen. Both Robertson and Clay were charmed when first introduced to him and their enthusiasm only deepened with time. 'I liked the marshal instinctively,' said Clay at the time. 'He was polite, even affable, with a sense of humour and with the obvious desire to seem friendly.'[32] The two men often dined together in the company of their wives, and undertook joint outings into the countryside.

One of their most memorable trips was to the Leipzig Fair: the Soviet and American commanders invited General Sir Brian Robertson to join them, along with a few others, and everyone enjoyed a convivial lunch washed down with copious quantities of vodka. When Clay returned to Berlin and opened the boot of his car, he found that Sokolovsky had filled it with gifts from the fair, including Meissen china and figurines. Such presents were swiftly reciprocated: the marshal was given cigars, pineapples and boxes of nuts.[33]

Lucius Clay was not alone in wooing Sokolovsky: General Robertson had also worked hard to cultivate the Soviet marshal. He and his wife, Edith, went so far as to take him to London, inviting him to their box at the Royal Opera House for a performance of Puccini's *Turandot*. Sokolovsky enjoyed the evening immensely and was even more grateful when Robertson secured him an invitation to a reception at Buckingham Palace, where he was granted a lengthy audience with King George VI. As his London visit came to a close, the Robertsons gave him a joyous private dinner at the Savoy Hotel. They felt that the visit had been a triumphant success. 'A new understanding had been cemented.'[34]

The Soviet marshal certainly knew how to entertain his fellow commandants in return. He presided over countless magnificent banquets, with the finest being held in commemoration of the October Revolution. Among the British invitees was Major General Bishop, Robertson's deputy chief of staff.

'We passed the Banqueting Hall where exotic dishes, including boars' heads with oranges in their mouths, were displayed in some profusion.' Noticing a veritable mountain range of caviar, Bishop turned to one of the Soviet officers and said that he had not eaten any since before the war. 'This shocked the Russian marshal, who told me that if I were a general in the Red Army, my wife would be able to deal at a special shop where she could buy, for example, twenty-three different sorts of caviar.'[35]

What neither Sir Brian Robertson nor Lucius Clay knew about Marshal Sokolovsky was that he was a conflicted man. This other Sokolovsky, noted one who had studied him at close quarters, 'known only to his aides, was often ill at ease: an insomniac who night after night prowled his bedroom, tormented by a World War I leg wound [and] who spoke by direct phone to Moscow for almost an hour each night.'[36] He chain-smoked eighty cigarettes a day – a clue to his nervous disposition – for he could scarcely function without a continual top-up of nicotine. His stress levels were not assuaged by the dispatches he received each fortnight from Marshal Aleksandr Vasilevsky, chief of staff of the Red Army's High Command in Moscow. These missives would order him to play an increasingly dirty game against his western counterparts, while all the time dissembling behind his mask of charm.

Alone among the western leaders in Berlin, Frank Howley was keeping a close eye on Sokolovsky. He was convinced that the bonhomie was contrived and that the marshal was as untrustworthy as all the other Kremlin appointees. On one occasion, Howley overheard a conversation in which Sokolovsky assured Clay that the Red Army would never be used as an instrument to force Communism on Germany. 'I had the funny feeling at the time that "Wise Guy" Sokolovsky was lying,' said Howley, 'and I said so.' Clay refused to accept Howley's opinion. 'I know Sokolovsky,' said Clay. 'He wouldn't lie to me.' Howley persisted. 'Wise Guy's attitude infuriated me,' he said. 'We were being pushed around . . . but Sokolovsky's remarks were taken in good part by our commanders.'[37]

The French representative on the Allied Control Council was General Koenig, a distinguished veteran of the Great War and an ardent supporter of General de Gaulle. He was adamantly opposed to Berlin becoming the capital of a revived Germany and determined to prevent any sort of central government. He had an intense dislike of the city and visited 'as infrequently as possible and always with reluctance'.[38] So wrote Lucius Clay, who was not yet aware that Koenig had created his own little paradise in Baden–Baden. There, in the beautifully landscaped grounds of his official residence, distinguished visitors 'were greeted with ceremonial guards of Algerian cavalry bearing lighted torches'.[39] When the *Daily Telegraph*'s Anthony Mann visited, he was astonished to be shown 'specially installed toys such as electrically operated portcullises, desk-drawers and curtains'. In a country that was virtually starving, it was a shocking example of 'squandermania'.[40]

In common with his French colleagues on the Kommandatura, General Koenig would frequently side with the Soviets over the months that followed, much to the frustration of the Americans and British. Yet there was little outward sign of discord in the early days of the Allied Control Council, and personal relationships remained warm and friendly. On one memorable evening the four well-lubricated commandants – Clay, Robertson, Sokolovsky and Koenig – linked arms in the gilded assembly room of the Kammergericht and sang the 'Song of the Volga Boatmen', stamping their feet in time with the band.

'It's *got* to work,' said Clay of the Allied Control Council. 'If the four of us cannot get together in running Germany, how are we going to get together in an international organisation to secure the peace of the world?'[41] It was a good question – and one that remained unanswered.

In these gloomy times there was a glimmer of political optimism – small in itself, but of such significance that it was to dominate life in Berlin for months to come. The prelude to the drama had taken place in the weeks that followed the Soviet capture of the city, when Walter Ulbricht and his Moscow comrades had re-established the Berlin Communist Party. By mid-October three other political parties had also been created: the Social Democrats, Christian Democrats and Liberal Democrats.

This led to a flurry of excitement amongst Berliners, who felt they might at last be given a voice in running their carved-up city. On Tuesday, 16 October, Ruth Andreas-Friedrich and two comrades from her resistance network spent the afternoon discussing which party they should support. Dr Walter Seitz had already made up his mind. 'Mass misery requires social solutions,' he said.[42] He was joining the Social Democrats.

Frau Andreas-Friedrich disliked the idea of being tied to a particular set of policies. 'It is not easy to join a party if, during all one's life, one has been against any kind of association, insignia or membership.' Yet she agreed to accompany Dr Seitz to the first meeting of the Social Democratic Party and reluctantly signed up for membership that very evening, wincing when someone addressed her as comrade. When she wrote her diary that night, she tried to convince herself she'd made the right decision. 'Daydreaming will not make the world any better,' she wrote.[43]

What neither she nor her friends realised was that they were walking headlong into a trap laid by Stalin. Only a few weeks earlier, the Soviet leader had summoned Walter Ulbricht to a secret meeting in Moscow and revealed his plan to seize control of Berlin through the ballot box. Stalin knew that the Berlin Communists were unlikely to win a majority in free and fair elections: electoral victory would go to the Social Democrats who were gaining widespread support in Berlin.

Stalin's idea was to engineer a merger of the Communist Party and the Social Democratic Party, and rename it the Socialist Unity Party. This would stand a far greater chance of winning an election, and thereby Walter Ulbricht and his supporters would be swept to power quite legally, just like Hitler thirteen years before.

The single figure who stood in his way was Otto Grotewohl, the earnest and bespectacled leader of the Social Democrats. When he heard rumours of the proposed merger he became an outspoken opponent. 'We are the party of the centre,' he said. 'We are the party of power.'[44] He wanted nothing to do with Ulbricht and his Communists.

Grotewohl was unremarkable in every sense – grey, dull and boorish. In his life before politics, he had been a builder of swimming pools and there were many who felt that this was the extent of his talents. He also had a flaw in his character that his Communist rivals were intending to exploit. Weak-willed and naive, he was the ideal candidate to be won over. Over the days that followed, Walter Ulbricht used every possible bribe to persuade Grotewohl to change his mind about the merger. First, a generous gift of art supplies was delivered to his home, for he was known to be a keen amateur artist. Next, he was offered a luxury villa in the Soviet-controlled district of Niederschönhausen. When this failed to do the trick, Marshal Zhukov promised to get his son released from a British prisoner-of-war camp. According to one in his circle, it was his bourgeois background that made Grotewohl such an enticing catch for the Soviets. 'The Communists wanted to have him as a kind of label for the middle class people they wanted to win over.'[45]

Slowly but surely, Ulbricht's drip-by-drip strategy began to work. 'He changed his mind from hour to hour,' noted one alarmed observer of the wavering Grotewohl.[46]

When Ruth Andreas-Friedrich heard what was taking place, she felt she was witnessing the first great showdown of the post-war period. 'If the Social Democratic Party in Berlin is swallowed up by the Communist Party, it will be the end of democracy in Berlin, the end of democracy in Germany and – sooner or later – the end of democracy in Europe.'[47] This was nothing short of a battle for the soul of the West.

Grotewohl soon received a summons to Soviet military headquarters in Karlshorst. There, he was subjected to intense discussions laced with menace. Among the threats was the reminder (as if he needed it) that the Soviets had recently 'surprised him with his confidential secretary' – an embarrassing indiscretion for the married Grotewohl.[48]

'The pressure increased and increased,' said young Wolfgang Leonhard, one of the Hotel Lux revolutionaries, 'and I had my first bad feelings.'[49] Yet there was to be no let-up. The journalist Curt Riess had insider information on what was taking place and said that the threats against Grotewohl continued for a full twelve days. At the end of it he 'almost collapsed from exhaustion and it was scarcely surprising that he changed his mind'.[50] The merger of the two parties at long last received his blessing.

Ruth Andreas-Friedrich was to describe it as Grotewohl's 'road to Damascus' moment, an episode that transformed him into 'a fanatical apostle of an immediate merger'.[51] He reappeared into the world as a born-again Stalinist and would soon be uttering sentiments that would have been unthinkable in his previous life. 'Comrade Stalin is the greatest socialist in the world,' he said in one speech. 'Comrade Stalin is the father of the world.'[52]

Politics is full of pitfalls and the best-laid plans can easily go awry. Just when it seemed that Stalin's scheme was working to perfection, an unforeseen spanner was thrown into the works. Ruth Andreas-Friedrich was attending an important party meeting when Otto Grotewohl found himself facing a furious backlash. The storm began with heckles and insults. 'Lackey!' yelled an angry voice in the audience. 'Go back to Karlshorst, Otto!' As Grotewohl rose to his feet, the audience began stomping their feet. 'Traitor . . . fraud . . . resign.'[53] And then, rising above the tumult, came a chorus of voices demanding a public vote on the merger.

Frau Andreas-Friedrich felt a cool shiver of excitement as the crowd dared to pass a motion declaring Grotewohl's merger invalid unless ratified by a vote of all party members. 'Everybody's face is glowing with pride and excitement,' she recorded in her diary that night. 'For the first time in thirteen years we have defended our freedom.'[54] She realised the significance of the moment. 'The battle has begun,' she wrote. 'No one knows how it will end.'[55]

Walter Ulbricht's team worked fast and furiously, targeting party members with propaganda leaflets printed at their Prinzenallee headquarters. Yet it soon became clear that the merger was going to be rejected by a large majority, who had seen through Ulbricht's ruse and preferred to remain with the status quo. Ulbricht's response was sudden, dramatic and decisive. On the day of the vote, Red Army soldiers were sent into the streets with orders to shut down all polling booths in the Soviet sector. When an outraged Frank Howley protested to his Russian opposite number, he was told that the organisers of the vote 'had failed to comply with certain mysterious regulations'.[56]

The vote went ahead in the British, American and French sectors of the city, where the anti–merger faction won by a landslide. More than nineteen thousand party members voted against the motion, while fewer than three thousand were in favour. Ruth Andreas-Friedrich was jubilant. 'Despite violence, threats and propaganda, the will towards self-determination triumphed.'[57]

She was not alone in realising the importance of what had happened. Frank Howley also felt that the result marked a turning point for Germany's capital, even though the electorate had been tiny. 'The first positive proof that the Germans no longer were political sheep,' he wrote of that day's events.[58]

Brigadier Hinde's intelligence officer, George Clare, was equally upbeat, noting that it was the Soviet Union's first serious setback in the German capital since the end of the war, one with important ramifications. 'Britain, France and the USA were now no longer just occupiers. They had become Berlin's defenders and protectors from totalitarian tyranny.'[59]

The ballot was not quite the end of the story, though, for there was to be a disturbing and unexpected postscript. Far from conceding defeat, the Soviets brazenly acted as if they had won the vote. Ruth Andreas-Friedrich was astonished to learn that they were heralding the outcome as a victory. 'What manner of mental gymnastics allowed them to reach that conclusion', she said, 'would remain puzzling even to a mathematical genius.'[60] She suspected a sinister stratagem to play fast and loose with objective fact, with the aim of making it impossible to determine what news was true and what was fake.

Just a few days after the poll, Walter Ulbricht orchestrated the formal merger between the Communist Party and the Social Democratic Party in the Soviet sector of Berlin, in blatant disregard of the election result. It was the first tangible sign that the city was splitting into two distinct halves. Ulbricht himself remained in the shadows during the ensuing festivities, for the two figureheads were to be Otto Grotewohl and Wilhelm Pieck, the ageing leader of the German Communist Party.

The ceremony was staged in the auditorium of the Berlin State Opera House, a carefully choreographed jamboree played out in front of more than a thousand party loyalists. As they waited in tense anticipation, a slim, clean-shaven man slipped into the building in order to observe everything that followed. Wilfred Byford-Jones, intelligence agent for the British, had come to keep tabs on this landmark event.

He had already witnessed a carnival atmosphere outside the opera house, where the street lamps and telegraph poles were decked with festive bunting. 'Red flags flew from high masts outside the theatre; red flags fluttered on the radiators of cars which brought delegates; crowds of white-gloved Russian-controlled police directed traffic.'

Once inside the building he was to witness a ceremony that was remarkably similar to the rallies previously organised by the Nazis. 'Instead of a bust of Hitler there were colossal busts of Marx, Engels and Stalin. Instead of the slogan, "One Land, One People, One Leader" there were the words "One Land, One Party, One Aim".'[61]

The orchestra pit was crowded with vetted broadcasters and floodlights lit the stage from all directions. Excitement mounted as rousing music was blasted through speakers. The entire scenario had been choreographed to perfection; the Nazi's favourite film director, Leni Riefenstahl, could not have done better. And then came the moment of high drama. The floodlights suddenly swept to each side of the stage as the two protagonists emerged from the backstage shadows. A triumphal roar greeted Otto Grotewohl as he addressed the crowd. 'I come from the right,' he bellowed. 'Pieck comes from the left. In the centre we meet.' As the invited crowd thundered their approval, he shouted, '*Nun sind wir vereint!*' (Now we are united!)[62]

Byford-Jones's jaw dropped with astonishment as the entire audience leaped to its feet. 'No two stars of the theatrical orbit of Berlin who had trod that famous stage had ever had such a reception.'[63] As the two leaders warmly embraced each other, a banner was unfurled to reveal the emblem of the newly merged party. The *Sozialistische Einheitspartei Deutschlands*, or Socialist Unity Party, was to be represented by two clasped hands in gold with a red flag fluttering behind them. Grotewohl himself had helped in the design, perhaps using the paint-set given to him by Walter Ulbricht.

Byford-Jones found the spectacle deeply depressing. 'The fact that the fusion meeting had been held in the presence of Red Army officers, and that future committee meetings would be held in territory administered by the Russians, was assurance enough that the party would run along proper ideological lines.'[64]

Brigadier Hinde was seriously alarmed by the new party's 'virile and dynamic leadership'.[65] He feared that Berliners might find themselves led 'into dangerous experiments' by Ulbricht and company, 'who are ready to take advantage of the present situation'.

The merger caused outrage at the next session of the Kommandatura, where the four deputies exchanged heated abuse. Frank Howley described it as 'the longest, brawlingest and perhaps the least productive of all our meetings'. At its heart was the unresolved issue of whether the three western Allies should recognise the new Socialist Unity Party in the Soviet sector.

'If this type of conference is to continue,' wrote a furious Howley, 'we should recognise the failure of the Kommandatura and find some other method of handling Berlin.' He was pessimistic about the months ahead. 'We were going downhill fast,' he said, 'and couldn't put on the brakes.'[66]

But, in truth, he didn't want to.

PART III

Breakdown

10

The Iron Curtain

EVER SINCE HIS defection in the summer of 1945, Igor Gouzenko had been in hiding with his family, holed up in Camp X on the frost-blasted shores of Lake Ontario. This forlorn spot, with its decaying shacks and rusting barbed wire, was where America's Office of Strategic Services had secretly trained its wartime saboteurs. Now, fogbound and eerily deserted, it was being used by the Canadian government as the securest possible location for safeguarding their first Soviet defector. In the early weeks of 1946, Gouzenko was moved to a restored farmhouse that adjoined the camp, along with his heavily pregnant wife, Svetlana, their young son and a team of security guards.

Gouzenko was questioned for many weeks by officers of the Royal Canadian Mounted Police, along with officials from the FBI, MI5, MI6 and the British Security Coordination, run by Sir William 'Intrepid' Stephenson. Everything was conducted in the utmost secrecy, and knowledge of Gouzenko's dramatic revelations was restricted to a handful of people, notably the Canadian prime minister, President Truman and British prime minister Attlee.

Over the weeks that followed, the Soviet spy ring was quietly dismantled and twenty suspects taken into custody. These included senior figures in Canadian public life, including a member of parliament, Fred Rose; Emma Woikin of the Department of External Affairs; and Kathleen Willsher of the UK High Commission. But the biggest name of all was the mysterious 'Alek', also known as 'Primrose': this was the British nuclear physicist, Alan Nunn May, who had joined Montreal's nuclear research laboratory three years before. May would eventually confess to having been handing over nuclear secrets since 1943, along with samples of the uranium isotopes 233 and 235.*

Mackenzie King knew that the ongoing investigation would be but the opening chapter in what was certain to prove a sordid affair. 'We are only at the beginning of the real disclosures,' he warned in private. 'It will grow into one of the major sensations of the day.'[1] He was appalled by what he already knew of Soviet treachery and felt personally humiliated by the fact that it had happened on his watch. He also foresaw the dangers of revealing to the public the enormity of the Soviet espionage ring, aware that it was certain to set the world on edge. 'It really is a terrifying business in what it reveals of a diabolical planned effort to produce a fifth column within a friendly country and to have all plans laid in readiness for another war.'[2]

The prime minister took it upon himself to accuse the key villains in person, summoning staff of the Soviet embassy to his office at 4 p.m. on 15 February 1946. Colonel Zabotin was unable to attend, for he had been recalled to Moscow; he was represented by the sinister second secretary, Vitali Pavlov. Also in attendance was the chargé d'affaires, Nikolai Belokhvostikov. They were to learn the extent of Gouzenko's revelations in an account read to them by Mackenzie King himself.

'When I began to read the statement,' the prime minister wrote in his diary, 'I noticed the young chargé d'affaires coloured up quite perceptibly. His countenance became very pink. There was no other evidence of particular emotion and his face gradually assumed its natural colour.' The second secretary behaved rather differently. 'The other man, Pavlov, however, sat throughout with his hands clenched tight and with a sort of dour, determined, indifferent appearance. I noticed that he kept pressing his thumbs on his fingers as I was reading.'[3]

Neither man had anything to say, for Gouzenko's defection had left them outflanked.

The Canadian enquiry was still underway when a gruff, heavy-jowled British gentleman could be seen boarding a train at Silver Spring

---

* The courier who took these samples to Moscow was unaware of the dangers of radiation and suffered such high levels of exposure that he needed blood transfusions for the rest of his life.

station in Maryland. It was the first week of March and the gentleman in question was Winston Churchill, leader of His Majesty's opposition. He was embarking on a twenty-four-hour overnight journey to Missouri in the *Ferdinand Magellan*, President Truman's armoured railcar.

Churchill had been invited to make a keynote speech in Truman's home state and he intended it to be his most important address since losing the 1945 election. He was accompanied on his journey by the American president himself, Truman's twenty-two-year-old daughter Margaret, and the usual entourage of aides and Secret Service men. Also in the party was the president's close adviser, General Harry Vaughan.

Churchill was in ebullient form during the voyage, drinking five large Scotches before the on-board dinner and reciting anecdotes about his youthful skirmishes against the Boers in the parched hinterlands of Natal. The two protagonists got along famously and agreed to call one another Winston and Harry; they played poker into the late hours and watched the darkening plains unfurl into the endless horizons of Indiana and Illinois. At one point Churchill put down his cards and gushingly expressed his desire to live in the United States, although he swiftly added that he deplored some of its more recent customs. When Truman enquired which customs he had in mind, Churchill said: 'You stopped drinking with your meals.'[4]

On the following morning, as the train chased the sluggish flow of the Missouri River, Churchill handed his speech to Truman and asked for his opinion. 'He told me he thought it was admirable,' wrote Churchill, 'and would do nothing but good, though it would make a stir.'[5]

The first stir of that historic day was caused by Churchill himself, and within minutes of his arriving in Fulton. '[His] desire for liquid refreshment became something of a problem, [for] Fulton was a dry town.' So wrote the young Margaret Truman, who was astonished by Churchill's capacity for alcohol. After a frantic search, General Vaughan managed to find both liquor and ice for the insatiable Winston. 'Well, General,' joshed Churchill as he poured himself a generous sharpener, 'I am glad to see you. I didn't know whether I was in Fulton Missouri or Fulton Sahara.'[6]

The speech was due to take place just a few hours later, in the gymnasium of Westminster College. Although Fulton was an unremarkable midwestern town, Churchill was performing on a world stage and he dressed to impress his audience, donning the scarlet robes and plush black cap of Oxford University. Thirty thousand locals had flocked to the streets in the hope of glimpsing this near-mythical beast, while the makeshift auditorium was packed to capacity with an expectant crowd.

Truman performed the introductory warm-up. 'I understand that Mr Churchill is going to talk about the sinews of peace,' he said. 'I know he will have something constructive to say to the world.'[7]

Once the president had finished his introduction, Churchill asked for the lights to be dimmed, plunging the auditorium into a gloomy twilight of giant shadows and snapping flashbulbs. This caused dismay among the assembled pressmen, who could pick out little more than Churchill's balding scalp. The British Movietone commentator apologised to viewers for the curtain of darkness that had fallen over the great auditorium. Yet the dark backdrop served its purpose, for the looming shadows merely heightened the drama.

The 'World Citizen', as Truman had called Churchill, made his way to the lectern. He had the air of an ageing warship going doggedly into battle, his stooping shoulders like great oak beams, his bones creaking as they sought to support the giant head. Yet the cannon were primed for action and the old galleon was more than capable of delivering a formidable broadside.

As Churchill approached the podium the three-thousand-strong crowd rose to their feet, clapping, cheering and shouting their praise. Churchill flung his foppish cap onto the nearby chair, nudged his tiny spectacles onto the bridge of his nose and slowly started to speak. 'I am glad to come to Westminster College this afternoon,' he began. 'The name "Westminster" is somehow familiar to me.'

Gone was the rambling Churchill of Yalta and Potsdam; gone were the digressions and interminable anecdotes. 'It is my duty . . . to state facts as I see them to you, to place before you certain facts about the present position in Europe.'

He then launched into the portentous heart of what would soon become the most famous speech of the post-war period. 'From

Stettin in the Baltic to Trieste in the Adriatic, an iron curtain has descended across the Continent.' He was unsparing in both words and actions, slicing the air with a theatrical chop as he growled the words 'iron curtain'. 'Behind that line lie all the capitals of the ancient states of Central and Eastern Europe. Warsaw, Berlin, Prague, Vienna, Budapest, Belgrade, Bucharest and Sofia, all these famous cities and the populations around them lie in what I must call the Soviet sphere and all are subject in one form or another, not only to Soviet influence, but to a very high and in many cases increasing measure of control from Moscow.'

Churchill next addressed the situation in the German capital, issuing a stern wake-up call to his audience. 'An attempt is being made by the Russians in Berlin to build up a quasi-Communist Party in their zone of Occupied Germany by showing special favours to groups of left-wing German leaders.'

Then, in words that could have come straight from the playbook of Frank Howley, he issued a stern injunction on how best to deal with the Soviets. 'I am convinced that there is nothing they admire so much as strength, and there is nothing for which they have less respect than for weakness, especially military weakness.' He called upon the western democracies to stand together in unity, for it was the only way of keeping the Soviet monster at bay. 'If however they become divided or falter in their destiny, and if these all-important years are allowed to slip away, then catastrophe may overwhelm us all.'[8]

Truman had said that Churchill's speech would cause a stir and it did rather more than that. The influential political commentator Walter Lippmann spoke for many when he called it an 'almost catastrophic blunder'.[9] Editorials across the country agreed with Lippmann's assessment: Churchill was accused of causing untold damage in relations between the United States and the Soviet Union. Eleanor Roosevelt, the late president's widow, declared herself outraged while the Wall Street Journal issued a fuming riposte to Churchill's suggestion of a western alliance against the Soviet threat. 'The United States wants no alliance, or anything that resembles an alliance, with any other nation.'[10] This, indeed, had been a corner-stone of American foreign policy ever since George Washington's

Farewell Address in 1796. Many viewed the speech as a deliberate repudiation of the White House's policy of working alongside the Soviets as allies.

Stalin added to the chorus of outrage, describing the speech as 'calculated to sow the seeds of discord between the Allied Governments and make collaboration difficult'. Indeed, he went so far as to label it 'a call to war'.[11] In Britain, too, there was widespread fury, with ninety-three Labour members of parliament tabling a motion of censure against Churchill. His speech, they said, was 'inimical to the cause of world peace'.[12] Even Anthony Eden discouraged Churchill from creating any more 'polemics with Stalin'.[13]

Churchill himself took such criticisms on the chin, confident that he was correct in his analysis. Among the few who did not join the chorus of criticism was the foreign secretary, Ernest Bevin, who was in complete agreement with Churchill's views on Soviet duplicity.

As the recriminations grew ever louder, President Truman did what any politician would do: he denied having any advance knowledge of what the former prime minister was going to say. When pressed on his opinion of the speech, he issued a lame 'no comment'.[14] But he did write to Stalin offering to send the *Missouri* to bring him to the United States so that he could also make a speech in the same venue as Churchill. Stalin declined to leave the snow-bound Soviet capital on grounds of health. 'Age has taken its toll,' he said. 'My doctors tell me I must not travel.'[15]

Winston Churchill's speech came as music to the ears of George Kennan, chargé d'affaires at the American embassy in Moscow. He had been unwell for weeks, laid low 'with cold, fever, sinus, tooth trouble and, finally, the after-effects of the sulfa drugs administered for the relief of these other miseries'.[16] Life was unremittingly depressing. His boss, the ambassador, was absent, his colleagues were on leave and he was beset by a profound malaise. 'Bed-ridden by these various *douleurs*, I suffered the daily take of telegrams and other office business to be brought currently up to my bedroom.'[17] These were indeed 'unhappy days', as he labelled them, and they were made all the more gloomy by news that the Soviets were engaging in yet more trickery, this time over the recently formed World Bank.

Kennan had a naturally retiring disposition and did not enjoy sticking his head above the parapet. Despite his conviction that Truman's performance at Potsdam had been lamentable, he had hitherto confined his frustrations to his wife and his private diary. Not any longer. When asked by Washington for an up-to-date appraisal of Soviet tactics, he threw caution to the wind and fired off a multi-gun salvo. 'It was no good trying to brush the questions off with a couple of routine sentences . . .' he later said. 'It would not do to give them just a fragment of the truth. Here was a case where nothing but the whole truth would do.' He relished the opportunity to do something momentous. 'They had asked for it,' he said. 'Now, by God, they would have it.'[18]

What followed was his 'Long Telegram', a spirited document designed to turn American foreign policy on its head. Blunt, concise and written 'like an eighteenth-century Protestant sermon' – complete with lashings of fire and brimstone – it unsparingly lambasted the Soviet regime.

'At the bottom of the Kremlin's neurotic view of world affairs', wrote Kennan, 'is the traditional and instinctive Russian sense of insecurity.' This insecurity manifested itself in a 'patient but deadly struggle for total destruction [of] rival power'.[19]

He warned that this was particularly the case in hotspots like Berlin, where the Soviets were not to be trusted on any level. 'Everything possible will be done to set major Western powers against each other,' he wrote. 'Anti-British talk will be plugged among Americans, anti-American talk among British.' The Soviets were masters of sowing seeds of mistrust. 'Where suspicions exist, they will be fanned; where not, ignited.'

So his telegram continued – an outpouring of insightful analysis about the extreme dangers of the Soviet regime. In one particularly resonant phrase, he warned that Soviet power 'is impervious to the logic of reason' and 'highly sensitive to the logic of force'.[20] Most importantly, the Kremlin would always back down 'when strong resistance is encountered'. Kennan's message was forthright: the Soviets must be confronted with total resolve.

He sent his Long Telegram to Washington just eleven days before Churchill's speech in Fulton and it was still being circulated, copied and studied. The timing could not have been more perfect, as Kennan himself was quick to point out. 'Six months earlier, this message would probably have been received in the Department of State with raised eyebrows and lips pursed in disapproval.' Six months later and it would have been 'preaching to the converted'. But in the spring of 1946, Kennan's missive was treated as a revelatory gospel. 'If none of my previous literary efforts had seemed to evoke even the faintest tinkle from the bell at which they were aimed, this one, to my astonishment, struck it squarely and set it vibrating with a resonance that was not to die down for many months.'[21]

Kennan's authorship was one reason for the Long Telegram's being taken seriously. Here was someone who had lived in Moscow for years; who knew the Soviet Union intimately; who had regular meetings with Stalin; and who was giving a damning verdict on Soviet machinations. But his warning also coincided with a further bombshell that spring. Hot on the heels of Kennan's telegram came the first report on the Gouzenko affair, released into the public domain by the Canadian Royal Commission in mid-March. This threw a stick of dynamite into the already tense relations between East and West. Articulate and filled with damning evidence, it accused the Soviets of committing espionage in North America and singled out the GRU for particular blame, exposing their efforts to steal atomic secrets.

The revelations caused a sensation around the globe, with lurid newspaper articles about a vast North American spy ring orchestrated by the Soviet regime. The press had got hold of the story in advance of the report's publication, which only heightened the sense of dark treachery. 'Moscow Steals Nuke Secrets!' screamed the *Toronto Daily Star*, while *The Gazette* reported that 'Canada's Exposure of Red Fifth Column Stirs World!'

Such histrionics were wholly absent in Kennan's Long Telegram, which provided a sober, forensic and devastating analysis of the Soviet Union's malign intentions. As its contents gathered traction, it began to change opinions amongst those in the Washington elite. The influential diplomat Charles Bohlen, interpreter at both Yalta and Potsdam, had long been urging a policy of accommodation with the Soviet regime. Not any longer. He now believed that the world was rapidly dividing into 'two irreconcilably hostile camps' and argued that the Americans 'should use every method at its disposal' to counter the Soviet threat.[22]

The Soviets knew nothing of Kennan's telegram, but they responded with manufactured outrage at the manner in which the Gouzenko revelations were being reported, accusing the West of exploiting them for political gain. An editorial in *Izvestia* accused the Canadian prime minister of launching 'this anti-Soviet campaign without considering that such action is contrary to normal relations between states . . .' His actions, it said, were certain to be doomed. 'King and his friends have forgotten the lessons of history, where there are a number of examples of failure of anti-Soviet adventures.'[23]

Over in Berlin, Frank Howley was planning his own anti-Soviet adventure, having grown increasingly infuriated by America's 'hands-across-the-Iron-Curtain cranks', as he called those who wanted to understand the Russians. 'Understand them?' he fumed. 'That's beyond the power of any Westerner.' But he warned that 'the Russians understand us perfectly' and knew exactly how to get what they wanted.[24] In Howley's opinion, enough was enough. It was time for confrontation.

II

Ministry of Lies

FRANK HOWLEY HAD grown used to expecting the unexpected in Berlin but even he was taken by surprise when he attended a meeting of the Kommandatura at the end of April 1946. The Russian team had undergone a radical purge. Lieutenant-General Smirnov had disappeared without a trace, never to be seen again, and his deputy had been removed due to 'terrible stomach wounds received during the war'.[1] Why these wounds had only now become an issue was unclear but it seemed likely that he, like everyone else, was being punished for the botched attempt to rig the party merger.

Other members of the Soviet entourage had also disappeared, departing on a one-way train to Moscow. Among the few who remained was the shadowy Mr Maximov, with his NKVD raincoat and sprig of white lilac. He had almost certainly played a malign role in the purge of his erstwhile comrades.

The incoming team was headed by a pugnacious heavyweight named General Alexander Kotikov, instantly recognisable by his mesmerising eyes, his quiff of silver hair and his blunted turnip of a nose, the latter the result of being kicked in the face by a horse when young. Howley knew nothing about General Kotikov when he first pitched up in Berlin and was unaware that he had been selected by Moscow because he could be trusted to punch hard and low. He was also a committed Communist. At the age of fifteen, he and his friends had ripped off their baptismal crosses as a gesture of solidarity with Lenin's Bolsheviks. 'By this act', said Kotikov, 'we were joining the revolution.'[2] It was the beginning of a blood-and-guts adventure that would see him fight the Nazis at both Moscow and Leningrad, before taking part in the capture of Berlin.

Kotikov was unusually gregarious for a Soviet general and had a flamboyant charm that was wholly absent in the other members of his team. His Berlin office was furnished with an impressive rank of ten telephones, the most striking of which was made from gleaming white Bakelite. 'It might have belonged to a Hollywood actress,' remarked the journalist Karl Schwarz. 'It wasn't quite like what I had expected a Communist general's office to be.'[3]

Kotikov was still an unknown quantity when introduced to his three Allied colleagues. Brigadier Hinde was determined to forge a good working relationship with him and went so far as to offer him a gift of three hunting dogs. 'In return,' said a gracious Kotikov, 'I would ask you to accept a sportsman's gift – a shotgun.'[4] Howley was more reluctant to engage with the Soviet newcomer because he sensed that the Kommandatura was at a turning point. 'Was the Russian policy to be softened towards the Western democracies?' he wondered. 'Was Kotikov sent in because of his knowledge of politics to effectively help the Communist Party?'[5]

The Soviet commander certainly made a favourable impression at his first Kommandatura meeting, addressing his fellow members with courteous charm. 'I'm new here to the Kommandatura,' he said. 'You, my colleagues, are doubtless more familiar with this question. Won't you let me have your words and advice on the matter?'[6]

Howley came close to being won over, but the fact that such words were coming from the mouth of a Soviet official gave him pause. Over the days that followed he began to wonder if Kotikov was actually a master of dissimulation, sent to Berlin because he 'was an expert on conference technique'.[7]

This was indeed correct. Kotikov was a highly skilled operator who outclassed all who had come before him. 'In striking contrast to his predecessors,' said Howley, 'he brought a new dialectical weapon to the Kommandatura. He was the first to use humility, and use it effectively.' He would feign ignorance, 'begging the speaker to expound more fully, please'. Howley soon saw through this deceit and immediately took against him. 'His humility was as unctuous as Uriah Heep's and, being as serpentine, was as poisonous as a sting.'[8]

Yet he remained captivated by Kotikov. It was as if this were the enemy he had wanted all along, a tough-playing fullback whose role was to expel the western Allies from Berlin. His gregariousness only added to the allure: Kotikov was to prove a most fulsome host, throwing lavish soirées at which the vodka flowed as swiftly as the Don.

'Well we've worked, we've talked, now let's eat,' he would roar as he led the others into the adjoining banqueting room. Curt Riess was witness to one of these feasts. Riess was no stranger to excess, but Kotikov's lavish entertainments outclassed those of everyone else. 'Along the whole length of an enormous table stood the slender towers of bottles: Moskowskaya brand vodka, red Crimean champagne, sweet wines, French cognac, Pilsner beers. There were bowls of Strasbourg pâté de foie gras, roast chicken, game, huge glass bowls of red and black caviar. There were lobsters, oysters, turkey with truffles, every imaginable fish, salads, salmon, sturgeon and mountains of white bread and butter.'

In the midst of the banquet was Kotikov himself, 'the personification of jollity', who repeatedly slapped everyone on the back as a sign of hearty goodwill. 'He was constantly toasting the health of someone,' noted Riess, 'the Mayor, the city administration, the progressive populace of Berlin, and with each toast everyone had to empty his glass.' By the end of the banquet, the entire room (with the exception of Kotikov himself) was completely drunk. 'Apparently, alcohol did not affect him.'[9]

Howley's opinion of the general would grow more damning with every passing month, but not everyone was so negative. Kotikov's adoring daughter, Svetlana, wrote a fulsome vignette about her father's love of children, his loyal dogs Rex and Ralph, and the wicked pleasure he took in haggling with Moscow's street vendors. With wincingly saccharine sentiment, she explained that her father encouraged Berliners to go to the opera 'because he thought that if your heart is open to beauty and honesty then goodness will prevail'.[10]

Kotikov's arrival in Berlin coincided with the departure of Howley's oft-absent boss, Major General Ray Barker. Barker held a farewell dinner at his villa on the shores of the Wannsee and invited Kotikov, Howley, Hinde and Lançon. No sooner had they sat down at the elaborately furnished table than Barker put his Soviet counterpart through a curious little mind-game. It was so peculiar, indeed, that it forms one of the few memorable passages in Kotikov's turgid memoirs. The Soviet general describes how General Barker picked up his artfully folded napkin, crushed it into a tight ball and then handed it to the Soviet general and asked him to refold it.

The challenge was laced with enough menace to give Kotikov an unexpected thrill. 'I took the crumpled napkin and examined it carefully. Some faint traces of creases were still just visible. Slowly and carefully, deliberately taking my time, I folded the napkin and passed it back to Barker.'

His napkin mission accomplished, Kotikov now made capital out of it. 'As far as I can see, general, sir,' he said with irreproachable politeness, 'you've entrusted your successor the task of messing up the napkins of Berlin. And you've assigned to me the role of the one to make them straight again.' The Soviet general clamped his steel-blue eyes firmly onto those of his host. 'Let's hope that this collaboration of ours will run as smoothly as your little joke did just now. But to be honest, I wish we applied our efforts elsewhere, rather than playing with dinner napkins.'[11]

Frank Howley was convinced that Kotikov had been despatched to Berlin for a specific mission. 'From the volume of notes he carried and his generally aggressive attitude, it was obvious he had been sent by Moscow with definite orders to get the new Communist Party going.' Not only that, he was also there 'to control Berlin and to harass the Western allies'.[12]

As the summer of 1946 approached, the heat inside the Kommandatura building intensified. While Brigadier Hinde remained scrupulously polite, the battles between Howley and Kotikov became intensely personal. This was exactly how Howley wanted it to be, for he had long believed that the biggest mouth made the loudest noise. 'Personalities', he said, 'determined which nation was most influential.'[13]

Kotikov's account of their feuding reads like a mirror image of Howley's. 'The allies were all smiles,' he said. 'They developed this deceitful diplomacy of smiles into an art form, perverted as it was.

They used it every time they wanted to mislead us, to conceal their true motives, to muddy the waters.' He expressed sadness at the steady breakdown in relations: 'What a striking difference there was between these "new" Americans and their compatriots whom we got to know in April 1945 on the River Elbe. There, on the Elbe, we shared a common sentiment, to crush fascism as soon as possible.'[14]

There were the occasional light-hearted moments, yet even these were fraught with tension. On one occasion, Brigadier Hinde invited everyone to accompany him on a wild boar hunt in Spandau forest, an invitation that was eagerly accepted. Howley and Hinde came equipped with hunting rifles and were aghast to discover that Kotikov and his men had come armed with submachine guns. As a troop of boar crashed out of the undergrowth, the Russians opened up with everything they had.

'I hit the dust,' recalled Howley as he found himself caught in a maelstrom of Soviet bullets. Hinde's British party also fell to the ground, 'frantically burying their heads in leaves to escape the Russian fusillade'. When they eventually looked up, the ground was covered with dead boar. 'It was practically the second Battle of Berlin,' said Howley, who noted that Kotikov's deputy had killed five of the animals and wounded many more.[15] The British were left speechless by the lack of fair play. 'The blighters!' fumed one as he went over to examine the massacre.[16]

Among the many challenges facing Brigadier Hinde that spring was that of purging the British sector of all remaining Nazis. Denazification was a cornerstone policy of the four occupying powers and every German over the age of eighteen was required to fill in a *Fragebogen*, or questionnaire, answering 130 questions about his or her previous employment, income and education. 'What political party did you vote for in the November election of 1932? What did you vote for in March 1933?' Some questions were as obscure as they were bizarre. 'What titles of nobility were ever held by you or your wife or by the parents or grandparents of either of you?'[17] Hinde's specialists assessed these questionnaires and placed each respondent on a sliding scale of guilt. At one end were the active henchmen of the Nazi regime: Gestapo members, prison guards and brutal SS thugs. At the other end were the unwilling travellers who had joined the Nazi Party because it was the ticket to a quieter life. Penalties ranged from imprisonment to exclusion from employment, while those found free of guilt were given a certificate that became known as a *Persil-Schein* or 'Persil Ticket' on the grounds that its holder was 'whiter' than the brand of washing powder to which it referred.

Hinde viewed denazification as a vital part of the post-war cleansing process. 'We should be guided by the principle that if denazification is worth doing, it is worth doing thoroughly.' He urged his team to read a pamphlet produced by Frank Howley's unit: it was entitled 'Are There Any Good Nazis?' 'When you have read it,' he said, 'you will probably agree with me that there are none.'[18]

Berlin's four ruling powers formed specialist bureaux to oversee the denazification process, a wise decision given the complexity of the task. One such bureau, 'Cultural Affairs', was tasked with vetting Berliners wishing to resume work in the world of the arts. No one was to be granted a licence unless they could prove they had a clean slate. It sounded easy enough on paper, but it was dependent upon agreement among the four powers, and this was in increasingly short supply in that fraught spring of 1946.

Brigadier Hinde's representative was Major Kaye Sely, a Munich-born bon viveur whose approach to denazification immediately raised eyebrows. Not only did he disagree with his American, French and Soviet colleagues, but he also criticised the unbending approach of his boss. He intended to take a far more relaxed approach than that of Brigadier Hinde, turning a blind eye to all but the worst offenders. 'What's it matter whether a road-sweeper, butcher, baker, candle-stick maker was or was not in the party?' he said. 'We waste time, energy and money catching those little fish in our net.'[19] Sely was hunting the big game and was not interested in the minor players. His laissez-faire approach threw him into immediate conflict with the American representative, Ralph Brown, who took his cue from Frank Howley. 'If there is the slightest smell of Nazism, out they go.'[20]

The French attitude was radically different, and perfectly encapsulated by their Gauloises-smoking representative, Michel Bouquet. He found the whole process a pointless chore. One of Hinde's men noted wryly that the French detested all Germans, not just those who were Nazis. 'If one could have degermanised the Germans, the French would have been enthusiastically for it.'[21] But they had no interest in determining the level of someone's guilt.

The Soviet approach was altogether more duplicitous. Anthony Mann conducted an undercover investigation into their activities and discovered a disturbing twin-track policy. In public, they were deeply hostile to former Nazis, but in private they took a very different approach. 'If any German had special skills or knowledge useful to the Soviet authorities,' he said, 'his Nazi past was irrelevant.'[22]

This was true enough. The Lux Hotel revolutionary, Wolfgang Leonhard, admitted that skilled Nazis were offered immediate employment: '[It was] a question of *how* can we use them.' If they were ready to co-operate, 'they immediately got high positions'.[23]

Former henchmen of the Third Reich were encouraged to switch sides by being offered a stark choice – incarceration or promotion: 'We have your documents, we can put you in prison for ten years, we can send you for ten years to Siberia. Or you can have a second chance. If you sign [a contract] that you will work with us, you can live in peace and, even more, we can promote you.'[24] It was a policy that worked. 'Thousands of former higher Nazis immediately became informers for the NKVD, the Soviet state security.'

The four powers forged a consensus of sorts in the early stages of denazification, but this was to be abruptly shredded by the arrival from Moscow of a Soviet colonel named Sergei Tiulpanov. Ruthless and intellectually brilliant, Colonel Tiulpanov quickly realised there was political capital to be made out of denazification. With a single-mindedness that stunned all who witnessed it, he set out to exploit this capital.

Tiulpanov was the incoming head of the Soviet Information Bureau, working closely with General Kotikov. It was a uniquely powerful post, for Tiulpanov was in charge of every aspect of culture, including theatre, cinema, journalism and propaganda. His fiefdom included the whole of Soviet-occupied Germany, but it was in Berlin that he was to fight his sharpest battles.

He cut an unmistakable figure in the streets of the capital on account of his punch-bag physiognomy. 'His face, his manner, his whole appearance immediately arrested my attention,' wrote the American information officer, Nicolas Nabokov. 'His head was clean-shaven and had large protruding ears. It was totally neckless, like an oversized billiard ball on a short, well-built body.'[25]

Tiulpanov eschewed military decorations, apart from a discreet red star, and looked so ill at ease in uniform that one acquaintance described him as 'a civilian in disguise'.[26] Unlike General Kotikov, he had turned down lodgings in the secure Karlshorst compound and opted instead for a sprawling villa in Weissensee. From here, he ran a mini-empire that inspired admiration and fear. 'If Tiulpanov so much as crosses the street, it means something,' said one terrified Soviet functionary.[27]

Charming but choleric, he did not suffer fools gladly. He lambasted a sycophantic Berlin theatre director for his praise of a dreadful Soviet movie. 'Why don't you tell us the truth?' he snapped. 'We've had quite enough arse-crawlers who find everything we do wonderful.'[28]

Tiulpanov's encyclopaedic knowledge of Germanic culture made him a formidable enemy to the Western allies. He had studied at the University of Heidelberg and could discuss Goethe's writings with the insight of an academic. He even kept a statue of the writer on his desk. By the summer of 1946, Tiulpanov was influencing public opinion in every sphere of culture. His principal mission was to win the hearts and minds of Berliners, not an easy task given the raping and looting that had taken place in the recent past. 'There was an urgent need', said one, 'to prove that the country of Pushkin, Tolstoy, Dostoevsky, Chekov and Gorki was cultured and civilised.'[29] Tiulpanov aimed to demonstrate that Russians and Germans shared a love of high culture, unlike the uncouth, gum-chewing Americans, or the middle-brow British with their preposterous Gilbert and Sullivan operettas.

To assist him in his task, he had picked a team of intellectuals who understood that culture was the perfect vehicle for propaganda. Tiulpanov's deputy, Alexander Dymshitz, was a former professor at Leningrad University with a deep knowledge of German history. Other recruits brought specific skills that would help them in the task ahead. 'Virtually all Russian culture officers were carefully selected specialists,' said the British officer, George Clare. 'They had a lot going for them.'[30]

They rapidly restored the city's principal concert halls and encouraged Berlin's finest performers to return to work, even if they had been enthusiastic Nazis. One of the first concerts they organised was Beethoven's *Fidelio* at the State Opera. It was a profoundly moving experience for the Berlin audience, for whom a night at the opera seemed to belong to the distant past.

Curt Riess studied Tiulpanov's manoeuvring with appalled fascination. The Soviet was a formidable enemy with an ambitious goal. 'He wanted to bring all of Berlin under Russian control,' said Riess. 'It was going to be a fast, surprise assault which would not give the Western powers a chance to recover their balance.'[31]

One of Sergei Tiulpanov's most powerful propaganda tools was Radio Berlin, whose studios had been captured intact in May 1945. None of the broadcasters was subjected to denazification. According to one American intelligence agent, the station continued 'with the same personnel that had been there under the Nazis . . . [They] just changed the colours of their shirts.'[32]

The Soviet colonel encouraged these broadcasters to sharpen their attacks on Frank Howley, by now the number one enemy in Berlin. Howley himself was quick to notice the change in tone. 'Any time that Soviet Radio Berlin could think up something defamatory or insulting about me,' he wrote, 'the air was full of my misdeeds.'[33] Tiulpanov was also the Svengali figure who pulled the strings of the Soviet-backed newspapers. He told editors that the Americans and British were no longer to be referred to as allies. Rather, they were to be described as 'imperialists' or 'aggressors'. Colonel Howley was once again his prime target. Newspapers began to refer to him as 'the brute colonel', 'dictator' or 'terrorist', monikers that brought Howley consider-able pride.[34] 'After being an "enemy of democracy," he wrote, 'I achieved the ultimate in perverse recognition when I was dubbed the "Beast of Berlin".'[35] One observer compared Tiulpanov's propaganda skills to those of Joseph Goebbels: 'Like Goebbels, he had almost unlimited power; like Hitler's Propaganda Minister, he could not bear being contradicted.'[36]

Frank Howley was not alone in being taken aback by the ferocity of Tiulpanov's propaganda. Lucius Clay expressed his concern at 'the constant unremitting daily attacks on everything American . . . our system of government . . . our president . . . the American military'.[37] He felt that the Americans were being comprehensively outflanked and needed to launch an immediate and sustained counter-attack. They did this by overhauling the existing American radio station, RIAS,* and using it to counter Tiulpanov's smears.

The ensuing war of the aerial waves was to prove every bit as dangerous as a military ground offensive. A sign of how seriously the Americans took this battle came when they appointed their Berlin intelligence chief, William Heimlich, to lead it. Not only was he an expert in intelligence, but he was also experienced in broadcasting and marketing. He immediately launched Operation Backtalk, an aggressive fight-back against Soviet propaganda.

Heimlich's first task was to transform RIAS into a round-the-clock operation. When fully powered, this self-styled 'free voice of the free world' could reach as far as Poland and Czechoslovakia.[38] When its signal was jammed by the Soviets, Heimlich sent RIAS loudspeaker vans into the streets in order to broadcast directly to Berliners.

Heimlich never broadcast straight propaganda. Rather, he offered Berliners something more seductive – news, special programmes for women, serials for children and witty cabaret shows of a sort that had never been heard before on German radio. Above all he offered humour, aware that this was his greatest weapon in the fight against Tiulpanov.

'When we were attacked, we never came back with vituperation.

* Radio In American Sector.

We came back with laughter. We made a joke of the attacks made upon us.' It was a recipe that worked. Within a few months, eight out of every ten Berliners were tuning into RIAS each day, a far greater number than those listening to Tiulpanov's Radio Berlin.

Heimlich even poked fun at Tiulpanov himself, especially when he learned that the colonel had quarrelled with William Pieck and threatened him with deportation to a gulag. 'We agree with Tiulpanov,' announced the tongue-in-cheek broadcaster. 'Germans who won't obey *should* be threatened.'[39] He added that the Americans would soon be deporting Berliners to Texas, a joke that raised many smiles as it was said that everyone's dream that summer was a one-way ticket to Texas.

Brigadier Hinde's officers were sorely out of their depth when facing Tiulpanov's team of experts. There were few German specialists serving in British Military Government and none who could match Tiulpanov's encyclopaedic knowledge of German art and culture. Hinde's theatre and music officer was a young Irishman named Pat Lynch who was chirpy, gregarious and full of jokes. But – said George Clare – he was 'no match for the Dymshitzes of Berlin'.

Lynch was said to have landed the job because he had once been an opera singer. 'Opera singer, me arse!' he scoffed when Clare asked him if this was true. He said he had spotted a newspaper advert for administrative jobs in Berlin and immediately applied, even though he had no idea what sort of employment was on offer.

At his interview, Lynch was asked if he was interested in music. 'I *love* it,' he said with his trademark grin, and explained how he had once sung in the chorus of the Ilford Amateur Operatic Society. He also 'went on a bit about Wagner', gabbling anecdotes in his thick Irish brogue.[40] After ten minutes of chatter he was offered the job of theatre and music officer in Berlin. Within a week he had taken up his post in the German capital, where he was to find himself competing with the intellectual powerhouse of Tiulpanov's inner circle.

The ensuing battle for Berlin's musical soul was to be focussed on a single man, the legendary conductor of the Berlin Philharmonic Orchestra, Wilhelm Furtwängler. 'Of all the famous names in German art,' said George Clare, 'there was none more illustrious, none more controversial.' He described Furtwängler as the 'most august of all Olympians'.[41]

Furtwängler was a household name in Germany and instantly recognisable because of his strikingly high forehead and deliberately dishevelled hair. Sixty-one years of age, and a towering presence in the cultural life of the country, he had also achieved global fame. In 1936 he had been offered (but turned down) the post of principal conductor of the New York Philharmonic, arguably the most prestigious musical role in the world.

Furtwängler had been compromised by his years under Nazism and opinion was sharply divided as to whether he should be allowed to return to his previous post. His supporters argued that he had done much to protect Jewish musicians in the capital, assisting them in getting immigration papers. 'Can you name me a Jew on whose behalf Furtwängler has *not* intervened?' sneered a director of the Nazi Ministry of Culture.[42] The conductor had also spoken out against the Nazi regime, refused to join the party and never gave the Nazi salute, even in Hitler's presence. But he had accepted the honorary title of Prussian state councillor and had performed at a number of Nazi functions, including the infamous Nuremberg Rally of 1935. He had also conducted a special celebratory concert for Hitler's fifty-third birthday. In the eyes of the western Allies, he was tainted by association.

Colonel Tiulpanov's team took a rather different approach, as Nicolas Nabokov was quick to note. 'The problem of "clean hands" in regard to the Nazis and collaborators didn't bother them,' he said. Although they claimed to follow the rules laid down by the Kommandatura, they 'disregarded them completely whenever they found them to be obstacles'.[43] Tiulpanov had no compunction about disregarding them when dealing with Wilhelm Furtwängler.

The German conductor was living in Vienna at the war's end and undertook the obligatory process of denazification. He was eventually given a clean record by the Viennese tribunal, his first step back into public life. This did not go unnoticed by Sergei Tiulpanov, who saw a unique opportunity to exploit Furtwängler's fame. His first act was to publish an open letter in the Soviet-backed *Berliner Zeitung*. 'Germany needs the artist Wilhelm

Furtwängler,' wrote Tiulpanov. 'Your birthplace appeals to you to return to it. The home of your true fame and world-wide successes, so indissolubly linked to the Berlin Philharmonic Orchestra, appeals to you to come back.'[44]

After intense lobbying and behind-the-scenes negotiations, Tiulpanov pulled off his greatest cultural coup and Furtwängler landed in Berlin. He did so on a Soviet plane at a Soviet airfield. He was given a hero's welcome. 'As his plane touched down, he was welcomed by representatives of the Soviet Administration . . . one of the Russian officers, a Captain Barski, immediately attached himself to Furtwängler as his "minder" and drove him to his grace-and-favour apartment.' This was in Frederick the Great's Sanssouci Palace in Potsdam. Tiulpanov had even installed Furtwängler's old grand piano, which they had 'to recover from some Red Army soldiers who had "borrowed" it'.[45]

George Clare was on hand to witness Furtwängler's arrival and realised that the Soviets had pulled off a masterstroke. 'Tiulpanov had his triumph,' he said. 'He was giving back to the German capital its most glorious living cultural monument.'[46]

The western Allies exploded when they learned what the Soviet colonel had done: this was a cultural coup too far. His American opposite number, General Robert McClure, issued a 'curt and icy statement' saying that the denazification certificate issued in Vienna was not valid in Berlin and that Furtwängler was banned from public life by Allied Control Council Directive No. 24. He would remain banned until cleared by Berlin's denazification committee.[47]

The Soviets simply ignored McClure and offered Furtwängler the directorship of the State Opera, which was in their sector (the Berlin Philharmonic was in the American sector). Furtwängler wisely declined any formal contract, but he swiftly resumed his conducting career with the backing of the Russians. Berliners were as ecstatic as Sergei Tiulpanov and his colleagues, who mocked the western powers for their strict adherence to the rules. 'It's ridiculous to force the world's greatest conductor to queue up like everyone else,' said one.[48]

Eventually even General McClure would relent. Furtwängler was permitted to conduct the Berlin Philharmonic at the American requisitioned Titania-Palast cinema. The orchestra played Beethoven to wild acclaim and Furtwängler was applauded for a full fifteen minutes. Many in the British and American administrations felt they had missed a trick in not backing Furtwängler from the outset. Not for the first time, and not for the last, Tiulpanov had gained the upper hand.

12

Crime and Punishment

BRITAIN'S FOREIGN SECRETARY, Ernest Bevin, worked tirelessly for the rebuilding of a shattered Europe throughout the spring and summer of 1946. In April and May he attended the Council of Foreign Ministers meeting in Paris, spending as many as nine hours a day in acrimonious arguments with his Soviet opposite number, Vyacheslav Molotov. Working alongside his American and French partners, James Byrnes and Georges Bidault, Bevin haggled over the future of Greece, the Balkans, Iran, Italian reparations and Trieste. A great deal was at stake. 'The choice', said the *Manchester Guardian*, 'is no longer between a good peace or a bad peace, but between a bad peace and no peace at all. And no peace is dangerously close to war.'[1]

The intensity of the negotiations took a physical toll on Bevin, an unfit man in his sixties. His physician, Dr Alec McCall, said that he didn't have a sound organ in his body, with the exception of his feet. He was suffering from angina pectoris, cardiac failure, arteriosclerosis, an enlarged liver, damaged kidneys and high blood pressure. He was also overweight and smoked heavily. His heart – 'the old ticker', as Bevin called it – was so weak that he could no longer cross the Atlantic by plane.[2]

In July 1946, Bevin returned to the French capital for a further two months in order to attend the Paris Peace Conference, at which the four foreign ministers were to negotiate peace treaties with Italy, Finland, Hungary, Romania and Bulgaria. Once the treaties were ratified, those nations that had been formerly aligned with the Axis were to be allowed to join the nascent United Nations.

The Peace Conference soon descended into a heated confrontation between the western Allies and the Soviets. Molotov opened the attack on 9 July when he accused the British and Americans of failing to disarm the German armed forces, as agreed at Potsdam. When he made further mischief at an alcohol-fuelled dinner that night, Bevin exploded in rage. According to Charles Bohlen, 'he rose to his feet, his hands knotted into fists, and started toward Molotov saying, "I've had enough of this, I 'ave."' Everyone present was astonished. 'For one glorious moment it looked as if the Foreign Minister of Great Britain and the Foreign Minister of the Soviet Union were about to come to blows.' Just in time, the security people closed in on Bevin 'and the incident was over'.[3]

On the following day, Molotov made a speech that was less confrontational but no less contentious. He said that the Soviet Union no longer wanted Germany split into two halves: rather, it sought a unified German state under a central administration. But this policy came with an unmentioned price tag – the envisaged administration was to be unabashedly pro-Moscow.

Bevin countered this proposal by arguing that rebuilding the German economy should be given priority over reparations. '*Nyet*,' was Molotov's curt response. This left the American secretary of state to spell out the agreed-upon response of the western powers.[4] The Americans and British would henceforth treat their zones of Germany as an economic whole, to be known as Bizonia, with jointly run agencies for food and the economy. Their intention was for the western half of Germany to be self-sufficient by the end of 1949.

This policy held particular appeal for Bevin, who was eager to start rebuilding countries shattered by the war. Yet the satisfaction of striking the Bizonia deal with the Americans did nothing to improve his health. He was sleeping little and drinking heavily – his secretary said he used alcohol like a car used petrol. On 25 July, after a heated debate in the House of Commons, Bevin collapsed with a heart attack.

This might have spelled the end of his political career but, remarkably, he was back at his desk in Whitehall after a fortnight's convalescence. He was not yet ready to abandon his task of forging the security of post-war Europe.

★

Walter Ulbricht had spent that spring and summer tightening his grip on Berlin. He had purged disloyal Communist activists and shoe-horned his own supporters into the judiciary and police. He had also ensured that local boroughs were in the grip of Communist allies. Berlin was almost in his pocket, but he now faced a major challenge: elections to the City Assembly, which were scheduled for 20 October 1946, threatened his hegemony over Berlin's most important institution. Ulbricht was a leader in need of a plan.

The election was to be the first formal showdown between east and west and its significance was lost on no one. For the first time since the collapse of the Third Reich, Berliners were being asked to vote for politicians to represent them. These politicians would, in turn, elect delegates to serve on the Assembly's executive body, the Magistrat, currently dominated by Ulbricht's appointees. It was clear to everyone that the very soul of Berlin was at stake. If the democratic parties came out on top, it would be a huge fillip for the western Allies. Ulbricht's cronies would be swept away and his ascent to power would be compromised, if not fatally stalled. But if the Socialist Unity Party won, it would be a triumph for the Soviets and their German Communist allies. The city would be theirs for the taking.

No sooner had the election been announced than the Soviet propaganda machine shifted into gear. Ulbricht knew that his best way of snatching victory from the western Allies was to use misinformation and dirty tricks. He was to do this with the enthusiastic support of General Kotikov and Colonel Tiulpanov, who both swung into action. 'They offered bribes, not on the niggardly scale of politicians handing out cigars, but like victorious Caesars fêting the Roman masses. Their bribes were city-wide, ranging from free notebooks for school children to food and electric power.'[5] So wrote Frank Howley, who added that 'the tricks the Russians concocted made other crooked political bosses look like Boy Scouts.'[6]

Curt Riess had never witnessed such blatant corruption occurring in the shadows of a supposedly democratic election. The Soviet regime was offering a simple transaction: bribes for votes. 'They distributed thirty million cigarettes, sixty thousand pairs of shoes for children; every man received a bottle of whisky and every woman a pint-sized bottle [of alcohol].' Riess overheard locals referring to the gifts as 'election bacon' – a play on the German proverb, 'Good bacon catches the mice.'[7]

But Frank Howley had some election bacon of his own. He had spent the summer developing a strategy for electoral victory, one he called Aggressive Neutrality. It was a disingenuous little oxymoron: while his strategy was certainly aggressive, it was never neutral and nor was it intended to be.

'The official American view was that we were in favour of no party and against no party,' he wrote. 'However, only a fool would say that the US would be indifferent to a Communist victory in Berlin.'[8] It was certainly no coincidence that the American secretary of state, James F. Byrnes, delivered a keynote speech in Germany on 6 September, six weeks before the election. He arrived in style, flanked by troops, armoured cars and tanks in order to convey a message of reassurance to both Berlin and the rest of Germany. 'I want no misunderstanding,' he said. 'We will not shirk our duty. We are not withdrawing. We are staying here.'[9]

Byrnes's speech was the launch-pad for a gloves-off election campaign that would see Ulbricht and his supporters pitching their formidable powers against Frank Howley and his team, with Brigadier Hinde and General Lançon playing supporting roles for the western Allies.

The first hint of trouble came when General Kotikov announced that fruit and vegetables imported into Berlin from the Soviet zone would henceforth be distributed only to the east of the city. It was his way of demonstrating to the populace that the Soviets had food whereas the western Allies did not. Howley delivered a swift counter-punch, warning that 'two can play at that game.'[10] He said that if Kotikov carried out this threat, he would hire a fleet of American planes and have huge quantities of fresh oranges, lemons and grapefruit flown in from California. These would then be distributed to every sector of the city, accompanied by leaflets informing Berliners of the Soviet mischief. Kotikov rarely backed down when dealing with Howley but on this occasion he chose prudence over rashness and withdrew his threat. But the damage was done, and Howley exploited it by using his formidable network of media contacts to inform Berliners of Kotikov's plan. 'As an electoral weapon', he said, 'the Russian plot boomeranged.'[11]

Kotikov next shut off electric power to the west of the city in order to boost it in the east, a simple enough manoeuvre given that one of the main generators was at Chernowitz in Soviet-occupied Germany. Once again, Howley informed the press.

Howley would later write with considerable glee about his exploitation of the media: 'We authorized an afternoon paper, *Der Abend*, and supplied enough paper for 100,000 circulation. We increased the circulation of *Der Tagesspiegel* to 400,000 and I saw to it that western, particularly American, ideas were expressed in these papers and expressed forcefully.'[12] He used this local media, as well as the Allies' radio station, RIAS, to highlight the weaknesses of Ulbricht's manifesto, which he described as being based 'upon falsehood, based upon lies, based upon intimidation, based upon phony promises of Utopia'.[13]

Howley provided few additional details about his behind-the-scenes practices, but Curt Riess was quietly investigating the political manoeuvring taking place on both sides and noted that the Americans had just as many electoral hand-outs as the Soviets. His tally of items distributed to voters in the west of the city included 'a million boxes of matches, 155,000 pairs of shoes, 16,000 bicycle tyres, 3,000 automobile tyres, 19,000 tons of cement, 1,200 square metres of window glass, 200 tons of paper and 5,000 tons of structural steel'.[14]

As election day approached, Colonel Tiulpanov's propaganda machine became a round-the-clock operation as it sought to gain votes for Walter Ulbricht's supporters. Ulbricht received additional help from General Kotikov's deputy, who blocked the centrist parties from holding rallies in the Soviet sector. Ulbricht's supporters were also aided in distributing cakes, biscuits and much-needed school notebooks. These notebooks were stamped with the Socialist Unity Party logo and bore a disingenuous message inside: 'This paper is being given to you, dear children, rather than being used for propaganda purposes, because we know of your great need for notebook paper.'[15]

Brigadier Hinde rarely lost his temper at the Kommandatura but he was apoplectic when shown one of these notebooks. He viewed the targeting of children as unforgivable and castigated Kotikov in thunderous tones, delivering 'a terrific oration against the pollution of children's minds'. He demanded that the notebooks be withdrawn, but Kotikov refused to back down insisting that they were nothing but 'an innocuous honest gift'.[16]

Harold Hays noted every twist and turn in the election campaign and saw that the situation was rapidly spinning out of control. When he walked through the eastern districts of the city on the eve of the vote he could scarcely believe the quantity of Soviet propaganda. 'So great was the supply of paper to the Communist Party that on the night before the elections, they were actually shovelling pamphlets into the streets from three-ton lorries, so that some areas were literally carpeted with paper.'[17]

Howley also took a trip into the Soviet sector, driving through the crowded streets in his black convertible Horch. 'The entire sector reminded me of a newsreel version of the Red Square celebrating the October Revolution,' he said, 'with Red banners and huge slogans strung across the streets.'[18] He noticed that the posters for the Socialist Unity Party were being defaced with flyers bearing a bitter-ironic slogan: 'Were you raped by the Russians? If so, of course vote for the SED.'[19]

At Walter Ulbricht's headquarters at 80 Prinzenallee the mood was upbeat as the final poll approached. Wolfgang Leonhard was monitoring events closely and felt that victory was assured: 'Every report came in here and we could at once form the best possible picture of what was going on. In anticipation of our victory . . . huge loud speakers had been put up in front of the editorial building to publish the results to the crowds assembled outside.'[20] No less optimistic was the Communist journalist Karl Schwarz, who was at party headquarters. 'Cases of liquor were already assembled for a victory celebration. It was expected that the Communists would win a clear majority.'[21]

Harold Hays decided to watch the unfolding results at the city's assembly hall, where there was to be a minute-by-minute update of the incoming results. 'At one end a great board had been erected on which the results were recorded. At the side of the hall, the girls worked on power machines, calculating the returns.'[22] The clock struck eight. The polls closed. Ballot boxes were sealed and despatched to the count. Hays detected a tangible sense of nervousness among the western Allies, prompted in part by the confidence of Ulbricht and his team.

The first results came just before midnight and it immediately became clear that this was to be a night to remember. There was a stunned silence at Ulbricht's headquarters. 'The announcer who was to publish the results to the crowds outside was tearing his hair.' The first counted ballots suggested that the Socialist Unity Party was about to suffer a catastrophic defeat. Wolfgang Leonhard could scarcely believe this reversal of fortune. 'One piece of bad news after another,' he said. 'Our faces became longer and longer . . . [and] with every few minutes that passed, the situation grew worse.'[23]

By the early hours of the morning, the results were clear. Ulbricht's party had suffered a massive blow, taking a meagre 19.8 per cent of the vote. Its centrist rivals had won a landslide 48.7 per cent. The campaign of propaganda, bribery and intimidation had backfired spectacularly and Wolfgang Leonhard thought he knew why. 'To the men in the street, we were known as the "Russian" party . . . They had voted against us because they saw in us a party dependent on the Soviet Union.'[24] Ruth Andreas-Friedrich expressed the same sentiment in her diary that very evening, only she overlaid it with pithy sarcasm. 'The women of Berlin have decided against their Russian lovers,' she wrote.[25]

Despite Allied fears of an electoral upset, the Americans had an extremely accurate idea of the likely result for they had hired the services of George Gallup, the analytics expert whose company had surged to fame after correctly forecasting the 1936 presidential election. Gallup's Berlin predictions were similarly accurate. 'His advisers had drawn up correct estimates to fractions of percentages.'[26]

While still at the count, Harold Hays bumped into Arthur Pieck, son of Wilhelm Pieck, the co-chairman of the Socialist Unity Party. Hays found Pieck utterly disheartened. 'He looked a shattered and disillusioned man . . . he mumbled something unintelligible and then blurted out: "We shall change this undemocratic result."' Hays himself was cock-a-hoop that the Soviets' corrupt practices had failed. 'Everything was tried in Berlin,' he said, 'and it is strange that despite economic bribery and the most intense propaganda by press and radio, they failed so miserably to convince the Berliners.'

Hays felt that the city's inhabitants had grown weary of Tiulpanov's incessant propaganda 'and considered that freedom was worth a little more than a few pounds of potatoes or a kilo of flour'. He also noted that most Berliners were elated by the result. 'Such jubilation applied not only to the three opposing political parties, but to democratic organisations and associations of every kind.'[27]

Also jubilant was Frank Howley, whose policy of Aggressive Neutrality had worked to perfection. He met up with General Kotikov and his team just hours after the announcement of the result. 'They were downcast: it was as great a personal defeat in a campaign they had directed with such fervour as it was a party defeat.'[28] But Howley knew that the battle was not quite over, for the city's executive body, the Magistrat, had yet to be appointed. Until that happened, Walter Ulbricht's supporters remained in place.

'They still had all the machinery of government in their hands through their appointed Red stooges,' said Howley. 'Here was a weapon they could use to obstruct the smooth functioning of the government machine.'[29]

Paul Markgraf's police force proved highly efficient at coercion that autumn, but it was rather less adept at stopping crime. Berlin had a soaring crime rate, with shootings and stabbings occurring on a nightly basis, often between inebriated soldiers. It was particularly bad in the American sector, where Frau Andreas-Friedrich had her apartment: 'A week ago a jeep was stolen from in front of our house, practically from under its owner's nose. The night before last the gasoline was taken out of Frank's [Dr Walter Seitz] car. Yesterday the car itself was stolen.' Crime was everywhere. 'The moment one turns one's back, a tyre is taken off, the battery removed or the entire car disappears.'[30]

Brigadier Hinde was increasingly troubled by the sinister manoeuvrings of Paul Markgraf's police force. 'There is too much political influence at work among the police,' he said. 'This we must gradually eradicate.' But this was easier said than done, for Markgraf had established his own police training school, which was tasked with producing ideologically sound officers. Hinde's response was to establish a rival school, but his eight hundred eager recruits were no match for Markgraf's thugs. Hinde conceded that there was 'a long way to go before the Force can be regarded as an efficient guardian of law and order'.[31] Until this happened, criminals had the run of the German capital.

The big-time criminals operated in the city's underground night-clubs, where they forged links with unsavoury elements in the four military governments. Some were former Nazis trafficking stolen goods; others were unscrupulous gangsters and pimps. Far from being constrained by a divided city, they found that the four different sectors offered a unique potential for large-scale corruption. There was opportunity – and money to be made – in chaos.

It was a dangerous world to enter, let alone investigate, but Curt Riess was to do just that. He had the advantage of having been born to German parents, and his fluency in the language enabled him to learn about the criminal underworld through its German participants.

At the bottom of the hierarchy were the street urchins who stole, smuggled and prostituted themselves. Riess infiltrated one gang of fourteen children, mostly orphans, who lived in a cellar. It was led by a cocky eighteen-year-old named Paul, a deserter from the Volkssturm.

'Would you like a glass of whisky?' he asked as he sluiced a generous measure of Johnnie Walker into a tumbler. 'You Americans drink nothing but whisky, I know.'[32]

Riess was amazed by the underground existence of this gang, whose chain-smoking girl members were dressed in trousers and bandannas. 'They showed me their supplies. There were hundreds of cans of meat, condensed milk and vegetables, piles of cigarettes, bales of cloth, cans of gasoline, several cameras.' When Riess asked about their daily routine, he was told they were engaged chiefly in smuggling food into the western sectors from Soviet-occupied Germany. 'Children can often get through places where adults would be caught.'[33]

But child gangs on the front line of crime were at greatest risk of getting caught, probably because they were the most conspicuous. They were also lowest on the food chain. At the other end of the spectrum were the big players, many of whom had been prominent figures in the Nazi regime. Powerful and well connected, they were using established criminal networks to procure rare metals, narcotics and jewels on a fabulous scale.

'The big black marketeers were the real dictators of Berlin,' said Riess. 'No one could seriously interfere with their business.' They bribed the police, paid off informers and confined themselves to the shadows: 'Sitting in offices scattered here and there throughout the city, they conducted their business by telephone. They had agents to carry out their orders and the men who were caught were usually the agents, only very rarely the men at the top.'[34] Those who ended up in jail still managed to prosper, for there was a thriving black market in the city's prisons, with the warders being their most valued clients.

The big-time operators were powerful and dangerous but relatively small in number. By far the largest criminal community in Berlin were the middlemen who dealt in stolen treasures. They had to be on their guard because they were being tracked by officers such as Captain Norman T. Byrne, a burly American professor sent to the capital with orders to hunt them down. An early recruit to Howley's A1A1 unit, Byrne had degrees from Harvard and the University of California and spoke Spanish, French and Chinese. His accomplishments were so impressive that he was soon promoted to a senior position in Monuments, Fine Arts and Archives (MFAA), an organisation tasked with safeguarding the city's treasures.*

'A versatile soldier of fortune' was how one acquaintance described Byrne,[35] a description that was to prove all too accurate, for the gregarious Norman Byrne was so versatile that he was successfully living a double life. By day, he was a diligent curator of looted masterpieces; by night, he was selling them off for his own personal benefit. His was a classic case of gamekeeper-turned-poacher and

---

* The employees of MFAA would later be celebrated by Hollywood in George Clooney's *The Monuments Men* (2014).

his story was to lift the lid on a complex network of criminals exploiting the chaos of a four-sector Berlin.

Byrne profited from his double life for many months and might have continued for long into the future had it not been for a sensational article published in *Newsweek*, alleging that large quantities of stolen art were being trafficked by American officers. The Soviets were not alone in profiting from the spoils of war; the western Allies were also culpable. The article was written by *Newsweek*'s chief Berlin correspondent, James O'Donnell, and was so scandalous that it prompted Berlin's American-run Criminal Investigation Division to launch an enquiry. This enquiry looked into cases of high-ranking American officers and civilians suspected of selling looted art. Captain Byrne's name cropped up with such frequency that he became a focus of the investigation.

On the afternoon of 12 August, Byrne was arrested in San Francisco while staying in the city during his 'rest and recreation' leave. Two weeks later he was accompanied back to Berlin by the two CID officers who had arrested him, Lester Kolste and Niklos Strauch. They had caught him with two valuable artworks in his possession and no satisfactory explanation. He now faced prosecution for his alleged crimes.

The ensuing trial was held in a courtroom at McNair Military Barracks in Berlin. Byrne was charged with seventeen counts of embezzlement and larceny, with one of his accusers being his former commanding officer, Colonel Frank Howley. Byrne's world of deceit was about to unravel in spectacular fashion.

Byrne's position at MFAA allowed him to search the properties of anyone suspected of trading in stolen goods. In the words of one senior American officer, Captain Byrne had 'practically unlimited authority to search out works of art'. He could enter private homes, seize rare objects and remove valuable works from damaged buildings. These were then stored in a collection centre, where they were examined and recorded in a central register. In the wrong hands, such sweeping powers were open to abuse.

One of his first seizures was a haul of six small Old Masters bearing the famous Goudstikker label on the back of their frames. These had originally been stolen from the Dutch-Jewish art dealer,

Jacques Goudstikker (probably on the orders of Hermann Göring), and had subsequently been acquired by a Berlin company director who was now trying to sell them. Byrne knew he could not filch such paintings; they were too well known. He acted entirely appropriately by having them transferred to the MFAA's storage facility.

But when he searched the director's apartment a day or two later, he found a valuable manuscript by the Florentine artist Agnolo Bronzino. This was a less obvious treasure and Byrne took it directly to his apartment at 10A Biesalskistrasse. On the following day he chanced upon a work by Albrecht Dürer. Eight by eleven inches, it was the original copper plate of his famous *Large Horse*, a work of art valued in 1945 at $100,000. This, too, was transferred to Byrne's flat. It was the beginning of an extraordinary season of looting and stealing, with the principal targets being the homes of wealthy Berlin collectors.

Every criminal needs an accomplice: Byrne had three – his lover, his assistant and his secretary. His lover was Margarete Loesche, a petite, dark-haired woman twelve years his junior. His assistant was Herta Waschow, whose hunger for money rendered her pliable in Byrne's criminal hands. His secretary was Helga von Corvin, whose membership of the Nazi party ought to have disqualified her from any job with the Allies. All three women were to find themselves accomplices in Byrne's wide-reaching international operation.

Much of his activity focussed on an art gallery owned by Colonel Alexander Kaminsky, a disreputable Russian aristocrat with a wealth of important connections. Kaminsky acted as a broker for paintings brought to him by impoverished Berliners, selling these works to American officers and taking a 15 per cent commission. His gallery was in the American zone of Berlin, at 3 Teltowerdamm in Zehlendorf, and it was turning over a staggering $200,000 a month. Kaminsky's trade had the veneer of legality and he always claimed that everything was above board, but he was widely suspected of dealing in trafficked art.

Kaminsky's high-level connections in the Soviet military were to protect him for many months, but the Americans eventually forbade him from trading in their sector of the city. He was described as 'a notorious black-marketeer who had for too long been protected in his business'.

Kaminsky's departure from the American sector did not lead to the closure of his business. It was officially reopened by the American Military Government, with the principal employee being Byrne's personal assistant, Herta Waschow. She had developed an infallible system for acquiring fine art at low prices. Impoverished Berliners would bring treasured items to the gallery, only to be given a debased valuation. When they balked and turned to leave, she would give them the option of selling the item through the gallery or having it seized by Captain Byrne.

In this way, Waschow and Byrne were able to accumulate a large collection of artworks, as well as porcelain and pottery from Meissen, Höchst, Frankenthal and Nymphenburg. Much of the Meissen was shipped directly to America where Byrne sold it to Colonel Harold Mercer, a collector of fine porcelain. Other items were resold in Berlin or taken to America by Byrne himself during his rest and recreation furlough.

When he was arrested, Byrne had Dürer's *Large Horse* and David Teniers's *Smoker* in his possession. His defence was unconvincing. He told the two officers that he was having the Teniers painting authenticated by an expert and said that 'the presence of the Dürer etching of the horse in his briefcase was accidental, unknown to him until after his departure from Berlin.' He was to prove a more masterful performer in the Berlin courthouse, arguing that he was allowed to send items to New York for appraisal by experts. 'Damn poor judgement,' was the opinion of Frank Howley.

As the case dragged on, the prosecutor grew increasingly impatient with Byrne. 'He always gives me a song and a dance about if, maybe, wherefore,' he said, '[but] he never answers the question.' It was a smart tactic on Byrne's part, for when the court's judgement was finally passed, to the astonishment of everyone, he was found not guilty (by majority verdict) of sixteen of the seventeen charges.

But that seventeenth charge was to prove his undoing. His acceptance of backhanders, along with small personal items that he had indisputably stolen, caused him to be censured for 'moral turpitude'. Although he escaped a prison sentence, he was dismissed from the army with immediate effect. Byrne's career, both professional and criminal, was at an end.

It was ironic that his downfall was caused neither by his criminal network nor because he had shipped large quantities of treasure to America. Rather, it was because he was found guilty of 'accepting' one pair of lady's boots, one fur jacket, three typewriters, some silk stockings, some leather and one handbag, 'of the value of more than fifty dollars, property of persons unknown'.

The wider enquiry into looted art soon stalled, with many suspects escaping investigation. One of Byrne's irreproachably honest colleagues, Everett Leslie, compiled a report on American looting, only to find himself castigated by General Lucius Clay. The general did not want his reputation tarnished by stories of improper practices taking place on his watch. 'The interview was protracted, sultry and painful,' said Leslie. 'The general accused me of every possible infraction of every possible article of war.'[36]

Lieutenant Colonel John MacNeil, the chief investigating officer in the Byrne case, wrote a report expressing his belief that scores of servicemen were involved in large-scale crime. 'It seems certain that others have acted improperly,' he wrote, although he declined to name any names. He would later add a cryptic afterword. 'I burned my notes as soon as this report was written. I didn't just throw them in the wastebasket, I burned them.'[37] Why he did this remains a mystery, but he may well have done so on the orders of higher authorities.

MacNeil's destruction of the evidence was not the only suggestion of a cover-up. The entire file on the looting of art by American servicemen was destroyed by the provost marshal's office in 1965, the very year in which it was due to enter the public domain.

The Byrne case was symptomatic of a city in moral collapse. Corruption was endemic and it was impossible to do business without paying bribes. 'Decent behaviour no longer mattered,' said Riess. 'You had to be cunning and adroit. Berlin had entered a state of absolute corruptibility – there is no other way to put it . . . An honest man would have been considered abnormal.'[38]

Into this criminal underworld stepped Detective Inspector Tom Hayward, a stocky police officer from Scotland Yard with twenty-two years of experience. He was on secondment to the German capital, with a mission to bust some of the biggest criminals in town. It was to prove the mission of a lifetime.

Hayward had spent much of his career with Scotland Yard's Criminal Investigation Unit, rising through the ranks until he was eventually promoted to detective inspector in the summer of 1944. His case-notes reveal a methodical investigator whose cases frequently ended in conviction. When told that police inspectors were being sought to work in Berlin, Hayward had seized the opportunity for a crime-busting adventure, even though it meant a long absence from his wife, Lilian. In August 1946 he was accepted for the job and set off for the German capital in the company of his colleague, Detective Superintendent Thorp.

The two men were stunned by what they found on arrival. Here was every detective's dream, a highly organised criminal underworld that had agents operating across the globe. Every section of society was involved, but Hayward's brief was to track down the big-time racketeers.

His initial researches soon revealed the focus of the most lucrative crime: Berlin was awash with rare metals and radioactive minerals, as well as narcotics, penicillin and priceless works of art. All were being illegally traded on the black market.

Within weeks of arriving in the capital, Hayward set to work on 'Operation Sparkler', an undercover mission to infiltrate the criminal networks and arrest the leading players. His file on the investigation, 'Operation Sparkler and Large Scale Black Market Activities', is frustratingly incomplete. Pages are torn or missing, identities concealed behind pseudonyms and the underworld networks so Byzantine that Hayward himself struggled to make headway. Yet the surviving papers offer a tantalising glimpse into Berlin's four-power criminal underworld.

Detective Inspector Hayward was aided in his work by Controller Bechter, an employee of Brigadier Hinde's Economic Information Section. Bechter had already spent several months investigating this underworld and his case-notes were to form the backbone of the ensuing operation.

It did not take much work to reveal the source of the most valuable booty. Until May 1945, gemstones and rare metals owned by the government had been held in secure vaults at the Reichsstelle für Edelmetalle, a Nazi-run agency dealing in the rarest commodities. The agency's holdings that spring had included half a million carats of industrial diamonds, 4,000 kg of gold and 800,000 kg of silver, as well as 1,000 kg of other rare metals such as palladium and radium. Much of this had gone missing at the time of the fall of Berlin, with the bulk of it disappearing into the criminal underworld. 'Thus', said the Operation Sparkler report, 'an organisation responsible for the control of great wealth had disintegrated, and its potential assets slipped beyond Allied control.'[39]

It was almost impossible to put a price tag on the missing material, although it was 'conservatively estimated to have a value of approximately 250 million pounds'. As the investigation proceeded, it became apparent that the true figure was considerably higher and it was revised upwards to 'somewhere in the neighbourhood of 300,000,000 dollars'. This was such a mind-boggling sum that it was said to present 'a major threat to the German and perhaps even European economy and financial stability'. It placed Detective Inspector Hayward at the centre of one of the greatest criminal investigations of all time.

The sheer complexity of Berlin's crime network caused the investigation to proceed agonisingly slowly. One group of Allied officers was believed to be involved in radium negotiations 'involving many millions of Reichsmarks', mostly with agents from the Yugoslav Communist underworld. The same group was also engaged in illegal transactions in drugs, 'such as opium and cocaine, as well as penicillin and other medications'. There was also an all-American network 'organising a large export and import business based in New York, with agencies in Paris and Brussels'.

As for the Soviets, Detective Inspector Hayward discovered that they were buying up a wide range of highly prized goods. According to the Sparkler report, 'a fairly large number of Germans, Poles, Yugoslavs and other nationals are acting as contact men between the Russians and sources of supply'. Two unnamed Soviet agents informed Hayward that the Russians 'had set up an official buying agency called Voyentorg in Berlin-Weissensee' that was paying the highest prices for black market metals. The Sparkler report warned that 'the interest shown by Soviet and other east European countries in metals and minerals forming the basis of atomic research are of sufficient consequence to merit a most immediate investigation.' This was indeed an alarming discovery. The Soviets were buying up everything needed to build a nuclear bomb.

The investigation did not confine itself to rare metals. 'Cameras, lenses, photographic equipment, binoculars and microscopes running into hundreds of millions of Reichsmarks are obtained from large stocks scattered over the zones.' Illicit deals were being done in shares, bonds and patents, as well as in currency and property. 'The question of buying up of real estate in Berlin by foreigners is again a chapter by itself.' Operation Sparkler also lifted the lid on the underworld trade in looted art, including Old Masters, sculptures, rare coins and Renaissance tapestries. 'Many of these are of priceless value and not readily available in Europe, but they appear to be finding interest in the United States.' This was all too true, as Captain Norman Byrne had been quick to discover.

By the autumn, Detective Inspector Hayward had a clearer understanding of the unprecedented scale of the criminal underworld, including the names of a few leading players. Several former SS members were profiting from their connections. Others, such as Fräulein Teach, were former employees of the Reichsstelle für Edelmetalle. Teach was known to be 'trafficking black diamonds from Bavaria into Switzerland'. And then there was Dr Reinhardt Heraeus, the principal agent of another large-scale diamond operation.

US Counter-Intelligence joined the investigation and undertook its first raid at the same time as the British. Hayward's team of uniformed German policemen targeted sixteen undercover addresses in the British sector of Berlin and a further sixty-eight in the British zone of occupied Germany. The Americans targeted a further 373 addresses where illegal activities were believed to be taking place. The aim, as described in an American report, was 'to strike the objective with surprise as the first glimmer of early dawn breaks through the dark sky'.[40]

The results of those first Sparkler raids were comparatively modest: in the British area, rare metals and stones to the value of £500,000 were recovered, along with £80,000 of industrial diamonds.* Thirty-eight people were arrested. The American raids were more successful, yielding some $8 million-worth of rare metals.†

Detective Inspector Hayward had produced results with impressive speed but he knew he had merely scratched the surface. 'Each individual investigation unearthed some new aspect of this black picture,' he said. Crime was so endemic that it was spiralling out of control and he called for a forty-strong team of Scotland Yard detectives to help smash the crime ring. Unless or until such a force were sent to Berlin, big-time criminals would operate with impunity selling rare and valuable metals to agents of the Soviet regime.

* Worth approximately £24 million today.
† Worth approximately $107 million today.

13

Playing Dirty

BERLIN WAS AN unpredictable place in the aftermath of the October 1946 election. As darkness descended each evening, the city's inhabitants scurried home through the shadows, eager to escape the criminals, robbers and vagabonds who had made the twilight hours their stalking ground. A new moon in the final quarter of October distilled the night into an impenetrable blackness. At such a time, it was safer to remain indoors.

Yet even locks and bolts brought little security to Berliners and the most frightening element of life in the city was the routine disappearance of neighbours, family and friends. The process invariably began with a visit from the NKVD, as had happened to the Hoecke family in Potsdam in May 1945, followed by a summons for questioning. And then came a deafening silence. Few of those arrested ever returned to tell their story.

Frau Irmgard Grötrupp had gone to bed early on the night of 21 October 1946 because her husband was away from home. She was sleeping deeply when the phone rang loudly and shrilly at 3 a.m. When she picked up the receiver, she heard the harassed voice of a friend who asked in breathless anguish: 'Have you got to leave for Moscow too?'[1]

Frau Grötrupp was still trying to make sense of her friend's question when events overtook her. 'There was the sound of powerful engines . . . [and] cars stopping at the door.' Aware that this could mean only one thing, she jumped out of bed and looked outside. 'From every window I could see Russians; the house was surrounded by soldiers with tommy guns. Outside were cars and lorries, nose to tail.'

Frau Grötrupp was terrified. A forced transfer to Moscow was the fear of every Berliner with technical skills, and her husband's brilliance as a rocket engineer made him an obvious target. The reality of what was happening was nevertheless hard to digest. She knew that there was no escaping the Soviet soldiers. Not only did she have nowhere to go, but her maid, Anni, and young son, Peter, were also in the house.

'Someone pressed the front doorbell and kept his finger on it – fists hammered on the door – the noise echoed through the house.' When she opened up, soldiers burst inside, inspected all the rooms and then began moving her furniture into the waiting lorries. It was menacing, traumatic, terrifying.

'The noise of heavy military boots going up and down, the clatter of broken glass, and Anni's scornful voice, screaming from the dining room.' Frau Grötrupp was permitted to telephone her husband, who warned her that he was being held under military guard. 'You do understand, don't you?' he said. 'There is nothing I can do.'

Their brief phone call at an end, Frau Grötrupp tried to step outside the back door for some fresh air. But a gun barrel was pointed at her face and the soldier in charge gave her a frigid stare. '*Nyet!*'

Frau Grötrupp was not alone in her predicament. There were hundreds of similar cases that night, right across the Soviet sector of Berlin. Experts, scientists and technicians – predominantly men, along with their wives and children – were woken from their sleep, bundled into cars and driven to the Schlesischer train station, from whence they were to be transported to Moscow. For many it was to involve a three-week journey by rail, punctuated by mind-numbing halts in sidings and stations. In Frau Grötrupp's case, it was a journey undertaken without her husband: she had no idea of Helmut's whereabouts and nor did she know if or when she would be reunited with him.

One of those on board managed to escape. The renowned physicist, Dr Ulrich Capeller, jumped from the train during the night and got away unseen. The story of his flight back to the German capital would eventually emerge in a British intelligence report. 'By various methods he made his way to Berlin where he arrived penniless, half-starved, possessing only the clothes he was wearing.'

When Frau Grötrupp's train stopped in yet another siding she peered out of the window and got the surprise of her life: her husband was being helped aboard. He had been transported by car from Berlin and now brought news of exactly what was taking place. 'Over two hundred men with their families and movables had been deported,' he told her. This was an understatement. Operation Osoaviakhim saw the rounding up of 1,900 German scientists living in Soviet-occupied Germany, along with a further four hundred from Berlin itself. There were so many of them, and their laboratory equipment was so cumbersome, that it required the use of seven hundred railway carriages. Frau Grötrupp felt a sudden envy of the rocket scientist Wernher von Braun, whom she knew to have been seized by the Americans. '*He* travelled on well-upholstered seats,' she said, '*we* on benches which are hard in spite of the upholstery'.

The reception they received upon finally arriving in Moscow went some way to brightening her spirits. The Grötrupps were assigned a large villa, formerly the home of a government minister. 'Not bad,' she admitted. 'Not without taste.'

Operation Osoaviakhim was a magnified version of what the Soviets had been practising for many months, plucking individual scientists from their sector of Berlin and despatching them to Russia. On this occasion it had been an efficiently coordinated exercise that lasted from 3 a.m. until 5 p.m. But the Soviet administration had also been kidnapping individual experts from the British and American sectors of the city over the previous months, using agents working for the police chief, Paul Markgraf. Among those seized was the director of the Staaken quartz-melting works. He was snatched by Markgraf's henchmen in the British sector, bundled into a car and driven to the east of the city where he was handed over to the Soviet authorities. He was never seen again.

Brigadier Hinde was kept apprised of what was taking place, with much of his information coming from his intelligence officers. Chief among these was Arthur Parkin, who headed an agency known as the Enemy Personnel Exploitation Section. It had two principal functions: to gather intelligence on German scientists in the Soviet sector and then to smuggle them out to the west. Parkin's office was staffed by seven experts in the field of intelligence, four of them women (Mrs E. J. Knapp, Miss J. Chapman, Miss E. Hearn, Miss J. Mitchell). They spent much of their time recruiting German agents who could report from inside plants and factories now under Soviet control. By October 1947, Parkin had a formidable network operating not just in the Soviet sector of Berlin, but in Soviet-occupied Germany as well. In 'Special Intelligence Report 3', covering the early weeks of that year, he revealed that 'in each factory we have an agent of whose reliability we are certain . . . [and] within the next months it will be possible to present a picture which will substantially cover the activities in Russian-occupied Germany.'

This proved to be the case. At a specialist colour-processing plant run by the photographic company, AGFA, forty miles from Berlin, Parkin's undercover agent was a certain Dr Ziegler. He reported on everyone who might be of value to Britain. At the V2 rocket plant in Sömmerda, the insider information came from one E. H. Schön, 'a very valuable agent', said Parkin, who revealed that many of the factory's specialists were keen to flee the Soviet yoke. 'There has been for some time a concerted determination to work for the western democracies.'

This intelligence work carried substantial risks. If caught by the Soviets, Parkin's German agents could have expected interrogation and worse. 'The families of those concerned will be arrested and held as hostages,' he noted in one of his reports.

His unit also had a network of local informers who intercepted mail and eavesdropped on the Soviets. In this way they were able to read the letters of scientists already sent to Russia. Among them was Manfred von Ardenne, the physicist taken to Moscow with his wife in May 1945. One of his letters, sent to an acquaintance in Berlin from von Ardenne's new home on the Black Sea, was intercepted. 'We have a very nice household and two Russian girls who do everything for us,' he wrote. 'All apparatus and instruments were brought here, but many pieces were badly damaged. It is so hot that one can hardly put a foot down on a stone floor during the day.'[2] He tried to put a brave face on his predicament but he was not enjoying himself.

By the time the Soviets had concluded Operation Osoaviakhim, some 150 German scientists had already applied to Parkin for help in fleeing the city, along with a number of Berliners being forced to work as informers for the Soviets. Among them was a Herr Malz, who told Parkin that he had been threatened with death if he refused to eavesdrop on British officers drinking at the Haus Stefanie, a hotel in Charlottenburg. Parkin offered Malz immediate protection, 'and he and his wife are now hiding in Berlin, pending an opportunity to escape to the Western zone'.[3]

Other scientists had lucky escapes, dodging Markgraf's henchmen and then informing British intelligence of what had happened. One such was Otto Heil, an expert in air navigation systems. He was strolling through the city's American sector when he heard his name being shouted from a limousine. 'Someone opened the door and called to me, "Hello Comrade Heil!" and stretched out his hand, as if to shake hands with me.' Heil moved towards the car and was about to greet the man when he noticed three other people in the vehicle. 'All of them had typical Russian faces,' he said, 'and therefore I ran away.'[4] It was a lucky escape.

The Soviets' principal targets in Berlin were those working for AEG (radar researchers), the Gema works (high-tech rocket engineers) and the Askania works (skilled technicians). In the aftermath of Osoaviakhim, Parkin received 'a flood of callers . . . all with the same aim in view, to escape the possibility of deportation and remove themselves as quickly as possible to the Western zone, the United Kingdom or the USA'.[5]

General Kotikov's role in snatching the Berlin scientists provoked uproar in the Kommandatura. Frank Howley was as implacable as ever when he broached the subject. 'I will not tolerate kidnapping in the United States sector of Berlin,' he thundered. 'I will not countenance your sending police or other agents into the United States sector for the purpose of arresting Germans or any other nationals under our jurisdiction.' He produced a thick dossier filled with the names of Berliners who had been arrested by Paul Markgraf's officers: it included judges, officials, journalists and businessmen. '[Here] is the record of thousands of hours of search and enquiry and protest,' he said as he slammed the dossier onto the desk, 'but most of the then–missing are still missing today.'[6] The British supported Howley in his protest and went so far as to accuse Kotikov of 'a violation of human rights'.[7]

General Kotikov did not deny what he had done. Rather, he brazenly admitted to snatching the scientists before voicing his disgust at the double standards of the western Allies, whom he knew to have removed hundreds of scientists. 'I am not asking the Americans and British at what hour of the day or night they took *their* technicians,' he said. 'Why are you so concerned about the hour at which I took *mine*?'[8]

Howley privately admitted that they were in 'a sticky spot', given that Kotikov was speaking the truth. An American team, led by the intelligence agent Boris Pash, had been the first to undertake a mission to capture Berlin's most prestigious scientists, many of whom had fled to the western zone of Germany in the first weeks of 1945. Aware that they were likely to be seized by either the Soviets or western powers, they preferred the latter as the lesser of two evils. Among those captured was Otto Hahn, awarded the Nobel Prize for his discovery of nuclear fission, and the Nobel laureate Werner Heisenberg, an expert in atomic science. Colonel Pash described Heisenberg as 'one of the world's leading physicists, and worth more to us than *ten divisions* of Germans'.[9] Scores of others were seized at the same time, including many who had previously worked for Berlin's prestigious Kaiser Wilhelm Society.

Boris Pash's mission was no more legal than that of General Kotikov; indeed the American colonel delighted in the underhand nature of his work, describing his team as 'Pancho Villa bandits, with ammunition tucked into pockets and in canvas bandoliers slung across our shoulders'. In one lucrative swoop they bagged no fewer than twenty-five Berlin scientists. They also seized a primitive nuclear reactor, drums of heavy water (deuterium-enriched water used in nuclear energy research), and what Pash described as 'nearly the entire core of the Nazi atomic pile in uranium ingots'.[10]

Colonel Pash's mission was but one of many, with the most spectacular being Operation Paperclip: it would eventually lead to the capture of more than 1,600 German scientists across Germany, including the rocket scientist, Wernher von Braun. Frank Howley was aware of this and wisely dropped the issue of the scientists snatched by Kotikov's agents. Yet the atmosphere in the Kommandatura remained poisonous and Howley warned the Soviets that they were treading on thin ice. 'Throughout the day, General Kotikov made many remarks bordering on insults,' he said at the end of one session. 'We no longer are conducting these meetings as gentlemen; they are developing into a series of dogfights.'[11]

He pointed the finger of blame directly at his Soviet counterpart, 'my number one antagonist', who disgusted him on both a personal and professional level. 'The epitome and the quintessence of the evil doctrines Moscow preaches,' he wrote. 'A big bulky man . . . with a mouth like a petulant rosebud, his mind turned on and off automatically with switches operated in the Kremlin.'[12]

Berliners faced a shivering future as a wintery blast snapped in from the Russian steppes. The waters of the Grunewald turned dark and sluggish, and thin skeins of ice formed on the boating lakes. By New Year's Eve the brooks that fed the Wannsee and Müggelsee had frozen to shining pearls. And then came a further knife-blade from the east and everything was locked into a hibernal freeze.

It was the coldest winter on record. In January 1947, the mercury struggled above zero on just eleven days. In February, the most brutal month of all, it remained far below freezing both night and day. When Ruth Andreas-Friedrich checked her thermometer on Wednesday, 5 February, it read minus seventeen. 'No water, no electricity, no heat, no potatoes,' she wrote. 'Freezing cold day and night . . . Icicles hang from the ceilings and all the door handles are white with frost.'[13] By the middle of that month, the city's air-raid shelters, hospitals and theatres were being turned into 'warming halls', half-heated spaces in which Berlin's frozen population could congregate.

'The hardest winter of Berliners' lives,' declared the Soviet sector newspaper, Berlin am Mittag.[14] It was no hyperbole. The city had run out of coal, firewood and power. Andreas-Friedrich watched people setting out for the Grunewald forest 'equipped with knapsacks, baskets and shopping bags . . . jammed together in overcrowded trains, and wast[ing] hour upon hour searching for one day's worth of firewood'.[15] It was dangerous work, for hunger had driven wolves from the woods onto the Berliner Ring, the network of roads that bordered the city.

In the famous Tiergarten, giant lindens were hacked into firewood by hollow-cheeked Berliners. Dorothea von Schwanenflügel watched in dismay as two-hundred-year-old trees disappeared 'into the iron stoves of freezing Berliners'.[16] Pathé newsreels showed spinsters dragging frost-blasted branches back to their ruined dwellings.

The elderly and the very young froze to death in their beds. 'The lower the temperature drops, the more ghastly the rise in the numbers of victims of the cold.'[17] When a Polish refugee train pulled into one of Berlin's stations, fifty-three people on board were found ice-rigid like statues. All had died of hypothermia.

Before long more than a thousand people had frozen to death, while a further 450 chose suicide over the lingering pain of frost-bite. Frozen water pipes meant there was no longer any running water. This, in turn, necessitated queuing at the public pumps. One mother would later recall throwing soiled nappies into a bucket of water that instantly froze solid. She had to hack them out and slowly thaw them on the meagre flame she managed to coax from the stove.

With no water and no flushing lavatories, bodily waste had to be taken outside and dumped in nearby ruins. Ruth Andreas-Friedrich tried to put a brave face on the hardship. She and her friends sat around a flickering kerosene lamp wearing thick fur coats and listening as one of them read poems by Goethe. 'And when you come to think about it,' she said, 'they seem even more beautiful at twenty below zero, and without electricity, water or coal.'[18]

And then the mercury plunged yet further, reaching an Arctic-low of minus twenty-nine degrees Celsius. Twelve-year-old Inge Gross was living at her grandmother's place in the American sector, in a flat that (like most buildings in Berlin) had no glass in the windows. She helped her grandma stuff the broken panes with cardboard, wood and rags, yet still the freezing wind whipped through these flimsy barriers. '[We] spent a lot of time in bed to keep warm. Our feather-beds' – a rarity in this post-war period – 'were our lifesaving possessions.'[19] There were no classes at Inge's local school, owing to the lack of heating, but she went there anyway because it meant she got her half-litre ration of watery gruel.

Hunger. It was gnawing, painful and ever-present. One million Berliners were still living off the 'hunger card' (ration card five) which provided them with just 1,500 calories a day. When Elfriede von Assel learned that a delivery of potatoes had been dumped in a nearby street, she rushed outside only to discover that they had frozen as hard as pebbles. 'We grated them and cooked them in water. They tasted disgusting . . . the grated potato was used to thicken a watery soup.'[20] Her only other daily sustenance was the ten grams of fat she obtained with her ration card. It was the equivalent of two small teaspoons.

There was an infamous murder case that winter. A man, who had lost his ration card and survived for days on scraps of dried bread, eventually grew so desperate that he killed a colleague for his card. It was the view of the Berlin court that there had been mitigating circumstances.

One city, two worlds. For the western Allies those long winter months were a time of endless merriment, especially as many officers had by now been joined by their wives. Frank Howley's wife, Edith, had moved into their enormous villa on Gelfertstrasse, along with their four children. She was delighted to have twelve servants, maids and cleaners to do the domestic chores and equally happy to have access to a wide range of food from the army commissary. One of her fellow Americans, Lelah Berry, reeled at the abundance. 'Gleaming meat counters chockfull of choice cuts; shelves stocked with canned goods, coffee, sugar and lard; refrigerators filled with butter, margarine, cheese, creamy bottles of milk and fresh eggs and stalls overflowing with fresh oranges, apples, crisp celery, cauliflower . . .' Her greatest concern was putting on weight: within a few months of arriving in Berlin she had gained ten pounds.

Mrs Berry confessed to having niggling concerns about her life of abundance. 'The sick dog of one of my American friends was put on a milk-sugar-white-bread diet by the veterinarian and eats every day as much sugar as a German child's entire Christmas bonus.' She also had the occasional pang of conscience about the elderly couple evicted from the villa she now occupied with her twenty-nine-year-old husband, Elmer. 'Sometime I feel like a thief, living cosily here in their home while they huddle in the concrete-floored garage.'[21] But such anxieties about the Germans never lasted for long. 'After all, they started it,' she reasoned. 'They asked for it.'

Others had more troubled consciences. Joan Crane, wife of an economics expert, felt as if she had landed 'in some colonial outpost' in which the Americans were lording it over the native Berliners. 'They exist only as a sea of hungry, silent faces,' she said, adding that 'the social status of a German, any German in our zone today, is on a level comparable to a negro in Mississippi.'

Mrs Crane would eventually voice her disgust in an excoriating article she wrote for Philadelphia's *Saturday Evening Post*, in which she laid bare the excesses of Americans lording it over the Germans. 'Housekeeper, cook, nursemaid, chauffeur, dressmaker, language tutor, masseuse, musicians for private entertainment – all who are not given to us free by the Government are to be had for a price so ridiculously low as to be negligible.'[22] A professional private orchestra, hired for an all-night soirée, cost one pack of cigarettes per player.

Joan Crane's greatest fear was that the behaviour of the western powers would backfire in spectacular fashion, causing such disgust among the populace that Berliners would eventually balk at voting for the western-supporting political parties. 'Our present short-sighted, punitive policies designed only for the humiliation, not the regeneration of Germany can only end by driving the Germans into the hands of a communist type of government,' she said. 'If we want Germany to remain as a part of Western democratic culture, we must quickly work out a program of liberal economic aid designed to get the German economy back on its feet.'

General Lucius Clay was appalled when shown an advance copy of Mrs Crane's article. It was so detailed, and so cogently argued, that it threatened to cause a storm. He applied such pressure on the editor of the *Saturday Evening Post* that the article was withdrawn shortly before it was to go to press. The only surviving copy is the one typed by Joan Crane herself.

No less critical was an official 1947 American report into Military Government in Germany, exhaustive in detail, which recorded numerous acts of unruly behaviour committed by off-duty soldiers. These included 'unprovoked and wanton brutality, brawling, drunkenness, thieving and acts humiliating the local authority sponsored by Military Government'. Rape alone remained a rarity: the report cited just one case, in the Zehlendorf district, where a soldier was arrested but released almost immediately. 'He returned to the scene of the crime and raped the same woman.'

The report concluded that Berliners held American troops in low esteem. 'They consider the GIs and officers as men who drink to excess, who do not wear uniforms as they should, who make a great deal of noise on the street at night, who beat civilians without reason [and] who engage in black marketeering.'[23]

Such criticism went unheeded. For most expatriates, the party continued throughout the winter, with few of them troubled by their profligate behaviour. Curt Riess attended many sumptuous dinners hosted by officers of Military Government. 'There would be canapés, tremendous quantities of Manhattans and Martinis, crème de menthe and aged French cognac and the best French champagne. Russian caviar, oysters and huge steaks would be served.'[24]

For those without partners there were nightclubs, bars and uproarious cabarets. Twenty-two-year-old Captain Richard Brett-Smith spent his evenings carousing with friends in Rio Rita, Bobby's and Chez Ronnie. Most outlandish of all was the Femina, whose trademark was a telephone on every table. This made for easy introductions between the sexes, although Brett-Smith wryly noted that 'the directness of both the Russian and the American approach to German women may have made [the telephones] superfluous.'[25] Frank Howley went to Femina for the 'big luscious steaks' that were of a size that he had never encountered outside North America.[26]

Club-life in Berlin had always been outlandish, with venues catering to every sexual persuasion. For those with fluid sexual identities there was the Tabasco Club, the most outré of Berlin's new nightspots. Captain Brett-Smith went there as an unabashed voyeur and found it 'genuinely impossible to tell who was a man or a boy and who was a girl'. Men danced with men and women with women, 'and sometimes, oddly enough in that atmosphere, men with women, but it was anybody's guess who was who'.

Such behaviour was nevertheless tame in comparison to the hedonistic activities taking place in private dwellings. Ordinary soldiers were not welcome at these soirées, not even captains, and Brett-Smith received only snippets of stories about excess and debauchery. 'As all these *exhibitions*, erotic games, drug parties and aphrodisiacal shows were illegal,' he said, 'any kind of uniform was anathema to their promoters.'[27] To those who did get invited, it felt like a return to the giddy days of the Roaring Twenties.

By the early months of 1947 the broad sweep of Stalin's foreign policy was progressing according to plan. The disastrous Berlin election had been a small blip on an otherwise impressive scoresheet. The Red Army was in possession of large swathes of Eastern Europe and had been followed into the occupied territories by the infamous NKVD and GRU, whose agents were proving ruthless in hunting down those deemed politically unreliable. Post-war elections were also being successfully rigged, with bribery and intimidation enabling the Communists to win with spectacular margins: 70 per cent in both Bulgaria and Romania, and 80 per cent in Poland.

Although these newly formed governments were often coalitions, all the positions of power went to the Communists. They would typically seize control of the Interior Ministry, Justice Ministry and ministries of Information and Propaganda. In this way, they were able to tighten their grip over the respective populaces. It was exactly the model that Walter Ulbricht had set out for Berlin: political control masked by a veneer of democracy.

Stalin had always intended to extend his rule over post-war Eastern Europe. When conversing with Tito's deputy, Milovan Đjilas, he was quite clear about his goal. 'Whoever occupies a territory also imposes upon it his own social system,' he said. 'Everyone imposes his own system as far as his army can reach.'[28] By February 1947, most of the cities mentioned in Churchill's Iron Curtain speech were firmly in Stalin's grasp, including Warsaw, Prague, Budapest, Belgrade, Bucharest and Sofia. The one city not yet in his hands was Berlin.

Britain's fortunes were rather bleaker than those of the Soviet Union that winter. The country was hit by major cuts to the power supply, with coal supplies falling so low that industrial production was halted for a full three weeks, something the Luftwaffe's bombing campaign had never achieved. Unemployment rose sharply, from 400,000 to 2.3 million, and the general misery was compounded by the freezing weather and the scant supplies of food. Bread – never rationed in wartime – had been on the ration books since the previous summer.

Just two years earlier, at Yalta, Churchill had striven to preserve the integrity of the British Empire. Now, the sun was rapidly setting on the country's imperial dominions. On 20 February, the prime minister announced to the House of Commons that Britain would be leaving India 'by a date not later than June 1948'. Ceylon and Burma would follow soon after.

Nor was the situation any easier closer to home. Ernest Bevin announced that Britain could no longer provide essential financial aid to Greece and Turkey, while the problem of Palestine was referred to the United Nations after two decades of British rule. The British Empire seemed to be on the brink of collapse, with the mother country so destitute that it was unable to halt the decline.

As the glacial winter at long last melted into spring, Brigadier Hinde had reason to be optimistic. The democratic parties had won the election, the Kommandatura was more or less holding together and the British sector was in better shape than it had been a year and a half earlier. More importantly, the brigadier's importation of medicines had prevented a much-feared pandemic.

On Sunday, 11 May 1947, he drove into the forest on the outskirts of Berlin in order to indulge his passion for birds. He was to have an unwelcome surprise as he crept through the undergrowth, when the sudden bark of a Soviet soldier demanded to know what he was doing.

'I am looking at birds,' snapped the brigadier, unaware that he had inadvertently strayed into the Soviet zone.

'You are looking at our airfield,' said the sentry.

'Utter rot, my dear fellow. I am Brigadier Hinde and I have not the slightest interest in counting your planes. I am looking at birds and you are frightening them away, dash it!'

The sentry did not believe him and called his captain. The captain ordered Hinde's arrest. Within minutes, the brigadier was bundled into a car and driven to Soviet military headquarters.

A lengthy interrogation ensued, with the Soviets insisting that Hinde's binoculars were clear evidence of espionage. His lack of identity papers, which he had inadvertently left at home, incriminated him still further. For a full two hours he faced threats and accusations, but he stuck to the line that he was deputy military governor of the British sector. His interrogators eventually decided to call his bluff by telephoning General Kotikov.

'What does he look like?' asked Kotikov.

When the brigadier's erect bearing and clipped moustache were described, Kotikov exploded down the phone.

'For God's sake apologize and turn him loose! That *is* Brigadier Hinde!'[29]

That spring brought a more agreeable surprise for the brigadier when two of his daughters, Elisabeth and Cathryn, came to stay. For the girls, seventeen and fifteen years of age, it was the trip of a lifetime: they took a ferry from Harwich to the Hook of Holland and then a steam train to Helmstedt, at the frontier of the Soviet-occupied zone of Germany. This was where the adventure began in earnest: the train was searched, the doors locked and the window blinds closed and sealed. For the next twelve hours the train crawled towards Berlin. Not until it arrived were the blinds reopened, revealing a city still in ruins. 'We couldn't swim in the river because it was still full of bodies,' said young Cathryn. Putrid and foul-smelling, these were just some of the hundred thousand corpses of Berliners that would eventually be pulled from the wreckage. The girls spent their evenings at dinner parties, cocktail soirées and dances. Elisabeth Hinde soon caught the attention of Michael Holland-Hibbert, aide-de-camp to General Sir Brian Robertson. 'I have

rather fallen for [her],' he confided to his diary. 'She is very attract-
ive and dresses well and is terribly sweet and very self-possessed,
without being know-all-ish or precocious.'[30] The two of them danced
through the night at a party hosted by the Macaskies, a military
family stationed in Berlin, and feasted on suckling pig.

But there was to be no long-term romance, for the Hinde girls
soon had to return to England. They spent their final evening
thumping out *Clementine* on the piano, with their brigadier father
singing along in unabashed joy.

General Kotikov brooded for weeks after the disastrous election, as
did the whole of his team. 'They were morose and took the voters'
rebuff personally,' said Howley, 'absenting themselves from Allied
cocktail parties and other social functions.'[31] Just a few months before,
Kotikov had been the life and soul of every party, pouring vodka,
proposing toasts and slapping everyone on the back as a sign of
hearty goodwill. Now, he didn't even show up.

The first sign of serious trouble came at the first meeting of the
Kommandatura to take place after the election, at which Kotikov
was even more aggressive than usual. Harold Hays could scarcely
believe the manner in which the Soviet general spoke that day and
felt that electoral defeat had changed everything, throwing each side's
differences into sharp relief. 'We were now in two violently opposed
camps.'[32]

Kotikov would soon get his sweet revenge. Howley had long
suspected that the Soviets would try to obstruct any new appointments to the Magistrat and this is exactly what now happened.
Kotikov declared that no one could be appointed without the
unanimous approval of all four commandants, a move that gave him
a veto over who could sit on the city's most important body.

Matters reached a head when the City Assembly came to select
a new mayor. It initially voted for a compromise candidate named
Otto Ostrowski, who promised to steer an even keel between east
and west. But as he increasingly sided with the Soviets, the Assembly
dramatically stripped him of office. When it came to choose his
successor, it threw caution to the wind and selected one of the few
figures whom the Soviets genuinely feared, a man whose towering

personality was destined to play a central role in shaping the future of both Berlin and Germany. Ernst Reuter won that second mayoral vote by a resounding 82 per cent, a stunning victory that gave him unrivalled authority. His platform was unambiguous: to defeat the Soviet menace. It seemed all but certain that General Kotikov would wield his veto and block Reuter's appointment.

14

Shifting Sands

Ernst Reuter was an unlikely figure to find fame in any eventuality. He was even less plausible as an inspirational hero for several million Berliners facing a volatile situation. Just short of sixty he had an uninspiring appearance, with a lumbering frame and heavy jowls. He walked unsteadily with the aid of a cane.

Curt Riess was underwhelmed when he visited Reuter at his home in Berlin's western suburbs. 'I had been expecting to see a revolutionary,' he said. 'The man before me was a rather portly, bourgeois-looking person.'[1] But no sooner had Reuter opened his mouth than Riess was forced to revise his opinion. The commanding voice, the rich tones, the emotional delivery, all added up to something unforgettable. 'He had a burning fire in himself,' explained Reuter's son, Edzard. 'A very, very sincere man.'[2] When Reuter spoke, everyone listened.

One of the first Americans to know him well was Karl Mautner, one-time intelligence officer with the 82nd US Airborne. Mautner singled Reuter out as the most important German in Berlin, and one with more than a touch of Winston Churchill about him. 'A heavy-set, serious, cigar-smoking man who dominated any room he was in . . . I saw him in rooms where there were very important Americans and allies, but the focus was always Reuter. He had this charisma.'[3]

Reuter's magnetism was but one reason why he was feared by the Soviets. He also came equipped with a weapon that had the capacity to inflict serious damage on the Soviet Military Administration. That weapon was his former life. Reuter had once been an ardent Communist, converted to the cause after his capture on the eastern front in 1916. He was soon introduced to Lenin, who was so impressed that he ordered Reuter's release from prison camp and appointed him leader of the Volga Germans. In this post Reuter became an intimate of Joseph Stalin, then serving as commissar for national minorities. It gave him first-hand knowledge of Stalin's inner thoughts.

Although Reuter won the approval of both Lenin and Stalin, he did not fit the mould of the archetypal Soviet revolutionary. 'Well versed in Marx and Lenin,' noted one, 'but inspired by Goethe and Homer.'[4] Reuter abhorred the bloodshed in Soviet Russia and was repulsed by the Kremlin's ever-tightening stranglehold on power. Eventually he snapped. First, he broke with the Communist Party and then he broke with Stalin's Russia. 'Moscow's desire to achieve total power was repugnant to me,' he later said.[5] By the mid-1930s, he felt the same about Nazi Germany and fled to Turkey, where he was granted asylum. He didn't return to Berlin until the end of 1946.

Reuter soon came to the attention of Frank Howley, who felt he ticked all the right boxes. The fact that he was hated by General Kotikov made him a yet more valuable ally. Here was a German figurehead who could be trusted by the three western powers.

The more Howley praised Reuter, the more Kotikov attacked him, describing his anti-Soviet outbursts as 'reminiscent in tone and content to those of the Goebbels propaganda ministry'.[6] Kotikov instructed the Soviet-controlled press to attack him and encouraged Walter Ulbricht and Wilhelm Pieck to join the fray. Ulbricht accused Reuter of being an American agent,[7] while Pieck declared him a traitor who needed to be silenced.

'Herr Reuter will never be permitted to take office,' thundered Kotikov in the aftermath of Reuter's election triumph and reiterated his demand that the four commandants should have the final say over the appointment of Berlin's mayor.[8] The western Allies vociferously disagreed, arguing that Reuter's thumping majority needed to be respected. Unable to reach a consensus, they kicked the issue upstairs to the Allied Control Council, where it was debated by the four overlords. To the astonishment of everyone, General Clay dramatically turned American policy on its head by declaring that General Kotikov was correct: the Kommandatura should have the final say.

Howley was appalled at such a catastrophic blunder. Clay's decision was certain to strip Reuter of his victory, making a travesty of democracy. It would also undermine his own authority. 'A great blow for me,' he said, 'because I had maintained consistently that the Russians would try to control Berlin's elected government by means of the veto.'[9] He described Clay's action as 'a new low for American prestige'.[10]

The British were equally dismayed and more than a little confused. An *Observer* editorial said that Clay's administration 'appeared to the onlooker like a magnificent high-powered car with the front and back wheels turning at full speed in opposite directions'.[11] The only conceivable explanation was that Clay hoped Kotikov would offer a quid pro quo, allowing all the other appointments to the Magistrat to go ahead in exchange for the veto over the post of mayor. Kotikov was having none of it. He refused to consider allowing his archenemy to be installed as mayor.

Ernst Reuter was the most furious of all, calling it the ultimate betrayal. 'This sudden decision of General Clay [is] the point of utmost compliance toward the Russian claims for dominancy,' he said. '[It is] if you like, a sort of Munich for Berlin.'[12] Smarting with anger, he printed visitor cards that read, 'The Elected but Unconfirmed Mayor of Berlin'.[13] In his stead, the post of mayor temporarily went to one of his deputies, Louise Schroeder.

Reuter waited on the sidelines, preparing for what he believed would be certain conflict with the Soviets. In the 1920s he had been director of Berlin's transport and public utilities; he had also been the architect of the sprawling transport and communications network that had transformed the city into one of the world's most efficient metropolises. This had given him invaluable knowledge of how Berlin lived and breathed.

Hidden among the Greek and Latin texts in Reuter's Zehlendorf apartment were dozens of large-scale blueprints of the city's water, gas and electricity supplies, subway lines and communication cables. He now smuggled these out of his flat and handed them over to the western Allies. His reasoning was typically pragmatic. Although Colonel Howley and Brigadier Hinde had a good working knowledge of their individual sectors, these plans revealed the inner anatomy of the city: its veins and arteries, its lungs and its lifelines. They would be priceless documents if ever the Soviets were to lay siege to the western districts of Berlin, for they contained the very information that could keep the city alive.

Lucius Clay's relationship with Frank Howley reached its lowest ebb in the aftermath of the Ernst Reuter debacle. The two men had five consecutive meetings, with each being more confrontational than the last. These clashes gave Howley food for thought. 'They reaffirmed my own feeling that my thinking was in complete dis-agreement with American policy in Berlin.' To his eyes, Clay was the embodiment of that troubled policy, one that he had opposed 'from the very first day in Berlin'. He began to toy with the idea of escaping the madness of Germany and returning to the United States. 'Even *I* could understand that anyone who was as far off the track as I, couldn't succeed in Berlin.'[14]

Lucius Clay agreed. He was incensed by Howley's free-wheeling approach to policy and curtly informed him that he would be 'invited to go home if I couldn't follow the orders of the commanding general'. Clay even went so far as to accuse Howley of running 'a Gestapo city', which led Howley to retort that he had done his best to follow Clay's misguided orders for the better part of two years.[15]

Despite his thoughts of returning home, Howley decided to make a final push for his aggressively anti-Soviet policy that spring, upping the tempo of his one-man battle against General Kotikov's admin-istration. When the city's Soviet-backed trade union threatened to cripple Berlin's food supply, he warned that such threats would be opposed with force. 'We'll fight to the finish,' he told union leaders. 'There will be people dead in the streets, but they won't be Americans. They will be Germans. And I will hold you, and your organisation, responsible for their murder.'[16] Kotikov responded by accusing Howley of running the American sector of Berlin as if it were his personal mafia empire, describing it as 'a waste-hole of crimes, a centre of kidnappings and employer of former SS soldiers in its police'.[17]

Throughout that spring of 1947, Colonel Howley argued for increasingly bold action against the Soviets, convinced that tit-for-tat retaliation was the only way of dealing with them. 'Counter-measures are the only thing the Russians understand and respect,' he said. 'If they made arrests in our sector, then we should make arrests in theirs. If they cut our telephone wires, we could cut theirs, and also pull the power switches which went through our sector into theirs.'[18]

Lucius Clay strongly disagreed, preferring dialogue, diplomacy and resolution. Ever since arriving in Berlin, he had worked hard to accommodate his Soviet colleagues on the Allied Control Council and quietly congratulated himself on forging a close personal relationship with Marshal Sokolovsky. 'Quiet, unassuming and dignified,' he said of his Soviet opposite number, adding that 'Mrs Clay and I both developed a genuine friendship for him and for Mrs Sokolovsky.'[19]

But now, to his alarm, that friendship had begun to falter. 'While the change was not immediately noticeable,' he said, 'it soon became apparent that fewer Russians were attending Allied social functions and informal meetings between senior representatives came to a standstill.' Before long, Clay was no longer invited to Soviet soirées. It was an unexpected development that seriously jeopardised his policy of rapprochement.

No less unexpected was the fact that his dealings with the aloof Sir Brian Robertson took a sudden upwards turn. Upon first meeting Robertson, Clay had viewed him as 'typical of what we have come to expect from the regular British officer – well groomed, poised, and reserved almost to the point of stiffness'. Try as he might, Clay found it almost impossible 'to break through this outward reserve'. But Robertson came equipped with two qualities that Clay admired greatly – loyalty and integrity. 'He proved a staunch associate,' Clay said of his British counterpart, and praised him for having 'the intelligence of the educated and disciplined mind'.[20] Clay was also in agreement with Robertson's imperious approach to both Germany and Berlin, an approach that was raising hackles in Whitehall. Mandarins disliked Sir Brian's Victorian sense of mission and accused him of running his territories as if they were the Raj. Robertson deftly turned such criticisms to his own advantage. 'We here *are* Empire builders . . .' he said. 'The Empire whose boundaries we struggle to extend is the Empire of true democracy, of peace and decency.'[21] It was a policy that chimed perfectly with that of Lucius Clay, and the two men actively promoted the fusion of the British and American zones of Germany into the single unit, Bizonia, agreed upon the previous summer. Before long the French had also joined the zone and Bizonia became Trizonia. It was the clearest signal that Germany was splitting into east and west.

When Lucius Clay studied the fast-changing geopolitical map that spring, he received an unpleasant surprise. Anti-Communist forces in Poland had been forced out of government; King Michael of Romania was being hounded into exile; the democratic parties in Czechoslovakia were in serious danger. Clay realised that 'the Communists, under direct control of the Kremlin, dominated most of eastern Europe.'[22] Stalin was also turning his attentions to Western Europe, encouraging a general strike in France and intervening in elections in Italy. More alarmingly, the Soviet leader had established the Cominform, whose programme was directed at the political domination of Europe.

Clay was also infuriated by the highly charged propaganda emanating from the offices of Colonel Tiulpanov, who launched a vicious press campaign that bragged of Soviet airpower. This was reinforced by an ostentatious display of fighter planes in the skies over Berlin. Clay was incensed by such a breach of trust and responded by ordering an American fighter formation to fly over the capital; he even got them to sketch out the letters US with their vapour trails. It gave him a kick of pleasure and 'diverted somewhat the trend in the war of nerves'. A month later, with relations strained yet further, he ordered a fly-past of a fleet of B29s – the planes that had delivered the atomic bomb to Hiroshima and Nagasaki. When Marshal Sokolovsky protested, Clay brazenly told him that he wanted to demonstrate 'the effectiveness with which we could participate in [Berlin's] security arrangements'.

There was no longer any place for quiet diplomacy. Clay's good relationship with Sokolovsky belonged to the past and the meetings of the Allied Control Council were becoming as fraught as those of the Kommandatura. 'It was in the Soviet interest to permit relationships to deteriorate,' he said that spring. 'To wage a war of nerves re-creating the fear in Europe, which alone could make possible the further advance of Communism.'[23]

In the capital itself, the talk was of war. Ruth Andreas-Friedrich found that it was dominating everyone's lives and she recorded snippets of overheard conversations in her diary: '"War," says the newspaper vendor. "War," says the streetcar conductor. "War," says the mailman, the grocer and the butcher's wife at the corner.' In the absence of any hard news, rumour spread like wildfire, with extravagant claims and counter-claims. 'All of Bavaria is one huge arsenal. Every night Russian troop transports roll westward. The Western Allies will be lucky if they manage to stop the Russian advance at the Atlantic.'[24] Before long, these rumours grew even darker. 'Increasing signs indicate that there will be a third world war,' Andreas-Friedrich wrote.

The Soviets were indeed tightening their grip on Berlin. Factories working for the western powers routinely had their power supplies shut off and the American parcel-post service was blocked, leading to a stockpile of 650,000 undelivered packages. The Soviets also held up goods crossing through the Soviet zone towards western Germany, causing acute shortages. Kotikov was repeatedly asked to explain the reason for such actions, but he never gave a straight answer. 'You might as well try to pin down a jellyfish as to try impaling a Russian on a reasonable question,' was Howley's memorable conclusion.[25]

Relations between the Soviets and the western powers reached their lowest ebb in the spring of 1947, when three of Germany's four overlords – Clay, Robertson and Sokolovsky – attended the Moscow Conference. Its purpose was to resolve issues outstanding since Potsdam, and it was to be led by the four foreign ministers. Lucius Clay was joined in Moscow by Truman's new secretary of state, George Marshall, while General Robertson was accompanied by Ernest Bevin. Georges Bidault and Vyacheslav Molotov were once again representing France and the Soviet Union, respectively.

Clay found the dreary Moscow weather a perfect reflection of everyone's mood, with the streets strewn with piles of dirty snow. Security was a serious concern, even at the residency of the American embassy. 'The experts, files, secretaries, clerks, and stenographers were all installed in the ballroom. The windows in this room were kept closed, with drawn shades.' There was good reason for this. One of the embassy's security officers told Clay of his fears 'that some acute hearing devices and long-distance cameras might otherwise record or photograph conversations and papers'.[26] Tensions were further heightened when the British contingent 'found six concealed plastic dictaphones in the walls of their office'.

Events took a brief comic turn on the eve of the conference when the American ambassador, Walter Bedell Smith, misunderstood the nature of the hair tonic that his local barber wished to administer. By the time he realised the mistake it was too late. '[He] fumed as he stared in the mirror at his newly pink hair.'[27] Whether or not this was deliberate on the part of the barber remains unknown, but Bedell Smith's hair remained pink for the duration of the conference and provided a rare moment of levity in an otherwise sombre gathering. The six-week conference proved no happier than the previous meeting in Paris, when Bevin had come close to punching Molotov. The Soviet foreign minister proved as obdurate as ever, demanding ever-larger reparations from Germany. Bevin summed up these demands as an attempt 'to loot Germany at our expense'.

There were forty-four main sessions and innumerable committee meetings, but no meeting of minds. As the conference reached its weary conclusion, the American secretary of state paid a courtesy call on Stalin, accompanied by Charles Bohlen. The Soviet leader was much changed in the twenty-one months since the Potsdam Conference, noted Bohlen: 'grayer, careworn and fatigued'. During their visit, which lasted an hour and a half, Stalin spent most of the time doodling wolf's heads onto a sheet of paper, using a red pencil. He told his American guests that he was untroubled by the lack of any agreement. 'We should be detached and even relaxed about the subject,' he said.

Bohlen had never trusted Stalin and suspected an ulterior motive. In a private memo to Truman, he warned the president that Stalin 'saw that the best way to advance Soviet interests [in Europe] was to let matters drift . . . Unemployment was widespread. Millions of people were on short rations. There was a danger of epidemics. This was the kind of crisis Communism thrived on.' George Marshall agreed and spent the entire journey back to Washington discussing with Bohlen 'the importance of finding some initiative to prevent the complete break-up of Western Europe'.

That initiative had, in fact, been taken in his absence, by President Truman himself. In an eighteen-minute address to the US Congress on 12 March, Truman had announced a dramatic shift in American foreign policy. 'I believe that it must be the policy of the United States', he said, 'to support free peoples who are resisting attempted subjugation by armed minorities or by outside pressures. I believe that we must assist free peoples to work out their own destinies in their own way.'[28] In short, he was calling for America to intervene in the affairs of the world. This policy was to become known as the Truman Doctrine.

Among the first practical steps was a massive financial aid package to Greece and Turkey – stepping in where Britain had stepped out – in order to stem the rise of Communism. But Truman's doctrine had a far wider scope than the eastern Mediterranean. Its purpose was nothing short of containing Soviet expansion and supporting all countries threatened by Communism. As such, it was exactly the policy shift that George Kennan had advocated in his Long Telegram thirteen months before. Kennan was now rewarded for his work with an influential new post as first director of the Policy Planning Staff. It would give him a decisive role over all future aspects of American foreign policy.

Secretary of State George Marshall added flesh to the bones of the Truman Doctrine on his return from Moscow, calling for the immediate rehabilitation of the German economy. In a radio broadcast to the American nation, he warned that the Soviets were intent on seizing control of the whole of Germany. If the country were to be saved from complete collapse, the western world needed to take immediate action. 'The patient is sinking while the doctors deliberate.'[29]

One of those doctors was George Marshall himself. Within weeks of his radio address he was sketching the outlines of his Marshall Plan. Not only did he intend to regenerate Europe, but he also wanted to send a clear signal to Stalin that America meant business. From his office in Berlin, Clay saw it as a drawing of the battle-lines. 'The thin screen of American and British soldiers in Germany symbolized the united will of two great nations that this far the threat of the Red Army would reach – and no further.'[30]

One of the first people in the capital to hear of the Marshall Plan was Ruth Andreas-Friedrich, who received the news within twenty-four hours of the American secretary of state making his first speech. 'A glimmer of hope appears from somewhere,' she wrote. 'Finally, a constructive proposal.'[31] The stakes could scarcely have been higher, as Marshall himself was aware. If his plan succeeded, Western Europe would be transformed into a bulwark against Stalin. But if it failed, there was 'a real danger that [the] whole of Germany will be drawn into [the] eastern orbit, with obvious dire consequences for all of us'.[32]

For Lucius Clay, Marshall's plan represented concrete proof that American policy had undergone a sea change. The document with which he had first arrived in Berlin, JCS 1067, was to be discarded forthwith. In its place was a master plan for rebuilding the German economy. As one newspaper put it, 'Clay came with a brief of destruction [and] stayed to execute a brief of reconstruction.'[33] Germany was to be rebuilt, with a resurrected Berlin at its heart.

By the end of June, Marshall's ideas were being discussed at the highest levels in London. American aid was to be made available to any country prepared to assist in the rebuilding of Europe. 'Dollars will not save the world,' said Marshall, 'but the world today cannot be saved without dollars.'[34] President Truman informed the American people that the Marshall Plan was the practical application of his Truman Doctrine. 'Two halves of the same walnut,' was how he put it.[35]

Moscow saw it as a declaration of war, with Molotov issuing a fiery denouncement. 'The intention of the Marshall Plan is to rob independent European countries of their self-reliance and place them under American control. Russia opposes the Marshall Plan because it splits Europe in two.'[36]

It was still not certain that Marshall's plan would pass through Congress, for there were powerful dissenting voices. Ironically, it was Stalin who ensured its success. The launch of a Soviet-backed coup in Czechoslovakia and the defenestration of the popular foreign minister, Jan Masaryk, in the second week of March, gave the Marshall Plan the push it needed. It passed rapidly through the Senate and soon afterwards completed its passage through the House of Representatives.

Lucius Clay saw this as a turning point. 'We were now engaged in a competitive struggle, not with arms but with economic resources, with ideas and with ideals.'[37] He did not know how long the struggle would last and nor did he know what form it would take. But he felt sure that the showdown would be focussed on Berlin.

It was ironic that Frank Howley decided to leave Berlin at the very time when American policy had swung into line with his own views. For some months he had let it be known that he was considering leaving his post and this had led to a flurry of employment offers. In Philadelphia, political leaders wanted him to run for mayor; in Washington he had offers from the State Department; in New York he had proposals from big business. All were promising an annual salary far in excess of the $10,000 he received in Berlin.

In spite of this, his decision to leave was taken with a heavy heart. For more than two years he had engaged in a near-constant battle with the Soviets, as well as fighting hard for the Berliners in the American sector of the city. He could look back on his time with pride, for he had brought stability to the sector under his control and overseen the restoration of power, water and public transport. Just a year ago he had been so optimistic about a long tenure in Berlin that he had brought his family here, placing his children in one of the new American schools. Now, everything was coming to an end.

Two days before his departure, on Thursday, 13 November, he was summoned to a valedictory meeting at General Clay's office. It ought to have been an emotional moment for both men, yet their exchanges remained strictly businesslike. Clay asked a few questions about the Political Affairs section and Howley answered as best he could, but he felt that Clay wasn't really listening. 'Apparently, he had something much more important on his mind.' As Howley turned to leave for the final time, Clay asked a question that stopped him in his tracks. 'Frank,' he said abruptly, 'how would you like to come back on active duty as commandant?'

Howley was astonished, flattered and knocked sideways. He was being offered the post he had always wanted: not that of deputy, but that of permanent, Berlin-based commandant of the American sector, a position that he could dominate and make his own.

Here was a promotion to be savoured, not to mention being a job for which he was uniquely qualified. The dramatic shift in President Truman's foreign policy also meant that Howley's views were now in accord with those of Washington. It was this, more than anything else, that had led to Clay's change of heart. Howley accepted the offer immediately, certain that the city was about to enter its most turbulent period. 'I did go to the United States,' he later wrote in his memoirs, '[but] three weeks later, I was back in Berlin.'[38] This time, he was fully in charge.

Marshal Sokolovsky's behaviour in the Allied Control Council changed so dramatically over the course of that autumn that it was as if he were a different person. Gone were the aphorisms, the witty asides and the quotes from Jane Austen. Gone, too, was any hint of friendship with his erstwhile partners. Lucius Clay was astonished to hear the marshal spit poison at the Americans and British. 'Sokolovsky really threw the book at us,' he said after one meeting at which the Soviet marshal accused the two powers of every conceivable crime, from hiding Nazi war criminals to deliberately dividing Germany.[39] It was not an off-the-cuff remark: the marshal brought along a carefully prepared statement that was calculated to offend. Clay said that he 'read it with the utmost gravity and I seemed to feel at the time a complete change in his attitude'.[40]

Molotov was to launch an equally blistering attack at the next meeting of the foreign ministers in Paris, with his ire directed at the Marshall Plan. 'Insults, insinuations and accusations,' snapped Ernest Bevin, as he listened to a series of charges levelled against the British and Americans.[41] After one particularly heated outburst, he turned to a Foreign Office mandarin and whispered excitedly, 'This really is the birth of the Western bloc.'[42] This was true enough. By the spring of 1948, the crisis had led to the creation of the

Western Union in which Britain, France, Belgium, Luxembourg and the Netherlands agreed to work together on issues of defence, economics and politics in post-war Europe.

Lucius Clay was convinced there would eventually be a showdown, but the opening shot was fired sooner than he was expecting. At a regular meeting of the four overlords, on 20 March 1948, Marshal Sokolovsky was even more bellicose than at the previous meeting. The Soviet Union held the rotating chairmanship of the Allied Control Council that month, enabling him to set the agenda. Sokolovsky was in no mood for niceties. As he lit the first in a chain of long-stemmed black cigarettes, he accused the western Allies of treating the German people with contempt.

Clay and Robertson exchanged glances: never before had Sokolovsky expressed himself with quite such force. Clay started to counter his charges but it was clear that Sokolovsky had no interest in what he had to say. The interpreter had scarcely finished translating his opening words when Sokolovsky interrupted him, pulled out a sheet of paper and read from a prepared statement. This repeated all the usual charges against the western powers, only 'in more aggravating language'.

The tone of Sokolovsky's attack proved too much for General Robertson. 'I wish to protest against the strong language the chairman has used in describing the attitude of his colleagues.'[43] He was brusquely silenced by Sokolovsky, who was no longer interested in what Robertson had to say. 'Rudely interrupting and without explanation, the Soviet delegation, following what must have been a pre-arranged plan, rose as one.' As their chairs scraped backwards across the parquet floor, Sokolovsky narrowed his eyes before dropping his bombshell. 'I see no sense in continuing the meeting,' he said, 'and I declare it adjourned.' Without further ado, the Soviet delegation stormed from the room. Lucius Clay was stunned. 'The Allied Control Council was dead,' he said. It was the end of four-part rule for Germany.[44] The Berlin Kommandatura was now the only channel of communication between the Soviets and the western Allies.

Clay immediately sent news of the rupture to Washington, appending a chilling postscript to his message. 'For many months I have felt and held that war was unlikely for at least ten years,' he said. 'But within the last few weeks I have felt a subtle change in Soviet attitude . . . [it] gives me a feeling that it may come with dramatic suddenness.'[45]

General Robertson also felt that Berlin was about to explode. For weeks he had been informing London of an 'intense war of nerves' being waged by the Soviets. Now, matters had reached a head. 'One foot wrong now,' he warned, 'and it's World War Three.'[46]

15

Breaking Point

IN SOVIET-RUN POTSDAM, Valerie Hoecke had received no news from her husband, Paul, since his arrest by NKVD officers three years earlier, in the spring of 1945. Now, she found that she was also under suspicion and was obliged to report each week to the local offices of the Soviet Military Administration, where KGB agents questioned her about parishioners of the Russian Orthodox Church. The Soviets' mistrust of the White Russian community deepened further when they learned that Potsdam's replacement priest, Father Theodore Gilyavski, had fled to the West.

It was around this time that a woman known only as Mrs X warned Frau Hoecke that she was in danger. How she knew this is unclear, but she urged Valerie Hoecke and her children to flee Potsdam while they still had the chance.

Ever since the closure of their local parish, the Hoeckes had travelled to the American sector of Berlin to attend services at the Russian church in Nachodstrasse. At the end of one of these services, Frau Hoecke fell into conversation with an American counter-intelligence officer named Captain Michael Shterbinine, also a Russian émigré, who listened to her account of weekly KGB questionings before giving her the same advice as Mrs X. She was in danger and must flee the Soviet zone as soon as possible.

Shterbinine was able to offer sanctuary at his house in the American sector, where Frau Hoecke and her children could lodge for as long as it took to arrange transit out of Berlin. Over the weeks that followed, the Hoeckes surreptitiously moved their most treasured possessions into the captain's house, transporting them in a little handcart.

Frau Hoecke managed to sell the family piano, which gave her some much-needed money, as well as the leather-bound books that her children had salvaged two years earlier. It was soon time for their final trip out of Potsdam. Young Hermann took a final glance at the toys he had to leave behind and bade farewell to the family home. 'It was a grey, overcast day when we left Leiblstrasse for the last time and walked through downtown Potsdam to the S-bahn station.'[1] The four of them could only pray they were not being watched or followed.

Brigadier Hinde received some devastating news that spring. His oft-absent boss was to be replaced by a new commandant, General Otway Herbert, who announced his intention of taking an active role in the work of the Kommandatura. The general was also bringing his own chosen deputy, Brigadier Edward Benson, which meant that Brigadier Hinde no longer had a role. His work in Berlin was at an end and, unlike Colonel Howley, there was to be no happy postscript.

Harold Hays was appalled when he heard the news. He had worked alongside Hinde for three long years and had seen the brigadier's accomplishments at close quarters. Not only had Hinde saved the British sector from complete collapse, but he had also 'worked long and tirelessly for the cause of unity'.[2] Without the diplomatic presence of Brigadier Hinde, the Kommandatura would certainly have broken up.

Hinde left Berlin as he had arrived, without fuss or fanfare, and headed to his new post in Lower Saxony. Honours would follow later in life, with a knighthood bestowed in 1956. Yet there was always a nagging sense that history had passed him by and it was only his loyal colleagues who kept his achievements alive in Berlin. His blueprint for the city is not to be found in the National Archives, nor in any other repository. His surviving family may well have the only copy.

His successor, General Herbert, was woefully ill-equipped for the momentous events about to hit Berlin. According to one observer, Herbert expected his work 'to be interesting and not particularly exacting, and brushed aside any talk of troublesome Russians'. Herbert had long held that old soldiers had enough discipline to get along in amicable fashion, 'whatever their differences in creed or even colour'.[3] He was in for a rude awakening.

Harold Hays disliked Herbert from the outset, finding him a fastidious martinet with an autocratic mind. 'Not quite the personality for delicate diplomatic adventures,' he wrote. 'Thrustful, intolerant or, at times, even impetuous and petulant.' The general was also caustic and unforgiving, characteristics that gained him few allies and even fewer friends.

There was a more serious problem with General Herbert, one that had not been foreseen when he was selected for the job. Frank Howley despised him, a fact that created a potential rift between the Americans and British at a highly sensitive moment. These two men 'were engaged in one of the most delicate diplomatic jobs in history', said Hays, 'but they appeared to tolerate each other only so long as the cohesive force of Russian intransigence bound them together'. From their very first meeting, it was 'a most uneasy partnership'.[4]

This was an understatement. Howley described General Herbert as 'gloom personified' and 'always the pessimist', and he would later write about their 'terrific head-on fights, far beyond mere academic disputes'. He also found Herbert to be relentlessly negative. 'Tension was high,' Howley said, 'and I considered his defeatist approach destructive to Western unity.'[5]

Colonel Howley's greatest concern that spring was that General Kotikov would cut supplies to the western sectors of the city and thereby starve its military garrisons into submission. To pre-empt this, he drew up a 'Basic Assumption Plan' that set out the minimum stockpile needed to keep those garrisons alive. His 'assumption' was that the Soviets would stop supplies of both food and fuel. If so, everything needed to support the 6,500 Allied soldiers, along with their families and staff, would have to be transported along the single-track railway that ran through Soviet-controlled territory from Marienborn to Berlin, a distance of 110 miles.

That was one logistical headache. A far greater challenge would be if General Kotikov also cut supplies to the two and a quarter million inhabitants living in the western sectors of Berlin. This would create an untenable situation. It was simply not credible that one could keep the city alive by the use of a single railway line.

On 25 March, Colonel Howley called a secret meeting with his British and French counterparts, General Herbert and General Jean Ganeval. The former listened with growing scepticism as Howley outlined his Basic Assumption Plan, now rechristened Operation Counterpunch, before dismissing the very idea of a Soviet blockade. 'Preposterous!' he said. 'They wouldn't dare.'

'Preposterous, my ass!' interjected Howley, but the British general was not yet finished. He said that if there were indeed a sustained blockade, as Howley was suggesting, then it was inconceivable for the Allied garrisons to remain in Berlin. 'We could never hold out,' he said. 'The Russians could have us out in a month, if they wanted to.'[6] His words prompted another furious riposte from Howley. 'We'll starve, we'll eat rats, rather than quit Berlin!'[7]

A week after this stormy meeting, General Herbert sent a report to Whitehall setting out the insurmountable problems that would be caused by the Soviets cutting supplies. It was 'highly improbable that the Western sectors could hold out through a winter', he said, and added that frequent power cuts would soon break the will of Berliners. In such a scenario, the city's inhabitants 'would prefer to have the Russians'.[8] It was a sentiment that displayed extraordinary ignorance of the resilience of Berliners.

General Herbert's assessment was not well received in London, where Ernest Bevin was increasingly strident about the Soviet threat. 'We *must* stay in Berlin,' he said, adding that he 'did not want with-drawal to be contemplated in any quarter'. He was even more outspoken in cabinet meetings, warning that the Soviet Union was 'actively preparing to extend its hold over the remaining part of continental Europe'. This, he said, would lead to one of two outcomes: 'either to the establishment of a World Dictatorship or, more probably, to the collapse of organised society over great stretches of the globe'.[9]

Bevin might have been even more alarmed had he known that on 19 March, Stalin had engaged in secret discussions with Wilhelm Pieck, the joint leader of the Socialist Unity Party. Pieck gave Stalin a frank warning that the Communists stood no chance of winning a fair and free election in Berlin. Stalin suggested they resort to more sinister means. 'Let's make a joint effort,' he said. 'Maybe we can drive them out.'[10]

Frank Howley's idea of supplying Berlin by train laid bare the problem of access to the city. For the previous three years, the western powers had been using one of two railway lines that linked the capital with the western-occupied sectors of Germany. The first of these lines crossed the British-Soviet border at Helmstedt (in Saxony) while the other crossed the American-Soviet border at Hof (in Bavaria).

The only other means of access was via the two sanctioned autobahns, which followed more or less the same routes as the railway. The drive was a bleak experience in the winter months when the difficulties of dealing with truculent Soviet border guards were compounded by snow, ice and Arctic conditions: 'The war-splintered road, the dense black forest lining much of the route, and the sinister absence of any signs of life (because Soviet Zone inhabitants were forbidden to approach the motorway) made the 200 kilometres into central Berlin seem at least double the distance.' So wrote journalist Anthony Mann, who said the surface of the road was covered in arrows 'marking emergency road-repairs or unexploded bombs'.[11] Such was the precarious state of the lifelines into western Berlin.

It soon became apparent just how precarious these were. In the small hours of 1 April, the Frankfurt–Berlin steam express, *Berliner*, was approaching the Soviet frontier town of Marienborn, the last stopping point before the German capital. The train was carrying three hundred American army officers and enlisted men, many of whom were rejoining wives and loved ones in Berlin. The *Berliner* shuddered to a halt at the border post, hissing steam and coal-dust into the freezing night air. As it did so, armed Soviet border police could be seen emerging from the dimly lit station office, their faces illuminated by their mercury vapour lamps. There was nothing unusual about this, for they had the right to check the documents of German passengers. But on this occasion, they also demanded to inspect the papers of the Allied military personnel.

The train's commander refused point-blank and warned that his military police would open fire if the Soviet border patrol dared to board the train. Among those on the *Berliner* that night was Captain Clarence Cummings, who listened in alarm to the escalating tension. Voices were raised and angry cries broke the silence of the night.

'If they want to shoot, we can shoot too!' shouted an American voice. 'Come on, Colonel, let's go through!'[12]

A tense stand-off ensued while the train's commander phoned Berlin in an attempt to get orders. The American troops grew increasingly bullish and declared their willingness to fight their way through to the capital. But when dawn broke they were still in Marienborn and as the day drifted towards noon it became clear there was to be neither shooting nor any progress towards the capital. At 8.20 p.m., more than eighteen hours after their arrival, the engines fired up steam and the train headed back to Frankfurt. It was a humiliating experience.

What no one on board knew was that they had been pawns in a ferocious shouting match between Lucius Clay and the joint chiefs of staff in Washington. Clay had spent much of that day in the telecom room of his subterranean bunker, arguing with his political masters. Both he and Howley wanted the train to force its way through to Berlin, firing weaponry if necessary. But the joint chiefs of staff refused to countenance such an idea. The Truman Doctrine was one thing, but this was a step too far. 'In no event shall there be shooting,' they said,[13] adding that it 'carried the risk of placing the onus on us for another world war'.[14]

Clay was dismayed by their response and shot back a defiant message. 'We have lost Czechoslovakia, Norway is threatened . . . [W]hen Berlin falls, Western Germany will be next.' He told Washington it was vital for America to stand firm. 'If America does not understand this now . . . then it never will, and communism will run rampant.'[15]

The American climbdown encouraged the Soviets in their harassment and they now began stopping every train and interrogating the passengers on board. Jean Eastham was a young member of the Auxiliary Territorial Service en route to Berlin just days after the *Berliner* incident. She had not anticipated that her journey would be quite so eventful. She and her four fellow travellers were ordered off the train by Soviet guards and bundled into dilapidated buses.

'Each bus had an officer and two soldiers, armed with revolvers and Sten guns.' The guards detained the little group for many hours before they were eventually allowed to proceed to Berlin, albeit without their luggage. The Soviet guards warned Miss Eastham that she and her friends wouldn't be in Berlin for long, because 'we weren't entitled to be there'.[16]

Ever since the western Allies had negotiated the use of two high-ways into Berlin, they had been allowed to establish Allied Autobahn Aid Stations at twenty-five-mile intervals along the roads. These precarious little outposts, deep inside Soviet-occupied territory, were surrounded by gateposts, searchlights and barbed wire: their purpose was to aid British, American and French drivers who were out of fuel, had punctures or had broken down. But now, as tensions once again increased, the Soviets ordered their closure.

Receiving orders to leave his station was a mournful occasion for Captain Desmond Haslehurst, and one that called for a little cere-mony. As the Union Jack was lowered for the last time, he snapped his arm into a military salute and kept it clamped into position while his comrade sounded the 'Last Post' on the trumpet. 'Pack up everything and return to base,' were the instructions. 'Leave nothing for the Russians, not even the barbed wire.'[17]

As travel by road and rail became increasingly fraught, the only reliable means of reaching the city was by plane, using one of the three air corridors agreed upon in 1945. But this brought its own dangers. At exactly 1.57 p.m. on 5 April 1948, a British-owned Viking passenger aircraft was making a scheduled flight from London when it plunged from the sky and crashed to the ground in the Soviet sector of Berlin. On board were fourteen passengers and crew, all of whom were killed. Seconds later, a Soviet Yak fighter also slammed into the ground, scattering burning debris into the British sector of the city. The Soviet pilot was killed instantly, with his abdomen and legs crushed into the wreckage.

Several eyewitnesses revealed that the Yak had been performing aerial acrobatics around the Viking when disaster struck. They described the Yak as making a steep upwards climb when it hit the Viking's starboard wing, ripping it off. Others would later corrob-orate this version of events.

General Robertson was outraged by such an avoidable tragedy and personally delivered a letter of protest to Marshal Sokolovsky, who stated that the crash was a terrible accident. But within twenty-four hours, the marshal had changed his tune and claimed that the pilot of the British Viking had deliberately rammed the Yak, causing the fatal collision.

The ensuing Anglo–Soviet enquiry was conducted in an 'electrical atmosphere of suspicion and mistrust', with Sokolovsky further igniting the tension by refusing to allow the British to investigate the debris of the Viking or even remove the charred bodies.[18] In such a poisoned climate it was inevitable that the commission of enquiry would fail. The Soviets declared that the crash 'was an accident for which the British side is to be declared guilty' and went so far as to demand compensation for the widow of the Russian pilot.[19]

The British pressed ahead with their own enquiry which drew on the testimonies of thirty-seven eyewitnesses, all of whom agreed on the essential detail: the Yak had been performing reckless aeronautics when it collided with the Viking. The two enquiries led to an uneasy stalemate and became one more grievance to stoke the simmering resentment between east and west, attracting widespread coverage in the press. Hays sensed that conflict was in the air. 'The already extremely tense situation became charged with foreboding,' he said; he feared that the smallest trifle could provide 'the initial spark of a third world conflagration'.[20]

The days that followed were marked by yet more curbs on transport, with the border crossing at Marienborn becoming a dangerous gamble. On 11 June, General Herbert was told that no more freight trains could enter the capital because of 'congestion in the Berlin yards'.[21] This was to cause severe problems for the few factories that had started to function, notably the Blaupunkt radio works and the Osram lightbulb manufacturer.

The ban was soon rescinded, but it was followed by restrictions on imports of coal and fuel. Next to be cut was the milk supply to the western sectors of Berlin. The first Frank Howley knew about this was when he received a visit from his medical officer. 'I'm sorry, Colonel,' he said, 'but the Russians have cut off our milk supply.

Unless we get that fresh milk, six thousand German babies in our sector will be dead by Monday.'

When Howley investigated the matter, he was told that the Russians would resume the milk supply if the Americans collected it in their own trucks, thereby reneging on the previously agreed-upon deal. This would use up precious gasoline, but Howley had no alternative but to back down. 'I had to admit I was licked,' he wrote. 'There was nothing to do but eat crow and submit, for the time being at least.'[22] But it taught him an important lesson: that very day, he ordered 200 tons of condensed milk and 150 tons of powdered milk to be flown into the capital.

Shortly after the milk debacle, the Russians closed the bridge over the River Elbe near Magdeburg, claiming it was in 'urgent need of repairs'.[23] This was a serious provocation, for the bridge carried all autobahn traffic from Helmstedt to Berlin. Henceforth, vehicles had to cross the river by hand-ferry, two at a time.

More sinister was the Soviet decree that any Berliner travelling to the western zones was obliged to buy their tickets at Friedrichstrasse station in the Soviet sector of the city. This would enable the authorities to keep track of people's precise movements. When General Kotikov also sent Soviet troops into the American sector to seize control of the German Railway administration headquarters, Howley's patience snapped. This building was the nerve centre of all railway operations in and out of Berlin and therefore of vital importance to western interests. Howley sent in American troops and told them not to hold back when evicting the Russian soldiers. His orders were followed to the letter: Kotikov's railway officer, General Vasily Petrov, was escorted from the building with an American tommy gun rammed into his stomach.

The Hoecke family successfully evaded Soviet intelligence agents on their valedictory journey from Potsdam to the American sector of Berlin and were soon safely installed in Captain Michael Shterbinine's Dahlem villa. After the hardships of Soviet Potsdam, they found themselves initiated into a world of material abundance. 'Rice Krispies and Shredded Wheat cereal for breakfast, with cardboard model planes in the box as an added bonus.' The children were also given bananas, orange juice and American comic books.

Young Hermann soon began to suspect that not everything with the American captain was quite as it seemed. Mysterious visitors spent hours in his study and there was an unnamed person living in the attic. Hermann later discovered that it was a Soviet air force pilot named Pavlik, who was also using the villa as a safe house while plotting his defection to the West.

After several weeks in hiding, Captain Shterbinine introduced nine-year-old Hermann to a group of work colleagues, probably fellow intelligence agents, and asked if he could run a few errands. These were routine at first (delivering papers and reports), but he was soon sent on more clandestine missions that involved his being driven across the city – probably into the Soviet sector – in an unmarked jeep. 'We would drive to a street corner in a deserted part of town, where I would get out and walk around the block to a specific house.' He was told to knock on the door, wait for it to open and then quickly slip the package through the gap. To a young boy, such missions were incredibly exciting. 'Could these packages have been instructions to agents on the other side?' he wondered. 'Were they fake documents intended for people trying to cross the line into the West?'

Hermann Hoecke was the only member of the family allowed out from the captain's villa. 'Aside from my secret agent activities, no one in our family ever left the safe house throughout our stay.'[24] Their most pressing task in those stressful days of spring 1948 was to find a way of getting out of Berlin and into the western zone of occupied Germany.

It seemed appropriate to everyone that the final official showdown between the Soviets and the western Allies should take place in the Kommandatura, scene of so many previous wrangles. Meetings had become so heated over the previous weeks that it no longer func-tioned as a debating chamber. 'It would take a wheelbarrow to bring here all the insults published about the Americans in the Soviet sector,' said Howley at one session. Kotikov's response was equally combative. 'A ten-ton truck wouldn't be enough to haul all the insanities and calumnies the press carries in your sectors.'[25]

Howley felt that the Soviets were doing everything they could to provoke a definitive crisis. 'Kotikov's attacks seemed all part of the new campaign by the Russians to kill the Kommandatura, blame the West for its demise and then try to drive us all out of the city.'[26]

A regular meeting had been scheduled for that Wednesday, 16 June, beginning, earlier than usual, at 10 a.m. It was an insufferably hot morning, leading one commentator to say that it was as if the weather itself 'had a role in the tragedy and the melodrama of things to come'.[27]

The three western representatives arrived at the Kommandatura for what they assumed to be a regular session, with the usual wrangling over trade unions, city governance and postal services. The first surprise came when General Kotikov failed to show up. They were told he had an illness and would be represented by his deputy, Colonel Andrei Yelizarov. More alarming was the presence of the sinister Mr Maximov.

The meeting was angry and ill-humoured, with the arguing continuing until around 7 p.m., when something most unusual occurred. The door to the chamber opened and in walked a strange-looking Soviet commissar. 'A man I had never seen before,' said Howley, 'and have never seen since.' He was not introduced, nor was it clear why he was there, but he certainly made an impression, for he was wearing a colourful embroidered Ukrainian blouse. He leaned over the table and whispered furtively to Yelizarov and Maximov.

His words had an electrifying effect. 'An emotion very close to excitement shook the two usually frozen-faced Russians and Yelizarov asked for a recess.' Howley and his British and French colleagues agreed and headed to the upstairs dining room, leaving the Russians to discuss matters in private.

'Looking out of the dining room window a few minutes later, I saw Maximov striding nervously up and down, puffing a black cigarette in a long holder.' He was wearing a thick 'Eisenhower' jacket under his woollen coat – strange attire for such a sweltering evening – and was chatting in animated fashion to the mystery commissar. 'Something was in the air,' said Howley. 'That was definite.'

The meeting continued as before, with another four hours of fruitless argument. 'Absolutely nothing had been accomplished,' said Howley. 'I was done in.'[28] At 11.15 p.m. he asked General Ganeval, the chairman of that day's session, if he could be excused. 'I'm tired,' he said. 'I'm going home and I'm going to bed. With your permission, General, I will leave my deputy, Colonel Babcock, to represent me.'[29] The general agreed and Howley moved towards the door, unaware of the extraordinary scenes about to unfold.

Lieutenant Colonel Hays observed everything that followed. 'For a brief moment the talking ceased,' he said, 'while all eyes were directed towards Colonel Howley through the thick haze of the tobacco smoke. The interpreters, for once caught completely off their guard, remained silent.'

Hays's eyes flicked left and right; something was afoot at the far end of the room. As Howley made his way downstairs, Mr Maximov whispered something to Colonel Yelizarov, who shot to his feet and slammed his papers onto the table. 'I consider it impossible to continue this meeting after an action that I can only claim as a hooligan action on the part of Colonel Howley,' he shouted. 'I will not remain here any more.'

He hurled abuse on the now-absent Howley, leading to such a slanging match that the stenographers were unable to keep up. Yelizarov then headed for the door, with Commissar Maximov right behind him. Hays had never witnessed anything like it. 'Frantic efforts were made to convince the Russians that they had made a mistake and to persuade them to return.'[30] But to no avail. Seconds later, the Soviet delegation stormed out of the room. It was later said that the last word spoken by Yelizarov was '*nyet*'. It was the perfect epitaph to the now-defunct Kommandatura.

Frank Howley would later write in his diary about the dramatic events of that evening: 'Personally, I say it is good riddance of bad rubbish. I think it has been a disgrace for an American representative to sit for six months and listen to the abuse of the American people, the American Army, and all our concepts of democracy.'

Later that night, at around 3 a.m., he gave a briefing to the American press, which had already picked up rumours of the drama. 'If any jokers think they're going to get the British, French and

Americans out of Berlin,' said Howley, 'they have another think coming.'[31]

The final act in that great spring showdown of 1948 took place in absolute secrecy. Frank Howley described it as 'a strictly cloak-and-dagger affair, with all the trimmings'. It was to involve a small team of men and women, none of whom was privy to the secret, along with an inner circle of experts residing inside a gilded cage at York House, a Military Government building in the British sector. 'It was a cage in the strictest sense of the word,' said Howley. 'We couldn't afford to allow the slightest hint of our intentions to reach the Russians.'

The experts included Germany's foremost financiers, plucked from their homes and transported to York House in order that their expertise could be exploited. 'No key physicists, with the dark secrets of the atomic bomb locked in their brains, were guarded and shrouded more carefully.'[32]

Operation Bird Dog was indeed a clandestine operation and it had begun at the Rhein-Main Airbase in the American zone of occupied Germany. On 23 June, Lieutenant Randolph Tully and a handful of American pilots were ordered to fly 'a load of merchandise' that had been stacked into sealed crates marked Bird Dog. These crates were to be flown to Berlin.

Tully and his men were mystified by the secrecy of the operation and their curiosity was further piqued when their briefing officer handed them primed grenades. 'If you have to crash land in Russian territory, blow up the ship,' he said, referring to the C-47 in which they were flying.

The flight itself was uneventful: as they prepared to land in Berlin, Lieutenant Tully transmitted to the control tower the cryptic message he had been given on taking off. 'Tempelhof tower, Tempelhof tower, we have New York on board.'[33] As the plane touched down, Tully and his men noticed jeep-loads of military police chasing down the runway to meet them.

Only later would Howley be able to reveal their cargo. It had been 250 million crisply printed Deutschemarks, an entirely new currency that the western powers were introducing into their zones of Germany. Those financial experts held under lock and key in York House had been tasked with studying the problem of introducing a new currency to Berlin without crippling the already broken economy. The western powers were not intending to launch this currency in Berlin, unless or until the Soviets carried out their threat to do the same. If so, they would simultaneously issue their Deutschemarks.

The drama had begun on 19 June, when Marshal Sokolovsky announced that the Soviet Military Administration was introducing a new currency in its zone of occupied Germany. It would also be the only one valid in the capital. 'Only one currency will circulate in Berlin,' he said, 'the currency of the Soviet zone.'[34] His intention was to use it to bring the city's banking and financial sectors under his control.

The western Allies responded with their secret master plan. Within hours of the Soviets introducing their currency, they injected their 250 million Deutschemarks into the economy at a fixed and stable exchange rate. This was to cause uproar at the City Assembly, where the elected members debated the currency issue amidst extraordinary scenes in the surrounding streets. An angry mob of Ulbricht supporters had gathered outside the building to denounce the western currency. Red flags fluttered in the wind and huge banners proclaimed that 'Only One Currency Will Save Berlin'.[35] The three-thousand-strong crowd was whipped into a frenzy by Ulbricht himself, whose grating voice reverberated from a loudspeaker van.

Ruth Andreas-Friedrich watched the band of activists in mounting alarm. 'People are yelling. Their faces twisted as if they're suffering convulsions. The crowd surges forward. Trampling, pressing and pushing ahead like a stream of lava.'[36]

Inside the Assembly chamber, Ernst Reuter's deputy, Louise Schroeder, still the city's acting-mayor, proposed that both currencies should be circulated on an equal basis, something that the western powers were prepared to accept. But the mob vehemently disagreed and now smashed its way into the building. Amidst scenes of chaos, assembly delegate Jeanette Wolff, a slight, sixty-year-old grandmother, shouted down Ulbricht's supporters. 'I spent six years in a concentration camp without being scared of the SS,' she yelled. 'I'm not going to run away from the Socialist Unity Party.' Her words were met with a torrent of abuse. 'Throw that bitch out . . . We'll shut your mouth for you . . . Traitors are to stay outside.'[37]

The deputies refused to be intimidated and agreed by a large majority to accept both currencies, despite the vehement opposition. Howley was delighted to have notched up yet another victory. 'Berlin's elected representatives refused to be bullied,' he said. 'The meeting ended with a major defeat for the Russians.'[38]

But he soon found himself with a further battle on his hands, one with a less certain outcome. Late in the evening of that same day, 23 June, the political editor of *Der Tag* newspaper, Margot Derigs, was checking the final set of the newspaper's galley proofs when she suddenly heard the Teletype machine of the Soviet ADN news agency starting its characteristic tac-tac-tac. A message was coming through on the Teletype paper and it was sensational: 'TRANSPORT DIVISION OF THE SOVIET MILITARY ADMINISTRATION IS COMPELLED TO HALT ALL PASSENGER AND FREIGHT TRAFFIC TO AND FROM BERLIN TOMORROW AT 06.00 HOURS BECAUSE OF TECHNICAL DIFFICULTIES.'[39] The Soviets were also stopping all deliveries of coal and food to the western sectors of Berlin and cutting off electricity supplies.

Frau Derigs knew that the Soviets meant business. The siege of Berlin had begun.

PART IV
The Siege

16

The Perfect Siege

A BESIEGED CITY requires a number of essentials if the inhabitants are to be kept alive. Clean drinking water is vital, as are
sufficient food, fuel and medication. An acute shortage of food
cost thousands of lives during the Siege of Leningrad, while a lack
of fuel caused extreme deprivation during the 1870 Siege of Paris.
A further requirement is that morale be kept up: if the besieged
inhabitants lose faith in their leaders, the will to resist is rapidly
undermined.

Western Berlin's stockpile of supplies was meagre indeed in the
spring of 1948. The small British garrison had enough food for
thirty-seven days, but the population of the city's western sectors,
some 2.4 million people, could be fed for just twenty-seven days.
There would be enough petrol for ten weeks, if it were severely
rationed, and coal for perhaps half this time. American warehouses
also contained 200 tons of condensed milk and a stockpile of
powdered milk, emergency supplies that Howley had prudently
imported to the city. Yet it was nowhere near enough. A report
written by General Herbert concluded that if the Soviets maintained
their siege for more than a few weeks, 'the German population will
suffer considerable hardship'.[1] This was a typically British understatement. They would starve.

The British and Americans had previous experience of jointly
breaking a siege. In the summer of 1900, their diplomatic legations
(and those of other nations) in Peking had been besieged by Boxer
revolutionaries. The leading powers had worked together to break
the siege, successfully deploying a multinational task force. Teamwork
had proved crucial to this success. Frank Howley's plan for breaking
the siege of Berlin also owed much to the idea of teamwork. He

knew that Allied unity would be the deciding factor in whether or not his siege-busting plan delivered the necessary results.

Grand historical parallels were uppermost in his mind in those opening days of the siege. 'The cold inhuman minds of the Kremlin had reached a wicked decision, the most barbarous in history since Genghis Khan reduced conquered cities to pyramids of skulls.'[2] Howley knew that the closing of the land routes had marked the end of the phoney war and the beginning of a battle for survival. 'June 24, 1948, is one of the most infamous dates in the history of civilisation,' he wrote, adding that it was the day on which 'the Russians tried to murder an entire city to gain a political advantage'.[3] It was conquest by starvation, pure and simple. 'There we were, in a land-locked city, trapped in the Bear's paws.'[4]

In the great castle sieges of the Middle Ages, the physical boundaries of the besieged city were its stone ramparts, buttresses and crenelated battlements. Nothing could be brought inside this defensive shield without first penetrating the ranks of the surrounding attackers. The tactical recognition flash of post-war Berlin, a cloth symbol sewn onto the sleeve of every Allied uniform, suggested a similar scenario for the German capital. The city was represented by a black dot surrounded by an encircling band of red. Berlin was indeed encircled by Red Army forces and the three western sectors were completely cut off. 'Overnight, the city became a remote island isolated one hundred miles within hostile Russian waters.'[5]

Ernest Bevin was on holiday in the Dorset resort of Sandbanks when he learned of the Berlin siege. He immediately headed back to London, travelling in a torpedo boat sent across the Solent to fetch him. He had no doubt as to the course of action he should follow. 'The abandonment of Berlin would have serious, if not disastrous consequences in Western Germany and throughout Western Europe,' he said.[6] There was no question of yielding to Soviet pressure.

Over in Washington, President Truman's response was similarly bullish. 'We are going to stay. Period.' He added that the western Allies were in Berlin 'by the terms of an agreement and that the Russians had no right to get us out by either direct or indirect pressure'.[7]

Yet Howley knew that the situation on the ground was close to checkmate. 'Militarily we didn't stand a chance. The Russians could have moved into the areas and liquidated us before you could say, "Politburo!"' The western Allies had only two battalions of troops inside the city, 'which would have been powerless against the Soviet panzer divisions'.[8]

The odds were indeed heavily stacked against the western powers. The Soviet sector of Berlin housed a garrison of 18,000 combat-ready troops, whereas the western sectors could muster just 3,000 American fighting men, 2,000 British and 1,500 French. This gave the Soviets a three-to-one advantage over their western rivals. They also had 300,000 soldiers camped out in eastern Germany, for they had not demobilised their armies with the same speed as the Americans and British. The Allied sectors of the capital were particularly vulnerable to surprise attack: the 341 square miles of greater Berlin were criss-crossed with lines of the underground U-Bahn and overland S-Bahn, now largely restored. There were no fewer than 158 commuter stations from which Red Army soldiers could pour into the western sectors. Districts like Kreuzberg, Tiergarten and Wedding could be overrun within a matter of hours. Any defensive action on the part of the Allies would have rapidly led to all-out war, with unpredictable consequences.

The situation in Berlin was different from all previous sieges in one important respect: only the western half of the city was block-aded and Berliners could still cross into the Soviet sector. True, there was a marked increase in the number of checkpoints – more than seventy on the main crossing points – and the Communist police were prone to confiscating food and goods. Yet the subway lines remained open and the besieged inhabitants of the west were enticed into the Soviet sector by the promise of extra rations. 'Bread and potatoes and all the things a German likes,' noted one British observer.[9] This came at a price. In order to claim those extra rations, inhabitants had officially to register with the Soviet Military Administration, a constraint that few were prepared to accept. Once registered, they would be forever under the Soviet yoke.

The situation seemed hopeless to most of the city's inhabitants, as well as to the Allied garrisons. Howley alone harboured a ray of optimism about the showdown that was about to follow. 'Although the Reds had succeeded in cutting us off completely by land, depriving us of the autobahn, the railroad and the canals,' he said, 'the blockade had one flaw. Moscow didn't control the skies.'[10]

The three air corridors to the capital had been agreed upon in writing back in 1945. The Soviets had no means of stopping the Allies from using these corridors, short of shooting down their planes. This was something that Howley gambled they would not dare to do. Yet supplying 2.4 million inhabitants by air was logistically impossible, as his Basic Assumption Plan had revealed. Absolutely everything needed importing: salt, milk, coal, potatoes, fat, sugar, medical supplies, gasoline. It could not be done.

Russia's insistence in 1945 that the western Allies feed their own districts of Berlin had given Howley a very precise idea of the city's daily requirements: 641 tons of flour, 150 of cereal, 106 of meat and fish, 900 of potatoes, 51 of sugar, 10 of coffee, 20 of milk, 32 of fats and 3 tons of yeast. He also knew exactly what he had in the city's warehouses: 17 days' supply of flour, 32 days' of cereal, 26 days' of milk.

But Berlin did not require just food: all fuel supplies had also been stopped by the Soviets. '*Coal shipments to Berlin from the Soviet zone are halted,*' announced the Soviet-run ADN news agency in its transmission of 23 June. '*The Soviet authorities have also ordered the central switching stations to stop the supply of electricity from the Soviet zone and Soviet sector to the Western sectors.*'[11]

Without coal, there could be no electricity. Without electricity, there could be no functioning sewage plants. No heating. No lighting. No clean water. Berlin's drinking water had to be pumped from deep underground aquifers up through a natural filter of sand and gravel. If the pumps failed, the water supply would falter; disease would run rampant and people would die. The Soviets had great experience with siege warfare, having been the besieged (at Leningrad and Stalingrad) and the besiegers (at Budapest). In blockading Berlin, they had indeed created the perfect siege.

In the weeks that preceded their blockade, the daily delivery of supplies to the capital's western sectors had been around 13,500 tons.

Howley reckoned the minimum subsistence requirement to be 4,500 tons. The carrying capacity of a Dakota C-47 Skytrain, workhorse of the Second World War, was two and a half tons. And therein lay the problem. It would require 1,800 flights a day to keep the city's inhabitants alive, with a plane landing every ninety-six seconds at each of the two airports in the western sectors.

The British had just six Dakotas at their airfield in Wunstorf in western Germany, with eight more on order from RAF Waterbeach in Cambridgeshire. The Americans were better equipped, with access to about fifty battered C-47s, or 'Goony Birds' as they were known; these had survived the battles for Sicily, Normandy and Arnhem. Such a motley collection of aircraft could not possibly keep Berlin alive.

This was the opinion of everyone with a stake in the crisis. General Brian Robertson was adamant that bad weather would soon bring an airlift to a halt – Tempelhof airfield was notorious for being fogbound – while the perennial pessimist, General Herbert, predicted that the western Allies would be defeated by October. 'Then we'll all have to leave Berlin,' he said. Frank Howley slammed Herbert for being 'shockingly defeatist' and dismissed his words as 'one jaundiced British officer's viewpoint'.[12]

Yet Howley's own masters in Washington were equally pessimistic. Secretary of State George Marshall dismissed an airlift as 'obviously not a solution', while America's ambassador to Moscow, the formerly pink-haired Walter Bedell Smith, said he had 'little faith in the ability of the airlift to supply Berlin'.[13] Even the Soviets believed it impossible, having witnessed the Luftwaffe's doomed attempts to supply the Wehrmacht's troops at Stalingrad.

Lucius Clay favoured a different means of breaking the siege: he wanted to thrust an armoured convoy through the Soviet zone, punching a road-route through to the capital. His idea was to deploy six thousand troops on a mission he had codenamed Operation Truculent. General Robertson was appalled by the idea, certain that it would ignite a major conflict. 'If you do that,' he told Clay, 'it'll be war – it's as simple as that.' He paused for a moment before adding an uncomfortable afterthought. 'In such an event, I'm afraid my government could offer you no support.'[14]

President Truman also vetoed the idea of an armoured column, as did all his advisers. Clay was told that 'all the military chiefs were against it.'[15] Powerful voices in Washington were also growing jittery about the dangers facing the American garrison in Berlin. Lieutenant General Albert Wedemeyer, the army general staff's director of plans and operations, advocated withdrawing American troops and their dependants. By the end of June, his voice had been heard and he was heading to Europe to investigate the practicalities of pulling out these people.

But his trip did not go to plan. As he passed through London on the morning of 28 June, shortly before a luncheon at Claridge's Hotel, events took an unexpected turn. Wedemeyer, the so-called master of operations, was to find himself comprehensively outflanked.

That late-June day saw Britain's foreign secretary, Ernest Bevin, in a combative mood. Brooding and pugnacious by nature, he had no qualms about thumping the diplomatic punch-bag. He even looked like a pugilist, with his thickly flattened nose and powerful fists; he had the heft and physique of one who had once earned his living by manual labour. 'His massive head and features', wrote his biographer, 'possessed an almost geological irregularity.'[16]

Bevin looked particularly adrift in the measured splendour of the Foreign Office, whose sweeping galleries stood as relics of a bygone age. Yet they were relics that Bevin liked to profane to his own advantage. When an American visitor asked him why he had a twice-life-size painting of King George III hanging over his desk, he received a no-nonsense response. ''E's my hero,' said Bevin. 'If he hadn't been so stupid, you [Americans] wouldn't have been strong enough to come to our rescue in the war.'[17]

Bevin was determined to take the lead on Berlin and he now found his chance. On the first full day of the siege, he hosted a meeting with Lieutenant General Wedemeyer and six other distinguished visitors from America. Wedemeyer was increasingly concerned by the 'cocky, irresponsible attitude' of Lucius Clay and particularly alarmed by the idea of supplying Berlin's inhabitants by air, something that he believed impossible. In the words of Frank Roberts, Bevin's private secretary, the lieutenant general had come to London 'to persuade him [Bevin] that it really wasn't on and couldn't be done'.[18]

But Wedemeyer was to be wrong-footed by Bevin's opening words. 'Gentlemen,' he boomed, 'I have news I believe you will find extremely interesting. I have just come from a meeting of the full Cabinet at which it was agreed that under no circumstances will we leave Berlin.'[19]

There was a stunned silence as everyone digested what he had just said. These were words that came with consequences, as Bevin knew all too well. If impoverished Britain were to resist the Soviet blockade, it would be unthinkable for America to withdraw unilaterally. The Allied partnership had been crucially important throughout the war and the foreign secretary's declaration of intent would surely require Truman to follow suit.

Wedemeyer repeated his conviction that an airlift was impossible, at which Bevin peered at him through his thick horn-rim spectacles. 'Well, General,' he said, 'I never thought I'd live to see the day when the Head of the American Air Force exclaimed to me that his Air Force can't do what the Royal Air Force is going to do.'[20]

Lucius Clay's special adviser, Lawrence Wilkinson, had also been invited to the meeting and he was the first to break rank. 'Well, Mr Secretary,' he said, 'on behalf of the Berliners, may I for one say that this is the best news we've had in a long time.'[21] His was a lone voice among many and the meeting soon broke up without agreement. Frank Roberts personally accompanied Wedemeyer to the door, noting that he seemed completely fazed by what had just happened. 'He sort of shook himself, rather like a dog coming out of a pond.'[22] His parting words were, 'I suppose we're meant to do it.' Roberts nodded vigorously. 'That was the message.'[23]

Bevin had had direct experience of dealing with Stalin at Potsdam and felt it imperative to show that Britain was prepared to punch hard and low. To this end, he now asked the American ambassador, Lewis Douglas, if President Truman would consider sending two squadrons of B29 Superfortresses to Britain. Based within reach of Moscow, the presence of such planes would, in Bevin's words, 'help to persuade the Russians that we mean business'.[24] He soon got his way: the National Security Council sanctioned the despatch of sixty B29s.

Just a few days after this request, Bevin rose to his feet in a packed House of Commons and delivered a defiant speech in which he vowed that Britain would prevent 'the ruthless starvation of two and a half million people'. He had none of the oratorical eloquence of his predecessor, Anthony Eden, yet he spoke with gritty conviction when he talked of defeating Stalin. 'His Majesty's Government and our Western Allies can see no alternative between that and surrender, and none of us can accept surrender.'[25] Eden agreed and generously repeated Bevin's words back to him: 'We are in Berlin as of right. It is our intention to stay.'[26]

The foreign secretary would become ever more strident in the days that followed. He spoke of building up the airlift to 'really sensational proportions', sending in hundreds of aircraft.[27] 'We must fill the sky with our planes,' he told his secretary of state for air, Arthur Henderson.[28] The prime minister, Clement Attlee spoke from the same page: 'Put everything into the sky that we've got.'[29]

It was easy to make promises yet so hard to fulfil them. Both men knew that they did not have the planes to feed 2.4 million Berliners for anything more than a few weeks. But saving Berlin's inhabitants was only one of Bevin's motives in promoting an airlift. The far greater prize, as he saw it, was to lock America's military might into the future defence of Western Europe. It was a prize he chose not to advertise.

The inhabitants of Berlin's western sectors absorbed news of the siege with a sense of impending doom. Harold Hays took a tour around the British sector and found morale at a low ebb. 'There was black despair in some quarters and a kind of paralysing, hope-less resignation in others.' Families were left reeling at 'the extraordinary and terrifying psychological shock of a sudden and complete blockade'. This shock was compounded by the mixed messages coming from the Allied information departments, whose officials were convinced that an airlift 'could not possibly even begin to alleviate the problem into which they had been dragged against their will, let alone solve it'.[30]

The effect of the Soviet blockade was instantaneous, as Anthony Mann noted on the very first evening: 'Lights went out, machinery and pumping stations stopped, trains came to a halt.'[31] He was astonished that an entire metropolis could so quickly be brought to a standstill. Within hours, untreated sewage was flowing into the rivers and canals. Mann had written extensively about the city's infrastructure and knew more than most Berliners about the catastrophe that awaited them: 89 per cent of the west's electricity supply was generated in the east. Ernst Reuter's plea to rebuild Kraftwerk West, the 228,000-kilowatt power plant at Spandau, had fallen on deaf ears. Now, the western sectors had just two small auxiliary generators to supply them with power.

Frank Howley said that the western sectors of Berlin 'seethed with excitement when the people fully realized they were in a state of siege', a rather different assessment to that made by Harold Hays.[32] It certainly didn't seem very exciting to Ruth Andreas-Friedrich. 'No radio, no light, no electricity for cooking, which means – like so many times before – no way of heating up a little water for coffee.' Such was her diary entry on that first night of the siege. Soon the water supply was also cut. 'Since the water purification plants have stopped functioning, it is advisable to drink only water that has been boiled.'[33] But boiling water was not easy. Power was only available for two hours in any twenty-four-hour period, often in the middle of the night. For Frau Andreas-Friedrich, as for many Berliners, it was like stepping back into the Middle Ages.

In the Klemm household, where young Inge Gross was living with her mother, a twenty-four-hour watch was kept over the power supply. As soon as it flickered on, day or night, there was instant activity. 'We got up and frantically worked . . . mending, darning socks, [doing] unfinished housework and, most importantly, cooking the next day's meal.'[34] There was a very short window in which to prepare food.

Fräulein Gross found everyone hovering between disbelief and despair. 'We cannot survive this, people exclaimed.' The Klemm family were not the only ones to feel helpless. The city was full of ashen-faced people who walked 'aimlessly about the streets hoping to hear bits and pieces of news'. There was a gallows humour across town. 'A quick death, please, not starvation.'[35]

The one glimmer of comfort came from Frank Howley, whose regular radio broadcasts assured the city's inhabitants that the Americans would never abandon Berlin. Ruth Andreas-Friedrich was comforted by Howley's friendly drawl, noting his words and her thoughts. '"*We shall not let the people of Berlin starve*," he affirms loudly and clearly . . . We are relieved . . . We hope again! Because so far, Colonel Howley has always kept his promises.'[36]

That same afternoon, Howley met up with Lucius Clay to discuss bringing in supplies by air. Clay was in an upbeat mood. 'Frank . . .' he said, 'I'm ordering some planes in. They won't be many, but they will be planes. How fast can you get ready to accept them and what do you want brought first?'[37]

Howley requested sacks of flour, on the grounds that it was 'a famine food' that filled people's bellies. Shortly afterwards, he drove down to Tempelhof airfield to watch the arrival of the first fleet of C-47s. 'Old, tired, patched, the planes had been hastily collected from military airfields in the western zones of Germany and rushed into the Berlin service.' Many still bore their camouflage paint from service in the deserts of North Africa; others had the three stripes painted on for the 1944 Normandy invasion. Howley felt a sense of acute pride. 'As the planes touched down and bags of flour began to spill out of their bellies, I realized that this was the beginning of something wonderful – a way to crack the blockade.' He returned to his office that afternoon 'almost breathless with elation, like a man who has made a great discovery and cannot hide his joy'.[38] Yet it was joy tempered with doubts about the future. An airlift was not a long-term solution to the crisis.

The imposition of the Soviet blockade affected different families in different ways. For most Berliners, the most immediate effect was a sudden worsening of their diet. Mercedes Wild was a seven-year-old schoolgirl for whom mealtimes had been a monotonous regime of watery potato soup. Now her diet was even worse. 'All was dried. Dried potatoes, dried carrots, dried eggs and dried milk, a new experience.'[39] Flying in pre-dried food was the idea of Frank Howley, who reasoned that it would be lighter to transport. But there were soon shortages of everything and hunger became a debilitating fact of life. After years of hardship and deprivation, Berliners were drained and exhausted.

Howley's greatest concern, and Lucius Clay's, was that the city's inhabitants would be unable to cope with indefinite hardship. To this end, the two men summoned Ernst Reuter to a meeting to ask his opinion about their steadfastness. 'General,' said Reuter, 'there can be no question of where the Berliners stand. Berlin will make all the necessary sacrifices and offer resistance, come what may.'

Reuter was accompanied to that meeting by an impressionable young Willy Brandt (later chancellor of West Germany), who noticed that Reuter's words wrought magic on both Clay and Howley. 'The gentlemen were visibly impressed. They had perhaps expected to hear complaints, reproaches, conditions – instead, they heard quite another sound.'[40] Reuter was defiant and bullish: his was the in-defatigable voice of Berlin.

Clay had hitherto been one of the few Americans not to warm to Reuter, finding him too authoritarian. He now revised his opinion, viewing him as a Churchillian figure who could act as guardian of the city's morale. 'Rugged, intelligent and courageous, he held the affection of the people of Berlin and was their logical leader in this crisis.'[41] Reuter had likewise changed his opinion of Clay, whom he had previously blamed for blocking his appointment as mayor. Now, he saw him as a man of rigid principles.

Reuter slipped comfortably into the role he was to play during the siege, acting as standard-bearer for the people of Berlin and lifting their morale. 'Berlin will be the German Stalingrad that will turn back the tide of Communist pressure,' he said. He had long admired Churchill's steadfastness in the summer of 1940; now, he saw Berlin as being in a similar predicament. He assured Howley and Clay that its citizens would also fight to the bitter end, 'if necessary alone'.[42] They were brave words, but Reuter knew it was hard to resist on an empty stomach.

There are times when the only solution to a problem is to summon the services of a British-born maverick. The Allies had done this in the months before D-Day, calling upon the eccentric inventor

Sir Percy Cleghorn Hobart to design amphibious tanks that could emerge from the sea onto the Normandy beaches. Now, another British maverick was once again to prove his worth, although on this occasion no one had solicited his help.

Air Commodore Reginald 'Rex' Waite, wiry forty-seven-year-old friend of Brigadier Hinde, was a flying-boat veteran who had first displayed his genius for logistics while serving on the D-Day planning staff. With his engaging smile and precision-clipped moustache, Waite quite looked the part of a jovial airman. '[He] bubbles with enthusiasm and imagination,' wrote one. 'Ideas are always flowing from him.'[43] This was true enough. Beneath the RAF beret was a brain hardwired for mathematical logic. While his fellow airmen dreamed of high-altitude dogfights, Waite pondered logarithms and polynomial algebraics. And now, as he examined the crisis facing Berlin, he began to jot down some equations.

Waite was head of what he liked to call the 'Berlin Air Ministry' – it was actually the Air Section Command Services Division – working as chief of staff to General Herbert, with a roving commission that included 'the complete rearrangement of life for siege conditions'.[44] In a letter to Brigadier Hinde at the outset of the siege, Waite wrote that 'tension has risen to about 90% of boiling point . . . It is anyone's guess on what will happen in the next few days and the situation is as interesting as it has ever been.' He congratulated Hinde for getting out at the right time. 'Your graceful exit was perfectly timed and nobody now envies Benson [Hinde's successor] who has been having a dreadful time.'[45]

Journalist Edwin Tetlow was fascinated to watch Waite at work. 'His head was bowed over a tiny pocket book and he was making drawings and calculations with the stub of a pencil.' His focus was absolute as he considered the application of mathematics to the idea of an airlift. 'He was devoting his technical brain, shaped by a long service career in every branch of flying, to the problem of getting coal into Berlin.'[46]

Waite had spent the previous weeks overseeing the import of essential army rations: 100 tons delivered each day by plane to the Allied garrisons, a mission with the unlikely codename of Operation

Knicker. It was derided by *The Times*, which remained firmly against an Allied airlift. 'Talk of an air bridge is merely picturesque.'[47]

Waite begged to differ. He was exhilarated by the scale of the crisis and was determined to find a mathematical solution. 'Two and a quarter million people is a lot,' he said. 'It's 22 times the size of Wembley Stadium full of people. Anyone who's seen Wembley when it's full and realizes [it holds] only 100,000 people . . . We had 22 times that to feed, and look after, every day, come fog and high water.'

Waite identified eight potential airbases in western Germany that could be used to supply Berlin. The capital's western districts had two airfields, Gatow and Tempelhof, which would require radical upgrades if they were to support the intensity of traffic that Waite was envisaging. The runways were to be extended; the foundations back-filled with two feet of rubble and covered with tarmac recycled from Berlin's streets. When his team asked how tarmac could be recycled without specialist equipment, he had a ready answer. 'By pouring burning oil on it and then shovelling the tarmac off the hot street and putting it on top of the stones.'[48]

Eight outbound airports and two inbound offered the possibility for a huge number of flights: Waite computed that Gatow alone could handle 288 flights a day, allowing for two and a half minutes for each aircraft. 'And that involves taxiing out, getting on the runway, taking off and getting a safe distance clear at the far end of the runway before another one could be told to come in.'[49]

Rapid unloading would be crucial. Waite wanted lorries stationed alongside the runway, engines running in readiness for their cargoes of food and fuel. The fuel would be driven to a waiting barge, which would receive its cargo by means of six chutes. Waite wanted each barge to be moving forwards as it passed under the chutes, so as not to waste precious seconds. His system was to work with absolute precision and he was confident it could break the siege, just so long as enough spare planes could be gathered from across the globe.

When he explained his plan to General Herbert, he was given the cold shoulder. 'It can't possibly work,' snapped Herbert.[50] He got a similar response from General Robertson, who 'thought it impossible'.[51] But when he showed the plan to Lucius Clay, he got a very different reaction. Clay read through Waite's blueprint, thought for a moment and then read it a second time. Suddenly his face lit up.

'Okay!' he said with a smile. 'I'm with you!'[52]

With these words, the Berlin Airlift was on.

The Soviets erected giant portraits of Stalin within days of capturing Berlin. In this photograph, three members of the US Women's Army Corps discuss the billboard on Alexanderplatz, 9 July 1945.

Berliners relied on the black market to buy food and essentials. Here, Berlin ladies exchange items in the Tiergarten, 1947.

Off-duty British soldiers chat to German girls at Berlin's Grunewald swimming pool, 1946. Fraternising, or 'fratting', was actively discouraged by the occupying powers.

The harsh daily reality for most Berliners. Gas and electricity supplies were intermittent, forcing families to cook outside on makeshift stoves. Food was strictly rationed and there was never enough.

Women collecting firewood in the outskirts of Berlin. Winter 1946–7 was the coldest on record, with temperatures plunging to minus twenty-nine degrees Celsius. The old and weak died of hypothermia.

The boundaries of Berlin's four sectors were marked by large signs in three languages.

General Lucius Clay was military governor of American-occupied Germany. A chain-smoking workaholic, he had a tense relationship with Colonel Frank Howley.

General Vasily Sokolovsky led the military administration of Soviet-occupied Germany. Affable and urbane, he eventually fell out with his western colleagues.

General Sir Brian Robertson was deputy military governor of British-occupied Germany. Aloof and austere, he was accused of running Germany as if it were the Raj.

Founding the Socialist Unity Party, Berlin, April 1946. German Communist leader
Wilhelm Pieck (*left*) shakes hands with Social Democrat Otto Grotewohl.
Walter Ulbricht (*bottom right*) led the Moscow-based group of German revolutionaries.

Ruth Andreas-Friedrich: a Berlin-based journalist
and leading member of the Onkel Emil resistance
group. She wrote an insightful diary of daily life
in the German capital from 1945 to 1948.

Colonel Sergei Tiulpanov headed
the Soviet Military Administration's
propaganda bureau from 1945 to
1948. Ruthless and intellectually
brilliant, he exploited German
culture for propaganda purposes.

The Berlin Airlift was a lifeline for two and a half million Berliners. Here, children in West Berlin watch American planes bringing essential supplies into Tempelhof airfield.

US Lieutenant Gail Halvorsen took pity on Berlin children and dropped packets of candy from his C-54. This act was a major propaganda coup and was soon extended to cover East Berlin as well.

General William 'Tonnage' Tunner was placed in charge of the Berlin Airlift. He transformed it into a highly efficient supply operation that kept Berlin's population alive.

Ernst Reuter, mayor of Berlin's western sectors, addresses a huge rally in front of the Reichstag on 9 September 1948. His historic speech was greeted with rapturous applause.

An estimated five hundred thousand Berliners gathered to hear Reuter's speech, the biggest demonstration in the city's history. 'Enough mass power to change the face of Europe', wrote *Time* journalist Emmet Hughes.

The Berlin blockade was lifted on 12 May 1949. Here, watched by the world's press, the first Berlin-bound jeep leaves the British checkpoint at the Helmstedt border post.

Britain's Foreign Secretary, Ernest Bevin, signs the North Atlantic Pact in the auditorium of the State Department in Washington. It marked the birth of NATO and the start of a new chapter in the Cold War.

17

Flying High

URGENT MESSAGES BEGAN clattering out of Teletype machines at airbases across the globe within minutes of Lucius Clay giving the green light to the full-scale airlift. Captain Clifford 'Ted' Harris was based on Johnston Atoll, a speck of steaming lushness in the Pacific Ocean. It was midnight when he saw a jeep's carbide headlights cutting through the darkness. 'Ted,' yelled the voice of his navigator, 'you've got to get yourself all together in thirty minutes. We're going to Berlin!'

Six hundred miles to the east, on Honolulu, Private William 'Greek' Glatiotis was seated in a bar sluicing ice-cold beer. He choked with surprise when a sergeant greeted him with the words, 'Hey, Greek, you're shipping out in two hours' time.'[1] It was the very last thing he was expecting. The news came as an equal shock to a party of air-force wives sailing from San Francisco to Honolulu in order to join their husbands. They looked up and saw the entire group flying over their heads.[2]

From Alaska to California, Massachusetts to Alabama, American airmen received similar calls to action. At Elmendorf Air Force Base in Anchorage, the pilots of the 54th Troop Carrier Squadron, the 'Eager Beavers', were hauled out of the camp cinema at 6 p.m. to be told the news. By 9.30 a.m. the following morning all 210 men were airborne.

British airmen received similarly curt summonses. Flight Lieutenant Dick Arscott was about to set off on a weekend's leave with his wife when his trip was abruptly cancelled. 'I've got news for you,' said his squadron commander. 'You're going to Germany.'[3] Within hours, Arscott and his comrades from 46 Squadron were heading for Berlin.

The incoming airmen touched down at airfields across the western zones of Germany, with the Americans landing into Wiesbaden and Rhein-Main (near Frankfurt) and the British coming into Wunstorf, Fassberg and Celle, in Lower Saxony. To the airmen from Johnston Atoll and Honolulu, it came as a shock to land in such places. Eighteen hours earlier they had been sweltering in the soupy climate of the Tropic of Cancer. Now, they found themselves at bleak air bases swept by wind and rain. Summer in Germany. On 2 July, it rained solidly for eighteen hours at Wunstorf.

Commodore Waite had selected eight suitable airfields in western Germany: these were situated in a sweeping arc between Lübeck on the North Sea and Wiesbaden in Hesse. They were to serve as giant larders for the inhabitants of Berlin, with food and fuel to be flown down the three air corridors that led to the besieged sectors of the German capital. Herein lay a potentially fatal flaw in Waite's airlift plan. The two serviceable airfields in Berlin – Gatow (in the British sector) and Tempelhof (in the American sector) would be receiving dozens of planes every hour.

Waite's calculations left no room for error. Nor did they take into account wind, rain and fog, elements that could play havoc with the all-important figure of 4,000 tons a day. It was an operation that hung on a wing and a prayer.

Dick Arscott was one of the first airmen assigned to the airlift, landing into chaos at Wunstorf. The rainswept airfield was churned to thick mud and the concrete dormitories were hopelessly inadequate for the hundreds of airmen pouring into the place. When Arscott looked for somewhere to sleep, he was told 'it was a matter of climbing up the stairs, finding a space and lying down'. Unfortunately, the upstairs dormitories were all full and Arscott spent his first night sleeping on a billiard table.

He and his comrades were to work a sixteen-hour day, seven days a week, with as many as three return trips to Berlin each day. They worked in revolving shifts: breakfast was served at 8 a.m. on day one, 4 a.m. on day two and midnight on day three.[4] It played havoc with Arscott's body clock, for there were days when he would eat breakfast in the evening and lunch in the middle of the night. Everyone was on a different timeframe, as was apparent in the washrooms. 'Men in uniform were washing next to men in pyjamas, quietly shaving as though it were early morning.'[5]

Day and night rapidly lost all meaning, for Wunstorf was lit electrically around the clock, with the bulbs emitting a piercing light that put a strain on the eyes. There was constant complaining about the food. Phyllis 'Pip' Parson, of the Women's Auxiliary Air Force, found the dried protein particularly disgusting: 'Dehydrated meat which looks like brown paper . . . You put it in a bowl and it swells up, and that's your meat ration.'[6] She ate it with Pom or Smash (both brands of dehydrated potato), also powdered. Dick Arscott found it virtually inedible: he lost a full two stone in his first fortnight.

Arscott sensed that the airlift was 'being run on sheer enthusiasm', with an amateurishness that pervaded everything.[7] One of his comrades, a young flight lieutenant, quipped that the entire operation was being run 'by guess and by God'.[8] The Wunstorf operations room certainly gave that impression, equipped with nothing more sophisticated than a Perspex plotting chart. Even the flight path into Berlin had to be negotiated with primitive and often faulty instruments. There were bleeping radar beacons to help pilots navigate the air corridors, but the final approach was always hellish. 'Nail-biting in bad weather,' said one pilot.[9]

Pilots also faced the additional menace of Soviet harassment, with Yak fighters swooping down on the lumbering Allied cargo planes in 370 mph dives. Their pilots had learned nothing from the fatal crash of the previous April. 'Like a swarm of wasps', thought ensign Bernald Smith as he counted twenty-two Yaks performing acrobatics in the sky around him.[10] When flight engineer Albert Carotenuto made his final approach into Berlin, the Yaks came so close that their piston-driven engines sent his plane into a violent shudder. 'One micro-second on either side and it would be mincemeat.'[11]

At Gatow, General Kotikov encouraged Soviet artillery to fire incendiary bullets between incoming planes; he also had powerful searchlights carefully positioned so as to blind incoming flights at night. Airman Gerry Munn was about to land when the sky seemed to explode into a million fragments of light. 'A blinding, blinding flash of bright white light.' Munn's eyes went into a spin. 'I couldn't see from here to the windshield, let alone ten miles ahead.'[12] It was a miracle that the control tower was able to talk him down to the ground.

Once on the ground, pilots had just seconds to get their planes off the landing strip before the next plane came in to land. Airman John Curtiss overheard an American pilot harassing the pilot of a Halifax already on the ground. The American shouted down the radio that if the other pilot didn't get 'his ass off the runway pronto, he's going to get 80,000 lbs of pulsating aluminium up his backside'.[13]

British pilots usually flew into Gatow airfield, in the south-west of Berlin, while the Americans landed at Tempelhof, a vast airport complex designed by Hitler's principal architect, Albert Speer. The latter had been intended as the aerial gateway to the envisaged Nazi capital of Germania, with a sweeping terminal almost a mile in length. But Tempelhof was an unfinished project in 1948, and it didn't even have a concrete runway. It also had a potentially lethal design flaw, for it was surrounded by five-storey apartment blocks. One of these was exactly in line with the final approach. In dense fog, this tower block was a brooding invisible menace.

'Interesting, to say the least,' noted the laconic American officer, Bill Voigt, on his first approach to Tempelhof. The tower block was less than a quarter of a mile from the runway, requiring him to perform an aeronautical leap before slamming the plane down to the ground. He soon learned how to vault his plane over the tower block, but his fellow pilots were sceptical when he explained his technique. 'As soon as your peripheral vision lost the buildings under the wing,' he told them, 'you clapped the power of all four engines.' It all happened with a shriek and a scream. 'Pull the throttles, all the way back to idle, and the aeroplane would settle like a rock.' It was dangerous, exhilarating and it worked – just. But it took a heavy toll on the aircraft. 'We were beating the heck out of brakes and tyres.'[14]

The Washington-based reporter, Chamber Roberts, arrived at Tempelhof on just such a flight. 'Incredibly dramatic,' he thought as the plane skimmed the roof of the tower block. 'The greatest adventure I've ever been on, like riding the rapids in the Nile.'[15]

Frank Howley watched the blockade-busting planes with a mixture of awe and pride. 'The airlift was a reality by the first week in July,' he said, 'acquiring strength with every succeeding day.'[16] By the end of that month, some 50,000 tons of food had been delivered to besieged Berliners. It was less than half the daily minimum – and meant that over a million people faced starvation – but Howley and Clay were already planning a massive increase in capacity.

Both men knew that coal was as imperative as food, for it was needed for everything from power stations to bakeries. 'Vital to our existence,' wrote Howley. 'Before the siege, 6,000 tons of coal had been delivered each day by train. Now, it was down to zero.'[17]

The blockade was not yet one week old when Lucius Clay called the Frankfurt-based General Curtis LeMay, commander-in-chief of the United States Air Force in Europe. It was a telephone call unlike any other.

'Curt,' asked Clay, 'have you any planes that can carry coal?'

'Carry *what*?' asked LeMay.

'Coal,' repeated Clay.

'We must have a bad phone connection,' said LeMay. 'It sounds as if you're asking whether we have planes for carrying coal.'

'Yes, that's what I said – coal.'

There was a moment's pause on the line before LeMay's voice boomed down the line. 'The air force can deliver anything.'[18]

Ernst Reuter's blueprints of the city's infrastructure soon proved their worth. It was almost certainly one of these plans that revealed the whereabouts of the cross-city gas mains, thirty-six inches in diameter and carrying a high-pressure supply. Commodore Waite, architect of the airlift, was quick to exploit this information. 'In the first week we burrowed down under some houses, where we knew the gas mains was, and we connected it up to ours, and the Russians supplied us with gas.'

It was a similar story with the electric power supply to Gatow airfield. The Soviets wrongly thought that the electricity was being generated by one of the British auxiliary stations. In fact, the power was coming from an underground cable that led from East Berlin to the British sector. Unknown to General Kotikov, that cable was keeping Gatow in operation. 'The Russians kept that switch working in our favour for the whole operation,' said Waite. 'They never knew.'[19]

Reuter's blueprints were also used to cause mischief, as Howley was to recount with glee. He had given the airlift the codename Operation Counterpunch and he intended it to be more than a resonant phrase. 'The counterpunch that pleased me most was directed at Sokolovsky himself. To my unbounded delight, I discovered that the gas for the Russian commander's house, in the Russian suburb, came from a plant in the American sector.'[20] Howley promptly cut the supply, rendering the house uninhabitable. 'Sokolovsky had to go house-hunting.'[21] When his furniture was being moved, the removal van inadvertently strayed into the American sector. Howley promptly arrested the driver and confiscated everything inside the van.

Clay joined in the baiting of Sokolovsky, having his LaSalle sedan stopped for speeding in the American sector. The marshal's armed bodyguards jumped out of the vehicle in a highly agitated state. 'Our patrol quickly put a gun in the pit of Sokolovsky's stomach,' said Clay, 'and his bodyguards calmed down.' The marshal was held for almost an hour before being released. Clay later felt he had overstepped the mark and called on Sokolovsky to express his regrets, but his words fell on deaf ears. 'The marshal was cold and indignant and charged that the arrest had been made as a plan to humiliate him.'[22]

The first days of the siege clearly exposed the fault-line between east and west, and nowhere more so than in the city's police force. Ever since the spring of 1945, it had been controlled by the former Nazi panzer captain, Paul Markgraf. Now, with the encouragement of Ernst Reuter, the Berlin Magistrat suspended Markgraf from office for being 'undemocratic, anti-social and unGerman'.[23] In his place, it appointed Dr Johannes Stumm, a man of firm moral standing who had the accolade of having been sacked from Berlin's police force by the Nazis.

The Americans, British and French immediately recognised Dr Stumm while the Soviets continued to back Paul Markgraf. In the ensuing fallout, Stumm established a new headquarters in the west of the city, with 1,100 policemen under him. This left a rump of 900 policemen serving under Paul Markgraf. Henceforth Berlin had two rival police forces and Markgraf made it clear that any of Stumm's men who strayed into the Soviet sector were liable to be arrested, beaten and imprisoned.

On the twenty-eighth day of the siege, 22 July, Lucius Clay was summoned from Berlin to Washington for emergency discussions with President Truman and his National Security Council. The meeting was scheduled to take place at 11 a.m. in the Cabinet Room of the White House and there was only one subject on the agenda: Berlin.

All the most important figures were in attendance including the three joint chiefs of staff, with General Omar Bradley representing the army, General Hoyt Vandenberg the air force and Vice Admiral Arthur Radford the navy. Everyone present had previously expressed opposition to any expansion of the airlift, believing it to be an unachievable operation that would end in humiliation for America. Clay, the general who had never done battle, now found himself in combat with the most experienced commanders in the American armed forces.

Matters were not helped by the fact that Clay was suffering from the onset of lumbago and experiencing such excruciating back pain that he could scarcely turn his head. Yet he valiantly took on the big guns of Washington, single-handedly fighting for a massive expansion of the airlift.

His opening words reminded everyone of what was at stake. 'Mr President and gentlemen,' he began, 'the abandonment of Berlin would be a serious if not disastrous blow to the maintenance of freedom in Europe.'[24] He warned that Stalin's troops would swiftly overrun any territories vacated by the Americans and pointed out that the airlift was already achieving miracles, with eighty C-47s and fifty-two C-54s flying 250 round trips each day. These were bringing in some 2,500 tons of food, a little more than half what was needed. 'Two months ago, the Russians were cocky and arrogant,' said Clay. Now, they were going 'out of their way to avoid incidents'.[25] The airlift, along with Howley's fiery radio broadcasts, was having an effect.

Having finished with the preliminaries, Clay launched an 'impassioned plea' for more planes.[26] And this was the point at which he ran into difficulties. He told the assembled generals that he needed to expand his fleet to 207 aircraft, which would require an immediate addition of seventy-five C-54s if he were to save Berlin from starvation.

There was an audible gasp in the room as everyone digested his words. Then, with the cautious conservatism of a senior commander, the air force chief of staff, General Vandenberg, refused Clay's request point-blank. 'That's more than half our fleet.'[27] The general warned that these planes could easily be destroyed on the ground in the event of war with the Soviet Union, and added that the diversion of so many aircraft to Berlin would 'seriously impair America's ability to wage strategic warfare'.[28]

Clay sidestepped Vandenberg's concern and reminded everyone of what was at stake. 'If we move out of Berlin, we have lost everything we've been fighting for. The airlift has increased our prestige immeasurably.' He said it was not only a question of saving lives. The German capital had become 'a symbol of American intent'.[29]

Truman said little, although he acknowledged Vandenberg's alarm about sending more planes to Berlin. After briefly reviving Clay's previous idea of sending in an armed convoy, he returned to the central problem: 'How to stay in Berlin without risking all-out war?'[30] No one had an answer.

The president now rose from his seat and announced that he had another appointment scheduled in his diary. The Berlin meeting was to continue with Secretary of State Marshall in the chair. Clay felt the battle was lost, for 'the Joint Chiefs and everybody else were opposed'. The only person in the room who might possibly have championed his cause, the president himself, was leaving. As Truman swept out of the Cabinet Room, he turned to Clay and said, 'Drop in by my office before you leave, General.'[31]

Clay returned to the White House the following morning, shortly before catching his flight back to Berlin. It was a sparkling summer's day and sunlight was tilting through the windows of Truman's office. But Clay's mood was downcast, and not just because of his lumbago.

'You look like you feel badly, General,' said Truman.

'Mr President, I'm very disappointed. Without those planes, I just don't think we're going to make it in Berlin.'

Truman looked up from his desk and smiled broadly. 'Oh you're going to get them,' he said. 'I've just overruled the Joint Chiefs.'[32]

General Hoyt Vandenberg had done his best to quash the idea of an expanded airlift, but now that it had presidential approval he dramatically changed his tune. No effort should be spared, he said, 'to make it an operation worthy of the name'.[33] Others fell swiftly into line. Less than four weeks earlier, General Wedemeyer had been in London explaining to Ernest Bevin why the airlift could not work. Now, he was its greatest champion. He even had his own idea as to how it might succeed, suggesting that the entire operation be placed in the hands of the aeronautical pioneer, Major General William Tunner, celebrated for his high-altitude adventures in the Second World War. General Vandenberg agreed with this proposal and summoned Tunner to his office. The major general was given a briefing about the situation in the German capital and then offered the job of a lifetime. 'OK, Bill,' said Vandenberg, 'it's yours. When can you leave for Berlin?'[34]

William 'Bill' Tunner – 'Tonnage Tunner' to his comrades – had a track record unlike any other. From autumn 1944 until the winter of 1945 he had commanded one of the most exhilarating aerial operations of the Second World War. His task had been to fly in guns and explosives to Kunming in China, where the beleaguered forces of Chiang Kai-shek were fighting a rearguard battle against the occupying Japanese.

The route necessitated flying over the eastern Himalayas, traversing some of the most desolate mountain ranges in the world. From an airfield at Dinjan in north-east India, Tunner's airmen had to steer their planes up the Brahmaputra valley before navigating the rasping windstorms of the Patkai Mountains. They then flew by compass through freezing fog until they reached the lonely Santsung Range

– known as 'The Hump' – with its 15,000-foot summits thrusting into the rarefied air. 'Thin and cold,' noted the laconic Tunner as he forced his plane over these peaks at an altitude of 18,000 feet. 'The oxygen was biting into my nose.'

His mission had been near-impossible, yet he successfully led a team of 20,000 men and 300 planes that delivered 650,000 tons of munitions to the forces of Chiang Kai-shek. 'The Hump Airlift', he said, 'proved the possibility of airlifting anything, anywhere.'[35]

Now he was to apply his talents to the German capital, accepting the Berlin job offer with alacrity. 'Right away, sir,' was his breezy answer to Vandenberg's offer of employment, and he headed directly to Wiesbaden in the American zone of Germany.[36]

His Dinjan base had been notable for its primitive facilities. He was somewhat taken aback, therefore, when he pitched up at the Wiesbaden headquarters of General Curtis LeMay. LeMay had requisitioned the palatial residence of the Henkell wine-producing dynasty, with its 102 rooms, fifteen-strong staff and collection of exquisite antiques. It was from there that he had been directing the American side of the airlift, with Brigadier General Joseph Smith running the day-to-day operations.

The meeting between Tunner and LeMay was frosty, as Tunner was later to recount. 'I was forty-two, cocky and confident . . .' he said. 'I wanted to be left alone – I knew best how the job should be done.'[37] LeMay was irked at having (as Tunner put it) 'some hot-shot come in and throw his weight around'.[38] Tunner had been appointed over LeMay's head and the general addressed him tersely as he chomped on his trademark cigar.

'Well, you'd better get started.'[39]

Tunner's response was equally terse: 'Tell Joseph Smith I'm here and I'm taking over.'

LeMay nodded through a cloud of cigar smoke. 'I expect you to produce.'

'I intend to.'

Brigadier General Smith was furious at being supplanted by Tunner and he unleashed a bitter personal attack on his rival. 'Tunner didn't create this command for anyone but himself, for his own glorification,' he said.[40] Tunner was disdainful of the criticism. 'Joe Smith was a good man. LeMay was a good man. But they didn't know anything about air transport. The thing was about to fall apart.'[41]

In dismissing their contribution, Tunner was displaying the blunt-spoken arrogance that enabled him to get things done. Proud, and often cantankerous, he was said to be efficient to an almost inhuman degree.[42] This made him a dangerous enemy to the Soviets, but it also won him few friends among the American commanders in Wiesbaden. When taken to his quarters, he found he had been assigned a makeshift single room in a half-ruined hotel. The door opened directly into the bathroom and the bedroom was accessible only by squeezing through a gap behind the bathtub.

Tunner got an even less welcome surprise when taken to his airlift headquarters. 'The floors were covered with debris, the walls were filthy. There were no desks, no chairs, no telephones.' But he snapped his fingers and the great clean-up began. 'Now look,' he said to his men. 'We came here to work. I'm not asking you men to put in twenty-four hours a day, but dammit, if I can work eighteen hours a day, you can do fifteen.'[43]

Tunner had arrived in Germany with many of the boldest adventurers from The Hump. The job of operations chief went to Robert 'Red' Forman, 'a barnstormer and crop-duster', whose brilliant red hair had earned him his nickname. Director of traffic went to Eddie Guilbert, 'the fun-loving rover of our crew'.[44] Other old hands included Orval McMahon (supplies), Kenneth Swallwell (construction) and Manuel 'Pete' Fernandez (communications). 'The world's premier scrounger', said Tunner of Fernandez. 'You name it and Pete could not only find it but come back with it and put it to good use.'[45]

Tunner was appalled by the amateurishness of the existing airlift, describing it as 'a real cowboy operation'. There were no schedules, no discipline, no sense of purpose. 'Everything was temporary,' he said. 'Confusion everywhere.' This confusion reached breaking point on Friday, 13 August, 'Black Friday', the day Tunner flew into Berlin in the company of Red Forman and Sterling Bettinger. It was the day on which the airlift would be forever transformed.

The weather was atrocious, with scudding black clouds and driving rain. Visibility over the Harz Mountains was down to zero. Tunner recalled the words of the comedian Bob Hope. 'Soup I can take, but this stuff's got noodles in it.'[46]

As they passed over the Fulda radar beacon, Tunner swung the plane's nose through fifty-seven degrees, aware that scores of aircraft were making a similar manoeuvre, each three minutes apart and each travelling at 180 miles per hour. The sky fell in as they made their final approach towards Tempelhof. The clouds dropped so low that the apartment blocks were obscured and the rain was sheeting sideways with such force that the radar was knocked out. One C-54 overshot the runway and crashed in a ball of flame. Another slammed on its brakes to avoid the fire and blew all its tyres. A third landed on an unfinished auxiliary runway and spun in ground-looping circles in the greasy mud.

The chaos on the ground forced the control tower to stack planes in the skies above Berlin, with scores of aircraft circling blindly in a 9,000-foot soup of cloud. As they bucked and shuddered, the pilots could be heard on the airwaves in a state of high alarm.

'This is a hell of a way to run a railroad,' snarled Tunner as he peered into the murk. Furious at being unable to land, he grabbed the aircraft mike and shouted down to the control tower: 'This is 5549 . . . Tunner talking, and you listen. Send every plane in the stack back to its home base.'

There was stunned silence from the control tower before an incredulous voice said, 'Please repeat.'

'I said, send everybody in the stack below and above me home. Then tell me when it's okay to come down.'[47]

The principal problem with the existing airlift was lack of discipline. Commodore Waite had envisaged a highly regimented system that would function with smooth efficiency. It was faultless as a work of theory, but it failed to take account of poor weather, high winds, grounded planes, and a finite number of airmen suffering from extreme fatigue.

No sooner was Tunner on the ground in Berlin than he went into overdrive, observing, criticising and barking orders. His directive to Red Forman and Sterling Bettinger was curt: 'Stay in Berlin until you've figured out a way to eliminate any possibility of this mess ever happening again – *ever*! I don't care if it takes you two hours or two weeks, that's your job.'[48]

Tunner was swift to instigate two cardinal rules that were to govern the airlift from that point on. Rule one was a standard practice that governed all flights. Henceforth, all planes were to fly an unchanging flight pattern, determined solely by instrument. Technology was to govern everything – a risky strategy at a time when radio compasses were often faulty.

Rule two was no less controversial. To avoid the hazard of stacking planes in the congested skies over Berlin, any pilot who missed his landing slot was to return immediately to base. 'It caused a great deal of comment,' noted Tunner, 'particularly among air traffic experts.'[49] But his rigid application of Waite's blueprint was a stroke of genius, for it enabled an unbroken succession of planes to land and take off. Aircraft flew into Berlin at five different altitudes and at intervals of 500 feet, with planes taking off and landing every ninety seconds. This enabled 480 planes to land each day at Tempelhof, the principal American airfield.

Tunner took great pride in the rhythmic drumbeat of his airlift. 'It is this beat, this precise rhythmical cadence, which determines the success of an airlift,' he said. 'This steady rhythm, constant as the jungle drums, became the trade-mark of the Berlin Airlift.'[50]

Tunner ordered an immediate upgrade to Tempelhof, which still had grass runways that dated back to 'the horse-and-buggy days of aviation'.[51] It was transformed into a three-runway air hub, equipped with all-weather steel and asphalt landing strips. The bulldozers required to transform the place were brought in by plane. Too heavy to be transported in a C-47, they were sliced into segments using oxyacetylene cutters and then welded back together once they were in Berlin.

Tunner was not impressed by the lax attitude of the airmen he met during that Black Friday visit. 'Crew members were drinking coffee, munching on doughnuts, smoking, talking and laughing.'[52] Not any longer. Henceforth they were forbidden to leave their planes as they were being unloaded.

The shortness of the pause between flights caused endless complaints from pilots, but Tunner's compensatory surprise was a snack bar on wheels equipped with hot dogs, doughnuts and coffee. It was also equipped with 'the most beautiful girls in Berlin to ride along in the mobile snack bar and dish out the goodies, along with enticing smiles'.[53]

Tunner knew from his Himalayan experiences that planes flying round-the-clock operations needed constant maintenance. This presented a serious problem, for he had a shortage of accomplished mechanics. His solution once again raised eyebrows. He approached the decorated Luftwaffe commander, Major General Hans-Detlef Herhudt von Rohden, an expert on maintenance and logistics, and asked for his help. Herhudt von Rohden's Nazi past mattered little to Tunner: 'I told him what I wanted and he delivered.'[54] Within days, Herhudt von Rohden had assembled a team of Luftwaffe mechanics who proved adept at keeping planes in good working order.

Tunner was fascinated to learn that the German commander had been one of the last Germans to get out of Stalingrad during the freezing winter of 1942. It had given him first-hand experience of the Luftwaffe's failure to break the siege. It was not the lack of planes that had caused this failure, he told Tunner, but the fact that there were too many. This had caused such congestion on the ground that supplies couldn't be efficiently landed. He agreed that a reliance on technology was the only way to run a siege-busting airlift.

There were still the occasional mishaps. One aircrew landed in Prague rather than Berlin after an unusually long flight. They got drunk with the Czech ground staff before clambering back into their plane and getting unsteadily airborne. A rather different mishap happened to Colonel Hal Austin, who took a quick nap while his co-pilot flew their C-54 into Berlin. When Austin awoke, he looked at the radio compass and saw that the needle was pointing backwards. This could mean only one thing: Berlin was far behind them.

'What the hell have you been doing?' he shouted to his co-pilot, Darryl Lamb, only to realise that Lamb was fast asleep. Austin swung the plane through 180 degrees and headed back towards the German capital, slotting the aircraft back into the flying pattern without anyone questioning why it was an hour and a half late.[55]

Tunner's shake-up of the airlift soon reaped dividends, with his fleet delivering increasingly large quantities of supplies to the city. He had access to a far greater number of planes than his British partners and could call upon a larger reserve of pilots. The British struggled constantly to catch up. Tunner's solution to this discrepancy was to take control of the British side of the operation and merge both into a combined force, one that could work with greater efficiency. General Curtis LeMay agreed with this proposition, for his initial doubts about Tunner had been replaced by an admiration for his work. Now, the two Americans broached the idea with their British counterpart, Sir Arthur Sanders.

Sir Arthur was distinctly unenthusiastic at the idea of being demoted, as Tunner was to record in his memoir. 'Erudite and urbane, [he] spoke eloquently and at length on the British position, offering alternative proposals and well-thought out compromises.' The air marshal was a stickler for the hierarchy of military life and made the mistake of addressing all his comments to General LeMay, hoping the senior commander might intervene on his behalf. It did him no good. 'LeMay just sat there puffing on his cigar and not giving an inch . . . Sanders might as well have been talking to his cigar.'[56]

Tunner was to get his way, as he always did. The two operations were merged into one and he was appointed overall commander. The new outfit was named the Combined Airlift Task Force, and Tunner's intention was to create the greatest airlift in the history of aviation. 'The sky was the limit,' he said that autumn.[57]

But he soon found that the sky over Berlin could be a capricious field of operations. While his system worked perfectly in the summer months, it was to be tested to the limit when snow blasted in from the steppes.

18

The Sky's the Limit

FRANK HOWLEY HAD not seen General Kotikov since the break-up
of the Kommandatura, yet scarcely a day passed without him
feeling the general's malign presence. Howley's house on Gelfertstrasse
had become the target for unpleasant Soviet antics aimed at intimi-
dating his wife, Edith, and their four children. 'I used to get strange
telephone calls late at night designed to break my rest and keep
my nerves jangling.' These calls were particularly irritating when
they occurred in the small hours, when everyone was fast asleep.
'Sometimes a strange voice out of the void would advise me to get
out of Berlin, [but] more often there was only silence when I picked
up the receiver.'[1] Howley had an armed sentry posted outside his
house, day and night, and also took the precaution of sleeping with
a pistol under his pillow. His son, Peter, would later recall his father
prowling around the house in the early hours of the morning, loaded
pistol in hand.

In spite of the ongoing menace, the colonel continued to drive
around town in his open-topped Horch. 'My theory was that an
open car was the best answer in the world to possible assassins. If
they wanted to shoot me, there I was, out in the open, not hidden
away in a bullet-proof limousine packed with guards.'[2]

There had been much talk of evacuating the spouses and dependants of American families living in Berlin, as it would decrease the
quantity of supplies needing to be flown in. Howley was strongly
against such a course of action, lest it send an unwelcome signal to
Berliners. 'It was necessary that they stick it out, if for no other
reason than to serve as a symbol of American determination not to
be driven from Berlin.'[3]

Yet many Allied dependants were worried about the future,

especially when the Soviet-run newspapers printed rumours that the same Asiatic troops who had sacked the city in 1945 were being returned to active duty. One Walter Ulbricht loyalist declared that when the Red Army seized the western sectors of Berlin, 'American families would be held in concentration camps "for further disposition".' As Howley noted curtly, 'everybody knew what that meant.'[4]

Edith Howley's fears for the future were not assuaged by her husband's abrupt manner of expressing himself. 'You know we don't stand a chance if the Russians come in,' he told her one evening when tensions were running especially high. 'I'll be killed and you know what will happen to you?' Mrs Howley nodded gravely. 'The Russians will throw me to the regiment.'[5] Yet still she refused to leave, as did most other American dependants.

British spouses also declined to leave the city. Over at 10 Höhmannstrasse, General Robertson's wife, also called Edith, instructed her butler to keep the family silver polished and displayed on the sideboard. It was her way of showing visitors that she had no intention of quitting Berlin. Yet she was nervous about the future, especially when she heard rumours of an imminent Soviet attack on the western sectors. Journalist Curt Riess went to investigate these rumours and was alarmed to discover that Soviet tanks were carrying out manoeuvres on the city's outskirts. 'By afternoon,' he said, 'they were parked in a semi-circle around West Berlin.'

Tensions increased yet further when Walter Ulbricht was spotted making his way to Soviet headquarters in Karlshorst, where it was said that he demanded that 'the tanks continue on into the city itself'.[6] The besieged sectors of western Berlin looked set to be on the brink of an invasion, yet it still didn't materialise. Allied intelligence agents informed Riess there was good reason for this. Stalin had warned both Sokolovsky and Kotikov not to push the game of brinkmanship too far. 'There must be no shooting in Berlin's western sectors.'[7]

Those early months of the siege were a time of extreme anguish for most Berliners, not least because there were so many questions that remained unanswered. Would there be enough food to keep them from starvation? Would they be abandoned by the western Allies? Everyone also wanted to know if the airlift would be able to keep them alive through the long months of winter.

Valerie Hoecke and her three young children were still hiding out in Captain Shterbinine's house and wondering if they would ever be able to get to Munich, where friends had offered them shelter. Ever since fleeing Soviet-controlled Potsdam, the Hoeckes had managed to keep themselves hidden from agents of the KGB and GRU, but only because they never left the security of the American captain's home. Apart from Hermann Hoecke's secret errands on behalf of Shterbinine, they remained behind closed doors at all times.

Whenever Frau Hoecke watched the never-ending procession of transport planes passing overhead, she felt a glimmer of hope. 'The airlift opened an escape route for us, enabling us to resume our journey to West Germany.'

Flying out of Berlin had not been possible at the beginning of the airlift, when Allied authorities permitted only stranded Germans to be returned to their homes in the western zone of the country. But a British-backed move led to small numbers of Berliners being flown out, predominantly the sick and the elderly. Numbers were strictly limited in the early weeks, but the initiative was soon expanded to include those with a pressing reason to leave the city.

Frau Hoecke had just such a reason and she now began gathering the necessary paperwork and raising money to buy the plane tickets. In the third week of July, just over a month since the start of the airlift, she got the nod from Captain Shterbinine: their paperwork had been processed and their places allocated. On the evening of their departure, the captain drove them to Tempelhof airfield in his army jeep. 'The sky was grey,' said Hermann, 'and rain appeared imminent.'[8]

It was evening by the time they boarded the converted C-54, whose propeller engines roared with menace as the plane hurtled down the runway. Hermann had never flown before and was fascinated as they circled upwards through the sky, tracing an outline of the city. The lights below winked, flickered and were lost to the night. For the Hoecke children, Berlin now belonged to the past.

In the course of three years they had lost their home, their possessions and their savings, but most of all they had lost their father. Hermann had last seen him on Sunday, 13 May 1945, being escorted from the family home by two officers of Soviet Military Intelligence. He would never see his father again: in common with so many abducted Berliners, Paul Hoecke's eventual fate is a mystery; his surviving family believe that he met his end in a prison camp in Kazakhstan.

William 'Tonnage' Tunner had always been confident about supplying Berlin by air during the summer months, but he knew it would be a far greater challenge during the long Berlin winter. One of his biggest problems was that Berlin had just two airfields, Tempelhof and Gatow. If he was to keep the city supplied with enough fuel to generate power throughout the colder months, he urgently needed a third landing strip. As autumn approached, he drove around the city's western districts in search of a suitable site amidst the bombed-out ruins. He soon found what he needed at Tegel in the French sector: an area of undeveloped wasteland used for anti-aircraft training during the war. He immediately summoned Kenny Swallwell, veteran of his gun-running operation in China, and set him to work on the challenge of his life: to build a major airport during one of the tightest blockades in history.

Swallwell proved himself quite up to the task, displaying an alchemist's ability to transform base metal into gold. Rubble was crushed into hardcore, bricks recycled as underlay and paving used instead of tarmac. 'Problems continually arose which would have stumped just about anyone else,' said Tunner. Swallwell even managed to conjure up a fleet of Caterpillar tractors – no one knew from where – and restore a couple of vintage steamrollers. One of his masterstrokes was to fire the enthusiasm of seventeen thousand German civilians, who worked in eight-hour shifts carting much-needed rubble to the Tegel construction site. 'The work began early in September when the weather was still hot,' wrote Tunner, 'and you could see women in bikinis and men in swimming shorts toiling away.'[9] Within seven weeks the airfield was nearing completion. Even Tunner admitted that Swallwell had pulled off an astonishing feat, although he helped himself to a slice of the credit. 'Once again I patted myself on the back for having brought him along.'[10]

There was but one remaining problem. Standing in the approach path of incoming aircraft was a 200-foot radio tower owned and operated by the Soviet-run Radio Berlin. The French commandant, General Jean Ganeval, repeatedly asked General Kotikov to dismantle the tower and move it elsewhere, offering him full financial compensation. But Kotikov – unsurprisingly, given the circumstances – ignored his requests.

General Ganeval made one final appeal and, when he was once more rebuffed, took matters into his own hands. Ever the showman, he invited Tunner to an inaugural meeting at Tegel airfield, along with twenty officers and men. Tunner had no idea why he had been summoned and grew even more perplexed when Ganeval offered everyone a celebratory drink. 'Somewhat strange,' he thought to himself, 'but the general provided such excellent refreshments, and exuded such Gallic charm, that all suspicions were allayed.' Tunner was still enjoying the impromptu drinks party when the room was rocked by an explosion of such magnitude that the foundations of the building shuddered violently. 'French and Americans alike dashed to the window just in time to see the huge radio tower slowly topple to the ground.'[11] As a billowing funnel of dust was siphoned upwards through the air, Ganeval turned to Tunner and smiled broadly. 'You will have no more trouble with the tower.'

The air was still thick with dust when General Kotikov pitched up at General Ganeval's office and screamed in fury at the French general. 'How could you do that?' Ganeval gave him an urbane smile before replying with deliberate misunderstanding. 'From the base,' he said, 'with dynamite.'[12]

Major Harold Hays had long feared that seething tensions inside the besieged city would prove impossible to contain, yet even he was taken by surprise by the orchestrated fashion in which the violence finally erupted. On Monday, 6 September, the City

Assembly was due to convene at the Stadthaus after a long period of absence. The building was in the Soviet sector and Hays headed to the Mitte district of the city in order to observe at first hand the ensuing events. His first surprise came when he passed a rabble of three thousand Communist-supporting labourers being 'herded like goats to the Stadthaus in trucks and other vehicles'. His second surprise came when he saw those labourers being greeted warmly by the Communist-controlled police 'who stepped obediently aside' as they prepared to storm the building.[13] For the second time in less than three months, the City Assembly was to come under attack.

The events that followed were so surreal that Hays had to pinch himself. The mob smashed down the plate-glass doors and then surged towards the chamber in which the delegates were assembled. After beating up several journalists, the insurgents went on the rampage. The delegates were forced to flee for their lives, escaping along the building's labyrinthine corridors and then barricading themselves into their offices. As they cowered behind locked doors, they could hear Colonel Paul Markgraf's thuggish policemen scouring the building. The police had a specific quarry: the forty-six western sector officers hired to protect the delegates of the democratic parties.

Those officers soon regretted crossing into the Soviet sector. One group was swiftly seized and dragged away for interrogation: the rest spent the next sixteen hours hiding out in the Allied liaison bureaux deep inside the building. Frank Howley was outraged to learn that a band of Markgraf's men had forced their way into the American bureau and seized a dozen or more of the policemen. 'The men were handcuffed and dragged, sobbing and screaming, out of the room, while an American lieutenant stood helplessly aside in the face of tommy guns brandished by Russian soldiers.'[14]

In the tense stand-off that followed, the French commandant, General Ganeval, worked through the night to find a resolution to the crisis. The good news came at 4 a.m.: General Kotikov gave his pledge that the remaining twenty-six western sector policemen would be allowed to pass freely through the cordon that Markgraf had thrown around the building. But as the policemen approached the cordon they were seized by Markgraf's henchmen and taken into custody. It was Kotikov's revenge for the destroyed radio tower. Some of the men were eventually freed, but others were to spend that autumn and winter incarcerated in the former Nazi concentration camp, Sachsenhausen, where they were mercilessly beaten. 'The clubs in the hands of the Russian and German camp personnel ruled night and day,' said one of the traumatised survivors.[15]

The storming of the Stadthaus was to have serious consequences. The western-supporting politicians now moved to the British sector where they established a new City Assembly, while the Communist delegates remained in the Soviet sector. The latter were to become, as Howley put it, 'the new rump government [that] the Russians were cooking up to shove down the throats of the people in East Berlin'.[16]

For the capital's inhabitants, the attack on the Stadthaus was the most tangible sign to date that Berlin was undergoing an irrevocable split. Ruth Andreas-Friedrich's diary entry in the aftermath of the attack was prescient. 'Two city parliaments, two police departments, two city governments,' she wrote. 'The Chinese wall along the sector boundary is rising slowly but surely.'[17]

When Curt Riess took a stroll through the fractured city, he was shocked to see that the Soviet administration had erected a steel-pipe railing across Potsdamer Platz. 'A real frontier in the middle of the city,' he said. He felt it was a harbinger of things to come.[18]

Everyday life became a constant struggle for Berliners in these desperate times. The daily ration was barely enough to keep people alive: one ounce each of fat and sugar, two ounces of powdered egg, two ounces of cereal, and seventeen and a half ounces of bread. But supplies were often so short that traders were unable to honour the ration coupons. Fuel and power were in equally short supply. The fortunate few with hand-operated generators put them to good use. One Berlin dentist got his wife to pedal hard on a bicycle generator so he could continue to use his drill.

The Allies reckoned they could allot just twenty pounds of winter coal supplies to each household. It worked out at a little more than a teaspoon a day. Candles fetched exorbitant prices.

Soap was a rarity and baths were always cold. In some districts of the city, customers lined up outside butchers' shops in the pre-dawn chill in order to get a bowl of broth made from boiled bones. Onions, once a staple, were no longer available. Everything was powdered. In such lean times, housewives became grimly creative. One engineer's wife, Herga Jungtow, made pancakes from potato peel, flour and powdered egg, frying the mixture in engine oil supplied by her husband.

There was little employment, for the economy had virtually collapsed. The only hope of a salary was to get work at one of the Allied-run airfields. 'If the people have no work they will lose heart,' warned Ernst Reuter. 'They will surrender to Communism.'[19] Some sixty-five thousand Berliners were taken on at Gatow and Tempelhof, most of them employed in unloading the precious cargoes of supplies flown in from the outside world. These supplies were stored in depots and warehouses before being transported under armed guard to distribution points in the western sectors. Flour, coal and salt were all pilfered whenever airport guards were called elsewhere. Additional rations could mean the difference between life and death.

Harold Hays had been shocked by the violence at the Stadthaus in the first week of September, but he now discovered that it was merely the prelude to a far more spectacular showdown. Berliners in the western sectors were outraged by General Kotikov's behaviour and vowed to have their voices heard. When Ernst Reuter called for a mass demonstration in the Platz der Republik there was feverish excitement throughout the city.

Hays was directly involved in what was to follow, for the Platz der Republik was in the British sector. It raised 'an immediate and ticklish problem of security', for the rally would also be within a stone's throw of the detested Russian War Memorial which had already been defaced and attacked. 'Here was a pretty kettle of fish!' wrote Hays. 'Heaven alone knew what might happen if the crowd decided on retaliatory measures.'[20]

Frank Howley gave his wholehearted support to Reuter's choice of venue and offered American assistance in clearing the remaining rubble from the square. This infuriated his British counterpart, General Herbert, who was against any form of demonstration backed by Howley. 'As provocative as you can get,' he snapped, when told of the chosen venue.[21] He would sanction the rally only if it took place in the Olympic Stadium, an unfortunate suggestion given that venue's previous associations with Nazism. Both Reuter and Howley stood firm, with the latter informing Herbert that 'only the Reichstag as a background would do, as symbolic of the resistance of the whole nation.'[22] When Sir Brian Robertson agreed with Howley, General Herbert had no option but to back down.

'What happened on the afternoon of the 9 September presented one of the most astonishing scenes imaginable,' wrote Harold Hays, who said that the ongoing blockade was momentarily forgotten as Berliners spilled into the streets in unprecedented numbers. 'They began to converge on the Platz der Republik in irregular sinuous columns which stretched for miles and raised the dust in a thin grey cloud.'[23]

American broadcaster vans began touring the streets, urging everyone to attend: 'Berliners from East and West, from Schöneberg, Wedding, Weissensee . . . today at five p.m. Berlin calling the world! Against the blockade, against the Markgraf police, against the Communist terror.'[24]

Hays spent much of that afternoon perched on the back of a lorry in Charlottenburger Chaussee, just a stone's throw from the Reichstag. 'Every approach road to the meeting place was jammed and every pathway through the Tiergarten disgorged thousands of laughing, singing or chatting people.' And still they came. 'When it seemed there could not possibly be room to hold more, they continued to arrive in vast numbers to swell the huge crowd.'[25] They came on foot, by bicycle, on buses, in lorries. 'Enough mass power to change the face of Europe,' thought *Time* journalist Emmet Hughes.[26] The number of Berliners who made their way to the rally that afternoon was calculated at somewhere close to half a million. It was the biggest demonstration in the city's history.

Among the crowd was Ruth Andreas-Friedrich, who noted approvingly that every section of society was represented. 'Housewives ran away from their stoves, the hairdresser abandoned his customer under the drying hood, the news vendor closed his newsstand.'[27] A few sharp-eyed observers noticed a menacing sight in the near distance. Monitoring the crowd through binoculars were Soviet officers stationed on the far side of the Brandenburg Gate.

Ernst Reuter had always vowed to lift the morale of his fellow Berliners and now he proved true to his word. That afternoon saw him in magnificent form with a soaring oration that was both raw and defiant. He began with a denunciation of the violence at the Stadthaus, with General Kotikov his principal villain: 'Before the cock crowed thrice, the Russian general broke his word.'[28] No less villainous were Walter Ulbricht's Communists who, in Reuter's eyes, personified another example of biblical treachery: '[Delegates] that want to sell themselves and their people to a foreign power for thirty pieces of silver.'

Then, with the unwavering conviction of an Old Testament prophet, he addressed his vast audience with a thumping drumbeat of rhetorical repetition: 'We cannot be bartered, we cannot be negotiated, we cannot be sold . . . whoever would surrender this city, whoever would surrender the people of Berlin, would surrender a world.' He urged every Berliner, young and old, to resist the Soviet menace. And then, in a sweeping phrase that was to resonate for years to come, he issued a heartfelt plea to the brotherhood of nations. 'People of the world, look upon this city! You cannot, you must not, forsake us!'

Reuter's speech was almost too effective, for it immediately ignited the excitable crowd. The trouble began when a Soviet police truck tried to make its way through the multitude. '*Ivan raus!*' roared the voices of thousands. '*Raus mit Kotikov!*'*[29] Within seconds, the truck was being pelted with bricks and rubble. Pistol shots rang out and the rally had its first casualty: a fifteen-year-old named Wolfgang Scheunemann was mortally wounded in the groin as he tried to shield a woman from the gunfire. There was chaos as more shots rang out. Even the war-hardened Curt Riess threw himself to the ground. 'A reflex action,' he later said. 'A memory of the war which

* 'Ivan [Russians] out! Out with Kotikov!'

seemed so long ago and which, as I was now slowly beginning to realize, perhaps had not stopped at all.'[30]

A Soviet policeman was beaten by the mob and might have been lynched had he not been rescued by British military police. And then the cries and the jeers were replaced by astonished gasps. A young lad had clambered to the top of the Brandenburg Gate and was ripping down the Red Flag that surmounted the monument.

'*Anbrennen!*' screamed the crowd. 'Burn it!'[31] As the lad tossed the flag to the ground he was shot dead by a Soviet marksman. He was the day's second casualty.

As a group of Red Army soldiers marched towards the nearby Russian War Memorial, they were pelted with yet more rocks. 'Let's drive the Russians back to Moscow!' shouted the crowd. 'Let's drive the Communists out of Berlin!'[32] The Russians recoiled, fired into the air and then continued their menacing advance. But they were to be stopped in their tracks by an intervention so singular that it was to be remembered by everyone who witnessed it. Out of the crowd there stepped a precision-dressed British military policeman named Major Frank Stokes, whose stiff deportment gave him the air of an imperial viceroy. 'Advancing coolly to meet the Russians, his swagger stick swinging loosely in his hand, the major beat a gentle tattoo on their gun barrels, like a schoolmaster admonishing refractory pupils.'[33] The Russians were so astonished that they beat a hasty retreat.

Hays realised that he was witnessing a pivotal moment in the history of Berlin. For three and a half years the inhabitants had been under 'almost inhuman pressure by the Russians'.[34] Now, in vast numbers, they had demonstrated that enough was enough. They did not want to be under the Soviet yoke. But the rally came at a cost. Frank Howley later learned that four Berliners had been killed and a further five sentenced to twenty-five years in a labour camp by a Soviet military court for alleged violence at the demonstration. 'That means death,' wrote Ruth Andreas-Friedrich in her diary. 'Sooner or later, in a concentration camp or a uranium mine.'[35] She knew, as did everyone else, that resisting the Russians carried a high price.

★

The British ground staff at Gatow airfield had grown used to witnessing the unexpected, but everyone was taken aback when a lumbering Avro Tudor aircraft landed without warning one September morning, ten weeks into the siege. The plane itself raised eyebrows, for the Tudor was a noisy beast with a dubious safety record. The pilot was to cause an even greater stir. One of Gatow's medical officers, Alf Johnson, did a double take when he saw the man jump down onto the tarmac, for he was dressed in pinstripe trousers and a homburg and was carrying a smart leather briefcase. He looked as if he was heading to a board meeting in the City of London.

It took less than a minute for his identity to become apparent. His name was Don Bennett and he had arrived in Berlin with a forceful personality and an illustrious wartime record. Bennett had been commander of the Pathfinder Force, the elite corps of the Royal Air Force that had been in the vanguard of every major bombing raid over Germany.[36]

Australian-born Bennett was born to fly. Planes had been his passion ever since childhood, when he watched the Wright brothers demonstrate their homespun flying machine at the racecourse of his native Toowoomba. During the war he had led a daring aerial attack on Hitler's greatest battleship, *Tirpitz*, from which he was lucky to make it back to England alive.

Bennett's wartime glories were to be overshadowed by a catastrophic post-war accident that occurred when he was managing director of British South American Airways. One of the Avro Tudor planes he owned had plunged from the sky, with the loss of thirty-one lives. Bennett had consistently praised the Avro Tudor's airworthiness, a lone voice of confidence at a time when many were lambasting its poor safety record. He was acrimoniously sacked, albeit with a generous severance payment, and he used this money to buy two more grounded Avro Tudors. He then established a new company, Air Flight, and hired the best technicians. 'We must prove that this is a good aircraft,' he told them. 'The best.'[37]

Now, in the autumn of 1948, Bennett saw a chance to redeem himself. The British government was determined to resume a leading role in the airlift, having been outperformed by the Americans for many months. The secretary of state for air, Sir Arthur Henderson, called upon Britons far and wide to turn the airlift into a national triumph. 'We shall use, as need demands, all the air resources which can usefully be brought to bear.'[38] To this end, he met with the directors of air charter companies established at the war's end. These 'sky tramps', as Henderson called them, were high-octane adventurers who scraped a lonely living by hauling cargoes to Britain's far-flung colonies.[39] Now, they were to support the efforts of the Royal Air Force in Berlin. Henderson viewed their mission as a second Dunkirk, to be undertaken with pluck and fortitude. Just as the little ships had aided the Royal Navy in the desperate days of 1940, so this aerial armada was to support the RAF in heroic if homespun fashion.

Edwin Whitfield of British European Airways was appointed to oversee the operation: the companies involved included Eagle Aviation, British Nederland Air Services, Aquila Airways, Kearsley Airways, Skyflight, Silver City Airways and Ciros Aviation. Among them they were able to muster an impressively large fleet of 104 planes, but when Whitfield inspected them he found himself in command of a gallimaufry of aerial machines that had been snapped up for scrap prices: twelve Hythe flying boats, two Wayfarers, several Haltons, a Liberator, a couple of Lancasters and Lancastrians, some Vikings, a decommissioned RAF Halifax and twenty Dakotas, none of which was sufficiently airworthy to carry a full load. Most still bore the dents and bruises of their wartime service and all were in a sorry state of repair, with leaking fuel tanks, fraying cables and faulty engines.

Standing proud among these patched and painted survivors was the former Air Vice Marshal Don Bennett and his two Avro Tudors, which began transporting freight shortly after Bennett's inaugural flight into Gatow. Bennett evinced the same can-do spirit that had been the hallmark of his leadership of the Pathfinders, not to mention a cavalier disdain for danger. On his first cargo-carrying flight into the German capital, one of the crew on board was horrified to see that the outer starboard engine was on fire. He immediately alerted Bennett, who dismissed the inferno with breezy confidence. 'The wind will blow it out,' he said, as indeed it did.[40]

Bennett worked around the clock, converting his second Avro

Tudor into an air tanker that could carry nine tons of diesel oil into the city. He flew three nightly sorties into Berlin for two months without a break, a feat that earned him the lasting admiration of Edwin Whitfield. 'An epic of human endeavour,' said Whitfield. '[It] can have few parallels in the history of aviation.'[41]

A further contribution to this aerial Dunkirk came from the ten Sunderland flying boats, used to import Berlin's daily requirement of thirty-eight tons of salt. Salt could not be carried in conventional planes because it leaked through the floor and corroded the plane's control wires. But Reginald Waite, the mathematical architect of the airlift, pointed out that Sunderlands were designed to land on salt water and that their wiring was in the roof. They now started using the River Havel as their airstrip, touching down, as one pilot put it, 'like a pelican landing on a puddle'.[42]

This was exactly the sort of British ingenuity that so quickened the pulse of Sir Arthur Henderson, but 'Tonnage' Tunner viewed it with a mixture of bemusement and disdain. 'Slow flying ponderous crates' was his dismissive opinion of the British Sunderlands, and he said he would be 'glad to see them go'.[43] When winter arrived, he ordered specially adapted Halifax bombers to fly in their stead, with the salt carried in vast panniers slung inside the planes' ammunition bays.

The British civilian effort was a laudable contribution from a country whose population was still living on rations similar to those of the inhabitants of Berlin. Sir Arthur Henderson's sky tramps successfully carried 150,000 tons of cargo into Berlin, including the most dangerous of all, gasoline and diesel oil. 'A magnificent achievement which has been a source of admiration and inspiration through the world,'[44] said Henderson.

Even Tunner expressed a grudging praise for the fleet of tanker planes. Yet it proved impossible for the British to match the American contribution to the airlift. A typical day saw Americans fly 5,000 tons into Berlin, whereas British planes rarely managed more than 1,000 tons.

Fog arrived at the end of October, threatening serious disruption to the airlift. 'Thick, impenetrable fog,' wrote Frank Howley as he stared out of his window into a zero-visibility blanket of whiteness.[45] Ice-cold fog had settled over four million square miles of Europe, from Finland to Italy, a 1,000-foot cloud that thickened with every passing day. Even Tunner grew alarmed. 'The weather closed in on us,' he wrote, only to learn that even worse conditions were on the way.[46]

On 3 November, the fog thickened to such an extent that all three of West Berlin's airfields had to halt their operations. Two hundred planes were forced to turn back as the runways were swallowed by the blanket, depriving Berlin of 1,500 tons of essential supplies. Visibility dropped from fifty yards to twenty, before dropping once again and rendering it impossible to see anything.

Airfields in Berlin, West Germany and across Europe were paralysed. Britain's supply hub for Berlin, Northfield airfield, was put completely out of action and most other airports were forced to close. 'The foggiest winter in eighty years,' wrote Ruth Andreas-Friedrich in her diary. 'The airlift does what it can. But neither can it do the impossible.'[47]

Tunner did his best to keep planes in the air, but it proved alarmingly hazardous. On 15 November, an American Skymaster attempted to land at Tempelhof but missed the runway and exploded into a fireball. It was a miracle that the crew escaped with minor burns. Three days later, an RAF Dakota crashed in the Soviet sector after losing its bearings in the fog. This crew was less fortunate than those on the Skymaster: all five were killed in the ensuing inferno. A third crash occurred when a Lancaster returning from Berlin smashed into woodland in Wiltshire, killing all on board. The fog was so dense that it took local residents an hour to locate the burning wreckage.

In any given twenty-four-hour period during the airlift, some 1,500 planes landed in Berlin. Not any more. As many as fifteen days of November proved impossible for flying, with scarcely any planes getting through to the city. On the worst-hit day, the capital received just ten tons of food instead of the 5,000 tons required to keep Berliners from starvation.

By the last week of November, the fog had reduced visibility to such an extent that even Tunner conceded defeat. 'On November 30th one of those pea-soup fogs closed in on Berlin,' he wrote. 'You couldn't drive a car in the city that day, much less land a plane.'[48] When young Inge Gross tried to catch a tram, visibility was so poor that she was unable to find her usual stop.

Frank Howley now feared the worst. 'We faced a grave situation,' he said. 'The frightening way in which our stocks were disappearing warned us that unless we replenished them at once, they would be exhausted within a week or – at the most – ten days.'[49]

Coal supplies were also dwindling, leading to ever-longer power cuts. Howley described this period as a time of 'continual, dreary darkness'. Light and power were available for just four hours a day and even then the supply was irregular and sporadic. 'Some house-wives had to get up at three o'clock in the morning to cook their meals,' he said. 'People couldn't read because there was no light most of the time. If they visited their friends, they did so in the dark.'[50]

Berliners were already pinched with hunger; now it was hard to get any food at all. When Inge Gross presented her family's ration card at her local grocer's she was greeted with an expression of regret. There was no food left. On the rare occasions when shops did get supplies, purchasing them required a six-hour queue in the damp air. The sick and the frail began to die in the neighbourhood of the Gross's lodgings. 'Emergency vehicles were frequently called to homes where old and friendless people were found starved to death.'[51]

A brief respite in the weather allowed the British to launch an emergency evacuation of seventeen thousand malnourished children to the western zones of Germany, where they were placed in special homes. Among those who left was Inge Gross's brother, ten-year-old Peter, whom she accompanied to the collection point at Gatow airport. It made for a sorry sight. 'Forty-five emaciated looking children, some of them without shoes, others without winter coats, had congregated with a parent or a guardian.' Among them were seven-year-old twins who weighed just sixteen kilos (thirty-five pounds) each.

The fog soon returned with a vengeance, causing a catastrophic disruption to the supply of fuel. 'We heard that coal supplies were dwindling and would be exhausted within days,' said Inge Gross. 'Then, Berlin would begin to die.'

And then came a sudden plunge in temperature that coincided with a complete rupture to West Berlin's power supply. The outage happened in abrupt and spectacular fashion. 'Everything ground to a halt,' said Fräulein Gross, who was travelling in a tram when it suddenly shuddered to a halt and gave up the ghost.

Frank Howley's worst nightmare had come to pass: Berlin had been brought to its knees.

19

Checkmate

THE AIRLIFT'S SEVEREST point of crisis led to a UN Security Council resolution demanding that the blockade be lifted. Stalin vetoed the resolution, confident that he would succeed in forcing the western Allies out of Berlin. The siege had by now been underway for more than four months and the city was only barely being kept alive.

The crisis also coincided with the American presidential election of November 1948. President Truman had such negative polling figures during the election campaign that no one expected him to win. His Republican contender was the distinguished governor of New York, Thomas E. Dewey, and he faced an additional challenge from Henry Wallace, a former vice president, who had split from the Democrats in order to found the Progressive Party. Wallace was standing on a foreign policy platform that sought to end hostile relations between America and the Soviet Union, whereas Dewey supported the continuation of Washington's foreign policy.

Truman remained the underdog, with plummeting popularity and hostility from within his own party. He ran an aggressive but poorly funded campaign, mocking Dewey as an ineffectual, do-nothing politician. Dewey preferred to play it safe, aware that he was ahead by miles in the polls.

Political pundits, newspapers and even those in Truman's inner circle predicted that the president was facing a crushing defeat. The *Chicago Daily Tribune* was so confident of Dewey's victory that it printed its banner headline, DEWEY DEFEATS TRUMAN, before polls had even closed. Truman alone was convinced he would win.

He was proven correct, winning both the Electoral College and the popular vote. It was a stunning victory, the like of which had never been seen before. The pollsters had missed the millions who swung behind the president in the closing days of the campaign and failed to account for the huge numbers of Democrats energised by Truman's assertive campaign. Truman won 303 Electoral College votes, while Dewey won just 189. Henry Wallace, the candidate who sought rapprochement with the Soviets, gained just 2 per cent of the popular vote.

Back in Berlin, General Alexander Kotikov had a fighter's respect for his enemy and was the first to acknowledge that Frank Howley and his team were accomplished operators. 'As skilful snipers they would watch over your every move, finding your weak spot, choosing the right moment to take an aim and shoot causing maximum damage.' They were also adept at conjuring clever solutions from thin air, 'knocking you off balance, sowing seeds of doubt, playing for time then suddenly forcing their own decisions on you'.[1] But Kotikov felt that in launching the airlift, the western Allies had bitten off more than they could chew. Not even 'Tonnage' Tunner could supply one of Europe's greatest capitals by air throughout an enduring, pea-soup fog.

The weather had indeed played into Kotikov's hands and he was confident that the siege would succeed if the Arctic freeze continued for a few more weeks. Berliners were already starving and it would not take much more hardship, along with the inducement of extra rations, to tip them into Soviet hands.

'Communist newspapers appealed to the residents of West Berlin to come and register for food,' fumed General Tunner, 'proclaiming that the fresh foods available were healthier than the dried and tinned foods we were bringing in by airlift.'[2] Kotikov also claimed to have so much coal that he didn't know where to store it. In the hands of Colonel Sergei Tiulpanov, such claims were turned into powerful propaganda that was starting to have an effect. Howley was troubled to learn that a trickle of desperate Berliners had been tempted into the Soviet sector in order to claim additional rations. He had no time for such weak-willed people. 'Spineless German backsliders!' he sniped, and vowed that they would never be allowed back into West Berlin.[3]

Just when the airlift reached its deepest point of crisis, at the

beginning of January 1949, there was a sudden and dramatic me-
teorological up-turn. 'The weather miraculously improved,' wrote a
relieved Howley, who saw the first glimmer of hope in the milder
temperatures. Planes began landing within hours of the improved
conditions and the city's empty warehouses were slowly but steadily
replenished. For the first time in months there was a renewed sense
of optimism. 'More planes began to arrive daily,' said Howley, 'our
new radar equipment reduced the weather hazard [and] we perfected
loading and handling techniques.' The tide was turning. If the Allies
could keep replenishing supplies throughout January, the Soviet
blockade would surely fail.

The renewed thunder of aircraft brought reassurance to Berliners,
who knew that their lives depended on an Allied plane landing
every few minutes. Howley said that people who had once
complained about the noise of the airfields were now welcoming
it, and he counted himself among the converts. 'To me, Tempelhof
was a stirring symphony. The roar of incoming planes, dropping
supplies and rushing back for more, was great music in my ears.' As
he lay in his bed listening to the noise reverberating throughout the
night, he felt increasingly confident about the future. 'The engines
seemed to repeat, "We're licking the blockade! We're licking the
blockade!" Every load that hit the ground meant another hole in
the stockade around Berlin.'[4]

Harold Hays noted that even the most sceptical Berliners were
starting to share Howley's confidence. The near-constant roar of
planes 'caused the Doubting Thomases to rub their eyes in wonder
at the amazing clockwork precision of aircraft landing and take-off
every three minutes [and] at the fortitude and great daring of the
crews'.[5]

General Tunner was steadily replacing Dakotas with the larger
American Skymasters; he was even eyeing up the possibility of
bringing in massive Globemasters which could carry 50,000 pounds
of supplies. As ever-larger planes flew into Berlin, so the scheduling
had to be revised. 'Times of loading, of landing, unloading and
take-off again were minutely scrutinized by experts,' said Hays, 'and
carefully adjusted to save precious minutes and, later, even precious
seconds.'[6]

The western Allies were also starting to triumph in the propaganda war, with General Tunner playing an important role. Most Allied officers argued that the daily tonnage figures should be kept secret, but Tunner had scented the propaganda value of advertising them. 'I not only wanted them unclassified, I wanted to publicize them, shout them from the housetops.' If Colonel Tiulpanov could play the propaganda game, then so could he. Indeed he saw the airlift as part of a wider strategy to win the hearts and minds of Berliners. 'If the Berlin Airlift was to be successful – and I never had any doubt but that it would be – then it would be more than just an airlift. It would be a propaganda weapon held up before the whole world. We should not hide it.'[7]

His second propaganda coup that winter began in an unlikely fashion, when a twenty-eight-year-old Mormon named Lieutenant Gail Halvorsen chatted to a group of emaciated children huddled by the Tempelhof perimeter fence. In broken English they told him how they liked to watch the never-ending convoy of planes coming in to land. Halvorsen was struck by the fact that none of the children begged him for candy, as they had always done during his wartime service in Africa. Filled with admiration for their self-restraint, he delved into his pockets and pulled out two sticks of gum, which he divided up as best he could. 'They looked like they'd just got a million dollars,' he said, 'they just couldn't believe it.'[8] Those who didn't get any gum gratefully received the wrapper, which they divided into pieces and licked with relish.

Their gratitude sparked an idea that was to have far-reaching consequences. 'Come back tomorrow,' Halvorsen told them. 'I'll drop enough that all of you can have some gum.' He said he would wiggle the wings of his C-54 during its final approach to Tempelhof, so they would know it was him, and then toss the candy out of the parachute exit.

That evening, he asked his co-pilot and engineer for their candy rations and spent the rest of the night making little parachutes so that the sweets would float gently to the ground.

On the following day, he spied the same group of children at the perimeter fence and duly dropped his candy. On the subsequent day there were even more children, who received a much larger delivery, and their numbers continued to grow until there were more than a hundred of them awaiting their bounty. When Halvorsen returned to Rhein-Main Airbase at the end of that week, he was told there was a huge sack of mail awaiting him. The envelopes of these letters were decorated with sketches of Skymasters dropping candy-bearing parachutes. Some of them were addressed to Onkel Wackelflügel (Uncle Waggle Wings), others to Der Schokoladen-flieger (The Chocolate Flyer).

'We're in real trouble,' said Halvorsen to his co-pilot, aware that such a stack of mail would not have gone unnoticed by the authorities. Sure enough, he was soon summoned to a dressing down with his commanding officer, Colonel John Haun.

'Halvorsen, what have you been doing?'

'Flying like mad, sir.'

'I'm not stupid, what else have you been doing?'

Halvorsen confessed everything, fully expecting to be court-martialled. But there was to be a very different outcome. Colonel Haun 'reached under the counter, pulled out a German newspaper, threw it down in front of me and there was my aeroplane on the front page with parachutes coming out of it'.

A smile spread over the colonel's face. 'You almost hit a German newspaper guy in the head with a candy bar in Berlin yesterday and he's got this story all over the world.'

Far from having him court-martialled, Colonel Haun ordered Halvorsen to drop candy in greater quantities. General Tunner himself had grasped the propaganda value of what was swiftly dubbed Operation Little Vittles: it was a public relations masterstroke that could be deployed with devastating effect against the Soviets. As a 'good news' story, it was hard to beat: smiling children devouring huge quantities of sweets supplied by caring pilots of the American Air Force.

The news spread rapidly across the globe, gaining widespread coverage in the local, national and international newspapers. Soon radio stations across the United States took up the cause, launching appeals for handkerchiefs so they could be turned into parachutes: 'Send in a handkerchief and we'll play your request tune.' Halvorsen was flown back to the States to appear on the popular radio show

We the People. 'The response from the millions of listeners to that program was fantastic,' said General Tunner, who was carefully monitoring the effect of the propaganda. 'Halvorsen's unit, the Seventeenth Air Transport Squadron, was daily flooded with candy and handkerchiefs for parachutes by the generous American people, as well as from some candy manufacturers.'[9]

When Halvorsen began receiving begging letters from children in East Berlin, Tunner realised he was onto something big. He now encouraged Halvorsen to drop sweets into the Soviet sector as well, aware that it would enrage General Kotikov. The Soviet Military Administration was indeed furious at such a simple yet successful stunt and issued a blistering complaint to the State Department in Washington, slamming the sweet drops as 'a capitalist trick . . . [and] a military operation to alienate the minds of these young people against our system'.

Halvorsen's candy mission was to run throughout the spring and was an undisputed triumph. It had infuriated the Soviets, delighted Berliners and transformed wavering public opinion in the United States. The *San Francisco Chronicle* celebrated one of Halvorsen's publicity trips to America with an editorial demanding that Congress increase its financial support for the airlift. 'A pivotal operation like the Berlin Airlift', the piece read, 'is not the place to start economising. On the contrary, we consider it would be cheap at ten times the price.'[10]

As the airlift proved increasingly successful, so the Soviet Military Administration tightened its grip on the perimeters of Berlin's western sectors. Along the seventy-seven-mile boundary between east and west there were now ninety-two checkpoints manned by Soviet police. Although it was still possible to cross from one sector to another, all food, contraband and western newspapers were routinely confiscated. Vehicles were checked, as were handcarts, and police began searching the purses, wallets and briefcases of passengers travelling on the subway and trams that crossed between East and West Berlin.

Yet it proved impossible for Soviet guards to seal the beleaguered western districts hermetically, and smuggling became a major source of additional supplies to the western section. Curt Riess saw eggs, caviar, automobile tyres and gasoline all being sold on the black market. 'Berlin was demonstrating that so huge and complicated a city could not be blockaded.'[11] He also noted that cash-hungry Soviet frontier guards were willing to let vehicles slip through their check-points for a fee of around 250 Deutschemarks. 'No papers needed,' he said, 'no questions asked.'[12] Once inside the city, any contraband could be secretly transferred, under the cover of darkness, to the western sectors.

Food trafficking was a particularly enticing occupation for those living in the Soviet zone of Germany, for the western-backed Deutschemark was far more valuable than the East German mark. Farmers living to the east of Berlin would smuggle sacks of potatoes onto the black market of West Berlin, where they were sold for the coveted Deutschemarks.

At the same time that food was being smuggled into the western sectors, the eastern zone of Germany found itself in dire economic straits. Throughout the early months of the blockade, the Soviet Military Administration had continued to receive reparations from western-occupied Germany, including pre-agreed supplies of coal and iron signed off at the Potsdam Conference. Now, Frank Howley reneged on these agreements and launched a full-scale counter-blockade.

The French commandant, General Ganeval, threw his support behind Howley's action, aware of the importance of the western Allies acting together. But Britain's General Herbert obstinately refused to take part, arguing that coal supplied to the Soviet zone was helping to sustain the British-run mines of the Ruhr. Howley blasted the general for his short-sightedness, but his anger was assuaged by the news that Herbert was to be relieved of his post that January. His successor, General Geoffrey Bourne, immediately joined the counter-blockade and the Soviet Military Administration found itself caught in a three-power economic vice. From the western zones they received no machinery, iron, steel, coal, chemicals, rubber, textiles, tools or spare parts. It was a setback that crippled industrial production in both East Berlin and Soviet-occupied Germany.

★

New city elections had been planned for that winter, but they were to be disrupted in spectacular fashion. Six days before the ballot, General Kotikov caused a sensation by declaring that the Soviet Military Administration was installing what he termed 'a provisional democratic Magistrat' in East Berlin.[13] This was to govern the Soviet sector of the city and would be headed by Friedrich Ebert, son of the first president of the Weimar Republic. Kotikov was hoping that Mayor Ebert would win the hearts and minds of the many Berliners who had loved his father.

Within hours of Ebert's appointment, the Russians had installed a complete puppet Magistrat for the Soviet sector filled with supporters of Walter Ulbricht. To its many critics it became known as 'the operetta council' because it always sang to the Soviet tune. Hays saw this as the decisive moment in Berlin's post-war history: 'the splitting of the city into two wildly hostile groups'.[14]

The election went ahead in the western sectors of the city, where 86 per cent of the population headed to the polling booths. Two-thirds of them cast their votes for the Social Democratic Party, a personal triumph for Ernst Reuter who was at long last sworn in as mayor of West Berlin. He was to prove a formidable counterfoil to Friedrich Ebert in the east.

Berlin's foreign correspondents struggled to explain the bewildering sequence of events to their readers. 'As a result of the election,' wrote Anthony Mann, 'the hapless Berliners acquired two rival Lord Mayors, two mutually hostile City Councils and two police forces, each of which issued warrants for the arrest of the other's senior officers.'[15] Mann's report was a concise synopsis of what had taken place: the city had definitively split in two, with opposing political systems operating in a highly charged atmosphere of mutual mistrust.

Frank Howley had one significant advantage over his Soviet rivals in that spring of 1949 and it was to cost them dear. Four years in Berlin had taught him that espionage is of vital importance when developing strategy. His principal source of intelligence was David Murphy, one of the few American intelligence officers in Berlin to speak fluent Russian. Murphy had arrived in Berlin less than twelve months before, but had rapidly established connections inside Soviet headquarters. These 'meat and potatoes sources', as he called them, included a senior Soviet political officer and several moles working in the Central German Administration for Internal Affairs. From these agents he was able to construct a highly accurate picture of life inside the Karlshorst compound, intelligence that was to prove 'vital to the policymakers'.[16]

The most pressing concern in both Washington and Whitehall was to know whether or not the Soviets would use military force to evict the western powers from Berlin. Frank Howley had long argued that they would not, but other senior figures were not so sure: this caused uncertainty over the long-term viability of holding out in Berlin. Now, David Murphy's mole provided some crucial intelligence. 'He was able to give us hard evidence on the state of morale in the Soviet forces in Germany. He made it quite clear that there was no indication that the Soviet army in East Germany during the blockade period was prepared to use force against us in West Berlin.'

That same mole added that the western Allies need not be unduly concerned by the military manoeuvres outside the city's boundaries. 'The very obvious Soviet troop movements . . . were simply meant to impress us, to frighten us, but they weren't real.' A further source dismissed the fighting capabilities of the Soviet-backed East German paramilitary organisations. 'The morale of these troops was so bad that they [the Soviets] didn't dare post them anywhere near the sector border because they would all desert.'

Such snapshots of intelligence were uniquely valuable, for they laid bare the problems facing General Kotikov's administration. 'This gave us really good solid information that we didn't have to fear an attack and that we could pursue the airlift operation without this happening,' said Murphy. He also received valuable political intelligence, with news that the Socialist Unity Party was intending to close down its offices in the city's western sector 'because they were not at all sure that the Soviet plans to get us to leave West Berlin were going to work'. It was the clearest sign yet that the Soviets themselves had recognised their policy was faltering.

Two years earlier, Brigadier Hinde had compared the situation in

Berlin to a high-level game of chess. David Murphy felt that the comparison was apt: General Kotikov had placed himself in such a situation that every move on the chessboard was leading him inexorably towards checkmate.

'Spring came back to blockaded Berlin, rustling her green skirts in the bright sunshine and radiant with resurrected hope.' So wrote an unusually poetic Frank Howley, who, by March 1949, knew he was on a winning streak. No longer did he anxiously scan the skies, as he had done during the forlorn period of fog and ice. Nor did he feel the need to make daily tours of Berlin's storage depots. Ever since January, planes had been landing every few minutes at each of Berlin's three airports, bringing in enormous quantities of food. 'The airlift was running like clockwork,' he wrote that spring. 'The swarm of planes overhead had become a noisy factor in humdrum metropolitan life.' Supplies were averaging 8,000 tons a day, more than was needed for subsistence, and on occasion it topped 10,000. 'Reserves were built to new highs. Rations were increased until they stood higher than in the Russian sector.'[17] Those Berliners who had crossed into the Soviet sector to get increased rations now begged to be allowed back.

'To hell with these weaklings!' snapped Howley. 'Let them stay where they are.' The British and French commandants begged him to reconsider, arguing that 'the very fact that people were shifting their allegiance was a victory for us, and that such persons should be allowed to reregister in our sectors.' Howley was not accustomed to back down, but on this occasion he did just that. Within days, the vast majority of these deserters had left the 'Made-in-Moscow paradise', as he put it, and crossed back into West Berlin.[18]

General Tunner was also feeling confident. He had a fleet of 379 aircraft flying round the clock, with a further seventy-five on the ground undergoing maintenance. In his airlift headquarters, fifty analytical charts were updated each minute with mathematical precision. 'A quick look, any hour of the day, would give me a clear picture of the entire complex.' As he studied the daily tonnage figures, one thing became apparent. 'We had the problem licked.'

Tunner had already pulled off two successful propaganda coups and now he planned a third, the biggest daily lift of supplies in the history of aviation. He described it as 'one big Gung Ho Day . . . with a far greater tonnage than we'd ever hauled before'. He had launched a similar stunt during his time on the Hump. On that occasion, it had been to instil a sense of competition in his men. This time round, it would be done as part of the propaganda war against the Soviets. Tunner chose Easter Day to be the record-buster. 'We'd have an Easter Parade of airplanes!' he said. 'An Easter Sunday present for the people of Berlin!' This airlifting blockbuster was to run from midday on Easter Saturday to midday on Easter Sunday – twenty-four hours to deliver something spectacular.

He placed his adrenaline-fuelled fixer, Red Forman, in charge of logistics. Forman instantly fired everyone's enthusiasm, telling them to set near-impossible targets on their 'how-go-zit boards'. Tunner looked on in admiration as pilots whistled their approval. All knew that 'this was going to be the biggest day yet.'[19]

As Easter Saturday approached Tunner felt the excitement building to a climax, noting that everyone was 'caught up in the exuberance of the mission'. He flew into Berlin in advance of the operation in order to monitor events from Tempelhof's control tower. He was to play a mischievous role that day, pitting the individual airports against one another. When the operations manager at Fassberg airfield told him they were running 12 per cent ahead of quota, he damned him with faint praise. 'That's fine,' he said, 'but of course it's not up to what they're doing over at Celle.'

Planes landed at West Berlin's three airports all that afternoon, evening and night, an uninterrupted stream of heavily laden aircraft. By 9 a.m. on Easter Sunday, Tunner knew they were going to break all records. Ten thousand tons of supplies had already been delivered to the city and there were still three hours to go. Scenting triumph, he asked General Clay to announce to the international press what they were doing. 'Any member of the press corps who hadn't smelled something in the air already got the official word . . . the correspondents descended on us in droves.'[20]

There were scores of journalists and cameramen in attendance as midday approached. A stack of aircraft could be seen in the clear skies above Berlin, with a plane landing at Tempelhof every sixty-three seconds. The very last plane of the Easter Parade came into land as the clock struck noon, bringing a final delivery of supplies. An officer quickly totted up the total tonnage flown into Berlin over the previous twenty-four hours before rushing outside to daub the figures in bright red paint onto the fuselage of that plane: TONS 12,941, FLIGHTS 1,398.

It was an astonishing achievement, with an average of one round trip for each of the 1,400 minutes in that twenty-four-hour period. Tunner was in celebratory mood. 'It was that day, that Easter Sunday . . . that broke the back of the Berlin blockade.'

Frank Howley had driven out to Tempelhof to witness the last C-54 coming in to land and found it an emotional moment. 'Less than a year ago I had stood at the same airfield and watched the old Gooney Birds bring in our first two hundred tons of flour, agonized at the prospect of feeding 920,000 families by air. It hadn't seemed possible at the time, but we were doing it.' Like General Tunner, Howley knew the battle was won. 'A succession of these record loads', he said, 'would see us holding out in Berlin until the Kremlin toppled into Red Square.'[21]

When it finally came, the end of the siege caught everyone by surprise. Frank Howley was seated in his office on Wednesday, 4 May when a sensational communiqué from the State Department clattered through the Teletype machine. 'AGREEMENT HAS BEEN REACHED BETWEEN THE THREE WESTERN POWERS AND THE SOVIETS REGARDING THE RAISING [OF] THE BERLIN BLOCKADE . . .'[22] The communiqué went on to say that the blockade was to end in eight days, on 12 May, and that the future fate of Berlin and Germany was to be decided at a specially convened council of foreign ministers.

Howley was immediately suspicious. 'I had received no orders on the subject, and therefore went out to military headquarters and called on everybody up to Clay himself.'[23] Lucius Clay was equally suspicious. His special adviser, Robert Murphy, had just returned from high-level meetings in Washington and had mentioned nothing about an end to the siege. Not until Clay laid his hands on a newspaper did he discover that the communiqué was indeed true.

Clay was piqued at not having been told in advance. 'While I understood the difficulties of maintaining secrecy when information passes through many hands,' he said, 'I was somewhat chagrined to hear the story this way.' He was even more infuriated to discover that Murphy knew about the truce negotiations, 'but had not felt free to tell me'.[24] Only now could Murphy inform Clay that negotiations between the Americans and the Russians had been underway for a full twelve weeks, negotiations so secret that only President Truman and a handful of State Department officials knew about them, along with Ernest Bevin and Clement Attlee. These had begun as casual discussions between two diplomats from the opposing camps, Philip Jessup and Yakov Malik, but their tempo and urgency had increased in the wake of General Tunner's Easter spectacular.

The first sign of a breakthrough had come when Stalin signalled that he was no longer troubled by the western Allies' introduction of the Deutschemark: in one stroke, the original casus belli had been dismissed. 'Watch this,' mooted Ernest Bevin when told of this unexpected development. 'Stalin may now raise the blockade.'[25]

The Soviet leader suggested that the future of Berlin and Germany should be discussed at a new council of foreign ministers, a proposal that the Allies were willing to entertain. Their only insistence was that there could be no strings attached, for they were well advanced in their plans to establish a West German government and they didn't want Stalin to stand in the way.

Events now proceeded rapidly, with the Soviets agreeing to lift their blockade if the Allies lifted their counter-blockade. After a flurry of additional meetings between Jessup and Malik, the deal was finally brokered on 27 April, and the news made public seven days later. The Soviet blockade was to end at 00.01 hours on 12 May 1949 – the end to a siege that had lasted 323 days.

Thousands of Berlin families stayed up that historic night in order to hear official confirmation that the siege was at an end. Waiting with them was Anthony Mann, reporting on the unfolding drama for the *Daily Telegraph*. 'West Berliners sat up by the light of such black market candles as were still obtainable,' he wrote, 'counting the minutes until the magic moment.'[26] As the midnight hour approached, they spilled onto the streets to hear the much anticipated

news announced through loudspeakers from radio vans. '*All communications, transportation and trade restrictions . . . will be removed.*'[27] As
radio operator Rudolf-Günter Wagner broadcast the news to the
crowds of newly liberated Berliners, his words were drowned out
by joyous whoops and shrieks. '*Hurrah!*' they shouted. '*Wir leben
Noch!*' (We're still alive!)[28] Berliner Manfred Knopf had lived through
four years of uncertainty. Now, he felt a sense of victory. 'We
belonged to the Western world!'[29]

Relief and gratitude were the overwhelming emotions that night,
along with a deep sense of joy. Ernst Reuter's son, Edzard, joined
the thronging crowds and saw genuine happiness on people's faces
for the first time in years. He knew why. 'Freedom had arrived.'[30]

Among those in the streets was Ella Barowsky, a member of the
Berlin City Assembly. After struggling to stay alive throughout that
terrible year of siege, she now found it hard to contain her emotion.
'We've done it!' she cried, before adding four words that gave her
the greatest lift of all. 'The West has won!'[31]

20

Fruits of Victory

O N THE NIGHT the siege came to an end, thousands drove to the British-American autobahn checkpoint that marked the frontier post of the city's Allied sectors. All wanted to glimpse the first vehicle to arrive from the west. 'Everybody was there,' said Curt Riess, 'actresses, beauty queens, boxers, six-day bicycle racers, famous writers, scientists.'[1] Many of the women wore full evening dress, while the men were in black tie. A phalanx of reporters from the international press had also assembled, along with cameramen and sound crews. American, British and French cars were parked everywhere. Berlin had not partied for four long years; now, everyone was determined to have fun.

As midnight approached, everyone was anxiously counting the seconds. At exactly one minute past the hour, the city lights in West Berlin snapped into life in accordance with the negotiated settlement. The Soviets had switched on the mains power that reconnected West Berlin to the gigantic Klingenberg power station in the eastern zone. At the exact same moment, 110 miles to the west of Berlin, floodlights lit up the Helmstedt border crossing. The wooden barriers that had blocked the Berlin autobahn for 323 days were lifted by the border guards and the assembled press correspondents rushed to their vehicles and fired the engines. The race was on. Everyone wanted to be first to reach the crowds known to be waiting in the capital.

According to one observer, it was a moment charged with emotion: 'As the leading jeeps of an Allied convoy passed under the Soviet barrier to the accompanying [sic] of much saluting, girls broke through the cordon with tears of joy running down their faces to throw armfuls of lilac into the laps of British and American servicemen.'[2]

There were equally delirious scenes as the first Allied military train entered the Soviet zone 'in the glare of cinema floodlights'.[3] This marked the beginning of a vast supply operation. A further twenty trains were soon rolling across Soviet-occupied German lands towards the capital that night with full loads of food, fuel and mail. Trains and vehicles alike were draped with flags – American, British and French – and given a triumphant send-off, with a band of British troops giving a lusty rendition of 'It's a Long Way to Tipperary'!

At the Berlin end of the autobahn, the ever-growing multitude in western Berlin strained necks and eyes as they peered into the darkness in the hope of glimpsing the first vehicle to arrive from Helmstedt. Everyone wanted tangible proof that their ordeal was finally at an end.

Half an hour passed, and then an hour and the crowd grew anxious and impatient. But at precisely 1.46 a.m., the glare of head-lamps could be seen through the darkness. The lead vehicle in the pack was a grey Ford convertible driven by United Press correspondent Walter Rundle. As he drew to a halt, the crowd mobbed his vehicle, pulled open the doors and thrust a wreath of roses around his neck. For Rundle, it was the finest reception he had ever received. He stepped out onto the road, his sharp Hollywood suit gleaming in the glare of the headlights, and gave a commanding wave to the crowd. They responded with a roar of approval, greeting him like a hero.

Rundle was soon joined by dozens more journalists and cars, followed by the first of a convoy of lorries, their high bonnets bedecked with garlands of spring branches. At long last, Berliners were convinced that the blockade was truly at an end.

Harold Hays spent much of that night in the office of General Geoffrey Bourne, the British commandant. It was approaching dawn when their meeting took an unexpected turn. The general 'suddenly cupped his hand behind his ears to listen, as he grinned beatifically at the sound of a shrill, penetrating blast which came shrieking through the air'. After listening quietly for a moment, he said, 'it's a grand sound.' What he and Hays had just heard was the whistle of the first goods train to steam into Charlottenburg station, pulling a huge line of food-laden wagons. 'That shrieking whistle was one of the most audible heralds which announced the end of one of the most brutal blockades in history,' said Hays. 'It was unquestionably the sweetest music we had heard for a great many months.'

He felt he was living through a key moment in European history, one that would forever change the world. 'The vicious Berlin Blockade had been completely broken by the stubbornness and grim determination of the Berliners and the Western Allies alike, and by the effectiveness of the counter-blockade.' He also felt that the breaking of the siege had a profound psychological significance, for it had shattered 'the last vestiges of respect which any freedom-loving individual could possibly have held for Soviet Russians or the German Communists'. The very idea of Soviet rule in West Berlin was now unthinkable. 'Their written and spoken word was now in such bad repute that no further reliance could be placed on anything they said or did.'[4]

On the following morning a special session of the City Assembly was convened to celebrate the triumph. Mayor Ernst Reuter opened the meeting in solemn tones, reading aloud the names of the seventy-nine men who had lost their lives in the airlift. Among them were distinguished wartime heroes such as thirty-six-year-old Lieutenant Robert von Luehrte from Covington, Kentucky, the veteran of fifty B-17 missions. There were also husbands, fathers and fathers-to-be, young men such as Frank Dowling, a Welsh RAF sergeant, who was killed when the Dakota he was in crashed in thick fog. He left behind a distraught widow, Hazel, and an unborn son who would be named Frank in honour of a father he never met.

After officially informing the assembled delegates that the West had won – and declaring 12 May a public holiday – Ernst Reuter stepped outside to address the crowd of three hundred thousand Berliners who had gathered outside the Schöneberg town hall to hear him speak.

'The blockade is ended!' he yelled to the sea of faces that packed the surrounding streets. The crowd responded with a thunderous cheer. 'The attempt to force us to our knees has failed, frustrated by our steadfastness and firmness. It has failed because the world heard our appeal and came to our assistance. It was frustrated because even though everything seemed against us, and even though it took faith to move mountains for us to survive, we have finally won.' He paused for a moment before delivering his pithy, five-word peroration. 'Berlin will always remain Berlin.'[5]

Sharing the grandstand with Reuter that day was Frank Howley. He remarked to one of his staff that the massed crowd fully deserved their triumph, for they had shown themselves 'willing to suffer and die for democracy'.[6]

The most immediate reward for the inhabitants of West Berlin was a massive influx of food and supplies at affordable prices. In the long months since the western Allies' currency reform, the economies of Germany's western zones had undergone a dramatic lift. 'The wholesalers had been waiting months for the end of the blockade,' said Curt Riess. 'As soon as it was lifted, they sent everything transportable to Berlin.' Berliners flocked to the shops, bought huge quantities of food, and ate in a fashion that had not been possible for years. Pork, cod, butter, eggs and coffee – all were once again available after four years of hardship. Riess described the days that followed the end of the blockade as 'orgies of gluttony'.[7]

General Lucius Clay left Berlin for good within three days of the end of the siege. Within a month he would also leave the army, thereby concluding a long and distinguished military career. He would later become a senior partner at Lehman Brothers, but he could never completely turn away from his service in Europe. As a founder of the influential publication, *Der Monat* (The Month), he sought to win the support of German intellectuals for America's aggressive Cold War foreign policy.

Four years earlier Clay had arrived in the German capital with orders to work in partnership with the Soviets. Now, those partners had become enemies and the world had split into opposing factions. Churchill's Iron Curtain had become a reality. Clay's relationship with Colonel Frank Howley had undergone a similarly dramatic shift. On first arriving in Berlin he had found Howley a dangerous troublemaker who treated the Soviets with contempt. But now, as he prepared to leave the capital, Clay saw eye to eye with Howley on virtually everything.

The colonel himself stayed in the city for a further four months, overseeing the transfer of many powers to the new city government under the capable leadership of Ernst Reuter. Howley was combative to the last. That post-blockade summer saw yet more wrangling over striking railway workers, the Markgraf police and the nefarious role of Kotikov's intelligence agents. General Kotikov himself emerged unscathed from the fallout of the airlift, a surprise survivor in a time of change, and he was to remain in his post for another year. He made repeated attempts to rejoin the Kommandatura in the aftermath of the siege, acting as if the break-up a year earlier had been merely an unfortunate hiatus.

Howley refused to countenance the idea of having the Soviets back on board, arguing that to do so 'would give tacit recognition to the illegal government the Russians had set up in East Berlin'.[8] Instead, the four commandants met irregularly and informally, often in the Kommandatura building, but declined to sign any agreements.

By September, Howley felt his work was done: he was ready to leave the city that had been his home since July 1945. The intervening years had brought a constant succession of challenges, yet he had overcome each new crisis with a mix of determination and humanity. When he looked back to where it all started, in the sleepy village of Barbizon, it seemed to belong to another era. His partnership with Brigadier Hinde; the long road to Berlin; the tussles in the Kommandatura – all were now firmly in the past.

The Kotikov-controlled media was overjoyed at the news of Howley's departure. 'The Soviet radio was popping its tubes with glee over my resignation as commandant,' wrote Howley. 'For some reason, I was suddenly "Howley, the Rough Rider from Texas".'[9] Every time his name was mentioned on the radio it was accompanied by a loud blast of cowboy music.

Berlin's correspondent for the Associated Press kept a close eye on the Soviet-backed media and was incredulous at the amount of vitriol it produced. 'Almost every day the Soviet army publishes new insults against Colonel Frank Howley. Red cartoonists lampoon him and if you believe what the Soviet newspapers say, it was Howley who almost single-handedly blockaded Berlin, split the city and destroyed the four-power Kommandatura.'[10]

Those newspapers had previously referred to him as the 'liar', 'terrorist' or 'black market knight'. Now, they simply called him 'the dictator'. The Soviet-licensed *Die Neue Zeit* published a damning assessment of his four-year regime in Berlin, describing it as inimical to peace. 'His name is most closely related to the Cold War and all those incidents that helped to create the Berlin crisis,' it said, adding that the break-up of the Kommandatura had been 'the consequence of one of those notorious hussar rides of the American commandant which sadly achieved such renown in Berlin's post-war policy'. Its conclusion was blunt: 'Howley is leaving his post at a time when western Berlin's policy of isolation discloses more and more clearly a complete bankruptcy.'[11]

The British press offered a rather different perspective, with one headline summing up Howley's departure in four words: 'A Legend Leaves Berlin'.[12] The American press was no less gushing in its praise for the man whom many held to have been the hero of the battle against the Soviets, 'a tough-skinned American who thrives on communist abuse'.[13]

Howley thrived on that abuse because it was tangible proof that the Soviets were rankled by his manner of doing battle. He also knew he was on the winning side. 'Communism has taken a terrible beating in Berlin,' he said. 'On one side of the street is the truth and on the other side is a lie, and the people can see for themselves which is which.'[14]

Howley packed up his villa in Dahlem at the beginning of September and prepared to take his wife and children back to America aboard the army transport vessel, *Maurice Rose*. But first, he wanted to say farewell to his most persistent enemy.

'I rather think that Kotikov will remember our farewell,' he wrote. 'The Kommandatura had just concluded its meeting and, as the departing chairman, I was host at the inevitable buffet in the next room.'[15] As he left the chamber for the final time, he allowed himself a brief moment to reflect on the constant sparring with his Soviet opposite number, a feud that had taken a physical toll on them both. 'My four years in Berlin gave me gray hair,' he said, 'but I have the satisfaction that I gave him stomach ulcers.'[16]

Now, he was to give those ulcers a final parting gift. As a waiter offered a tray of drinks, Kotikov confessed that he was in too much pain to drink his usual vodka. A gleeful Howley recounted in his memoirs what happened next.

'Champagne?' someone asked.

Kotikov puffed out his cheeks and shook his head. 'Makes me belch,' he said.

'Have a Martini,' I said shrewdly.

'What is a Martini?' Kotikov asked.

I pointed to the lethal drink on the tray. Innocently, Kotikov picked it up. I took champagne. Kotikov raised his glass . . . To my astonishment, [he] gulped the entire contents of his glass, Martini, olive and all. A look of wonder crossed his face. I proposed a toast. Another Martini clanked down to the Russian's ulcers. There were two more toasts and two more rapid Martinis for Kotikov. I looked at him curiously. His disarmingly cherubic face was twisted. Obviously his stomach was on fire.

I nodded toward another Martini.

'*Nyet!*' he gasped.[17]

On the day before Howley was due to leave Berlin, there was a grand send-off from the army at the US military compound, with a parade, a brass band and lots of speech-making. Senior generals from the British and French armed forces were also in attendance, along with leading members of the West Berlin city government, with Ernst Reuter a guest of honour. After taking the salute from precision-marching American infantrymen and cavalry, the new American high commissioner for Germany, John J. McCloy, pinned a Distinguished Service Medal to Howley's chest.

President Truman had written a special panegyric for the ceremony, declaring that Colonel Howley had been an inspiration to the people of Berlin. 'Exceptional meritorious service in a duty of great responsibility,' said the president, who added that Howley had displayed 'superior leadership and devotion to duty'.[18] He, more than anyone else, had saved Berlin from catastrophe.

When the ceremony was at an end, Howley moved across to his waiting Horch motorcar. As he did so, the cheering crowd broke through the security cordon and feted him as a departing hero. Arms were outstretched as everyone sought to shake his hand. One face particularly caught Howley's attention. Pushing through the crowd was a determined young woman, her hair scraped back from her face, her features pinched and wan. She looked like so many exhausted Berliners, yet there was something about her that held his attention. Her eyes were alive, despite the deprivations, and in her arms she clutched a healthy blue-eyed baby. She gave Howley the warmest of smiles as she told him that her child owed its life to the supplies he had imported to Berlin at the outset of the siege. 'This is my baby you saved when the Russians would not give us milk,' she said, the tears welling in her eyes. 'We will never forget you, sir. Goodbye and good luck!'[19]

Howley was to receive many honours upon his return to America: a spectacular fanfare in New York Harbour, a triumphant motorcade through the city and a summons to a private audience with President Truman. His conversation with the president was to remain private, although Truman's previous message to the Berlin farewell ceremony gives an idea of what he might have said. It was left to Howley himself to write the epitaph to his victory in Berlin, a victory made possible by the joint efforts of the three western Allies. 'Here's to the Yanks,' he wrote in his memoir, 'who, working day and night with our British and French allies and with democratic Germans, made the Berlin victory possible.' He praised the garrison soldiers of Berlin, the gallant pilots of the airlift and his inner circle of supporters, as well as his wife and four small children, 'who took the daily insults, threats and privations of the Communist rats [and] who walked like bears'.

Never shy to blast his own trumpet, he also praised himself. He had been the first to recognise that Berlin faced a grave danger from the Soviets and he had also been quick to realise that you need to punch hard and low if you are going to win. When summing up his four years in Berlin, he was characteristically frank. 'Only a fool would say that I had not done a good job.'[20]

As so often with Howley, the statement was cocky, brash and outrageous. But it was also true.

Epilogue

A S THE SIEGE of Berlin had been drawing to its close, a drama of global significance was unfolding in Washington. In the austere splendour of the State Department, President Truman's new secretary of state, Dean Acheson, was presiding over an unprecedented gathering of the world's most influential figures.

The date was Monday, 4 April 1949, and Washington was playing host to 1,300 distinguished invitees and a radio audience of millions. The US State Department predicted that the day's events would attract the biggest global audience in radio history.

It was shortly after 2 p.m. when the first grandees began filing into the vast auditorium of the State Department: senior officials of the United States government and select members of the Senate and House of Representatives. They were followed into the hall by the ambassadors of a dozen nations, along with high-ranking diplomats and their aides. All eyes were fixed on the raised dais. Close by stood the world's press.

As 3 p.m. approached, the band of the US Marines began playing jaunty Gershwin melodies that included 'Bess, You is My Woman Now'. It was intended as a compliment to the First Lady, Mrs Truman, seated in the front row, but a few senior diplomats could be seen shaking their heads in disapproval.[1] It seemed too frivolous a song for such an august occasion.

The American secretary of state, Dean Acheson, was the first to appear on the raised dais. Elegant and urbane, he carried himself with the dignified grandeur of an elder statesman. He was followed onto the stage by the foreign ministers of the other eleven nations, who took their seats beside a flank of national flags.

Acheson had played a central role in shaping American foreign policy since the end of the war. As tensions brewed in Berlin, so the West's policy towards the Soviet Union had hardened and sharpened. Acheson had been quietly driving that policy. As one commentator put it, he was 'the true begetter of the Marshall Plan, the champion of the Truman Doctrine, the moving force behind the post-war decision to arrest Soviet expansion in Europe'.[2] This was true enough, but it neglected the vital, behind-the-scenes role played by George Kennan, author of the Long Telegram.

Dean Acheson had also worked closely with Ernest Bevin, with the two men being the principal architects of the North Atlantic alliance, NATO, that was to be constituted that very afternoon. The gathering in Washington was for the formal signing of the North Atlantic Treaty by the foreign ministers of Belgium, Canada, Denmark, France, Iceland, Italy, Luxembourg, the Netherlands, Norway, Portugal and the United Kingdom. Acheson himself was to sign for the United States. In the words of one broadcaster, these twelve powers 'were sworn to stand together against aggression. An attack against one would be an attack against all.' This was the key commitment of the NATO signatories, as set down in Article Five of the treaty.

Moscow's response had come some days earlier: an outpouring of withering outrage, with the Kremlin slamming the treaty as an illegal act of aggression. 'It runs counter to the Yalta and Potsdam agreements, in which Britain and the United States assumed the obligation to co-operate in the consolidation of peace.'[3] The British government sent a stinging rebuke, castigating the Soviet authorities for violating every clause of the Potsdam Agreement, acts that had culminated in the eleven-month blockade of Berlin.

The proceedings in Washington formally began when the State Department's chaplain offered prayers for 'this day of destiny' – a day on which the famous Liberty Bell, which had once rung for the first thirteen states of America, was now heard 'by as many imperilled nations around the threatened earth'.[4]

Secretary of State Acheson was first to take the rostrum. The son of a bishop, he thundered a prophecy of doom against any country that threatened hostilities against the twelve signatory nations. 'If offences come, then woe unto them by whom the offence cometh.'[5] He mentioned no country by name, but everyone knew he was speaking of the Soviet Union.

One by one, the eleven other foreign ministers addressed the audience before signing the treaty. 'My country has had forced upon it two world wars against aggression within a period of a quarter of a century,' said Ernest Bevin. Now, thanks to NATO, British citizens would be able to 'sleep safely in their beds'.[6]

Dr Dirk Stikker of the Netherlands injected a more sober note into the day's proceedings. 'The treaty we are about to sign marks the end of an illusion,' he said, 'the hope that the United Nations would by itself ensure international peace.'[7] This had been President Roosevelt's cherished dream, the big idea he had brought to the Yalta Conference four years earlier. But the United Nations had proved unable to guarantee the peace in such turbulent times. 'A charming dream', said one, 'from which we had awakened gradually into a grey reality.'[8] A new, more robust organisation was needed – one so powerful that it would deter the Soviet Union from ever risking war with the West.

The founding of NATO marked the end of America's cherished policy of isolation. In a speech six years earlier, Truman had blamed the outbreak of the Second World War on America's isolationist attitude in the aftermath of the Great War. Now, his vision was for America to embrace the world and he would use his second term as president to bring this to fruition. As one commentator put it, the United States abandoned economic isolation with the Marshall Plan, abandoned political isolation by joining the United Nations and abandoned military isolation by joining NATO.

The foundation of NATO was not the only momentous event to take place that spring. On the very day that the western sectors of Berlin were celebrating their liberation from the Soviet blockade, American, British and French military governors signed off a constitution for the western-occupied zones of Germany. This marked the birth of the Federal Republic – West Germany – and was a turning point in the history of the post-war world. In the democratic elections held later that summer, Konrad Adenauer won the chancellorship on a clear platform: the creation of a stable democratic state irrevocably allied with the West. His overriding ambition, born of a deep mistrust of Stalin, was to 'integrate Germany completely into Western Europe'.[9] He got his way in the spring of 1955 when West Germany became a signatory of NATO. Ten years after Nazi Germany's humiliating defeat, the old enemy had become a trusted friend.

Berlin was not to be part of the new state of West Germany. It was to remain in legal ambiguity, officially under four-nation control although many of the Kommandatura's powers in the western sectors were delegated to Ernst Reuter's capable city government. A few Berliners entertained hopes that their city might yet become capital of the Federal Republic, but it was not to be. Chancellor Adenauer, a Catholic Rhinelander, was an outspoken critic of the historical influence of Prussia: in his eyes, Berlin was an unappealing symbol of that influence. He intended the republic's new capital to be the provincial town of Bonn, best known (if at all) as the birthplace of Beethoven.

Although West Berlin became increasingly aligned with the Federal Republic over the years that followed, the three-power Kommandatura continued to function until its final meeting on 2 October 1990, the eve of German reunification, when it voted to dissolve itself. Just eight months later, the new German parliament, the Bundestag, decided to re-establish Berlin as the country's capital.

The eastern sector of the city was to have a very different narrative from that of the western. In response to the establishment of the Federal Republic, the Soviet Military Administration announced the creation of the German Democratic Republic (East Germany) on 8 October 1949. It was to have East Berlin as its capital, in direct contravention of the Potsdam Agreement. The top jobs went to a familiar trio of revolutionaries. The elderly Wilhelm Pieck was appointed president of the new state, with Otto Grotewohl as chancellor. Walter Ulbricht was initially appointed deputy prime minister, but he was soon named as first secretary of the Socialist Unity Party, becoming the de facto leader of the country. After the brutal crushing of the East German uprising in 1953, the Kremlin threw its weight behind Ulbricht and allowed him to increase his grip on power.

Eight years after leaving the Hotel Lux in Moscow, he had secured the autocratic authority he had for so long craved.

Under his lacklustre leadership, East Berlin would undergo economic stagnation and decline, along with a haemorrhaging of its dynamic young population. Those living in the east of the city could cross into the western sectors and see the conspicuous wealth on display in lavishly stocked shop windows. Many chose to leave, a trickle that soon turned into a flood. Ulbricht's dramatic response came in 1961, when he ordered the construction of the Berlin Wall. The city was now physically split into two separate halves and it became virtually impossible for any inhabitant in the eastern sector to cross over to the west.

Twelve years earlier at the height of the siege of Berlin, Ulbricht had made a speech in which he said, 'As a German people, we will do everything in our power to support the Soviet Union.'[10] He proved true to his word, serving as a loyal Communist ally until his death in 1973.

The Soviet Union gave a swift response to West Germany's accession to NATO in the spring of 1955. Within eight days, it had signed a defensive treaty with Poland and six other Eastern Bloc countries: Albania, Bulgaria, Czechoslovakia, East Germany, Hungary and Romania. Officially called the Treaty of Friendship, Cooperation and Mutual Assistance, it soon became known as the Warsaw Pact. With its creation, the world had officially divided into two opposing camps that were to glower at each other over the dividing line of Berlin for the next thirty-four years.

That dividing line had already been scored into the ground when Colonel Frank Howley roared into town on 30 June 1945. He was the first to recognise that the Soviets were no longer an ally; that Stalin was plotting the seizure of both Berlin and western Germany. Howley saw Soviet duplicity in razor-sharp focus, with kidnappings, looting, murder and espionage being a daily reality in Berlin, along with lurid propaganda and the rigging of elections. Howley spent much of his tenure urging Washington to instigate tough measures against 'the Reds'.[11]

The rambunctious colonel had always believed that you could

successfully shout down your opponent only if your words were backed up by military might. The Soviets would always use force, he said, if they needed it to get their way. But he would later add an important caveat, one born from his experiences in Berlin. 'They'll only use force if they have a more-than-reasonable chance of succeeding.'[12]

With the creation of NATO, they had lost that more-than-reasonable chance.

Acknowledgements

W HEN I WAS very young my family made frequent outings to visit Great Aunt Irene, a formidable Victorian relic who had served in the British military and wound up in Berlin at the end of the Second World War. She would tell us how she had clambered into Hitler's ruined bunker and hacked a slab of red marble from the wall. This was later turned into a paperweight that sat atop her writing desk. Stuck onto its underside was a scrap of paper with the words, 'For Giles when I die' – a promise that was sadly not fulfilled.

I would like to say that Great Aunt Irene plays a role in *Checkmate in Berlin*, but I only half-listened to her stories. It wasn't until I started researching the book that I realised why she was so keen to talk about her post-war service in a city overrun with criminals, ex-Nazis, black-marketeers, kidnappers and pimps. She must also have witnessed at close quarters the political showdown that forms the narrative of this book.

Much of *Checkmate in Berlin* is drawn from first-hand accounts and I owe a debt of gratitude to the archives and archivists who have aided me in my work. My thanks to Rodney C. Foytik of the US Army War College Library, Carlisle, Pennsylvania, for his help with navigating the collection during my visit. The library's huge array of Frank L. Howley papers proved essential in telling the story of Cold War Berlin.

Staying in America, my thanks also go to the extraordinarily helpful archivists at the National Archives and Records Administration (NARA) in Washington DC, where I was able to sift through thousands of records from American Military Government. I am grateful to Kate Mollan at the Center for Legislative Archives for locating an important US Senate report into the behaviour of American forces in Germany.

In the UK, my thanks are extended to the staff of the National Archives, home to so many documents about Berlin, and to staff of the Imperial War Museum, which contains many diaries, memoirs and oral interviews. My thanks to Geoffrey Browell, head of archives at King's College London (which houses the Liddell Hart Centre for Military Archives); he provided me with access to their extensive collection of Cold War primary source material. The staff of the British Library were particularly helpful when it came to locating obscure newspaper and magazine articles; and Clare Smith of the Metropolitan Police helped source biographical information about Detective Inspector Tom Hayward.

Thank you as ever to the diligent team at the London Library, where so much of this book was written. A chat with one library member, Adrian Wilsdon, led me to the Field Security Section files in the National Archives; these contain the secret intelligence reports of undercover agents in Berlin.

In Berlin itself, my thanks to the staff and curators of the Alliierten Museum and the Militärhistorisches Museum Flugplatz Berlin-Gatow. I am also grateful to the President's Office of the Free University of Berlin for an unscheduled tour of the building which formerly housed the four-power Kommandatura.

Thank you to Eddie Ide from the Berlin Airlift Veterans Association for sharing documents and stories, and to Martin Bisiker of Legasee for providing transcripts of interviews. Warm thanks are also due to Kenneth Alford, author of *The Spoils of World War II*, for kindly sending me the extensive transcripts of the trial of Norman T. Byrne.

I am grateful to the estate of Curt Riess for permitting me to quote from his book, *The Berlin Story*, and to Paragon House and Suhrkamp Verlag for allowing me to quote from the English and German editions of Ruth Andreas-Friedrich's *Battleground Berlin* and *Der Schattenmann: Tagebuchaufzeichnungen 1938–1948*.

The children of several principal characters in the book proved both welcoming and extremely helpful. My sincere thanks to Peter Howley, for sharing memories of his childhood in Berlin and permitting me to quote from his father's writings; and to the rest of the Howley family for proving so obliging. My thanks are also extended to Brigadier Hinde's daughters: Cathryn Cawdor, who kindly invited me to stay at her home in the Scottish Highlands (the venison was delicious); and Victoria d'Avanzo, who twice invited me to her Wiltshire home. Both shared memories of their father and of Berlin.

My heartfelt thanks to Irina Scorer (née Hoecke) for sharing her childhood memories of Potsdam and Berlin, and to her husband, the late Peter Scorer, for providing the warmest of welcomes into their home.

I am grateful as ever to Georgia Garrett, my literary agent at RCW, and to the entire team there, where a special mention goes to Laurence Laluyaux, Stephen Edwards, Tristan Kendrick and Katharina Volckmer in the foreign rights department for working so diligently at selling my books around the world. My thanks are also due to Rob Kraitt at Casarotto Ramsay and Associates for being so assiduous in selling the TV and film rights to my books.

As ever, the team at John Murray have proved highly professional: a huge and heartfelt thank you to my two editors: managing director, Nick Davies, and editorial director, Joe Zigmond. Their editorial suggestions and advice were invaluable, and I am deeply grateful for the time and effort they put into editing the book. My American editor at Henry Holt, Caroline Zancan, also provided superb editorial input: it was a rare and uplifting experience to have three such experienced hands collaborating on the editing of my book.

Back to John Murray: thank you to the rest of the team there who have worked so hard on the book: Caroline Westmore, Yassine Belkacemi, Emma Petfield, Diana Talyanina, Howard Davies, Ellie Wheeldon, Juliet Brightmore, Caroline Jones and copy-editor, Candida Brazil. Equal thanks to the New York team at Henry Holt: Catryn Silbersack, Steven Seighman, Jenna Dolan and Chris O'Connell.

I am grateful to Masha Bozunova for finding little-known Russian documents about the capture of the Berlin Reichstag and for translating sections of General Alexander Kotikov's memoirs. I am also grateful to fellow London Library member, John McNally, who (once again) kindly read a very early version of the manuscript.

Lastly, my heartfelt thanks go to my family, who have lived through three long years of my near-total immersion in the early years of the Cold War: my daughters, Madeleine, Héloïse and Aurélia, and my ever-supportive and multilingual wife, Alexandra. She provided solutions to problems, translated documents from German into English and was the first to read the finished manuscript. *Vielen dank! Merci beaucoup!* Thank you!

Magny, Burgundy, February 2021

Picture Credits

Notes and Sources

Prologue

1. Cited in Laurence Rees, *World War Two: Behind Closed Doors, Stalin, the Nazis and the West*, BBC Books, 2008, p. 333.
2. W. Averell Harriman and Elie Abel, *Special Envoy to Churchill and Stalin 1941–1946*, Random House, 1975, p. 390.
3. Charles Bohlen, *Witness to History, 1929–1969*, Weidenfeld & Nicolson, 1973, p. 173.
4. Sarah Churchill, *Keep on Dancing*, Weidenfeld & Nicolson, 1981, p. 74.
5. Sir Alexander Cadogan, *The Diaries of Sir Alexander Cadogan, 1938–45*, Cassell, 1971.
6. Sarah Churchill, *Keep on Dancing*, p. 74. See also Lord Charles Moran, *Winston Churchill: The Struggle for Survival, 1940–65*, Constable, 1966, in which he mentions bed bugs biting Churchill's feet.
7. Cited in S. M. Plokhy, *Yalta, The Price of Peace*, Viking, 2010, p. 47.
8. *Foreign Relations of the United States: Diplomatic Papers, Conferences at Malta and Yalta, 1945*, United States Government Printing Office, 1955, p. 715.
9. A. H. Birse, *Memoirs of an Interpreter*, Michael Joseph, 1967, p. 182.
10. Milovan Djilas, *Conversations with Stalin*, Harcourt, Brace & World, 1962, p. 70.
11. Bohlen, *Witness to History*, p. 180.
12. Cited in R. Hopkins, *American Heritage*, Vol. 56, No. 3 (June–July 2005).
13. Bohlen, *Witness to History*, p. 180. See also Harriman and Abel, *Special Envoy*, p. 394.
14. Cited in Studs Terkel, *The Good War: An Oral History of World War Two*, Hamish Hamilton, 1985, p. 331.
15. Ibid., p. 122.

16. TNA FO 1079/13. See also Lucius Clay, *Decision in Germany*, William Heinemann, 1950, p. 11ff.
17. Cited in Diana Preston, *Eight Days at Yalta*, Picador, 2019, p. 138.
18. *Conferences at Malta and Yalta*, pp. 612 and 614.
19. Harriman and Abel, *Special Envoy*, p. 401.
20. *Conferences at Malta and Yalta*, p. 617.
21. Edward Stettinius, *Roosevelt and the Russians*, Jonathan Cape, 1950, p. 121. See also Harriman and Abel, *Special Envoy*, p. 401 and *Conferences at Malta and Yalta*, p. 617.
22. Cadogan, *Diaries*, p. 706.
23. Anthony Eden, *The Eden Memoirs: The Reckoning*, Cassell, 1960, p. 514.
24. Cadogan, *Diaries*, p. 706.
25. Cited in Jim Bishop, *FDR's Last Year*, Hart-Davis, MacGibbon, 1975, p. 384.
26. Bohlen, *Witness to History*, p. 183.
27. Andrei Gromyko, *Memories*, Hutchinson, 1989, p. 98.
28. *Conferences at Malta and Yalta*, pp. 797–8.
29. Winston Churchill, *The Second World War*, Cassell, 1954, Vol. 6, p. 316.
30. Ibid.
31. Cadogan, *Diaries*, p. 707.
32. Winston Churchill, *Second World War*, Vol. 6, p. 343.
33. Cited in Preston, *Eight Days*, p. 361.
34. Cited in Rick Atkinson, *The Guns at Last Light*, Henry Holt, 2013, p. 519.
35. Winston Churchill, *Second World War*, Vol. 6, p. 351.
36. Cited in Robert E. Sherwood, *Roosevelt and Hopkins*, Ishi Press, 2020, p. 870.

Chapter 1: The Road to Berlin

1. 'Frank Howley, *Berlin Command*, G. P. Putnam's Sons, 1950, p. 18.
2. Howley, Frank, unpublished diary and miscellaneous papers, USAWC Frank Howley archives, Box 5.
3. Ibid.
4. Howley, *Berlin Command*, p. 20.
5. USAWC Frank Howley archives, Box 2.
6. Ibid., Box 3.
7. Brigadier Hinde, miscellaneous papers, Hinde family archive.
8. Ibid.
9. Cited in Max Hastings, *Overlord: D-Day and the Battle for Normandy*,

Michael Joseph, 1984, pp. 134–5. See also Victoria d'Avanzo, 'My Father, the Loony Hero', *Scottish Daily Mail*, 16 January 2015.

10. Brigadier Robert Hinde, *Military Government: British Troops Berlin*, Printing and Stationery Services, Berlin, July 1945, Hinde family archive.

11. Private papers of Lieutenant Colonel H. Hays MBE, IWM Documents 20927.

12. Ibid.

13. Howley, *Berlin Command*, p. 19.

14. Hays papers, IWM Documents 20927.

15. USAWC Frank Howley archives, Box 2.

16. Ibid.

17. Hays papers, IWM Documents 20927.

18. USAWC Frank Howley archives, Box 2.

19. W. Byford-Jones, *Berlin Twilight*, Hutchinson, 1947, p. 19.

20. George Clare, *Berlin Days: 1946–47*, Macmillan, 1989, p. 5.

21. Howley, *Berlin Command*, p. 20.

22. Hays papers, IWM Documents 20927. See also USAWC Frank Howley archives, Box 2.

23. All Jim Kane quotes from https://nsarchive2.gwu.edu/coldwar/interviews/episode-1/kane1.html

24. All Alfred Aronson quotes from https://nsarchive2.gwu.edu/coldwar/interviews/episode-1/aronson1.html

25. http://news.bbc.co.uk/onthisday/hi/dates/stories/april/27/newsid_3563000/3563723.stm

26. Hays papers, IWM Documents 20927.

27. Goronwy Rees, *A Bundle of Sensations: Sketches in Autobiography*, Chatto & Windus, 1960, pp. 173–90.

28. USAWC Frank Howley archives, Box 2.

29. Howley, *Berlin Command*, p. 27.

30. Ibid.

31. Ibid., p. 16.

32. Ibid., p. 24.

33. Atkinson, *Guns at Last Light*, p. 578.

34. USAWC Frank Howley archives, Box 2.

Chapter 2: Flag on the Reichstag

1. Gyula Hays, *Born 1900*, Hutchinson, 1974, p. 160.
2. Cited in Wolfgang Leonhard, *Child of the Revolution*, Collins, 1957, pp. 297 and 303ff.; this sets out the broad sweep of Ulbricht's policy.
3. Ibid., p. 288. See also 'The Boss of East Germany', *Observer*, 7 December 1958.
4. Hays, *Born 1900*, p. 165.
5. Terence Prittie, 'Europe's Last Stalinist Ruler', *Guardian*, 19 August 1963.
6. Curt Riess, *The Berlin Story*, Frederick Muller, 1953, p. 188.
7. 'The Boss of East Germany', *Observer*, 7 December 1958.
8. Leonhard, *Child of the Revolution*, pp. 289–90.
9. Wolfgang Leonhard, interview transcript, https://nsarchive2.gwu.edu/coldwar/interviews/episode-2/leonhard1.html
10. Leonhard, *Child of the Revolution*, p. 284ff and interview transcript, https://nsarchive2.gwu.edu/coldwar/interviews/episode-2/leonhard1.html
11. Hermann Hoecke, 'The Hoecke-Southard Chronicles', unpublished typescript, 2011, p. 74.
12. Ibid., p. 75.
13. Helga Schneider, *The Bonfire of Berlin*, William Heinemann, 2005, p. 105.
14. Ibid., p. 142.
15. Anon. (Marta Hillers), *A Woman in Berlin*, Virago, 2011, p. 36.
16. Elfriede von Assel, interview transcript, KCLMA GB0099 Cold War.
17. Schneider, *Bonfire of Berlin*, p. 145.
18. Ibid., p. 153.
19. Ibid., p. 154ff.
20. Ibid., p. 160ff.
21. Riess, *The Berlin Story*, p. 16. See also 'Anonymous Account of the Last Days of the Second World War by an English Woman in Berlin', IWM 4029.
22. Friedrich Luft, oral interview, IWM 2966.
23. Cited in Norman M. Naimark, *The Russians in Germany: A History of the Soviet Zone of Occupation, 1945–1949*, Belknap Press, 1995, p. 72.
24. Cited in Corelli Barnett, *The Lords of War*, Praetorian Press, 2012, p. 256.
25. Obituary of Mikhail Minin, *The Times*, 25 January 2008.
26. See https://www.business-gazeta.ru/article/132054 (in Russian) for a detailed account of the assault. See also V. Sevruk (ed.), *How Wars*

End: Eye-Witness Accounts of the Fall of Berlin, University Press of the Pacific, 2005.

27. https://www.business-gazeta.ru/article/132054

28. See https://www.nytimes.com/1997/01/31/arts/beyond-battle-a-soviet-portrait.html and https://www.nytimes.com/1997/10/09/world/yevgeny-khaldei-80-war-photographer-dies.html. Also http://content.time.com/time/world/article/0,8599,1809018,00.html

29. Ruth Andreas-Friedrich, *Battleground Berlin*, Paragon House, 1990, p. 12.

30. Anon., *Woman in Berlin*, p. 107.

31. Andreas-Friedrich, *Battleground Berlin*, p. 13.

32. Konstantin Simonow, *Kriegstagebücher 1942–1945*, Vol. 2, Verlag Volk und Welt, 1979, p. 796ff.

33. Andreas-Friedrich, *Battleground Berlin*, p. 9.

34. Anon., *Woman in Berlin*, p. 84.

35. Ibid., p. 263.

36. Hildegard Herrberger, interview transcript, KCLMA GB0099 Cold War.

37. G. A. Tokaev, *Comrade X*, Harvill Press, 1956, p. 290.

38. Naimark, *Russians in Germany*, p. 79.

39. Anon., *Woman in Berlin*, p. 43.

40. Ronald Mallabar, oral interview, IWM 11211.

41. Winston Churchill, *Second World War*, Vol. 6, p. 343.

42. TNA CAB 20/691 Russia Threat to Civilization.

43. Ibid. See also Richard Norton-Taylor, 'Churchill Plotted invasion of Russia', *Guardian*, 2 October 1998.

44. Jonathan Walker, *Operation Unthinkable*, The History Press, 2013, pp. 64 and 68.

45. Ibid., p. 102.

46. TNA CAB 20/691 Russia Threat to Civilization.

47. Cited in Walker, *Operation Unthinkable*, p. 111.

48. John Toland, *The Last 100 Days*, Bantam, 1997, pp. 442–3.

Chapter 3: Red Berlin

1. Leonhard, *Child of the Revolution*, p. 288ff.

2. Leonhard, https://nsarchive2.gwu.edu/coldwar/interviews/episode-2/leonhard1.html

3. Leonhard, *Child of the Revolution*, p. 378.

4. Cited in Giles MacDonogh, *After the Reich: From the Liberation of Vienna to the Berlin Airlift*, John Murray, 2007, p. 105.

5. Emmet Hughes, 'Berlin Under Siege', *Life*, 19 July 1948.

6. Schneider, *Bonfire of Berlin*, p. 176ff.

7. Hoecke, 'The Hoecke-Southard Chronicles', p. 77.

8. Vasily Grossman, *A Writer at War*, Pimlico, 2006, p. 335.

9. Ibid., p. 338.

10. Douglas Botting, *In the Ruins of the Reich*, Methuen, 2005, p. 325.

11. Grossman, *A Writer at War*, p. 338.

12. Dorothea von Schwanenflügel Lawson, *Laughter Wasn't Rationed*, Tricor Press, 2009, p. 432.

13. Anon., *Woman in Berlin*, p. 245.

14. Ibid., p. 231.

15. Andreas-Friedrich, *Battleground Berlin*, p. 42.

16. Ibid., p. 39.

17. Riess, *Berlin Story*, p. 19.

18. Friedrich Luft, oral interview, IWM 2966.

19. Gregory Klimov, *The Terror Machine*, Faber & Faber, 1953, p. 113.

20. Ibid., p. 297.

21. Yelena Rzhevskaya, *Berlin 1945*, published in translation in Sevruk, *How Wars End*, p. 252. See also Rzhevskaya, *Memoirs of a Wartime Interpreter*, Greenhill Books, 2018.

22. https://www.cia.gov/library/readingroom/docs/HITLER%2C%20ADOLF%20%20MEDICAL%20ASSESSMENT%20%28DI%20FILE%29_0008.pdf

23. Ibid.

24. All from Rzhevskaya, *Berlin 1945*.

25. https://nypost.com/2018/07/14/how-the-woman-who-identified-hitlers-dental-remains-ended-up-in-prison/.

26. David Roll, *The Hopkins Touch*, Oxford University Press, 2015, p. 392.

27. Robert E. Sherwood (ed.), *The White House Papers of Harry L. Hopkins*, Eyre & Spottiswoode, 1949, p. 880.

28. Howley, *Berlin Command*, p. 26.

29. Ibid., p. 11.

30. Hays papers, IWM Documents 20927.

31. Hinde, *Military Government*, pp. 4–5.

Chapter 4: Loot

1. Toland, *The Last 100 Days*, pp. 442–3.
2. Grigori Tokaev, *Stalin Means War*, Weidenfeld & Nicolson, 1951, p. 86.
3. Tokaev, *Comrade X*, pp. 289–95. Colonel Tokaev's professed shock should be viewed with caution, for he wrote his memoirs after defecting to the West – although that the looting occurred is not in doubt.
4. Andreas-Friedrich, *Battleground Berlin*, pp. 21 and 25.
5. Riess, *Berlin Story*, p. 20.
6. Hoecke, 'The Hoecke-Southard Chronicles', p. 82.
7. Konstantin Akinsha and Grigorii Kozlov, *Stolen Treasure*, Weidenfeld & Nicolson, 1995, p. 68.
8. Interview with Andrei Belokopitov is in ibid., p. 80ff.
9. Akinsha and Kozlov, *Stolen Treasure*, p. 82.
10. Ibid., p. 85.
11. Tokaev, *Comrade X*, p. 290.
12. Cited in Aleksandr Shirokorad, Великая контрибуция. Что СССР получил после войны (*Great Contribution: What the USSR Received After the War*), Veche, 2013, p. 17.
13. Cited in an article on Zhukov's looting: https://www.bagira.guru/ussr/pobednye-trofei-marshala-zhukova.html
14. The following narrative about the von Ardenne family is from Manfred von Ardenne, *Ein glückliches Leben für Technik und Forschung*, Verlag der Nation, 1973. There is an interesting British intelligence report on von Ardenne in TNA FO 1031/59.
15. Andreas-Friedrich, *Battleground Berlin*, p. 59.
16. Ibid., p. 60.
17. Clay's account is from Clay, *Decision in Germany*, p. 20ff.
18. Ibid., p. 24.
19. Byford-Jones, *Berlin Twilight*, p. 130.
20. Ibid., p. 161.
21. Clay, *Decision in Germany*, p. 22.
22. 'Notes of a Meeting between Marshal Zhukov and Soviet Representatives, General Clay and US Representatives', unpublished typescript, USAWC Floyd L. Parks papers.
23. Georgii Zhukov, *The Memoirs of Marshal Zhukov*, Jonathan Cape, 1971, p. 661.
24. Clay, *Decision in Germany*, p. 23.
25. Ibid.

Chapter 5: Arrival of the Allies

1. USAWC Frank Howley archives, Box 2.
2. Ibid.
3. Howley, *Berlin Command*, p. 27.
4. USAWC Frank Howley archives, Box 2.
5. All from Howley, *Berlin Command*, pp. 28–31.
6. USAWC Frank Howley archives, Box 2.
7. Ibid.
8. Howley, *Berlin Command*, p. 33.
9. USAWC Frank Howley archives, Box 2.
10. Ibid.
11. Howley, *Berlin Command*, p. 35.
12. Ibid., p. 41.
13. Lucius D. Clay, interview transcript, Harry S. Truman Library, https://www.trumanlibrary.gov/library/oral-histories/clayl
14. Anthony Mann, *Comeback: Germany 1945–1952*, Macmillan, 1980, p. 32.
15. Hays papers, IWM Documents 20927. Sir Brian Robertson said it was 'simply fantastic to have permitted Berlin to become an island in the Soviet zone', as quoted in Mann, *Comeback*, p. 32.
16. Howley, *Berlin Command*, pp. 42–3.
17. Ibid., p. 43.
18. William Stivers and Donald A. Carter, *The City Becomes a Symbol: The US Army in the Occupation of Berlin, 1945–1949*, Center of Military History, United States Army, 2017, p. 62.
19. Howley, *Berlin Command*, p. 45; see also USAWC Frank Howley archives, Box 2.
20. Helen Woods, interview transcript, USAWC Frank Howley archives, Box 3.
21. William Heimlich, interview transcript, https://nsarchive2.gwu.edu/coldwar/interviews/episode-4/heimlich5.html
22. Riess, *Berlin Story*, p. 27.
23. USAWC Frank Howley archives, Box 5.
24. USAWC Frank Howley archives, Box 2.
25. Howley, *Berlin Command*, p. 100.
26. All from ibid., p. 45.
27. Ibid., p. 46.
28. USAWC Frank Howley archives, Box 2.
29. Ibid.

30. Howley, *Berlin Command*, p. 44.
31. Cited in Raymond A. Millen, *'Bury the Dead, Feed the Living': The History of Civil Affairs/Military Government in the Mediterranean and European Theaters of Operation During World War II*, US Army Peacekeeping and Stability Operations Institute, 2019, p. 187.
32. Howley, *Berlin Command*, p. 48.
33. Ibid.
34. Ibid.
35. USAWC Frank Howley archives, Box 2.
36. Ibid.
37. Howley, *Berlin Command*, p. 48.
38. Ibid.
39. USAWC Frank Howley archives, Box 2.
40. All from Howley, *Berlin Command*, p. 49.
41. USAWC Frank Howley archives, Box 2.
42. Ibid.
43. Howley, *Berlin Command*, p. 49.
44. Ibid., p. 50.
45. Richard Brett-Smith, *Berlin '45*, Macmillan, 1966, p. 36.
46. Edwin Tetlow, 'Cossacks Welcome the British to Berlin', *Daily Mail*, 4 July 1945.
47. Brett-Smith, *Berlin '45,* p. 39.
48. Hays papers, IWM Documents 20927.
49. Brett-Smith, *Berlin '45*, p. 41.
50. Edwin Tetlow, 'Desert Rats Lead British Troops into Berlin', *Daily Mail*, 5 July 1945.
51. Brett-Smith, *Berlin '45*, p. 43.
52. Manfred Knopf, interview transcript, KCLMA GB0099 Berlin Airlift.
53. Brett-Smith, *Berlin '45*, p. 44.
54. Ibid., p. 45.
55. All from Hays papers, IWM Documents 20927.
56. Ibid.
57. *Time* magazine, 'City of Death', 16 July 1945.
58. Cited in Alexandra Richie, *Faust's Metropolis*, HarperCollins, 1998, p. 609.
59. Hilda L. Witchell, interview, http://www.bbc.co.uk/history/ww2peoples war/stories/92/a5325392.shtml
60. James Chambers, oral interview, IWM 11329.
61. All from Hays papers, IWM Documents 20927.
62. Hinde, *Military Government*. By the time his pamphlet was published, the army's initial ban on fraternisation had been relaxed.

63. Byford-Jones, *Berlin Twilight*, p. 134.
64. Howley, *Berlin Command*, p. 54.
65. Ibid.
66. Clay, *Decision in Germany*, p. 29.
67. All from Howley, *Berlin Command*, pp. 52ff. and p. 12.

Chapter 6: Life on the Edge

1. Andreas-Friedrich, *Battleground Berlin*, pp. 65–6.
2. Hildegard Herrberger, interview transcript, KCLMA GB0099 Cold War.
3. All from Brett-Smith, *Berlin '45*, pp. 60–1.
4. Riess, *Berlin Story*, p. 38.
5. All from von Schwanenflügel Lawson, *Laughter Wasn't Rationed*, pp. 393–4.
6. All from Brett-Smith, *Berlin '45*, p. 159.
7. All from Andreas-Friedrich, *Battleground Berlin*, pp. 86–8.
8. Ibid., p. 91.
9. All from Howley, *Berlin Command*, p. 56.
10. Ibid., p. 71.
11. All from Brett-Smith, *Berlin '45*, p. 155.
12. James Chambers, oral interview, IWM 11329.
13. All from Howley, *Berlin Command*, p. 68.
14. From Howley, *Berlin Command*, p. 68 and USAWC Frank Howley archives, Box 2.
15. Howley, *Berlin Command*, p. 69 and USAWC Frank Howley archives, Box 2.
16. USAWC Frank Howley archives, Box 2.
17. Brett-Smith, *Berlin '45*, p. 173.
18. Byford-Jones, *Berlin Twilight*, p. 142.
19. Hays papers, IWM Documents 20927.
20. Brett-Smith, *Berlin '45*, p. 106.
21. Byford-Jones, *Berlin Twilight*, p. 39.
22. Botting, *Ruins of the Reich*, p. 18.
23. Cited in ibid., p. 19.
24. Cited in ibid., p. 18.
25. Interview with Christopher Leefe, cited in ibid., p. 307.
26. See Richie, *Faust's Metropolis*, p. 639ff. for examples of prices and values.
27. Hinde, *Military Government*, p. 7.
28. All from Byford-Jones, *Berlin Twilight*, p. 27ff.

29. Andreas-Friedrich, *Battleground Berlin*, p. 78.
30. Clare, *Berlin Days*, p. 34.
31. Ibid., p. 56.
32. Byford-Jones, *Berlin Twilight*, p. 27.
33. Ibid.
34. Ibid.
35. Hinde, *Military Government*, p. 7.
36. Interview with Len Carpenter cited in Botting, *Ruins of the Reich*, p. 293ff. See also Trevor Blore, '£160 Million a Year to Teach the Germans to Despise Us', *Daily Mirror*, 8 July 1946.
37. James Chambers, oral interview, IWM 11329.
38. Hinde, *Military Government*, p. 7.
39. All from Clare, *Berlin Days*, p. 55.
40. All from Brett-Smith, *Berlin '45*, p. 95.
41. Byford-Jones, *Berlin Twilight*, p. 153.
42. Ibid., p. 38.
43. Ibid.
44. Howley, *Berlin Command*, p. 61.
45. Leonhard, *Child of the Revolution*, p. 319.
46. Byford-Jones, *Berlin Twilight*, p. 158.
47. Ibid.
48. Ibid., p. 156.
49. Hays papers, IWM Documents 20927.
50. Howley, *Berlin Command*, pp. 11–12.
51. Ibid., p. 87.

Chapter 7: Dividing the Spoils

1. James MacGregor Burns, *Roosevelt: The Soldier of Freedom, 1940–1945*, Weidenfeld & Nicolson, 1971, p. 587.
2. Joan Bright Astley, *The Inner Circle: A View of War at the Top*, Little, Brown, 1971, p. 213.
3. Cited in Botting, *Ruins of the Reich*, p. 151.
4. Charles L. Mee, *Meeting at Potsdam*, André Deutsch, 1975, p. 73.
5. George Mallaby, *From My Level: Unwritten Minutes*, Hutchinson, 1965, p. 134.
6. Moran, *Winston Churchill*, p. 267.
7. Eduard Mark (ed.), 'Today Has Been a Historical One: Harry S. Truman's Diary of the Potsdam Conference', *Diplomatic History*, Vol. 4, No. 3, 1980, p. 320.

8. Ibid.

9. Moran, *Winston Churchill*, p. 273.

10. Cited in Mee, *Meeting at Potsdam*, p. 85.

11. Moran, *Winston Churchill*, p. 270.

12. James P. O'Donnell, *The Berlin Bunker*, Dent, 1979, p. 6.

13. Moran, *Winston Churchill*, p. 270.

14. George F. Kennan, *Memoirs, 1925–1950*, Hutchinson, 1968, p. 279.

15. Mee, *Meeting at Potsdam*, p. 94.

16. Hugh Trevor-Roper, *The Last Days of Hitler*, Papermac, 1995 (seventh edition), p. xlix. See also William D. Leahy, *I Was There*, Gollancz, 1950, p. 463 and James F. Byrnes, *Speaking Frankly*, Harper and Brothers, 1947, p. 68.

17. O'Donnell, *Berlin Bunker*, p. 302.

18. Eduard Mark (ed.), '"Today Has Been a Historical One": Harry S. Truman's Diary of the Potsdam Conference', *Diplomatic History*, Vol. 4, No. 3, summer 1980, p. 322.

19. George Elsey, interview transcript, https://nsarchive2.gwu.edu/coldwar/interviews/episode-1/elsey1.html

20. Mee, *Meeting at Potsdam*, p. 100.

21. Harry S. Truman, *Memoirs*, Vol. 1, Hodder & Stoughton, 1955, p. 275.

22. All from Mee, *Meeting at Potsdam*, p. 107.

23. Cited in ibid., p. 100.

24. Cited in Mark (ed.), *Diplomatic History*, p. 323.

25. Mee, *Meeting at Potsdam*, p. 100.

26. Ibid., p. 140.

27. Cited in Botting, *Ruins of the Reich*, p. 149.

28. Ibid.

29. Moran, *Winston Churchill*, p. 166.

30. Botting, *Ruins of the Reich*, p. 150.

31. Ibid.

32. Mee, *Meeting at Potsdam*, p. 221.

33. Botting, *Ruins of the Reich*, p. 150.

34. Moran, *Winston Churchill*, p. 285.

35. Cited in Mee, *Meeting at Potsdam*, p. 233.

36. Dean Acheson, *Present at the Creation*, W. W. Norton, 1969, p. 270.

37. Lord Hastings Ismay, *The Memoirs of General, The Lord Ismay*, William Heinemann, 1960, p. 403.

38. Bright Astley, *The Inner Circle*, p. 223.

39. Hugh Lunghi, interview transcript, https://nsarchive2.gwu.edu/coldwar/interviews/episode-1/lunghi7.html

40. Winston Churchill, *Second World War*, Vol. 6, p. 315.
41. Klimov, *Terror Machine*, p. 147.
42. Walter Isaacson and Evan Thomas, *The Wise Men*, Faber & Faber, 1986, p. 722.
43. Kennan, *Memoirs*, pp. 279–80.
44. Ibid., p. 258.
45. Isaacson and Thomas, *Wise Men*, p. 150.
46. All from Kennan, *Memoirs*, p. 258.
47. As cited in Howley, *Berlin Command*, p. 74.
48. Ibid.
49. Ibid., pp. 74–5.
50. USAWC Frank Howley archives, Box 2.
51. Howley, *Berlin Command*, p. 75.
52. Ibid.
53. Cited in Justin Mackeurtan, unpublished typescript, KCLMA GB0099 Williamson.
54. USAWC Frank Howley archives, Box 2.
55. Howley, *Berlin Command*, p. 76.
56. Zhukov, *Memoirs*, p. 656.
57. Howley, *Berlin Command*, p. 76.

Chapter 8: Let Battle Commence

1. Igor Gouzenko, 'Stalin Sent Me to Spy School', *Coronet* magazine, March 1953, p. 86.
2. Ibid., p. 87.
3. Igor Gouzenko, *This Was My Choice*, Palm Publishers, 1968, p. 138.
4. Ibid., p. 142.
5. Ibid., p. 195.
6. Ibid., p. 142.
7. Gouzenko, *Coronet* magazine, p. 90, and see Gouzenko, *This Was My Choice*, p. 142.
8. Gouzenko, *This Was My Choice*, p. 172.
9. Ibid., p. 171.
10. Ibid., p. 221.
11. Ibid., p. 222.
12. Ibid., p. 219.
13. Ibid., p. 225.
14. Ibid.

15. Ibid., p. 231.
16. Ibid., p. 234.
17. J. W. Pickersgill and D. F. Forster, *The Mackenzie King Record*, University of Toronto Press, 1970, pp. 8–9.
18. Cited in H. Montgomery Hyde, *The Quiet Canadian: The Secret Service Story of Sir William Stephenson*, Hamish Hamilton, 1962, p. 233.
19. Pickersgill and Forster, *Mackenzie King*, p. 12.
20. Ibid., p. 38.
21. All from ibid., p. 40.
22. USAWC Frank Howley archives, Box 3.
23. Howley, *Berlin Command*, p. 13.
24. Ibid., p. 7.
25. Ibid., p. 157.
26. *Historical Report*, Office of Military Government, Berlin District, USAWC Frank Howley archives.
27. William Heimlich, interview transcript, https://nsarchive2.gwu.edu/coldwar/interviews/episode-4/heimlich1.html
28. *New York Alumni Bulletin*, March 1949, USAWC Frank Howley archives.
29. Hays papers, IWM Documents 20927.
30. Ibid.
31. USAWC Frank Howley archives, Box 2.
32. Ibid., Box 3.
33. Hinde, *Military Government*, p. 3.
34. Stivers and Carter, *The City Becomes a Symbol*, p. 93.
35. Hinde, *Military Government*, p. 4.
36. Renée Bédarida, *Une Française à Berlin en 1945*, Cahiers de l'Institut d'histoire du temps présent, 1989–1990.
37. USAWC Frank Howley archives, Box 2.
38. Ibid., Box 3.
39. Ibid.
40. Cited in Mann, *Comeback*, p. 74.
41. USAWC Frank Howley archives, Box 2, but see also Barbara Fauntleroy, *The General & His Daughter: The Wartime Letters of General James M. Gavin*, Fordham University Press, 2007.
42. USAWC Frank Howley archives, Box 2.
43. Ibid.
44. Mann, *Comeback*, p. 55.
45. Howley, *Berlin Command*, p. 125.
46. TNA FO 1112/53.
47. TNA FO 1112/53.

48. All from Howley, *Berlin Command*, p. 63.
49. USAWC Frank Howley archives, Box 2.
50. Howley, *Berlin Command*, p. 87.
51. Ibid., p. 83.
52. USAWC Frank Howley archives, Box 2.
53. Hays papers, IWM Documents 20927.
54. General-Major A. G. Kotikov, Записки военного коменданта Берлина (*The Notes of the Military Commander of Berlin*), Veche, 2006, p. 229.
55. Hays papers, IWM Documents 20927.

Chapter 9: Enter the Overlords

1. Clay, *Decision in Germany*, p. 7.
2. Barry Turner, *The Berlin Airlift*, Icon Books, 2017, p. 18.
3. Cited in Jean Edward Smith, *Lucius Clay: An American Life*, Henry Holt, 1990, p. 5.
4. Jean Edward Smith (ed.), *The Papers of Lucius D. Clay: Germany 1945–1949*, Indiana University Press, 1974, p. xxxiii.
5. Peter Grose, 'The Boss of Occupied Germany, General Lucius D. Clay', *Foreign Affairs*, Vol. 77, No. 4 (July–August 1998), p. 179.
6. 'Profile: General Clay', *Observer*, 22 February 1948.
7. Clay, *Decision in Germany*, p. 254.
8. Nigel Nicolson (ed.), *Harold Nicolson Diaries and Letters, 1907–1964*, Weidenfeld & Nicolson, 2004, p. 151.
9. Smith (ed.), *Papers of Lucius Clay*, p. xxxv.
10. Ibid., p. xxxvi.
11. Robert Lochner, interview transcript, https://nsarchive2.gwu.edu/coldwar/interviews/episode-4/lochner1.html
12. Ibid.
13. Edloe Donnan, interview transcript, https://nsarchive2.gwu.edu/coldwar/interviews/episode-4/donnan1.html
14. Both from Grose, 'The Boss of Occupied Germany', p. 182.
15. Cited in Stivers and Carter, *The City Becomes a Symbol*, p. 3.
16. Heimlich, interview transcript, https://nsarchive2.gwu.edu/coldwar/interviews/episode-4/heimlich1.html
17. Edloe Donnan, interview transcript, https://nsarchive2.gwu.edu/coldwar/interviews/episode-4/donnan1.html
18. Howley, *Berlin Command*, p. 12. Karl Mautner, Howley's intelligence chief, provides insight into their relationship. Mautner said Clay found

Howley 'too Irish' and blocked his promotion. See Mautner, interview transcript, KCLMA GB0099 Cold War.

19. Both from an unpublished memorandum by D. L. Stewart, KCLMA GB0099 Williamson.

20. Ibid.

21. Mark Arnold-Forster, *The Siege of Berlin*, HarperCollins, 1979, p. 27.

22. Letter from Hugh Browne, recalling Anne Jackson's life in Berlin, January 1996, private collection.

23. 'The End of An Epoch', *Manchester Guardian*, 21 June 1950. See also 'Profile: General Robertson', *Observer*, 8 December 1946.

24. General Brian Robertson, speech transcript, TNA FO 1030/69.

25. Major General Sir Alec Bishop, 'Look Back with Pleasure: The Memoirs of Major General Sir Alec Bishop', unpublished typescript, IWM 98/18/1, p. 150.

26. David Williamson, *A Most Diplomatic General: The Life of General Lord Robertson of Oakridge*, Brassey's, 1996, p. 101.

27. Mackeurtan, unpublished typescript, KCLMA GB0099 Williamson.

28. Turner, *Berlin Airlift*, p. 70.

29. Mackeurtan, unpublished typescript, KCLMA GB0099 Williamson.

30. Bishop, 'Look Back with Pleasure', p. 175.

31. Thomas Falco, 'Berlin's ACA Building Example of Allied Efforts to Extend Wartime Unity through Occupation Period', *Military Government Weekly Information Bulletin*, 17 June 1946, KCLMA GB0099 Waite.

32. Clay, *Decision in Germany*, p. 24.

33. Letter from Clay to Colonel McCawley, NARA RG 260.

34. Richard Collier, *Bridge Across the Sky*, Macmillan, 1978, p. 3.

35. Bishop, 'Look Back with Pleasure', p. 152.

36. Collier, *Bridge Across the Sky*, p. 4.

37. Howley, *Berlin Command*, p. 58.

38. Clay, *Decision in Germany*, p. 105.

39. Tusa, *The Berlin Blockade*, Hodder & Stoughton, 1988, p. 51.

40. Mann, *Comeback*, p. 73.

41. From John H. Backer, *Winds of History: The German Years of Lucius D. Clay* (1983), cited in Tusa, *Berlin Blockade*, p. 50.

42. Andreas-Friedrich, *Battleground Berlin*, p. 98.

43. Ibid.

44. Wolfgang Leonhard, interview transcript, KCLMA GB0099 Cold War.

45. Ella Barowsky, interview transcript, KCLMA GB0099 Cold War.

46. 'Profile: Otto Grotewohl', *Observer*, 11 March 1951.

47. Andreas-Friedrich, *Battleground Berlin*, p. 117.

48. 'Profile: Otto Grotewohl', *Observer*, 11 March 1951.
49. Leonhard, interview transcript, KCLMA GB0099 Cold War.
50. Riess, *Berlin Story*, p. 77.
51. Andreas Friedrich, *Battleground Berlin*, p. 113.
52. Naimark, *Russians in Germany*, p. 299.
53. Andreas-Friedrich, *Battleground Berlin*, pp. 114–15.
54. Ibid., p. 115.
55. Ibid.
56. Howley, *Berlin Command*, p. 105.
57. Andreas-Friedrich, *Battleground Berlin*, p. 121.
58. Howley, *Berlin Command*, p. 106.
59. Clare, *Berlin Days*, pp. 93–4.
60. Andreas Friedrich, *Battleground Berlin*, p. 121.
61. Byford-Jones, *Berlin Twilight*, p. 166.
62. Ibid., p. 167.
63. Ibid.
64. Ibid., pp. 168–9. See also Leonhard, *Child of the Revolution*, p. 354ff.
65. Hinde, *Military Government*, p. 9.
66. Howley, *Berlin Command*, p. 104.

Chapter 10: The Iron Curtain

1. Pickersgill and Forster, *Mackenzie King*, p. 134.
2. Ibid., p. 144.
3. Ibid., p. 140.
4. David McCullough, *Truman*, Simon & Schuster, 1992, p. 488.
5. Cited in Martin Gilbert, *Winston S. Churchill*, William Heinemann, Vol 8, 1966, p. 865.
6. Margaret Truman, *Harry S. Truman*, Hamish Hamilton, 1973, p. 311.
7. Ibid.
8. All from https://winstonchurchill.org/resources/speeches/1946-1963-elder-statesman/the-sinews-of-peace/
9. Ronald Steel, *Walter Lippmann and the American Century*, Bodley Head, 1980, p. 429.
10. Gilbert, *Winston S. Churchill*, Vol. 8, p. 868.
11. McCullough, *Truman*, p. 490.
12. Gilbert, *Winston S. Churchill*, Vol. 8 p. 868.
13. Cited in Andrew Roberts, *Churchill: Walking with Destiny*, Viking, 2018, p. 896.

14. McCullough, *Truman*, p. 490.
15. Margaret Truman, *Harry S. Truman*, p. 313.
16. Kennan, *Memoirs*, p. 292.
17. Ibid.
18. Ibid., p. 293.
19. Ibid., p. 549.
20. Ibid., p. 556.
21. All from ibid., pp. 294–5.
22. Cited in Isaacson and Thomas, *Wise Men*, p. 355.
23. *Izvestia*, 22 February 1946, TNA FO 1012/97.
24. Howley, *Berlin Command*, p. 13.

Chapter 11: Ministry of Lies

1. Howley, *Berlin Command*, p. 124.
2. Kotikov, *Notes of the Military Commander*, p. 239ff.
3. Cited in Riess, *Berlin Story*, p. 67.
4. Letter from Kotikov to Hinde, private collection.
5. USAWC Frank Howley archives, Box 2.
6. Ibid.
7. Howley, *Berlin Command*, p. 100.
8. Ibid., p. 101.
9. Riess, *Berlin Story*, pp. 67–8.
10. Kotikov, *Notes of the Military Commander*, p. 239ff.
11. Ibid.
12. Howley, *Berlin Command*, p. 108.
13. USAWC Frank Howley archives, Box 2.
14. Kotikov, *Notes of the Military Commander*, pp. 223–4.
15. USAWC Frank Howley archives, Box 5.
16. Ibid.
17. Cited in Mann, *Comeback*, pp. 63–4.
18. Hinde, *Military Government*, p. 8.
19. Cited in Clare, *Berlin Days*, p. 72.
20. USAWC Frank Howley archives, Box 2.
21. Clare, *Berlin Days*, p. 106.
22. Mann, *Comeback*, p. 62.
23. Leonhard, interview transcript, KCLMA GB0099 Cold War.
24. Leonhard, interview transcript, https://nsarchive2.gwu.edu/coldwar/

interviews/episode-2/leonhard1.html. And Leonhard, interview transcript, KCLMA GB0099 Cold War.

25. Nicolas Nabokov, *Old Friends and New Music*, Hamish Hamilton, 1951, p. 224.

26. Riess, *Berlin Story*, p. 79.

27. Both from ibid., pp. 80–1.

28. Clare, *Berlin Days*, p. 63.

29. Ibid., p. 62.

30. Ibid., p. 63.

31. Riess, *Berlin Story*, p. 82.

32. Heimlich, interview transcript, https://nsarchive2.gwu.edu/coldwar/interviews/episode-4/heimlich1.html. See also Jurgen Graff, interview transcript, KCLMA GB0099 Berlin Airlift.

33. Howley, *Berlin Command*, p. 221.

34. USAWC Frank Howley archives, Box 5.

35. Howley, *Berlin Command*, p. 5.

36. Riess, *Berlin Story*, p. 79.

37. Clay, *Decision in Germany*, pp. 134–5, 157–8 and 161.

38. Turner, *Berlin Airlift*, p. 152.

39. Heimlich, interview transcript, https://nsarchive2.gwu.edu/coldwar/interviews/episode-4/heimlich1.html

40. All from Clare, *Berlin Days*, p. 63.

41. Ibid., p. 78.

42. Fred K. Prieberg, *Trial of Strength: Wilhelm Furtwängler and the Third Reich*, Quartet Books, 1991, p. 94.

43. Nabokov, *Old Friends*, p. 217.

44. Cited in Clare, *Berlin Days*, p. 78.

45. Ibid., pp. 79–80.

46. Ibid., p. 79.

47. Ibid., p. 80.

48. Ibid., p. 103.

Chapter 12: Crime and Punishment

1. Leading article, 'Paris', *Manchester Guardian*, 25 April 1946.

2. Dr McCall's diagnosis is cited in Allan Bullock, *The Life and Times of Ernest Bevin*, William Heinemann, 1960–83, Vol. 3, p. 288.

3. Bohlen, *Witness*, p. 255.

4. As cited in Bullock, *Bevin*, Vol. 3, p. 284.

5. Howley, *Berlin Command*, p. 118.

6. Ibid.

7. Riess, *Berlin Story*, p. 83.

8. Howley, *Berlin Command*, p. 133.

9. Turner, *Berlin Airlift*, p. 54.

10. Howley, *Berlin Command*, p. 122.

11. Ibid., p. 123.

12. USAWC Frank Howley archives, Box 3.

13. Ibid.

14. Riess, *Berlin Story*, p. 83.

15. USAWC Frank Howley archives, Box 3.

16. Ibid.

17. Hays papers, IWM Documents 20927.

18. Howley, *Berlin Command*, p. 129.

19. Riess, *Berlin Story*, p. 84.

20. Leonhard, *Child of the Revolution*, p. 359.

21. Riess, *Berlin Story*, p. 84.

22. Hays papers, IWM Documents 20927.

23. Leonhard, *Child of the Revolution*, p. 359.

24. Ibid.

25. Andreas-Friedrich, *Battleground Berlin*, p. 136.

26. Riess, *Berlin Story*, p. 84.

27. All from Hays papers, IWM Documents 20927.

28. Howley, *Berlin Command*, p. 131.

29. Ibid., p. 138.

30. Andreas-Friedrich, *Battleground Berlin*, p. 106.

31. Hinde, *Military Government*, p. 7.

32. Riess, *Berlin Story*, p. 72.

33. Ibid.

34. Ibid., pp. 64–5.

35. 'Record of Trial of Norman T. Byrne', Headquarters Berlin Command, Office of Military Government, United States, 18 February 1947. See also Kenneth Alford, *The Spoils of World War II*, Carol Publishing, 1994, which gives a highly detailed account of the arrest and trial of Byrne. See particularly chapters 1 and 4–7.

36. Cited in Alford, *The Spoils of World War II*, p. 4.

37. Cited in ibid., p. 65.

38. Riess, *Berlin Story*, p. 93.

39. All quotes taken from 'Operation Sparkler and Large Scale Black

Market Activities', TNA FO 936/741. See also Patricia Meehan, *A Strange Enemy People: Germans Under the British, 1945–50*, Peter Owen, 2001. And Christopher Knowles, *Winning the Peace: The British in Occupied Germany 1945–1948*, Bloomsbury, 2017, which has much on crime in the British sector and zone.

40. D. Steinmeier, 'The Constabulary Moves Fast', *Army Information Digest*, Vol. 2, No. 11, November 1947, p. 7ff.

Chapter 13: Playing Dirty

1. All from Irmgard Gröttrup, *Rocket Wife*, André Deutsch, 1959, pp. 15–21.
2. TNA FO 1031/53.
3. TNA FO 1031/60.
4. TNA FO 1031/53.
5. TNA FO1031/60.
6. 'US Says Russians Admit Kidnappings', *New York Times*, 22 May 1949.
7. Paul Bretherton, *Daily Mail*, 26 October 1946.
8. Howley, *Berlin Command*, p. 137.
9. Leslie Groves, *Now It Can Be Told: The Story of the Manhattan Project*, Harper & Brothers, 1962, pp. 243–4.
10. Colonel Boris T. Pash, *The Alsos Mission*, Award House, 1969, p. 227.
11. Stenographic notes from record of Kommandatura meeting held Friday, 31 January, NARA RG 260.
12. Howley, *Berlin Command*, pp. 14–15.
13. Andreas-Friedrich, *Battleground Berlin*, p. 150.
14. Paul Steege, *Black Market, Cold War: Everyday Life in Berlin, 1946–1949*, Cambridge University Press, 2007, p. 108.
15. Andreas-Friedrich, *Battleground Berlin*, p. 153.
16. Von Schwanenflügel Lawson, *Laughter Wasn't Rationed*, p. 458.
17. Andreas-Friedrich, *Battleground Berlin*, p. 153.
18. Ibid., p. 147.
19. Inge Gross, *Memoirs of World War II and Its Aftermath*, Island in the Sky Publishing, 2005, p. 122.
20. Assel, interview transcript, KCLMA GB0099 Cold War.
21. Lelah Berry, 'An Army Wife Lives Very Soft – In Germany', *Saturday Evening Post*, 15 February 1947.
22. Joan Crane, 'Malice in Blunderland', unpublished typescript, NARA RG 260.

23. United States Congress, Investigation of the National Defense Program: *Hearings before a Special Committee Investigating the National Defense Program, Part 42, Military Government in Germany, April 1946–October 1947*, United States Government Printing Office, 1948, p. 26,145.

24. Riess, *Berlin Story*, p. 66.

25. Brett-Smith, *Berlin '45*, p. 105. See also Julian Bach, 'America's Germany', *Life*, 13 May 1946.

26. Howley, *Berlin Command*, p. 89.

27. Brett-Smith, *Berlin '45*, p. 103.

28. Đjilas, *Conversations with Stalin*, p. 105.

29. 'Russian Zone Spy a Very Hot Potato', *New York Times*, 13 May 1947.

30. Michael Holland-Hibbert, unpublished diary, KCLMA GB0099 Williamson.

31. Howley, *Berlin Command*, p. 138.

32. Hays papers, IWM Documents 20927.

Chapter 14: Shifting Sands

1. Riess, *Berlin Story*, p. 95.

2. Edzard Reuter, interview transcript, KCLMA GB0099 Cold War.

3. Karl Mautner, interview transcript, KCLMA GB0099 Cold War.

4. Tusa, *Berlin Blockade*, p. 75.

5. Riess, *Berlin Story*, p. 95.

6. Ibid., p. 97.

7. Speech made on 17 May 1949, quoted in Steege, *Black Market*, p. 274.

8. 'General Kotikov on the Berlin Situation: An Interview with the Soviet Commandant', *Tägliche Rundschau*, 10 July 1947, NARA RG 260.

9. Howley, *Berlin Command*, p. 147.

10. Ibid., p. 149.

11. 'Profile: General Clay', *Observer*, 22 February 1948.

12. Stivers and Carter, *The City Becomes a Symbol*, p. 197.

13. Ibid., p. 201.

14. USAWC Frank Howley archives, Box 3.

15. Ibid.

16. Howley, *Berlin Command*, p. 154.

17. Cited in Arthur L. Smith, *Kidnap City: Cold War Berlin*, Greenwood, 2002, p. 27.

18. Howley, *Berlin Command*, p. 169.

19. Clay, *Decision in Germany*, p. 107.

20. Ibid., p. 106.
21. Cited in Williamson, *A Most Diplomatic General*, p. 105.
22. Clay, *Decision in Germany*, p. 160.
23. All from Clay, *Decision in Germany*, pp. 159–60.
24. All from Andreas-Friedrich, *Battleground Berlin*, p. 172.
25. Howley, *Berlin Command*, p. 174.
26. Clay, *Decision in Germany*, p. 147.
27. Thomas Parrish, *Berlin in the Balance, 1945–1949*, Perseus Books, 1998, p. 113.
28. President Truman's speech is available online: https://avalon.law.yale.edu/20th_century/trudoc.asp
29. Cited in Tusa, *Berlin Blockade*, p. 81.
30. Clay, *Decision in Germany*, p. 344.
31. Andreas-Friedrich, *Battleground Berlin*, p. 175.
32. Turner, *Berlin Airlift*, p. 93.
33. 'Profile: General Clay', *Observer*, 22 February 1948.
34. Parrish, *Berlin in the Balance*, p.132.
35. Turner, *Berlin Airlift*, p. 88.
36. Andreas-Friedrich, *Battleground Berlin*, p. 178.
37. Clay, *Decision in Germany*, p. 348.
38. Howley, *Berlin Command*, p. 157.
39. Clay, *Decision in Germany*, p. 161.
40. Ibid.
41. Desmond Donnelly, *Struggle for the World: The Cold War, 1917–1965*, Collins, 1965, p. 248.
42. Tusa, *Berlin Blockade*, p. 83.
43. Cited in Collier, *Bridge Across the Sky*, p. 5.
44. Clay, *Decision in Germany*, p. 356.
45. Cited in Turner, *Berlin Airlift*, p. 103.
46. Collier, *Bridge Across the Sky*, p. 3.

Chapter 15: Breaking Point

1. Hoecke, 'Hoecke-Southard Chronicles', p. 90.
2. Hays papers, IWM Documents 20927.
3. Cited in Robert Rodrigo, *Berlin Airlift*, Cassell, 1960, p. 7.
4. All from Hays papers, IWM Documents 20927.
5. Howley, *Berlin Command*, p. 201.
6. Ibid.

7. Cited in Collier, *Bridge Across the Sky*, p. 14.

8. TNA FO 1030/60.

9. Turner, *Berlin Airlift*, p. 100.

10. Stalin to Pieck, cited in Roger G. Miller, *To Save a City: The Berlin Airlift 1948–1949*, Airforce History and Museums Program, 1998, p. 1.

11. Mann, *Comeback*, p. 48.

12. Collier, *Bridge Across the Sky*, p. 18.

13. Cited in ibid., p. 20.

14. Cited in Tusa, *Berlin Blockade*, p. 112.

15. Cited in Turner, *Berlin Airlift*, p. 107.

16. Jean Eastham, interview transcript, KCLMA GB0099 Berlin Airlift.

17. Collier, *Bridge Across the Sky*, p. 23.

18. Robertson, *Most Diplomatic General*, p. 121.

19. 'The True Causes of the Air Collision', *Tägliche Rundschau*, 22 April 1948, NARA RG 260.

20. Hays papers, IWM Documents 20927.

21. Collier, *Bridge Across the Sky*, p. 35.

22. Howley, *Berlin Command*, pp. 3–4.

23. Collier, *Bridge Across the Sky*, p. 36.

24. All from Hoecke, 'Hoecke-Southard Chronicles', p. 92ff.

25. Both Howley and Kotikov are cited in Parrish, *Berlin in the Balance*, p. 152.

26. Howley, *Berlin Command*, p. 174.

27. Lowell Bennett, *Berlin Bastion: The Epic of Post-War Berlin*, Fred Rudl Publishers, 1951, p. 19.

28. Frank Howley, 'Payoff in Berlin', *Collier's*, 3 December 1949.

29. All from Howley, *Berlin Command*, p. 180ff.

30. All from Hays papers, IWM Documents 20927.

31. Howley, *Berlin Command*, p. 183.

32. Ibid., p. 187.

33. Collier, *Bridge Across the Sky*, p. 43.

34. Michail M. Narinskii, 'The Soviet Union and the Berlin Crisis 1948–1949', in *The Soviet Union and Europe in the Cold War 1945–53*, ed. Francesca Gori and Silvio Pons, Palgrave Macmillan, 1996, p. 66.

35. Collier, *Bridge Across the Sky*, p. 46.

36. Andreas-Friedrich, *Battleground Berlin*, p. 225.

37. Cited in Collier, *Bridge Across the Sky*, p. 47.

38. Howley, *Berlin Command*, p. 192.

39. Cited in Collier, *Bridge Across the Sky*, p. 48.

Chapter 16: The Perfect Siege

1. TNA FO 1030/60.
2. Howley, *Berlin Command*, p. 3.
3. Ibid., p. 196.
4. Ibid., p. 10.
5. Ibid., p. 197.
6. Cited in Bullock, *Bevin*, p. 576.
7. Cited in James Forrestal, *The Forrestal Diaries*, Viking, 1951, p. 427.
8. Howley, *Berlin Command*, p. 10.
9. Air Commodore Reginald Newnham Waite, 'The Berlin Airlift', unpublished typescript, KCLMA Waite.
10. Howley, *Berlin Command*, p. 205.
11. Collier, *Bridge Across the Sky*, p. 48.
12. Howley, *Berlin Command*, p. 207.
13. Both Howley and Bedell Smith quotes from Turner, *Berlin Airlift*, p. 123.
14. Collier, *Bridge Across the Sky*, p. 55.
15. Clay, interview transcript, Harry S. Truman Library, https://www.trumanlibrary.gov/library/oral-histories/clay1
16. Bullock, *Bevin*, Vol. 3, p. 81.
17. Cited in Richard Reeves, *Daring Young Men*, Simon & Schuster, 2011, p. 36.
18. Frank Roberts, interview transcript, https://nsarchive2.gwu.edu/coldwar/interviews/episode-1/roberts6.html
19. Cited in Collier, *Bridge Across the Sky*, p. 65.
20. Cited by Frank Roberts, interview transcript, https://nsarchive2.gwu.edu/coldwar/interviews/episode-1/roberts6.html
21. Cited in Collier, *Bridge Across the Sky*, p. 65.
22. Cited by Frank Roberts, interview transcript, https://nsarchive2.gwu.edu/coldwar/interviews/episode-1/roberts6.html
23. Ibid.
24. Cited in Tusa, *Berlin Blockade*, p. 154.
25. Hansard, 30 June 1948, https://hansard.parliament.uk.
26. Ibid.; see also Collier, *Bridge Across the Sky*, p. 73.
27. Turner, *Berlin Airlift*, p. 125.
28. Collier, *Bridge Across the Sky*, p. 102.
29. Ibid., p. 77.
30. Hays papers, IWM Documents 20927.

31. Mann, *Comeback*, p. 132.
32. Howley, *Berlin Command*, p. 198.
33. Andreas-Friedrich, *Battleground Berlin*, p. 226.
34. Gross, *Memories*, p. 163.
35. Ibid., p. 160.
36. Andreas-Friedrich, *Battleground Berlin*, p. 230.
37. Howley, *Berlin Command*, p. 204.
38. Ibid., p. 205.
39. Mercedes Wild, interview transcript, KCLMA GB0099 Berlin Airlift.
40. Quotes drawn from Willy Brandt, *My Life in Politics*, Hamish Hamilton, 1992, p. 15 and Willy Brandt, *My Road to Berlin*, Peter Davies, 1960, p. 186.
41. Clay, *Decision in Germany*, p. 379.
42. As quoted in Brandt, *My Life in Politics*, p. 114.
43. Cited in Reginald Waite, papers, KCLMA Waite (Addn 1).
44. Ibid.
45. Ibid.
46. Edwin Tetlow, 'Russia Had Planned to Get Us Out of Berlin by Aug 1', *Daily Telegraph*, 9 July 1948.
47. *The Times*, cited in Turner, *Berlin Airlift*, p. 111.
48. Cited in Reginald Waite, papers, KCLMA Waite (Addn 1).
49. Ibid.
50. Cited in Jessamy Waite, interview transcript, KCLMA GB0099 Berlin Airlift.
51. Cited in Anon., 'The Berlin Airlift, June 1948–May 1949' (a miscellaneous collection of documents), KCLMA Waite (Addn 1).
52. Ibid.

Chapter 17: Flying High

1. Both from Collier, *Bridge Across the Sky*, p. 76.
2. William H. Tunner, *Over the Hump*, Duell, Sloan and Pearce, 1964, p. 179.
3. Dick Arscott interviews: oral interview, IWM 18708; interview transcript, KCLMA GB0099 Berlin Airlift; and interview transcript, www.legasee.org.uk.
4. Arscott, interview transcript, www.legasee.org.uk.
5. Hammond Innes, *Air Bridge*, Pan, 2004, p. 133.
6. Pip Parsons, interview transcript, KCLMA GB0099 Berlin Airlift.

7. Arscott, interview transcript, KCLMA GB0099 Berlin Airlift.

8. Air Vice Marshal Larry Lamb, cited in Turner, *Berlin Airlift*, p. 131.

9. John Curtiss, oral interview, IWM 17771.

10. Cited in Collier, *Bridge Across the Sky*, p. 146.

11. Albert Carotenuto, interview transcript, KCLMA GB0099 Berlin Airlift.

12. Gerry Munn, interview transcript, KCLMA GB0099 Berlin Airlift.

13. John Curtiss, oral interview, IWM 17771.

14. Bill Voigt, interview transcript, KCLMA GB0099 Berlin Airlift.

15. Chamber Roberts, interview transcript, KCLMA GB0099 Berlin Airlift.

16. Howley, *Berlin Command*, p. 209.

17. Ibid.

18. Cited in Collier, *Bridge Across the Sky*, p. 61.

19. Reginald Waite, Papers, KCLMA Waite (Addn 1).

20. Howley, *Berlin Command*, p. 204.

21. Ibid.

22. Clay, *Decision in Germany*, p. 373.

23. Cited in Tusa, *Berlin Blockade*, p. 194.

24. Cited in Collier, *Bridge Across the Sky*, p. 90 and Clay, *Decision in Germany*, p. 368.

25. Cited in Stivers and Carter, *City Becomes a Symbol*, p. 235.

26. Clay, interview transcript, Harry S. Truman Library, https://www.trumanlibrary.org/oralhist/oral_his.htm

27. Cited in Reeves, *Daring Young Men*, p. 75.

28. Cited in Collier, *Bridge Across the Sky*, p. 91.

29. Cited in Turner, *Berlin Airlift*, p. 156. President Truman gives a detailed account of the meeting in his *Memoirs*, Vol. 2, p. 125.

30. Collier, *Bridge Across the Sky*, p. 91.

31. Clay, interview transcript, Harry S. Truman Library, https://www.trumanlibrary.org/oralhist/oral_his.htm

32. Cited in Collier, *Bridge Across the Sky*, p. 92.

33. Ibid., p. 93.

34. Tunner, *Over the Hump*, p. 162.

35. Ibid., p. 158.

36. Ibid., p. 162.

37. Ibid., p. 189.

38. Ibid., p. 162.

39. Parrish, *Berlin in the Balance*, p. 219. Tunner's published account, as related in *Over the Hump*, claims there was 'no sign of rancor'. But his later interviews – candid and unguarded – are more likely to reflect the reality.

40. Cited in Reeves, *Daring Young Men*, p. 83n.
41. Ibid.
42. Reeves, *Daring Young Men*, p. 65.
43. Tunner, *Over the Hump*, p. 166.
44. Ibid., p. 163.
45. Ibid., p. 164.
46. Ibid., p. 152.
47. Ibid., p. 154.
48. Ibid.
49. Ibid., p. 172.
50. Ibid., p. 174.
51. Ibid., p. 170.
52. Ibid.
53. Ibid., p.171.
54. Ibid., p. 183.
55. Colonel Harold 'Hal' R. Austin, interview transcript, https://riversideca.gov/library/history_vet_austin.asp
56. Tunner, *Over the Hump*, p. 187.
57. Ibid.

Chapter 18: The Sky's the Limit

1. Howley, *Berlin Command*, p. 221.
2. Ibid., p. 197.
3. Ibid., p. 221.
4. Ibid., p. 199.
5. Cited in ibid., p. 222.
6. Riess, *Berlin Story*, p. 131.
7. Ibid.
8. All from Hoecke, 'Hoecke-Southard Chronicles', p. 94.
9. Tunner, *Over the Hump*, p. 212.
10. Ibid., p. 211.
11. Ibid., p. 212.
12. Cited in Collier, *Bridge Across the Sky*, p. 146. See also Tusa, *Berlin Blockade*, p. 305 and Tunner, *Over the Hump*, p. 212, for slight variations on the story.
13. Hays papers, IWM Documents 20927.
14. Howley, *Berlin Command*, p. 216.
15. Cited in Tusa, *Berlin Blockade*, p. 229.

16. Howley, *Berlin Command*, p. 215.

17. Andreas-Friedrich, *Battleground Berlin*, p. 247.

18. Riess, *Berlin Story*, p. 119.

19. Cited in Rodrigo, *Berlin Airlift*, p. 31.

20. Hays papers, IWM Documents 20927.

21. Collier, *Bridge Across the Sky*, p. 116.

22. USAWC Frank Howley archives, Box 3.

23. Hays papers, IWM Documents 20927.

24. Collier, *Bridge Across the Sky*, p. 118.

25. Hays papers, IWM Documents 20927.

26. Collier, *Bridge Across the Sky*, p. 119.

27. Andreas-Friedrich, *Battleground Berlin*, p. 243.

28. Ernst Reuter's speech can be read in German here: https://www.berlin.de/berlin-im-ueberblick/geschichte/artikel.453082.php

29. Collier, *Bridge Across the Sky*, p. 120.

30. Riess, *Berlin Story*, p. 121.

31. Collier, *Bridge Across the Sky*, p. 120.

32. Howley, *Berlin Command*, p. 218.

33. Collier, *Bridge Across the Sky*, p. 121.

34. Hays papers, IWM Documents 20927.

35. Andreas-Friedrich, *Battleground Berlin*, p. 244.

36. For background information about Bennett see Archie S. Jackson, *Pathfinder Bennett: Airman Extraordinaire*, Terence Dalton, 1991, and Air Vice-Marshal D. C. T. Bennett, *Pathfinder*, Müller, 1958.

37. Cited in Collier, *Bridge Across the Sky*, p. 105.

38. *Manchester Guardian*, 14 July 1948.

39. Collier, *Bridge Across the Sky*, p. 102.

40. Cited in Tusa, *Berlin Blockade*, p. 237 and Rodrigo, *Berlin Airlift*, p. 156.

41. Cited in Tusa, *Berlin Blockade*, p. 316.

42. Cited in Collier, *Bridge Across the Sky*, p. 79.

43. Tunner, *Over the Hump*, p. 205.

44. *The Times*, 1 August 1949.

45. Howley, *Berlin Command*, p. 231.

46. Ibid.

47. Andreas-Friedrich, *Battleground Berlin*, p. 253.

48. Tunner, *Over the Hump*, p. 194.

49. Howley, *Berlin Command*, p. 231.

50. Ibid., p. 231.

51. Gross, *Memories*, p. 177.

Chapter 19: Checkmate

1. Kotikov, *Notes of the Military Commander*, p. 239ff.
2. Tunner, *Over the Hump*, p. 217.
3. Howley, *Berlin Command*, p. 259.
4. Ibid., pp. 220ff. and 237ff.
5. Hays papers, IWM Documents 20927.
6. Ibid.
7. All from Tunner, *Over the Hump*, p. 180.
8. Halvorsen story compiled from: Gail Halvorsen, *The Berlin Candy Bomber*, Horizon, 1997; Halvorsen, interview transcript, KCLMA GB0099 Berlin Airlift; interview transcript, KCLMA GB0099 Cold War; and https://nsarchive2.gwu.edu/coldwar/interviews/episode-4/halvor1.html
9. Tunner, *Over the Hump*, p. 208.
10. Cited in Reeves, *Daring Young Men*, p. 209.
11. Riess, *Berlin Story*, p. 145.
12. Ibid., p. 147; see also William Stivers, 'The Incomplete Blockade: Soviet Zone Supply of West Berlin, 1948–49', *Diplomatic History*, Vol. 21, Issue 4, October 1997, p. 571.
13. Cited in Stivers and Carter, *City Becomes a Symbol*, p. 283.
14. Hays papers, IWM Documents 20927.
15. Mann, *Comeback*, p. 141.
16. David Murphy, interview transcript, KCLMA GB0099 Berlin Airlift. See also David E. Murphy, Sergei A. Kondrashev and George Bailey, *Battleground Berlin: CIA vs KGB in the Cold War*, Yale University Press, 1997.
17. All from Howley, *Berlin Command*, p. 258.
18. Ibid., p. 259.
19. Tunner, *Over the Hump*, p. 220.
20. Ibid., p. 221.
21. Howley, *Berlin Command*, p. 259.
22. Announcement made public by RIAS broadcaster Rudolf-Günter Wagner. See Collier, *Bridge Across the Sky*, p. 155.
23. Howley, *Berlin Command*, p. 263.
24. Clay, *Decision in Germany*, p. 390.
25. Bevin quote is in memorandum 'New York to Foreign Office', TNA FO 371/76549.
26. Mann, *Comeback*, p. 145.

27. As quoted in Collier, *Bridge Across the Sky*, p. 155.
28. Ibid.
29. Manfred Knopf, interview transcript, KCLMA GB0099 Berlin Airlift.
30. Edzard Reuter, interview transcript, KCLMA GB0099 Cold War.
31. Ella Barowsky, interview transcript, KCLMA GB0099 Cold War.

Chapter 20: Fruits of Victory

1. Riess, *Berlin Story*, p. 162.
2. Cited in Mann, *Comeback*, p. 145.
3. Ibid.
4. All from Hays papers, IWM Documents 20927.
5. Cited in Reeves, *Daring Young Men*, p. 266.
6. Cited in Tim McNeese, *The Cold War and Postwar America, 1946–1953*, Chelsea House, 2010, p. 27.
7. Riess, *Berlin Story*, p. 164.
8. Howley, *Berlin Command*, p. 270.
9. Ibid.
10. Cited in USAWC Frank Howley archives, Box 5.
11. Ibid.
12. Ibid.
13. Ibid.
14. Ibid.
15. Howley, *Berlin Command*, p. 271.
16. Ibid., p. 15.
17. Ibid., p. 270.
18. Ibid., p. 4.
19. Cited in ibid., p 5.
20. USAWC Frank Howley archives, Box 3.

Epilogue

1. Among those disapproving was Sir Nicholas Henderson, assistant private secretary to Ernest Bevin. See Sir Nicholas Henderson, *The Birth of NATO*, Weidenfeld & Nicolson, 1982.
2. Alistair Cooke, 'Dean Acheson: NATO's Architect', *Guardian*, 14 October 1971.
3. 'Moscow's Judgment on the Pact', *Guardian*, 2 April 1949.

4. 'Atlantic Pact Signed by 12 Nations', *The Times*, 5 April 1949.
5. Alistair Cooke, 'The End of An Illusion', *Manchester Guardian*, 5 April 1949.
6. 'Speeches at the Signing of the Atlantic Pact', *Manchester Guardian*, 5 April 1949.
7. Cooke, 'The End of An Illusion', *Manchester Guardian*, 5 April 1949.
8. Ibid.
9. Cited in Richie, *Faust's Metropolis*, p. 676.
10. Cited in Naimark, *Russians in Germany*, p. 56.
11. Howley, *Berlin Command*, p. 65.
12. Howley, 'Longines Chronoscope interview of Major General Frank L. Howley', 1953, https://www.youtube.com/watch?v=A4RiE19ZAjA

Bibliography

Abbreviations

IWM: Imperial War Museum archives
KCLMA: King's College, London, military archives (Liddell Hart)
TNA: National Archives, UK
NARA: National Archives and Records Administration, USA
USAWC: United States Army War College archives

Primary Sources

Oral interviews, transcripts, letters, diaries and unpublished typescripts

Anon., 'Anonymous Account of the Last Days of the Second World War by an English Woman in Berlin', unpublished typescript, IWM 4029
Aronson, Alfred, interview transcript, https://nsarchive2.gwu.edu/coldwar/interviews/episode-1/aronson1.html
——, audio interview IWM 19290
——, interview transcript KCLMA GB0099 Cold War
Arscott, Dick, oral interview, IWM 18708
——, interview transcript, KCLMA GB0099 Berlin Airlift
——, interview transcript, www.legasee.org.uk
Ashley, Clifford, oral interview, IWM 21636
Assel, Elfriede von, interview transcript, KCLMA GB0099 Cold War
Atkins, H., unpublished private papers, IWM 92/28/1
Austin, Colonel Harold 'Hal' R., interview transcript, https://riversideca.gov/library/history_vet_austin.asp
d'Avanzo, Victoria (née Hinde), author interview, 13 January 2020
Barowsky, Ella, interview transcript, KCLMA GB0099 Cold War

Bishop, Major General Sir Alec, 'Look Back with Pleasure: The Memoirs of Major General Sir Alec Bishop', unpublished typescript, IWM 98/18/1

Carotenuto, Albert, interview transcript, KCLMA GB0099 Berlin Airlift

Cawdor, Cathryn (née Hinde), author interview, 4 December 2018

Chambers, Alec, interview transcript, www.legasee.org.uk

Chambers, James, oral interview, IWM 11329

Clay, Lucius D., interview transcript, Harry Truman S. Library, https://www.trumanlibrary.org/oralhist/oral_his.htm

Crane, Joan, 'Malice in Blunderland', unpublished typescript, NARA RG 260

Curtiss, John, oral interview, IWM 17771

Dankwardt, Frederick, interview transcript, www.legasee.org.uk

Doernberg, Stefan, interview transcript, KCLMA GB0099 Cold War

Donnan, Edloe, interview transcript, KCLMA GB0099 Cold War

——, interview transcript, https://nsarchive2.gwu.edu/coldwar/interviews/episode-4/donnan1.html

Eade, C. A., oral interview, IWM 20742

Eastham, Jean, interview transcript, KCLMA GB0099 Berlin Airlift

Eddy, John, interview transcript, KCLMA GB0099 Berlin Airlift

——, interview transcript, www.legasee.org.uk

Edwards, David, interview transcript, www.legasee.org.uk

Elsey, George, interview transcript, https://nsarchive2.gwu.edu/coldwar/interviews/episode-1/elsey1.html

——, interview transcript, https://www.trumanlibrary.gov/library/oral-histories/elsey7#375

Farge, Douglas, interview transcript, KCLMA GB0099 Berlin Airlift

Graff, Jurgen, interview transcript, KCLMA GB0099 Berlin Airlift

Halvorsen, Gail, interview transcript, KCLMA GB0099 Berlin Airlift

——, interview transcript, KCLMA GB0099 Cold War

——, interview transcript, https://nsarchive2.gwu.edu/coldwar/interviews/episode-4/halvor1.html

Hampton, Captain K. B., private papers, IWM 18/3/1

Hanson, Donald, interview transcript, KCLMA GB0099 Cold War

Hargrave-Wright, Joyce, interview transcript, www.legasee.org.uk

Hastings, Martin, oral interview, IWM 10453

Hatcher, Leo, interview transcript, www.legasee.org.uk

Hays, Lieutenant Colonel H., 'Nach Berlin', unpublished typescript, IWM 13/39/1

Heimlich, William, interview transcript, KCLMA GB0099 Cold War

——, interview transcript, https://nsarchive2.gwu.edu/coldwar/interviews/episode-4/heimlich1.html

Herman, Ken, interview transcript, KCLMA GB0099 Berlin Airlift

Herrberger, Hildegard, interview transcript, KCLMA GB0099 Cold War

Hoecke, Hermann, 'The Hoecke-Southard Chronicles: A Family History', unpublished typescript, 2011

Holland, Tom, interview transcript, KCLMA GB0099 Berlin Airlift

——, interview transcript, www.legasee.org.uk

Holland-Hibbert, Michael, unpublished diary, KCLMA GB0099 Williamson

Holtum, George, interview transcript, KCLMA GB0099 Berlin Airlift

Howley, Frank, unpublished diary and miscellaneous papers, USAWC Frank Howley archives

——, 'Longines Chronoscope interview of Major General Frank L. Howley', 1953, https://www.youtube.com/watch?v=A4RiE19ZAjA

Howley, Peter, author interview, 5 April 2019

Johnson, Alf, interview transcript, KCLMA GB0099 Berlin Airlift

Kane, Jim, interview transcript, https://nsarchive2.gwu.edu/coldwar/ interviews/episode-1/kane1.html

——, interview transcript, KCLMA GB0099 Cold War

Kennan, George, interview transcript, https://nsarchive2.gwu.edu/coldwar/ interviews/episode-1/kennan1.html

Knopf, Manfred, interview transcript, KCLMA GB0099 Berlin Airlift

Kondrashev, Sergei, interview transcript, KCLMA GB0099 Berlin Airlift

Laker, Freddie, interview transcript, KCLMA GB0099 Cold War

——, interview transcript, https://nsarchive2.gwu.edu/coldwar/inter views/episode-4/laker1.html

Lehmann, Geoffrey, oral interview, IWM 18755

Leonhard, Wolfgang, interview transcript, KCLMA GB0099 Cold War

——, interview transcript, https://nsarchive2.gwu.edu/coldwar/inter views/episode-2/leonhard1.html

Lochner, Robert, interview transcript, KCLMA GB0099 Berlin Airlift

——, interview transcript, https://nsarchive2.gwu.edu/coldwar/inter views/episode-4/lochner1.html

Luft, Friedrich, oral interview, IWM 2966

Lunghi, Hugh, interview transcript, https://nsarchive2.gwu.edu/coldwar/ interviews/episode-1/lunghi1.html

Mackeurtan, Justin, unpublished typescript, KCLMA GB0099 Williamson

Mallabar, Ronald, oral interview, IWM 11211

Manning, James, interview transcript, KCLMA GB0099 Berlin Airlift

Mautner, Karl, interview transcript, KCLMA GB0099 Cold War

Melvin, Alan, interview transcript, KCLMA GB0099 Berlin Airlift

Morrissey, Bill, interview transcript, KCLMA GB0099 Berlin Airlift

Munn, Gerry, interview transcript, KCLMA GB0099 Berlin Airlift

Murphy, David, interview transcript, KCLMA GB0099 Berlin Airlift

Parks, General Floyd L., unpublished papers, USAWC Parks

Parsons, Pip, interview transcript, KCLMA GB0099 Berlin Airlift

Pastore, Don and Valerie, interview transcript, KCLMA GB0099 Berlin Airlift

Reuter, Edzard, interview transcript, KCLMA GB0099 Cold War

——, interview transcript, https://nsarchive2.gwu.edu/coldwar/interviews/episode-4/reuter2.html

Roberts, Chamber, interview transcript, KCLMA GB0099 Berlin Airlift

Roberts, Frank, interview transcript, KCLMA GB0099 Berlin Airlift

——, interview transcript, https://nsarchive2.gwu.edu/coldwar/interviews/episode-1/roberts1.html

Samuel, Wolfgang, interview transcript, KCLMA GB0099 Berlin Airlift

Schitzler, Karl von, interview transcript, KCLMA GB0099 Cold War

Schutz, Klaus, interview transcript, KCLMA GB0099 Cold War

Scorer, Irina (née Hoecke), author interview, 28 February 2019

Sicklemore, Stan, interview transcript, KCLMA GB0099 Berlin Airlift

——, oral interview, IWM 18759

Smith, Geoff, interview transcript, KCLMA GB0099 Berlin Airlift

Sokolovsky, Marshal Vasily, interview transcript, *Soviet News*, 5 October 1948, https://www.cvce.eu/en/obj/interview_with_marshal_vassili_sokolovsky_in_soviet_news_5_october_1948-en-c7690f9c-b46b-4a95-b881-52a3318f3e5e.html

Travett, Norman Arthur, oral interview, IWM 10462

Voigt, Bill, interview transcript, KCLMA GB0099 Berlin Airlift

Waite, Jessamy, interview transcript, KCLMA GB0099 Berlin Airlift

Waite, Air Commodore Reginald Newnham, papers, KCLMA Waite

Weber, Heinz, interview transcript, KCLMA GB0099 Cold War

Wild, Mercedes, interview transcript, KCLMA GB0099 Berlin Airlift

Willett, Hazel, interview transcript, KCLMA GB0099 Berlin Airlift

Zeidler, Lothgar, interview transcript, KCLMA GB0099 Berlin Airlift

Published memoirs, journals, diaries and memoranda

Acheson, Dean, *Present at the Creation*, W. W. Norton, 1969

Andreas-Friedrich, Ruth, *Battleground Berlin*, Paragon House, 1990; for biographical information, see the German edition: *Der Schattenmann: Tagebuchaufzeichnungen 1938-1948*, Suhrkamp Verlag, 1984

Anon. (Hillers, Marta), *A Woman in Berlin*, Virago, 2011

Ardenne, Manfred von, *Ein glückliches Leben für Technik und Forschung*, Verlag der Nation, 1973

Barwich, Heinz and Elfi, *Das rote Atom*, Scherz, 1967

Bédarida, Renée, *Une Française à Berlin en 1945*, Cahiers de l'Institut d'histoire du temps présent, 1989–1990

Bennett, Air Vice-Marshal D. C. T., *Pathfinder*, Müller, 1958

Berry, Lelah, 'An Army Wife Lives Very Soft Life – in Germany', *Saturday Evening Post*, 15 February 1947

Birse, A. H., *Memoirs of an Interpreter*, Michael Joseph, 1967

Bohlen, Charles, *Witness to History, 1929–1969*, Weidenfeld & Nicolson, 1973

Brandt, Willy, *My Road to Berlin*, Peter Davies, 1960

——, *My Life in Politics*, Hamish Hamilton, 1992

Brett-Smith, Richard, *Berlin '45*, Macmillan, 1966

Bright Astley, Joan, *The Inner Circle: A View of War at the Top*, Little, Brown, 1971

Butcher, Harry, *Three Years with Eisenhower*, William Heinemann, 1946

Byford-Jones, W., *Berlin Twilight*, Hutchinson, 1947

Byrnes, James F., *Speaking Frankly*, Harper and Brothers, 1947

Cadogan, Sir Alexander, *The Diaries of Sir Alexander Cadogan, 1938–45*, Cassell, 1971

Chambers, Alfred and Louis Galambos (eds), *The Papers of Dwight David Eisenhower: Occupation*, Vol. 6, Johns Hopkins University Press, 1978

Churchill, Sarah, *Keep on Dancing*, Weidenfeld & Nicolson, 1981

Churchill, Winston, *The Second World War* (6 vols), Cassell, 1954

Clare, George, *Berlin Days: 1946–47*, Macmillan, 1989

Clay, Lucius, *Decision in Germany*, William Heinemann, 1950

Djilas, Milovan, *Conversations with Stalin*, Harcourt, Brace & World, 1962

Eden, Anthony, *The Eden Memoirs: The Reckoning*, Cassell, 1960

Fauntleroy, Barbara, *The General & His Daughter: The Wartime Letters of General James M. Gavin*, Fordham University Press, 2007

Forrestal, James, *The Forrestal Diaries*, Viking, 1951

Gollancz, Victor, *In Darkest Germany*, Victor Gollancz, 1947

Gouzenko, Igor, *This Was My Choice*, Palm Publishers, 1968

——, 'Stalin Sent Me to Spy School', *Coronet* magazine, March 1953

Gromyko, Andrei, *Memories*, Hutchinson, 1989

Gross, Inge, *Memoirs of World War II and Its Aftermath*, Island in the Sky Publishing, 2005

Grossman, Vasily, *A Writer at War*, Pimlico, 2006

Gröttrup, Irmgard, *Rocket Wife*, André Deutsch, 1959

Groves, Leslie, *Now It Can Be Told: The Story of the Manhattan Project*, Harper & Brothers, 1962

Halvorsen, Gail, *The Berlin Candy Bomber*, Horizon, 1997

Hargrave-Wright, Joyce, *The Bridge of Wings*, Abilitywise, 2015

Harriman, W. Averell and Elie Abel, *Special Envoy to Churchill and Stalin 1941–1946*, Random House, 1975

Hays, Gyula (also known as Julius Hay), *Born 1900*, Hutchinson, 1974

Henderson, Sir Nicholas, *The Birth of NATO*, Weidenfeld & Nicolson, 1982

Hinde, Brigadier W. R. N. Hinde, *Military Government: British Troops Berlin*, Printing and Stationery Services, Berlin, July 1945

Horrocks, Brian, *A Full Life*, Collins, 1960

Howley, Colonel Frank, *Berlin Command*, G. P. Putnam's Sons, 1950

——, 'Payoff in Berlin: Concluding My 4-Year War with The Reds', *Collier's*, December 1949

Ismay, Lord Hastings, *The Memoirs of General, The Lord Ismay*, William Heinemann, 1960

Kardorff, Ursula von, *Diary of a Nightmare, Berlin 1942–1945*, Rupert Hart-Davis, 1965, London

Kennan, George F., *Memoirs, 1925–1950*, Hutchinson, 1968

——, 'George Kennan's "Long Telegram"', http://digitalarchive.wilson-center.org/document/116178

Klimov, Gregory, *The Terror Machine*, Faber & Faber, 1953

Kotikov, General-Major A. G. (генерал-майор А.Г.Котоиков), Записки военного коменданта Берлина (*The Notes of the Military Commander of Berlin*), Veche, 2006

Large, David Clay, *Berlin*, Allen Lane, 2001

Leahy, William D., *I Was There*, Gollancz, 1950

Leonhard, Wolfgang, *Child of the Revolution*, Collins, 1957

Lowe, Yoshika, *Cold War Memories: A Retrospective on Living in Berlin*, Brats Books, 2014

Mallaby, George, *From My Level: Unwritten Minutes*, Hutchinson, 1965

Mann, Anthony, *Comeback: Germany 1945–1952*, Macmillan, 1980

Mark, Eduard (ed.), '"Today Has Been a Historical One": Harry S Truman's Diary of the Potsdam Conference', *Diplomatic History*, Vol. 4, No. 3, summer 1980

Moran, Lord Charles, *Winston Churchill: The Struggle for Survival, 1940–65*, Constable, 1966

Murphy, David E., Sergei A. Kondrashev and George Bailey, *Battleground Berlin: CIA vs KGB in the Cold War*, Yale University Press, 1997

Nabokov, Nicolas, *Old Friends and New Music*, Hamish Hamilton, 1951

Nel, Elizabeth, *Mr Churchill's Secretary*, Hodder & Stoughton, 1958

Nicolson, Nigel (ed.), *Harold Nicolson Diaries and Letters, 1907–1964*, Weidenfeld & Nicolson, 2004

O'Donnell, James P., *The Berlin Bunker*, Dent, 1979

Owings, Alison, *Frauen: German Women Recall the Third Reich*, Pergamon, 1995

Pash, Colonel Boris T., *The Alsos Mission*, Award House, 1969

Pocock, Tom, *1945: The Dawn Came Up Like Thunder*, Collins, 1983

Rees, Goronwy, *A Bundle of Sensations: Sketches in Autobiography*, Chatto & Windus, 1960

Riess, Curt, *The Berlin Story*, Frederick Muller, 1953

Rzhevskaya, Yelena, *Memoirs of a Wartime Interpreter*, Greenhill Books, 2018

——, *Berlin 1945*, published in translation in V. Sevruk, *How Wars End*

Schneider, Helga, *The Bonfire of Berlin*, William Heinemann, 2005

Schwanenflügel Lawson, Dorothea von, *Laughter Wasn't Rationed*, Tricor Press, 2009

Sevruk, V. (ed.), *How Wars End: Eye-Witness Accounts of the Fall of Berlin*, University Press of the Pacific, 2005

Sherwood, Robert E. (ed.), *The White House Papers of Harry L. Hopkins*, Eyre & Spottiswoode, 1949

Simonow, Konstantin, *Kriegstagebücher 1942–1945*, Vol. 2, Verlag Volk und Welt, 1979

Smith, Jean Edward (ed.), *The Papers of Lucius Clay, Germany 1945–49*, Indiana University Press, 1984

Spender, Stephen, *European Witness*, Hamish Hamiton, 1946

Stettinius, Edward R., *Roosevelt and the Russians*, Jonathan Cape, 1950

Strang, William, *Home and Abroad*, André Deutsch, 1956

Terkel, Studs, *The Good War: An Oral History of World War Two*, Hamish Hamilton, 1985

Thorp, Chief Superintendent Arthur, *Calling Scotland Yard*, Allan Wingate, 1954

Tokaev, Grigori, *Stalin Means War*, Weidenfeld & Nicolson, 1951

——, *Comrade X*, Harvill Press, 1956

Trevor-Roper, Hugh, *The Last Days of Hitler*, Papermac, 1995

——, *The Wartime Journals* (ed. Richard Davenport-Hines), I. B. Tauris, 2012

Truman, Harry S., *Memoirs* (2 vols), Hodder & Stoughton, 1955

Truman, Margaret, *Harry S. Truman*, Hamish Hamilton, 1973

Tunner, William H., *Over the Hump*, Duell, Sloan and Pearce, 1964

United States Congress, Investigation of the National Defence Program, *Hearings before a Special Committee Investigating the National Defense Program, Part 42, Military Government in Germany, April 1946–October 1947*, United States Government Printing Office, 1948

Zhukov, Georgii, *The Memoirs of Marshal Zhukov*, Jonathan Cape, 1971

Secondary Sources

Journals, magazines and articles

Adler, Karen H., 'Selling France to the French: French Zone of Occupation in Western Germany, 1945–c.1955', *Contemporary European History*, Vol. 21, No. 4, Cambridge University Press, November 2012

Control Commission for Germany, *British Zone Review*, Public Relations and Information Services Control Group, 1945–9

Falco, Thomas A., 'Berlin's ACA Building Example of Allied Efforts to Extend Wartime Unity Through Occupation Period', *Military Government Weekly Information Bulletin*, 17 June 1946, KCLMA GB0099 Waite

Fraser, Blair, 'Blair Fraser Keeps a Rendezvous with Igor Gouzenko', *Maclean's* magazine, September 1953

Gouzenko, Igor, 'New Soviet Spy Rings at Work in Canada', *New World* magazine, May 1947

Grose, Peter, 'The Boss of Occupied Germany, General Lucius D. Clay', *Foreign Affairs*, Vol. 77, No. 4, July–August 1998

Hannant, Laurence, 'Igor Gouzenko and Canada's Cold War', *The Beaver*, October 1995

Hughes, Emmet, 'Berlin Under Siege', *Life*, 19 July 1948

Lang, Will, 'Wind in Berlin', *Life*, 17 May 1948

Lönnendonker, Siegward, Betina Meissner and Angelika Stubert, *Kaiserswerther Strasse 16–18: Zum Einzug der Freien Universität in die frühere Alliierte Kommandantur*, Freie Universität Berlin, 1994

Merer, Air Commodore J. W. F., 'The Berlin Airlift', *Aeronautical Journal*, Vol. 54, Issue 476, August 1950, pp. 513–33

Military Government, 'Notes on the Blockade of Berlin 1948', *HQ British Troops Berlin*, Printing and Stationery Services, Berlin, 1949

Morgan, Edward P., 'Heels Among the Heroes: There Are Too Many Peck's Bad Boys in Our Occupation Forces', *Collier's*, 19 October 1946

Mosely, Philip, 'Dismemberment of Germany: The Allied Negotiations from Yalta to Potsdam', *Foreign Affairs*, Vol. 28, No. 3, April 1950

——, 'The Occupation of Germany: New Light on How the Zones Were Drawn', *Foreign Affairs*, Vol. 28, No. 4, July 1950

Ruffner, Kevin Conley, 'The Black Market in Postwar Berlin', *Prologue* magazine, Vol. 34, No. 3, 2002

Smith, Jean Edward, 'Berlin Confrontation', *Virginia Quarterly Review*, Vol. 42, No. 3, 1966, pp. 349–65

Steinmeier, D., 'The Constabulary Moves Fast', *Army Information Digest*, Vol. 2, No. 11, November 1947

Stivers, William, 'The Incomplete Blockade: Soviet Zone Supply of West Berlin, 1948–49', *Diplomatic History*, Vol. 21, Issue 4, October 1997, pp. 569–602

Books and monographs

Akinsha, Konstantin and Grigorii Kozlov, *Stolen Treasure*, Weidenfeld & Nicolson, 1995

Alford, Kenneth, *The Spoils of World War II*, Carol Publishing, 1994

Arnold-Forster, Mark, *The Siege of Berlin*, HarperCollins, 1979

Atkinson, Rick, *The Guns at Last Light*, Henry Holt, 2013

Barnett, Corelli, *The Lords of War,* Praetorian Press, 2012

Bennett, Lowell, *Berlin Bastion: The Epic of Post-War Berlin*, Fred Rudl Publishers, 1951

Bessel, Richard, *German 1945*, Simon & Schuster, 2009

Bishop, Jim, *FDR's Last Year*, Hart-Davis, MacGibbon, 1975

Botting, Douglas, *In the Ruins of the Reich*, Methuen, 2005

Bruce, Gary, *Through the Lion Gate: A History of Berlin Zoo*, Oxford University Press, 2017

Bullock, Allan, *The Life and Times of Ernest Bevin* (3 vols), William Heinemann, 1960–83

Burns, James MacGregor, *Roosevelt: The Soldier of Freedom, 1940–1945*, Weidenfeld & Nicolson, 1971

Chuev, Felix, *Molotov Remembers*, Ivan R. Dee, 1993

Clemens, Diane, *Yalta*, Oxford University Press, 1970

Cobain, Ian, *Cruel Britannia*, Portobello, 2012

Collier, Richard, *Bridge Across the Sky*, Macmillan, 1978

Donnelly, Desmond, *Struggle for the World: The Cold War 1917–1965*, Collins, 1965

Emsley, Clive, *Exporting British Policing During the Second World War*, Bloomsbury Academic, 2017

Feigel, Lara, *The Bitter Taste of Victory*, Bloomsbury, 2016

Fenby, Jonathan, *Alliance*, Simon & Schuster, 2006

Foreign Relations of the United States: Diplomatic Papers, Conferences at Malta and Yalta, 1945, Bryton Barron (ed.), United States Government Printing Office, 1955

Gere, Edwin A., *The Unheralded*, Trafford, 2003

Gilbert, Martin, *Winston S. Churchill*, William Heinemann (8 vols), 1966–83

Hamilton, Stephen A., *Bloody Streets: The Soviet Assault on Berlin, April 1945*, Helion and Company, 2009

Hastings, Max, *Overlord: D-Day and the Battle for Normandy*, Michael Joseph, 1984

Hyde, H. Montgomery, *The Quiet Canadian: The Secret Service Story of Sir William Stephenson*, Hamish Hamilton, 1962

Innes, Hammond, *Air Bridge*, Pan, 2004

Isaacson, Walter and Evan Thomas, *The Wise Men*, Faber & Faber, 1986

Jackson, Archie S., *Pathfinder Bennett: Airman Extraordinaire*, Terence Dalton, 1991

Knight, Amy, *How the Cold War Began*, Basic Books, 2007

Knowles, Christopher, *Winning the Peace: The British in Occupied Germany 1945–1948*, Bloomsbury, 2017

Lange, Karl-Heinz, *A General Description of Events at the Elbe River in Torgau between April 10 and May 6, 1945*, Historical Association of Torgau, 1995

Le Tissier, Tony, *The Battle of Berlin, 1945*, Jonathan Cape, 1988

Lowe, Keith, *Savage Continent*, Viking, 2012

McCullough, David, *Truman*, Simon & Schuster, 1992

MacDonogh, Giles, *After the Reich: From the Liberation of Vienna to the Berlin Airlift*, John Murray, 2007

McNeese, Tim, *The Cold War and Postwar America, 1946–1953*, Chelsea House, 2010

Mee, Charles L., *Meeting at Potsdam,* André Deutsch, 1975

Meehan, Patricia, *A Strange Enemy People: Germans Under the British, 1945–50*, Peter Owen, 2001

Millen, Raymond A., *"Bury the Dead, Feed the Living: The History of Civil Affairs/Military Government in the Mediterranean and European Theaters of Operation During World War II*, US Army Peacekeeping and Stability Operations Institute, 2019

Miller, Roger G., *To Save a City: The Berlin Airlift 1948–1949*, Air Force History and Museums Program, 1998

Naimark, Norman M., *The Russians in Germany: A History of the Soviet Zone of Occupation, 1945–1949*, Belknap Press, 1995

Narinskii, Michail M., 'The Soviet Union and the Berlin Crisis, 1948–9', in *The Soviet Union and Europe in the Cold War 1945–53*, ed. Francesca Gori and Silvio Pons, Palgrave Macmillan, 1996

Page, Norman, *Auden and Isherwood, The Berlin Years*, Macmillan, 1998

Parrish, Thomas, *Berlin in the Balance, 1945–1949*, Perseus Books, 1998

Pickersgill, J. W. and D. F. Forster, *The Mackenzie King Record*, University of Toronto Press, 1970

Plokhy, S. M., *Yalta, The Price of Peace*, Viking, 2010

Preston, Diana, *Eight Days at Yalta*, Picador, 2019

Prieberg, Fred K., *Trial of Strength: Wilhelm Furtwängler and the Third Reich*, Quartet Books, 1991

Rees, Laurence, *World War Two: Behind Closed Doors, Stalin, the Nazis and the West*, BBC Books, 2008

Reeves, Richard, *Daring Young Men*, Simon & Schuster, 2011

Richie, Alexandra, *Faust's Metropolis*, HarperCollins, 1998

Roberts, Andrew, *Churchill: Walking with Destiny*, Viking, 2018

Rodrigo, Robert, *Berlin Airlift*, Cassell, 1960

Roll, David, *The Hopkins Touch*, Oxford University Press, 2015

Sandford, Gregory W., *From Hitler to Ulbricht: The Communist Reconstruction of East Germany 1945–46*, Princeton University Press, 1983

Schachter, Judith, *Legacies of a Hawaiian Generation: From Territorial Subject to American Citizen*, Berghahn Books, 2013

Schivelbusch, Wolfgang, *In a Cold Crater: Cultural and Intellectual Life in Berlin 1945–1948*, University of California Press, 1998

Sherwen, Nicholas (ed.), *NATO's Anxious Birth*, C. Hurst, 1985

Sherwood, Robert E., *Roosevelt and Hopkins*, Ishi Press, 2020

Shirokorad, Aleksandr, Великая контрибуция. Что СССР получил после войны (*Great Contribution: What the USSR Received After the War*), Veche, 2013

Sloan, Stan, *Permanent Alliance? NATO and the Transatlantic Bargain from Truman to Obama*, Continuum Books, 2010

Smith, Arthur L., *Kidnap City: Cold War Berlin*, Greenwood, 2002

Smith, Jean Edward, *Lucius Clay: An American Life*, Henry Holt, 1990

Staercke, André de, *NATO's Anxious Birth*, C. Hurst, 1985

Stafford, David, *Camp X*, Lester and Orpen Dennys Publishers, 1986

Steege, Paul, *Black Market, Cold War: Everyday Life in Berlin, 1946–1949*, Cambridge University Press, 2007

Steel, Ronald, *Walter Lippmann and the American Century*, Bodley Head, 1980

Stivers, William and Donald A. Carter, *The City Becomes a Symbol: The US*

Army in the Occupation of Berlin, 1945–1949, Center of Military History, United States Army, 2017

Taschereau, Robert and R. L. Kellock, *The Report of the Royal Commission . . . June 27, 1946*, Stationery Office, 1946

Taylor, Frederick, *The Berlin Wall, 13 August 1961–9 November 1989*, Bloomsbury, 2007

——, *Exorcising Hitler*, Bloomsbury, 2011

Toland, John, *The Last 100 Days*, Bantam, 1967

Turner, Barry, *The Berlin Airlift*, Icon Books, 2017

Tusa, Ann and John, *The Berlin Blockade*, Hodder & Stoughton, 1988

Walker, Jonathan, *Operation Unthinkable*, The History Press, 2013

Wilson, Squadron-Leader G. D., *History of Gatow*, privately published, 1971

Williamson, David, *A Most Diplomatic General: The Life of General Lord Robertson of Oakridge*, Brassey's, 1996

Winterton, Paul, *Inquest on an Ally*, The Cresset Press, 1948

Ziemke, Earl F., *The US Army in the Occupation of Germany, 1944–1946*, Center of Military History, United States Army, 1990

Index